MANIFESTATIONS
OF APPREHENSION

MANIFESTATIONS OF APPREHENSION

A MEMOIR

WILLIAM A. CIMINO

Archway Publishing books may be ordered through booksellers or by contacting:

Archway Publishing
1663 Liberty Drive
Bloomington, IN 47403
www.archwaypublishing.com
844-669-3957

Front Cover Photo provided by the author.

ISBN: 978-1-6657-4606-9 (sc)
ISBN: 978-1-6657-4607-6 (e)

Library of Congress Control Number: 2023911580

Print information available on the last page.

Archway Publishing rev. date: 09/12/2023

DISCLAIMERS

To my brother, Rob, and his memory
1956–2020
"Big Little Bro"
He was the sweetest man I have ever known.

ARLINGTON NATIONAL CEMETERY
DECEMBER 2, 2021

I stood there, in turn, at the final resting places for these men. It was quiet as the sun gained dominance over a cloudy morning, and the fallen leaves were scattered over the acres of headstones as far as the eye could see. I am not ashamed to admit I shed a few tears as the reality of their passings took over my thoughts. I delivered a final respectful salute to them both before I leisurely walked back to the main building that contained beautiful exhibits of the cemetery's history.

As I made my way home, my thoughts were focused on our nation's most hallowed ground, where more than 400,000 people are laid to rest. I turned my attention to all those friends who served with me, supported me, made me laugh, may still be alive, or may no longer be with us. There are some friends I was not able to find in my search. I regret that but must emphasize that they are in my thoughts and prayers, and I am grateful for having them in my life. They may be gone but never forgotten.

CONTENTS

INTRODUCTION

A yearning emerged—a need to write a story—a true story, and one I knew well and reflected on now and then. This memoir begins in 1963 and terminates in early 1993. It contains information I believe to be factual, which embraces my best recollections, reflects my records, and contains details expressed in many personal letters between me and my spouse, Fran, when I was assigned away from my family for a time during my military career. I introduce real people, especially those most important and influential to me, when I want to emphasize their contributions to my military experience, friendship, support, and the strength of their characters and actions, which deserve merit and praise. I firmly believe one should evaluate his or her career through an appreciation of those whose influence contributed to its success.

I sought and received permission to use their names, photos, and other information either directly or through a surviving family member, if that became necessary and possible. I used fictitious names, however, to describe a few individuals who annoyed me and whose actions or behaviors deserve scrutiny or criticism. You find these types everywhere in life, and they, too, contributed to my experience.

I authored this book primarily because, at this stage in my life, I have found it enjoyable and necessary to preserve some family history. I realize now that there is so much more I would love to know about my ancestry—my grandparents, great-grandparents, and beyond—more about their lives. Their roots come from Italy, and that alone makes me wish I could speak, read, and understand the beautiful language of that land. And so, family history preservation became important to me, and I took action to record some significant family events.

Over the last few years, I have produced several family treasures:

2017: *Fran & Bill—50ᵗʰ Wedding Anniversary, June 24, 1967–June 24, 2017;* a thirty-four-minute video that begins with our childhoods.

2018: *Bill—50ᵗʰ Birthday Celebration, June 3, 2018* (Bill is our first son); a twenty-three-minute video that begins with his birth.

2019: *Costa-Cimino, Our Family Story, A Son's Perspective* (A tribute to my parents who both died young): a 127-minute video that begins with a reach back for both families, some as far as the mid-1830s.

2023: *The Joey Story, September 11, 2023* (Joe is our second son); a thirty-four-minute video that begins with his birth fifty years ago.

These were labors of love and have earned family-wide appreciation.

During the eleven-month effort to produce the 2019 video, I learned to appreciate the extent to which my paternal grandfather and uncles from my mother's and father's sides of the family contributed to military service in World Wars I and II and the Korean War. The "Special Tributes" section of this book briefly acknowledges their service, as well as others who deserve respect and admiration.

I envision more videos to add to the Cimino Video Library, but for now, I sought a bit of diversity. So I focused on this book, which primarily highlights my military career. I hope that in the future, perhaps a grandchild or great-grandchild might read it and embrace its message, which is far more important than anything I may have accomplished.

Inspiration and *encouragement*. These two words have a slight overlap in meaning and, more important, a distinction I hope to make clear. This book is not meant to inspire; that is, to present a vision, an environment of creativity, or provide deep insight and motivation. I do not think I can inspire anyone based on this book, and that is not my intention.

There are countless other stories and military careers, many of which are much more exciting, that *are* inspiring. I believe, however, that my story can be an encouragement—perhaps a boost, reinforcement, or even a reassurance that failure is only a bump in the road that you can put in the rearview mirror.

The life road ahead may be uphill, even tortuous at times, and it may have many "failure bumps" along the way. Recognition of a failure as an opportunity may eventually enable you to move beyond your misfortune and proceed toward success and achievement.

My purpose is simply to convey the notion that failure is something that needs to be digested for a time. It can be a few days or even years before you realize its full impact and how it may have influenced you to act, pursue your career, or live your life. That failure may become dormant, and it may take time to realize that it may also be the seed of an opportunity. In life, opportunities come and go. It's essential to recognize opportunities and to carefully assess whether to embrace them or not.

Manifestations of Apprehension embodies what I consider a significant failure in my life, one that pulled me down and made me feel worthless, incompetent, and a host of other negative descriptors. It caused me to question myself, my decisions, my future, and even my value to others. Processing this failure took time. And at a point later in my military career, then and only then did I realize how this deficiency truly impacted me and influenced me to navigate my way beyond it. It provided me with an opportunity to find my way ahead. I did not do it alone. Many others provided the support I needed over the years.

After a few years of military service, I genuinely appreciated that this downfall was an opportunity in disguise, a challenging but enabling component that led to a better-than-expected path for my career in the US Air Force. If I could emphasize my message right from the start, I would say, "Never allow a failure, no matter how severe, to characterize your life. Use it as a catalyst, a means to a greater goal, and to define better who you are."

A wise man once said, "Don't be afraid to start over again. This time, you're not starting from scratch; you're starting from experience."

A MEMORABLE DECADE

■ THE SIXTIES CHARACTERIZED

The 1960s was a decade of revolution and change across politics, music, and society in America. It was a tumultuous period of distinct characteristics in our country's history that is defined as turbulent, and violent, but also colorful. There were memorable moments, national crises, cultural and social evolutions, the emerging generation gap, and divisiveness. There were flower children, civil rights movements, pop fashion, anti-war protests, and the Space Race.

It is sometimes known as the "swinging sixties" because of its youthful and flavorful focus on music, art, and fashion. It gave us uniquely identifiable personalities such as Goldie Hawn, the bubbly blonde from the TV comedy series *Rowan & Martin's Laugh-In*; The Beach Boys, a group formed in 1961 in Hawthorne, California, with easy-listening hit tunes like "Surfer Girl," "Fun, Fun, Fun," "I Get Around," and "Good Vibrations"; the thriller director, Alfred Hitchcock, who produced many movies in the fifties, but perhaps remembered most for 1960's *Psycho*, which featured a creepy guy, Norman Bates (played by Anthony Perkins) who thought his dead mother was his best friend; James Marshall—Jimi Hendrix—one of the most influential electric guitarists; and Twiggy, a supermodel who gained international recognition.

Also referred to simply as "the sixties," some of the most favored trends were Afro hairstyles, the Barbie doll (every little girl's dream), bell-bottom pants, go-go boots, miniskirts, and lava lamps. And without a doubt, Beatlemania, characterized as the "British Invasion" when the Beatles touched down in New York on February 7, 1964, and debuted on the *Ed Sullivan Show*.

The era was defined by groovy fads, including peace signs and symbols, tie-dyed shirts, fallout shelters to offer protection against the threat of nuclear attack with the cloud of the Cold War and exposure of the Cuban missile crisis, and the dance craze created in Chubby Checker's number one song, "The Twist." It was the first modern dance style that did not require a partner, and couples did not have to touch each other while dancing. Checker said, "It's like putting out a cigarette with both feet and coming out of a shower and wiping your bottom with a towel to the beat."

The range of emotions in the sixties covered the entire spectrum from national shock and mourning with the November 22, 1963, assassination of our thirty-fifth president, John F. Kennedy, in Dallas, Texas, to euphoria and pride with the Apollo 11 moon landing on July 20, 1969, inspired by Kennedy's challenge to America to put a man on the moon, where Neil Armstrong made, "one giant leap for mankind." Emotions continued to fester with more assassinations during this period: Malcolm X on February 21, 1965; Martin Luther King Jr. on April 4, 1968; and Robert Kennedy on June 5, 1968. All were leaders of their time who were killed for their actions and beliefs.

■ COLLEGE: I'M READY

With the constitution of the decade unfolding, I graduated from an all-boys school, Saint Anthony's High School, in Smithtown, New York, in June 1963. I contemplated attending the Colorado School of Mines in Golden, Colorado, with a major in geology. My experience at Saint Anthony's was good as one among a total school population of about four hundred students taught by the Franciscan Brothers. They were tough but could be a lot of fun as well.

Over the years, Saint Anthony's left Smithtown and moved to Huntington, New York, where it became coed and grew to tremendous numbers. My interest in geology had a foundation in my dad's love of rock collecting, secondary to his interest in fishing for trout. During my younger years, he included me in both, and I consider myself truly fortunate to be his student in these pastimes.

The rock collecting took us to numerous quarries, riverbeds, old mines, and well-researched areas as we searched for semi-precious minerals, primarily in New York State, but on occasion, to locales as far as the West Coast. Dad developed a skill for using his lapidary machine to slice rock specimens and mark them for specific trimming, enhancement, polishing, and final quality for jewelry settings. He made many unique jewelry items for Mom, skillfully displaying another facet of his artistry; he was a commercial artist by trade.

Now, with great anticipation for college, I needed to decide where to go and what major course of study would be best for me. I do not recall any pressure from anyone that influenced my decision to attend Saint John's University (SJU) in Jamaica, New York. SJU is a private Catholic university founded in 1870 by the Congregation of the Mission (CM, the Vincentian Fathers of the Roman Catholic Church) to provide a growing immigrant population with higher-quality education.

I selected math as a major course of study with a minor in physics. I always liked these subjects but had no idea how I would use them after college. My godmother, Dorothy Connor—we called her Aunt Dot even though she was not connected by family—was elated since she majored in math and received both bachelor's and master's degrees in the subject. She was my mom's lifelong best friend. My focus at this point in my life, and certainly in my academic experience, was one year at a time, perhaps one semester at a time, and probably more appropriately, one day at a time.

Our family had moved from Brooklyn, New York, to a newly built home in Hicksville on Long Island in the summer of 1959. Shortly afterward, I started high school and commuted by bus daily. But now, my commute to the SJU campus in Queens was by a car driven either by my father, after which he continued to his work location in New York City (NYC), or by myself when a vehicle was available to me. At times I commuted by train.

As I look back at those college years, 1963–1967, certain events on the SJU campus and nationally stand out in my memory. I am no stranger to the memory of the Kennedy assassination in November 1963. Everyone knew where they were when that tragedy occurred. I was sitting in a math class when someone came into the room to announce that the president had been shot. It was difficult to concentrate on anything else after this terrible news. Students and faculty assembled in student halls and other centers to watch and hear the news unfold.

With a growing number of student friends with whom I shared the anxiety of such events, concern for our country grew as it became more immersed in the war in Vietnam, the escalation of civil unrest, and other negative trends that troubled our nation. On the other hand, as students, we always embraced the positive offered by the cultural and societal changes and the mere togetherness that our common goals presented.

I shared two classes with another student. One was a math class, the other an English class. She majored in early childhood education and was one of the students I often met with in the student lounge at a table we called the "frarority table," it being neither a fraternity nor sorority table, since none of us at that time were interested in either.

Her name is Francine Margaret Mary Micucci. Fran lived in Jamaica, New York, within walking distance of SJU, and I sometimes met her as she arrived on campus and walked with her until we parted for classes. It was September 1963, the beginning of our freshman year at SJU, and I liked the college experience from the get-go! We shared the two classes and always had much to talk about as we developed our friendship with each other and among a common group of student peers.

Fran had her list of interests beginning in that first year, including the Booster Club, the Italian Cultural Society, some intramural activities, and the Glee Club—a choir group. My friendship with Fran grew during the fall semester, but we did not date until the following year. I seldom dated others. As I recall, none were dated more than once or contributed further to my interests.

My study environment at home was not conducive to learning as I shared a small, one-hundred-square-foot bedroom with my younger brother of ten years, Rob. This sweet kid was never a problem or impediment to my learning. Still, I often did homework sitting on the edge of my bed, not at a desk with proper posture and lighting, and only sometimes at the kitchen table where there were constant but unintended interruptions.

My grades were not the best, but I struggled through the first year with a GPA of 3.89. At first, this may sound great, but it wasn't. The grades were calculated at a maximum GPA of 8.0 instead of the traditional 4.0. My parents were able to pay for my first year of tuition and books at SJU. However, they struggled with bills even though they both worked very hard at their jobs. Therefore, I needed to take a low-interest government loan with deferred payments for the remaining three years.

Back to Fran. It took me eight months before I asked her for a date, and I was determined to make it special. Why did it take me so long? I have no idea. Can't explain it. I asked her to go to the 1964 New York World's Fair at Flushing Park, not far from SJU. We went there on May 1, 1964, and marveled at the various attractions—over 140 pavilions, numerous restaurants, and exhibits from many nations, corporations, and states surrounding the famous Unisphere, a twelve-story, stainless steel globe, which remains there today.

There was a great deal to take in and enjoy, and we had a great day! If I remember anything about that day, it was not any particular exhibit, ride, or attraction. I remember that as we walked hand in hand, I suddenly turned to Fran with a serious look on my face.

"Did you ever steal anything?" I asked.

She turned to me with a puzzled look and replied, "No. Have you?"

Then I kissed her.

"Yes. I just stole a kiss," I said. Smiles formed on our faces in unison, and we held hands tightly. That is my best memory of that beautiful day. You could say that day launched a lifetime!

■ VIETNAM

I do not think a day went by during my years at SJU when there was not some headline story in the newspapers or news coverage on TV about the escalation of the war in Vietnam. This war was marked in history with a beginning date of November 1, 1955, and an end date of April 30, 1975. However, the US Congress considers the Vietnam era to have begun on February 28, 1961, ending May 7, 1975.

While most historians relate that the war started in the 1950s, the conflict in Southeast Asia originated with the French colonial occupation in the late 1800s. Over the next half-century, a timeline of complex political and military issues among the United States, France, China, the Soviet Union, and South Vietnam contributed to the emergence of the Vietnam War as we think of it most recently.

From the early 1950s to mid-1954, a founding principle of the Truman Doctrine stated that US foreign policy is to assist any country whose stability is threatened by communism. In January 1950, the People's Republic of China and the Soviet Union formally recognized the communist Democratic Republic of Vietnam. They provided economic and military aid to communist resistance fighters within the country. In June of that year, the United States stepped up military assistance to France. In early 1954, the French were defeated, and their rule in French Indochina ended. President Dwight D. Eisenhower recognized that this defeat presented a severe threat in Southeast Asia and that there could be a domino effect from communism. This domino theory would guide US thinking toward Vietnam for the next decade.

The Geneva Accords established North and South Vietnam with a division at the 17th parallel and an agreement that elections would be held within two years to unify

Vietnam under a single democratic government. The elections never happened. The United States began backing South Vietnam as North Vietnam built supply routes, later known as the Ho Chi Minh Trail, through Laos and Cambodia to support guerrilla attacks in the south.

In July 1959, the first US soldiers were killed during a guerrilla raid on their quarters near Saigon. In May 1961, President Kennedy sent helicopters and four hundred Green Berets to South Vietnam to perform secret operations against the Viet Cong, short for Vietnam Cong-san or Vietnamese communists. In January 1962, US aircraft began spraying Agent Orange in Operation Ranch Hand in an effort to kill vegetation that offered cover and food to guerrilla forces. Over the next year, South Vietnamese troops continued to be defeated as more civilians and Buddhist protesters fell victim to attacks. South Vietnam then went through a period of military coups and government replacements.

America entered the Vietnam War in August 1964, when the USS *Maddox* was allegedly attacked by Vietnamese patrol boats in the Gulf of Tonkin. This led President Johnson to enable airstrikes on the patrol boat bases. Two US aircraft were shot down, resulting in the first US airman, pilot Everett Alvarez Jr., being taken prisoner by North Vietnam. He endured eight years and seven months of brutal captivity by the North Vietnamese at the Hỏa Lò Prison (sarcastically known as the Hanoi Hilton by fellow POWs), where he was repeatedly beaten and tortured.

The Gulf of Tonkin Resolution, passed by Congress, authorized the president to use any measures required against the aggressors. In response, the Soviet Union and China contributed aircraft, arms, troops, and other resources to counter American actions. In 1965, President Lyndon B. Johnson launched Operation Rolling Thunder, a three-year campaign of sustained bombing in the north and along the Ho Chi Minh Trail. From this point on, more American ground troops were sent to Vietnam, and the draft increased to thirty-five thousand each month. Troops rose to 400,000 in 1966 and 500,000 in 1967. The trend in Vietnam was going in the wrong direction.

■ A RELATIONSHIP IS TESTED

During these turbulent and chaotic years, I continued my studies at SJU, my relationship with Fran, and began some part-time work because, like every other teenager, I needed some cash. I got my first job at Minute-Man Burgers in Hicksville. It was like a poor man's McDonald's, serving hamburgers, roast beef sandwiches, fries, milkshakes—all that good stuff! I worked primarily on the weekends, trying to make my schedule of education, work, and fun somewhat manageable.

After some time, I became the night manager there, which enabled me to make a few more cents per hour. During my tenure at this fine eating establishment, I developed a habit of ingesting an occasional meal on the house—everything from juicy roast beef sandwiches to burgers and beyond. I would also step outside to call Fran from the phone booth, and at times, our conversations went a bit long. One of the employees ratted on me regarding my free meals and personal phone calls. I could not deny the allegations, and I did not choose to lie. My excuse for eating the profits was that I was taste-testing the food, which did not go over very well with the owners. They fired me! So it was goodbye Minute-Man Burgers, hello JCPenney. It did not take me long to turn this unfortunate event into something positive and convince myself that I had moved up.

Since I could save a little cash, I bought my first car—a used 1956 Chevy convertible, with a coral and white body and a white top—for $400. I later sold that car, which I highly regret, for $300. I wish I had that classic today. My social scene increased, as one would expect, progressing from the frarority table to pizza joints, Community Gardens—a beer hall (the drinking age in New York State was eighteen at that time) with this group of friends, at parks to do some picnicking and rental boating on the lakes, and, of course, to the beach in the Chevy with the top down. We had a good crowd, and everyone got along great.

Fran and me, beachbound, September 1964.

The college years progressed, sometimes seemingly slowly and other times amazingly fast. It depended on the perspective of the volume of work or the fun times. In my sophomore year, I joined the Glee Club, not because I wanted to sing so much, but because it allowed more opportunities to see Fran and be in concerts with her. I had met her parents, Mr. and Mrs. Micucci, at a concert Fran was in during our freshman year. I liked them immediately, and they seemed to like me as well.

Joseph Vincent Micucci was born in Italy and immigrated to America when he was only eighteen years old. He learned to read and write English on his own and worked hard to provide for his family in Italy—his mother and younger siblings; and later, his wife, Fran, and her brother, Vince, older by four years. Mrs. Vincenza Micucci, who went by Jean, was born in the Little Italy section of NYC. She was the oldest of four daughters born to Mr. and Mrs. Pietro Marino. She went to Hunter College in the city and became a schoolteacher. Both she and Joseph valued education very highly and provided educational support and encouragement to their children, Vince, and Fran.

Fran and I often dated after that first date at the World's Fair. We went into the city, usually by subway when the fare was only a fifteen-cent token. We loved the city and embraced its numerous sights, museums, restaurants, and Central Park. One could never exhaust the possibilities. Most attractions then were free, not so today. We dated throughout our sophomore and junior years. Several formal dances were included. Fran always looked absolutely beautiful in her attire and would graciously accept the corsages I brought to her as an extra touch.

One time, however, a glitch formed when I heard that someone expressed a desire to ask Fran to a school-sponsored dance. I quickly established my strategy in this regard and let it be known to the potential perpetrator, as well as a host of other male candidates, that they could not take Fran to the dance.

They all asked, "Why not?"

My reply was simple—and accompanied by a serious look: "Because she is going with me!" So they backed off. The truth is that I had not asked Fran to go yet, but I did shortly after that. And with great confidence, I might add.

As our relationship matured, I spent more time at SJU after classes to do some homework in the library, so I could stop by to see Fran at her home before I left in the evening, sometimes early, sometimes late … very late to catch the subway to connect with the Long Island Railroad (LIRR) eastward bound to Hicksville. While there are eighty-one NYC subway stations in Queens, only one mattered—the one closest to Fran's home—the station at 169th Street and Hillside Avenue, about nine city blocks away.

I took the subway westbound two stops to the Sutphin Boulevard/Archer Avenue station, five blocks from the LIRR on Jamaica Avenue. From there, the ride to Hicksville station was about twenty-five minutes. On arrival in Hicksville, I would walk or run home, 2.1 miles from the train station. So I occasionally did my share of aerobic exercises.

It only happened once. I needed to carefully plan my departure to ensure I could get home. The subway ran 24/7, so it was never a problem. However, the LIRR schedule to Hicksville had its last departure around 1 a.m. On this one weeknight, I overextended my visit with Fran and had to dash to the subway and then to the LIRR. To my horror, I did not miss "The Last Train to Clarksville" (a 1966 song by The Monkees), but I did miss the last train to Hicksville! *Now, what do I do?* I wondered.

I had no choice. I called home and told Mom I was stuck and needed Dad to pick me up. They had already retired to bed for the evening. I occasionally arrived home late, and they were not normally very concerned about that. They trusted me. After all, I was a college kid now! Dad came to the phone. I cringed at the thought of asking him to pick me up. He was not happy. After all, he needed his sleep and had to rise early in the morning to go to work in NYC the next day. No, that day! He drove to the station, picked me up, and after a well-deserved tongue-lashing, we arrived home at about 2:30 a.m. Most of the way home was in silence as I stared out the window. I made sure I never did that again!

In the summers of '63, '64, and '65, Fran worked part time at Mark Cross, an up-scale leather goods store on Fifth Avenue and Fifty-Fifth Street in NYC. Her father ran the men's department there. Many celebrities would enter the store, and Fran had the occasional opportunity to show the store's goods to them. They included Hugh O'Brien, who played the leading role in the TV western series *The Life and Legend of Wyatt Earp*, Frank Sinatra, and Mia Farrow.

September 1965, the start of our junior year.

Fran dedicated her summer of '66 to the Head Start Program, which provided safe and positive environments for children to learn, play, and build the skills that prepared them for kindergarten and beyond. As I mentioned, I began flipping hamburgers and then eventually progressed to my next job at JCPenney in nearby Plainview, New York. I worked in the men's and boys' sections, keeping the clothing aisles and racks organized and presentable, and marking suits, slacks, and sport coats for alterations.

During my time at SJU, I had the opportunity to meet and talk with Fran's brother, Vince. He had attended ROTC at Notre Dame, and after graduation, he entered active duty as an officer in the US Air Force (USAF). I asked many questions about service in the AF and became increasingly interested. I did more research, focusing on numerous areas of expertise, called Air Force specialty codes—AFSCs.

Naturally, one thing comes to mind when one thinks of the AF—flying, and beyond that, becoming a pilot. With the war in Vietnam heating up, that became a concern when I received a draft notice from the US Army. I had forgotten to notify them that I was a student, which would have delayed any draft during college. Once I straightened that out, thank goodness, it bought some time. But more than likely, the inevitable would have to happen with an assignment in the army at some point after graduation.

I initiated some discussions with Fran as our relationship became more serious. I was trying to wrap my head around life after graduation, and many elements commingled: Where do Fran and I end up? What will be my job in the future? Where will that job take place? What job will Fran have, and where will that happen? Will I be drafted immediately? So many unanswered questions!

My discussion centered around that perhaps the best choice was to enter the AF immediately and return after initial training at Officer Training School, a three-month course of study and training at Lackland Air Force Base (AFB) in San Antonio, Texas, where I would earn my officer's commission. At that point, we could get married. I did not ask Fran to marry me at this juncture, but the subject slowly emerged, and Fran's reaction was, well, to put it mildly, no!

She raised some excellent points that once I became AF property, I would not have much control over my schedule, and we would not be confident that we could set a wedding date with any assurance. As I describe later, it turned out she was right on the money with that concern. As this discussion unfolded over the latter half of our spring semester in 1966, Fran decided it might be best to take a pause and date others, and there was a period over the summer when Fran and I stopped dating. It was sort of mutual agreement, with the thought that perhaps we should date others. After all, we were still in college and very young, so what was the rush?

Fran's mother understood this completely. However, I heard later that Fran's father was not supportive. He basically presented a dilemma to Fran. He told her, "You can marry anyone you want as long as you only go out with Bill!" Now that's an Italian father's logic for you. But it did not work. Fran *did* date others over the summer of 1966, before the start of our senior year. These other relationships went nowhere. I refrained from dating others, convinced I would get back with Fran. I loved her very much, and I knew she loved me. The foundation of our relationship was set more firmly than one might have thought.

NO WEDDING
IN OCTOBER

◾ FALL SEMESTER, 1966

The summer of 1966 offered me an opportunity to add to my mediocre savings account. I changed employers once again and worked in a clothing store called Bonds in Plainview, New York, repeating my sales skills in the men's and boys' clothing departments. With some mentoring, I extended my utility in the departments to fit the customers, young and old, for suits, slacks, and sport coats. It was especially gratifying to help parents in their purchase of a young son's first suit.

I was now cranked up to enter senior year at SJU, focus more on what was ahead, and most assuredly rekindle my relationship with Fran. It never really ended during the brief hiatus after junior year, but it felt weird not spending that time with her. Academics were now under way. Some of the math classes were difficult for me as they gained in intensity and depth, both in theory and application. Despite the greater effort needed in that regard, I still participated in the Men's Glee Club for the third year in a row. Student friendships were renewed and matured, the social environment brightened, and my time with Fran increased steadily. We participated in double dates with a few select couples. There were more dances, more corsages, and more visits with our families.

I had invited Fran to my paternal grandparents' apartment in Brooklyn to meet some of my family. My father was the oldest of seven children; he had four brothers and two sisters. The older sister was a Sister, a nun. She went by the name of Sister Gerard then but later reverted to her given name, Marie—Sister Marie. I told Fran that she would be there and that I would love to have them meet. Shivers ran up and down Fran's spine, as she could only recall many unpleasant experiences with nuns during her elementary school and high school years. However, once she met Sister Gerard, she was absolutely relieved with this extremely sweet member of my family.

"Why can't all nuns be like her?" would be her rhetorical question.

On another occasion, I invited Fran to my house in Hicksville, where she would meet my maternal grandmother, among others. It went something like this. No, it went *exactly* like this. We drove up to my house. Grandma Costa was already there, and with great anticipation, she was outside, where she usually perched herself when she knew someone was coming to visit. As I parked the car, Grandma hurried down the driveway, grabbed me in a body-swallowing hug, and kissed me all over my face.

"Bellie-Jay," she said. She understood English and spoke it well but had some difficulty saying some words, so "Billy" came out "Bellie-Jay". She then grabbed Fran, hugged her, and kissed her for an extended time. Then she suddenly stopped and pulled back her head a bit while she still held on to Fran. "Bellie-Jay, whosa dis?"

"Grandma, this is my girlfriend, Fran," I said with a smile aimed at Fran.

Grandma pulled Fran in for round 2 of her special love. "Oh, Francie, Francie!"

At this point, Grandma had twenty-four grandchildren, but she always made you feel you were the most important. And without a doubt, that now extended to Fran. She was a hug-and-kiss-first, ask-questions-later, lovable grandma. As a greater number of family introductions happened, the seriousness of Fran and my relationship became more apparent. So from a family and social perspective, life was looking better in the fall of 1966.

Nationally, however, by the end of 1966, American forces in Vietnam would total 385,000 men, with an additional 60,000 sailors stationed offshore. More than six thousand Americans had been killed that year, and thirty thousand had been wounded. Vietcong casualties were much higher, with an estimated sixty-one thousand killed, and their troops now numbered over 280,000. The cloud of the war grew darker. The need to formulate a post-college plan was becoming more intense.

■ UNCONVENTIONAL PROPOSAL

I do not remember the exact date, but I *do* remember the exact place. I was bowling with some friends in Plainview, a few miles from my house. It was early evening when we ended, and before I left for home, I went outside to call Fran. No one had mobile phones at that time, and phone booths were still available everywhere. I dialed Fran, and we spoke. I don't remember anything about our lengthy conversation except one thing.

I asked, "Will you marry me?"

Without hesitation, Fran replied, "Yes!"

I did not plan any venue for this, no special setting or dinner, no special day, no otherwise romantic environment. It just evolved into our conversation. It just happened. I understood how well our relationship matured and was confident in the outcome when I popped the question. I *did* get down on one knee in the phone booth to propose. People coming out of the bowling alley gave me a funny look as they walked by. Hey, who is to say that did not happen? There was no FaceTime; there were no witnesses! There also was no proof that it did or did not happen.

As the news spread to our families, we decided to get engaged on Christmas Eve and targeted October 1967 for our wedding. This would give us ample time to plan. The church was a no-brainer; it would be at Immaculate Conception Church in Jamaica Estates, Queens. We would select a reception facility that would accommodate about 150 guests.

I had a few hundred dollars to put toward an engagement ring. Fran's father had a friend in NYC who worked in the Diamond District, which runs on Forty-Seventh Street between Fifth and Sixth Avenues in Manhattan. So we went to see Mr. Barashino.

I put my money on the table. "This is all I have. What can you do for me?" I asked. He was gracious and extremely helpful, suggesting we put the money toward a quality diamond with a simple white gold setting. I purchased a one-carat round diamond with beautiful clarity and color. He further suggested a nearby shop to find a matching wedding band.

We found the perfect ring, and Mr. Barashino added a tiny diamond to the wedding band. The unique curvatures of the two rings fit adjacent to each other. They were a perfectly matched set—like us. I presented the engagement ring to Fran at her home next to her Christmas tree in the living room. We celebrated our engagement with our families and enjoyed the holiday break. Our final semester at SJU was on the horizon.

▪ THE HOME STRETCH

With academics in full swing, Fran continued her senior year student teaching, a critical component of her courses and grades. Student teaching required spending every day at a local public school in a classroom setting with elementary schoolchildren and covering varied subjects. She also attended an evening class.

I had four classes remaining, twelve credits, to obtain my bachelor's degree. I took two required math classes and two elective sociology classes. Our academic load was set for the final semester. Since we were going to marry, I also ramped up my work schedule to forty hours/week—full-time—at Bond's to build a bank account and strive for an initial level of financial independence. A full-time job and college classes kept me busy, no doubt!

I contacted a local AF reserve recruitment center to apply for training and avert any army draft. I selected UPT—undergraduate pilot training as the AFSC. There were approximately 125 AFSCs in the AF, but the choice was clear in my mind. If I was going to be in the AF, then flying was the goal. Being selected for pilot training was not a guarantee, and there was required testing in addition to a college degree.

Candidates must complete a comprehensive physical exam, qualify for and complete the three-month OTS in San Antonio, Texas, and achieve a satisfactory grade on the Air Force Officer Qualifying Test (AFOQT). I completed all the written test requirements and spent a full day at McGuire AFB near North Hanover, New Jersey, for the physical.

The AF informed me they would contact me after graduation and notify me when to enter active duty if all prequalifications were met. When I told them that Fran and I intended to marry in October, they advised that we move that to an earlier date to avoid any draft by the army and that the AF would target my entry into service in the summer months. Based on that information, we moved our wedding date to Saturday, July 15, 1967. The second half of 1967 was beginning to take shape.

■ AF ORDERS

Shock comes in many forms. Mine came via a letter dated 20 March 1967 (the date is formatted in military-speak, which I use going forward) from the "Department of the Air Force, Headquarters Lackland Military Training Center (ATC), Lackland Air Force Base, Texas. The subject: Officer Training School [OTS] Selection Letter (Male Candidate)," indicated that Maj. Johnsrud, chief, Student Selection Division, was pleased to inform me that I, "have been selected for Officer Training School. Upon graduation, your initial assignment will be to the Pilot utilization career field."

As I read this, I was thrilled with the news. I continued reading the requirements to accept the assignment. There were necessary reply forms, Armed Forces Security Questionnaires, a personal history statement, FBI fingerprint cards, and so on. All had to be returned to the nearest air force recruiter within five days of the letter. I needed to act fast!

The letter further dictated that I must bring a certified college transcript from the SJU registrar's office indicating the degree awarded, date, and major area of study to be presented when I enlisted at OTS. Candidates entering OTS start with an enlistment grade of staff sergeant. On graduation, they are commissioned as second lieutenants in the AF Reserves.

The recruiter had fifteen days from the date of the letter to submit all my forms and initiate a National Agency Check (NAC). The NAC is required as a background investigation for access to confidential or secret information. The check includes a review of the FBI criminal history repository, a credit check, and a check of local law enforcement agencies. No problem there; I had no history that would discredit me. It was up to the recruiter to get this done. Otherwise, my application would go on inactive status.

The final paragraph served the blow:

> Upon completion of the above requirements, this letter is authorization for your Recruiter to enlist you in the United States Air Force specifically for Class 68-B. You are to be enlisted so as to provide the proper amount of travel time and report not earlier than 0700 hours 5 Jul 67 and not later than 1300 hours 6 Jul 67 to the Officer Training School Wing Headquarters, Building 146, Lackland Training Annex. (See OTS Informational Brochure for a map showing Lackland Training Annex). In no instance will the Recruiter enlist you earlier for Officer Training without written authority from this Headquarters.

What, 5 July? Wait, I'm getting married on 15 July. I wondered, *How do I tell Fran? How do I tell the family? How do I fix this?* The letter closed with, "Best wishes to you for a successful career in the United States Air Force."

Holy crap! *Holy crap!*

◼ CHANGE IN PLANS

I called the school where Fran was student teaching, identified myself as her fiancé, and stated it was very important that I talk with her immediately. I could imagine what went through her mind when a school staff member interrupted her class and directed her to the phone.

Fran's reaction was what you would suspect and echoed mine: moderate to extreme panic! How would we ever find a church and reception facility in New York for a date before my enlistment? In New York, people usually needed to plan a wedding at least a year in advance, and there we were with a mere three months to find something available. We did not hold out much hope but tackled the issue immediately.

It was as if the stars aligned, and someone in a high place was on our side. Fran and her mother checked with the church first. And when the priest opened the church schedule for weddings, miraculously (no pun intended), there was an opening at 11 a.m. on Saturday, 24 June. The location for our wedding reception also fell into place as our good fortune continued. We managed to secure the Salisbury Country Club in East Meadow, Nassau County, Long Island. Today the area surrounding that former facility is known as Eisenhower Park.

Whew! We were on the calendar! The pace would go from a jog to a full sprint immediately as we needed to address all the significant events of the next few months: complete our final semester at SJU, graduate and celebrate on 11 June, and cement all the details of the wedding ceremony and venue, guest list, honeymoon; the list was dizzying. Fran and her mother worked especially hard.

As weddings go, the guest list is usually a major topic of dispute. One of my principal jobs was to democratically limit the number of guests from my side of the family, which was immense compared to Fran's. One of my mother's four brothers alone had twelve children, and I had difficulty convincing her that we could not invite them all. We asked the oldest of the children, my cousin, and his wife to represent that family.

I didn't have a cousin named Vinny. It would have been cool to say, "My cousin Vinny came to our wedding," but the movie didn't come out until 1992. Anyway, all other matters seemed minuscule.

As I looked back on my college experience, I recall a challenging workload with a couple of failed courses I needed to repeat and pass. I attended additional classes in the summers of '64, '65, and '66. I sustained the daily commute and less-than-optimal study environment and complemented school with outside work to earn some income. I maintained an average performance and graduated with 134 credits. The culmination of all this effort would finally come to a close.

■ SJU GRADUATION

Sunday, 11 June 1967, was a beautiful day with mild breezes and sunny skies over the rows and rows of white folding chairs spread over the SJU Queens campus and facing the stage and podium. Our families were there, ready with their cameras and movie-taking devices. The ceremony was exceptionally long as there were graduates from several departments at the SJU campus: School of Education (Fran's), St. John's College (mine)—the oldest of the schools, Department of Nursing Education, College of Business Administration, and the College of Pharmacy. There was an SJU Brooklyn campus with its own six distinct departments and ceremony.

Degree in early childhood education.

Fran and I walked together. We waved to our families after receiving our temporary degree parchments. Our official diplomas would arrive later, expressed in traditional Latin. It would not only be a reminder of all the hard work we endured and the birthplace of our relationship, but perhaps more important, and something we appreciated much later in life, that there is so much more to learn. What we accomplished by earning our bachelor's degrees was the tip of the iceberg as we came to recognize that learning never stops. It was a better understanding of the word "graduate"—to advance, move up. There is always more to know.

Degree in math.

With the ceremony complete and the abundance of congratulations winding down, our full-time focus was on our wedding day. The days ahead were a frenzy of activities—finalizing the guest list, ordering tuxedo rentals, flowers, the limousine, confirming honeymoon reservations, and on and on. While all this took place, we maintained a perspective of what life would be like after the wedding and honeymoon. My schedule was set with entering the air force, and since Fran had tested and qualified in the NYC Public School System for a teaching position in the fall of '66, she would do some substitute teaching during the summer and begin the new school year as a kindergarten teacher while I was away.

A visit to SJU in July 2022.
Nearly fifty-nine years after we met.

▪ THIRTEEN DAYS LATER

The time between graduation and our big day flew by in a flash. It was time to "execute the mission." (I was feeling the military influence already!) My best man and Fran's maid of honor arrived at our respective homes early to assist in their supportive roles. They both graduated from SJU a year before Fran and me and had dated. We knew them from the Glee Club and extended our social ties with them on many double dates. Their relationship did not progress as ours did. Over time, they went their separate ways and were currently dating others. It must have been a bit awkward for them in their roles at our wedding, but they never let that be a distraction.

My best man and I were squirreled away in a side room at the church while an earlier wedding ceremony was underway. As family and guests arrived, they were forced to wait outside the church until the current wedding was over and the church was vacated. It was a bit of a nuisance as that wedding did not end on time. It extended past the 11:00 a.m. start time for our wedding. With the wind whipping up and more people gathering, impatience and anxiety were on the rise. Eventually, that all became an afterthought as our ceremony became open for business.

I stood at the altar with the other men in the wedding party. Everyone was seated, and Fran's mother was escorted to her place on the left side of the aisle in the first row. When the "Wedding March (Here Comes the Bride)" began, Fran's father proudly walked her down the aisle behind the maid of honor and bridesmaids. My focus was on a single point in the entire space of the church.

Fran looked absolutely beautiful, and it was enhanced by the contrast of her recently acquired suntan against her white wedding dress. Her mother was apprehensive when, prior to the wedding, Fran went to the beach. She warned Fran that a tan would not go well with the wedding dress. But I thought she looked amazing, especially complemented by her broad smile and sparkling white teeth.

With the wedding vows taken, and photo sessions outside the church and at the Salisbury Country Club grounds behind us, we celebrated with friends and family at a reception with great music, a delicious dinner, and a wedding cake. Well, we *heard* the dinner was delicious. We could not verify that because we were so busy making the rounds to greet guests at tables and indulging in extended conversations that we missed our wedding dinner.

Wedding day, 24 June 1967.

We were starving when we arrived at the Americana Hotel in NYC for our first evening as husband and wife. We ordered room service and quickly gobbled our food before we moved on to the business of being married. The next day we left the city and headed to our rustic cabin at Alpine Village at the southern section of Lake George, New York—a 212-mile, three-and-a-half-hour drive upstate for our weeklong honeymoon.

USAF OTS

■ ELEVEN DAYS LATER

> I, William A. Cimino, do solemnly swear that I will support and defend the Constitution of the United States against all enemies, foreign and domestic; that I will bear true faith and allegiance to the same; and that I will obey the orders of the President of the United States and the orders of the officers appointed over me, according to regulations and the Uniform Code of Military Justice. So help me God.

Along with a roomful of other military candidates—men and women—I stood at attention at Fort Hamilton Army Base, located in the southwestern corner of Brooklyn, surrounded by the communities of Bay Ridge and Dyker Heights. It was in direct view of the Verrazano-Narrows Bridge, which connects the boroughs of Brooklyn and Staten Island. With our right hands raised, we repeated those words with our names inserted. In those few short seconds, I became the property of the USAF. They would tell me where to go and when, and when to jump and how high.

Fran had driven me to the installation that Wednesday morning on 5 July 1967. All the recent events—SJU graduation, wedding, honeymoon, and a brief few days in Jamaica, New York—seemed to happen at warp speed and were now in the rearview mirror. We knew that in a short while, my training would separate us for a time. We said our goodbyes at the airport and realized that the next three months would be difficult being apart. We promised we would write to each other as often as possible.

Once we completed our official enlistment, our group set out to our first assignment locations via various transport methods. I departed from LaGuardia Airport and landed in Dallas, Texas, at 2100 hours CDT. I thought I would have time to call Fran, but there was a quick turnaround to catch the next flight to San Antonio. On arrival, an AF officer lined us up to wait for a bus to take us to the Medina Annex at Lackland AFB. Lackland was an essential component of the massive AF's Air Training Command (ATC). I got to bed at 0300 on 6 July. It was a long day, the first of many, and I was ready for some sleep.

■ OTS—THEN AND NOW

AF OTS began at Lackland in November 1959. The first class (60-A) had eighty-nine trainees, including eleven women, who graduated and were commissioned as second lieutenants on 9 February 1960. Before OTS, other programs enabled civilians and enlisted to progress to officer status, but they were phased out as OTS became the sole AF organization for training future AF officers. OTS graduates varied through the years, from eighty-nine in the first year to a high of nearly 7,900 in 1967 as the war in Vietnam continued.

On 1 July 1993, ATC merged with Air University (AU) to form the new Air Education and Training Command (AETC). This command contained both OTS and the AF Reserve Officers' Training Corp (ROTC) conducted at colleges and universities across the country. During the spring and summer of 1993, OTS gradually relocated to Maxwell AFB in Alabama, the home of AU.

■ IT'S MILITARY TIME

If I didn't realize that my world had changed at Fort Hamilton when I took my oath, there was no doubt once I arrived in Texas, and indeed confirmed once I arrived at Medina. I shared room 231 in a three-floor building with two other officer trainees (OTs). One was from Philadelphia, the other from Kansas City. Both men were married. There was one single bunk and one double; I took the top bunk of the double. We each had a small locker and shared a desk. I claimed a section of the desk for Fran's photo. When the others saw her picture, no one complained or said I couldn't keep it there.

We became friends quickly as we shared a common emptiness: We missed our wives. And oh yes, we had a common goal: We needed to work our way to 0900 hours on 29 September 1967, OTS graduation.

I was well into dreamland when we were awakened at 0530 hours sharp. *What? I need more sleep than a couple of hours*, I thought. I quickly learned that our "normal day" would be from 0530 to 2400 hours. Our daily routine would begin soon enough, with classes on Monday, 10 July. We received an orientation on 7 July and were given our first assignment: We had to memorize four chapters in the OTS manual and the chain of command beginning with President Johnson (commander in chief) to OTs by Saturday, 8 July. There were thirty-five positions on that list.

I processed into class 68-B, Squadron 2, Flight 5 of the 3645th Student Squadron. There were 230 OTs in the class broken into squadrons and flights. This was just one of several classes that started every six weeks to train and attain commissioning as officers in the USAF. For the first six weeks, new OTs were lowerclassmen, known as C-men. In the second half of training, OTs became upperclassmen. OTS is student-run for the most part, with student ranks from second lieutenant to colonel.

The upperclassmen didn't harass us too much, but we quickly learned our duties and the need for discipline, meticulousness, cleanliness, and the school's code of honor: "I will not lie, cheat, steal, nor will I tolerate among us those who do." This was Article 133 of the *Uniformed Code of Military Justice.* Case in point. One day someone left some money on a table in our building's dayroom on the first floor, a place to lounge with others or study. The money remained there for several days, until word got around, and the rightful owner claimed it.

I immediately liked the order and structure instilled at the school. I believe it played a huge part in developing my personal life going forward and to this day. I became very organized and detailed; I routinely worked off lists. Later assignments enhanced these procedures in my everyday life.

My daughter, Jeannie, teases me about my regimen frequently. For example, when she and her family (husband and two children) were coming to Virginia to visit us from Colorado, I told her I had everything planned for their stay with Fran and me.

Jeannie jokingly but lovingly said, "Dad, do you have a spreadsheet for that?"

"No. I thought a PowerPoint would be better this time," I said. Lots of laughs. I am convinced she will tease me about this for the rest of my life, right up until I plan my funeral if that is possible.

There was more discipline: at meals. We would be four to a table. No talking. Feet must be flat on the floor with heels together. One hand must be under the table, leaving one hand to maneuver the food into your mouth. We were allowed eight minutes for breakfast and ten minutes each for lunch and dinner. No food was allowed in the room.

You were allowed to eat all you wanted at the chow hall, but the time limit prevented any serious attempt at making it a marathon session.

We spent most of our time on Sunday applying about fifteen coats of black polish to our shoes, spit-shining them until we could see our faces in the reflection. All three of us finger-dusted our room since inspections could be either announced or at random. (I don't think I will demand these measures when my daughter and family come to visit. That's a bit harsh!)

Clothing (uniform) issue, briefings on the rules, the schedule, haircuts—short ones—and the emphasis on teamwork, discipline, and standardization were all quickly prioritized at the outset. Our training would include drills, ceremonies, and room and uniform inspections that taught attention to detail and the need to form and operate as a team. We would need to stand at "parade rest," or, "attention," as directed during inspections. Any infractions would result in demerits called "gigs." An accumulation of too many gigs was not a good thing.

Training encompassed a wide variety of subjects, physical and mental endurance, and camaraderie among a group with a common goal. The phrase, "Cooperate and Graduate," which captured the need for teamwork, was an instant motto in OTS and would resonate in many other AF training programs ahead.

Classroom courses included the fundamentals of leadership, military management, the structure and mission of the AF, how to function in multicultural environments due to the nature of being an expeditionary air force, as well as basic combat skills, although OTS was not as rigorous in this regard as basic military training (BMT). Each training day would include physical training (PT), classroom instruction, field teamwork, and challenging situations that required leadership, methodology, cooperation, and stamina.

PT in Texas in the summer was brutal and challenging, with temperatures reaching one hundred degrees or higher. The worst was August. We would need to complete a series of exercises in a specified time and run the mile in eight minutes or less, which we would need to achieve by training day 50. By mid-July, I had worked up to a 3.5-minute half mile. By the end of July, I ran the mile in 7.5 minutes. Although not considered fast, it was certainly fast for me. One day, one of the members of our flight did not have his name tag, so the whole flight had to run in fatigues and combat boots. We made sure that didn't happen again!

I also completed medical exams, eye tests, dental checks, and immunizations during training. The shots were given by an "air gun" blast into the upper arm. There were times when I didn't feel well or up to par, and it was reflected in my physical training performance. I even fell down some stairs one day due to being overtired. There was minor soreness for a few days, but nothing major. Thank goodness for that. It would not have been good to fall back to another class due to any serious injury.

No one wanted to delay graduation. This reminds me of one day when our class completed a parade for graduation practice. We were told to remain at attention for an important announcement. A senior training officer stated that after reviewing the Army Officer Training Program, which was so superior and effective, the AF decided to extend the AF OTS, and our class would graduate in December. *What?* After a long pause, we learned that was not true. The training officer said it was an example of being ready to accept that things change. Whew! We almost did a group faint!

There were exams every week and assigned duties. We had to give speeches on topics like discipline, leadership, and military justice. Our classes ended at 1620 hours, when we would go back to our rooms to fall in for chow. After that, our evenings included studying until the lights went out at midnight. During the week, a few minutes before midnight was the usual time I could write a letter to Fran. We would have some time to talk on the phone on the weekends, and it couldn't come fast enough.

By mid-August, our flight had moved to upperclassmen status. We had two OTs per room and were now on the ground floor. It was our turn to switch roles and treat the lower classmen as we were treated, teach them what we learned, and make our expectations very clear.

It gave me great pleasure when we were up early as a new class arrived and one C-man reached his assigned room at 0515 hours. He threw his bag down and was ready to claim a bunk and jump into bed.

I shouted, "Don't go to bed. You have to get up in fifteen minutes!" I think he was in shock. His eyes widened, and his jaw dropped. *Yep. Get used to it, buddy!*

I wrote to Fran as often as I could to say I loved and missed her and to keep her updated on my training. I sent forty-seven letters and added some cards. Fran wrote to me every day, sending numerous cards and seventy-seven letters. They were a source of my strength during training and helped to keep me motivated. I never thought that I would not complete OTS, but there were times when the stress levels were extremely high in this nonstop physically, mentally, and psychologically demanding program. I dedicated myself to the training and looked forward to seeing her again when she would travel on 23 September ahead of the OTS graduation scheduled for the twenty-ninth.

I realized much later in my career that OTS fundamentals provided me with a foundation to build what drives my actions and behavior today in terms of organization, discipline, interaction with others, appreciation for authority and diversity, and love of country. While my parents always taught me to be respectful, truthful, and kind, I also highly valued those characteristics engendered and enhanced by my military experience. OTS established a bedrock.

■ PCS ORDERS AND GRADUATION

As graduation day became closer, every OTS student became anxious to hear news of their next assignment in the career fields they chose. We would quickly learn that the AF had forms and special orders that addressed every active-duty status and assignment change.

On 15 September, Special Orders AB-12990 stated I would be appointed in the Reserve AF as a second lieutenant for an indefinite term effective 29 September. There were twenty-one other OTS students in this order. Dated the same day, Special Orders AC-682 addressed a list of forty-eight staff sergeants, yours truly being one of them, stating we were relieved from assignment at OTS and honorably discharged effective 28 September 1967 (the day before commissioning). An honorable discharge certificate was also issued on the twenty-eighth. These two documents effectively transitioned me as an enlisted member in the regular AF and started my active-duty reserve status as an AF officer.

There was also an ATC letter dated 29 September, subject: Appointment as Reserve Officer of the Air Force addressed solely to me, 2nd Lt. William A. Cimino Jr., followed by my official AF number. Even though I never used the "Jr." after my name, since the AF somehow got that on my official records from the first day, it has stuck throughout my military career. The letter informed me that I completed OTS and was tendered the reserve officer appointment. Lots of paperwork, all addressed the transition.

Notice of my assignment arrived in Special Order AB-13193, dated 19 September 1967 from ATC, ten days before graduation. The order had several components: appointment in the AF Reserve (as if I didn't know this by now); assigned AFSC 0006, which is a code for pilot trainee; estimated departure date of 29 September; security clearance of secret; and authorization to move dependents (Fran) and household goods.

The final information contained the organization assignment—3645 Student Squadron, ATC, Laughlin AFB, Texas—to attend a fifty-three-week pilot training course, class 69-04, which would convene on 25 October 1967. This assignment was in Del Rio, Texas. Laughlin was one of several pilot training bases across the United States. My report date was NLT 24 October 1967.

COMMISSIONING CEREMONY

OTS Class 68-B (partial photo)—230 officer trainees entered, 105 graduated.
2nd Lt. William A. Cimino, fourth row, eighth from the left.

I performed well in OTS. My overall grades were in the mid-80s in this rigorous program, and my officer trainee effectiveness reports (OTERs)—issued in the fourth, seventh, and tenth weeks of training—were very good.

The day we all worked hard to reach was here—Friday, 29 September 1967. Fran traveled from New York on 23 September and was able to stay in guesthouse accommodations on the base. She would be among many proud families and friends who came to see their loved ones march by the viewing stand as the band played patriotic music, listen to the comments and accolades from the OTS commander, and witness the commissioning of each new AF officer as they walked up to accept their rewards while executing sharp salutes.

After all the new officers were commissioned, in unison, they threw their uniform wheel hats into the air as whistles and shouts could be heard loudly and clearly. Fran pinned on my shiny new second lieutenant bars. It was done. OTS was just one of many more training sessions to follow, one of many more training courses with a specific objective and goal that would add to military experience, knowledge, and refinement.

The day ended with a party that evening to celebrate with each other and with those who traveled far and wide to share in the joy of our accomplishments. That was the first AF party Fran and I attended. Many more followed in the years ahead, each with a diverse group of men and women, some married, some single, from all corners of the country, and with different faiths, ethnicities, and backgrounds. But all were united for common service in the USAF.

I loved the diversity and was excited about the future. I thought, *I'm ready! I'm pumped! UPT, here I come!*

UPT ASSIGNMENT

■ LAUGHLIN AFB, DEL RIO, TEXAS

Fran and I spent a few days in Texas after OTS graduation to have some time together before traveling back to New York to visit family and prepare for our return to the Lone Star state, where we would live for the next year. We took in some sites: the Alamo, the Chinese Sunken Gardens, and the San Antonio River Walk. We also visited Alamo Village, a movie set and tourist attraction near Brackettville, about two and a half hours west of San Antonio.

At the Village, Fran met Dean Martin's horse that appeared in the movie *Bandolero*, which would come out in 1968. We have a photo! During a filming break, I had the opportunity to meet and shake hands with Jimmy Stewart, who played Dean Martin's brother in the movie. If I remember anything about Stewart—other than that he was an actor, served in the military, and was a brigadier general in the USAF Reserve—it was his height, about six feet three inches, and his rich blue eyes.

After arriving back in Jamaica, New York, in early October, we visited with family and friends. Fran's parents had given us a car for our graduation and wedding gifts—a red, 1967 Corvair convertible with a black top. It was the Chevy that Ralph Nader, a noted consumer protection activist, viewed as dangerous, primarily due to the rear engine design. As far as I recall, we loved it and never had any issues with it.

We planned our road trip to Del Rio by a direct route through the southeastern and southern states. As we drove further to the south and west, it was disturbing to see signs of racial discrimination: "No Colored Allowed," "White bathroom only," and similarly divisive statements. That did not sit well with us. We would learn there are not only open displays such as these but even more subtle ways to discriminate, discredit, and alienate African Americans and other people of color.

When I reflect on all the years of my service and beyond and the diverse composition of the men and women in the military, while it has its share of social problems, it has been an environment of teamwork, mission-oriented actions, and devotion to duty and country from all members—Black, White, Latino, Asian; the list goes on.

We arrived in Del Rio a few days before my pilot training would start. It was an eye-opener! Coming from the boroughs of NYC, it certainly had an immediate and unambiguous impact on us both. We drove past Laughlin AFB before we reached our destination. A road sign ahead said, "Welcome to Del Rio."

We asked, "Where is it?" We continued driving and eventually found what we believed to be Del Rio. It is a city in southwestern Texas, 152 miles from San Antonio, and only 6 miles from the Mexican border and the city of Acuña. It did not take long to drive through the main parts of town and recognize all it had to offer. We both thought, *This is going to be an interesting year!*

We checked in at the base to get some information on housing. We learned that we would need to find off-base housing. The student pilot numbers in the 1967–68 time frame, with the war in Vietnam continuing to surge, were around three thousand per year, which would come from all UPT bases across the United States. Given that statistic and contributory share that Laughlin made to those numbers, it became clear why we would need to find off-base housing. The airbase could not accommodate all the trainees. We received some recommendations from Base Housing Services and began the search for a temporary home. When you are in the military, your home is always your temporary home because, without a doubt, you are going to move to a new assignment before too long.

We found a small corner duplex apartment to rent on the eastern edge of town. It had the essentials: a small kitchen, a small family room, two small bedrooms, a bath, and a one-vehicle carport. Emphasis on "small." Our address was 1214 Bedell Avenue in Del Rio, directly across from a bowling alley and only fifteen minutes, about eight miles, from the base.

We didn't have much clothing, furniture, or personal articles, so we fit perfectly into the duplex. The challenge would be how Fran spends her days and keeps busy while I worked through UPT. She quickly learned her way around town and the base. It was a force function. Here's a map. Go explore!

Eventually, we would expand our curiosity into Mexico and the city of Acuña, with its many shops, restaurants, and attractions. We usually went there with friends we met from the UPT class, all looking for the same variety of life in a new and remote place. These casual times proved to be a pleasant diversion from the new Cooperate and Graduate environment of pilot training. I was about to learn the intensity and depth of this phase in my AF training.

■ UPT COMPONENTS

It was Wednesday, 25 October 1967, day 1 of pilot training. And in a few days, I would turn twenty-two years old. I thought, *When I graduate from UPT, I will be twenty-three, a young pilot in the USAF. The war in Vietnam is not likely to end anytime soon, so I just may end up flying into Southeast Asia!* But putting those thoughts aside, it was time to get to the business of learning about flight and flying. I emphasize both because the training consisted of academics *and* flying.

There would be testing for both. The grades would be compiled for an overall grade and placement in the class. Additionally, there would be routine PT and field exercises, like PLFs—parachute landing falls—that enable you to minimize or eliminate any injury during contact with the ground after aircraft ejection. Daily classroom instruction started early and was typically a minimum of ten-hour days.

Before a pilot trainee even enters the cockpit, he (it was all male back in 1967) or she (more recently) would complete some basic academics. Initially, training was primarily classroom instruction. I was eager to learn all about aerodynamics and the principles of flight, the way air moves around an aircraft and its effects on the flying machine. A fascinating topic.

Myriad flight-related topics included airmanship; aviation physiology (T-37); physiological support; flight instruments; principles of flight, with a focus on the four primary forces—lift, weight (or gravity), thrust, and drag; VFR and IFR navigation; aural visual code; flying safety; aviation physiology (T-38); and radar. We would also learn the structure of controlled airspace, flight planning, weather, the FAA, and air traffic control.

Air traffic control included a diverse set of topics relative to flight: area control centers/en-route centers, classes (levels) of controlled airspace, approach and terminal control, ground control, flight traffic, mapping, and air navigation aids. Each topic had classroom instruction, study guides, and literature that we needed to consume. There was frequent testing, and instructors frequently informed us that a wash-out rate would apply to those who underperformed in the program. Other training hours focused on orientation and processing, duty, counterinsurgency, physical development, and condition, and marksmanship training.

Flying training would begin on the tenth day of class, after we established a good foundation of basic flight knowledge. Even though a shift to the flight line and the aircraft would occur at that point, academics would continue throughout the program and focus more on the aircraft systems germane to each phase of flight training. Instructor pilots (IPs) covered the unique features of three training aircraft: the Cessna T-41, the military version of the Cessna 172; the Cessna T-37 Tweet; and the Northrop T-38 Talon.

Initial flights in each aircraft varied between sixty and ninety minutes, We focused on basic flight characteristics and simple aerial maneuvers. On subsequent training flights, the IP quickly advanced to more intense and complicated aircraft maneuvers such as stalls and falls, spins, aileron rolls, barrel rolls, loops, and situations that encompassed specific aircraft emergencies requiring recovery actions.

The first week of pilot training had my complete attention. There was never a dull moment as IPs covered the topics in detail. My head was in the game, and I made sure I didn't fall behind in the many workbooks and academic exercises for each subject. After a long academic day, I returned home to have dinner with Fran only to jump back into learning mode lasting into the late-evening hours. The weekends gave us some respite but would not go without more hours devoted to studying.

We had a diverse group of trainees from across the country, as you would expect. Some trainees had some flight experience, but most did not. We had study groups to discuss topics or strive for answers to common questions. In my few short months in the AF, I could recall those characters that stood out for whatever reason. OTS had a few, and it was no exception in UPT.

There was this one guy from somewhere in Texas. He had a deep Texan drawl. It sounded odd, especially since I was born in Brooklyn and had my own accent, which I am sure *he* noted. We often teased each other in a friendly manner. He knew I was of Italian descent, so he greeted me with, "Hey, Gooombah," in the thickest drawl you can imagine.

"Hey, y'all," I responded and added as much Brooklyn as I could throw back at him.

For the remainder of October, my performance in academics was good. I tested well and felt confident in understanding the fundamentals of flight and all associated subjects. It was time to transition to flight training in the T-41. This aircraft is a short-range, high-winged trainer with a small, six-cylinder piston engine of 145hp and equipped with avionics and other systems consistent with military needs. The goal was to complete about twenty hours of flight instruction and flight check before a solo flight.

Once a trainee completed the T-41 phase, he would advance to the T-37, a small twin-engine jet trainer with side-by-side seating/controls and ejection seats. This was considered the USAF primary trainer, which IPs and students liked for its agility and responsiveness, although it was not overpowered. Part of the training required the student to intentionally place the aircraft in a spin. The IP would demonstrate the steps to recover to controlled flight. Students would practice these maneuvers until they became proficient.

Other training areas included T-37 policies and procedures, contact flying, instrument flying, navigation, and formation. A synthetic trainer—the T-4—enabled simulator training, the practice of emergency procedures, and normal flight. Once again, a series of flight checks eventually led to a solo flight in the Tweet.

T-41   *T-37 Tweet*

Photos: Courtesy of the National Museum of the USAF.

T-38 Talon

Photo: Courtesy of DVIDS—Defense Visual Information Distribution Service, MSgt. James May, 20 November 2020.

The last phase of flight training would be in the T-38, a two-seat, twinjet, super-sonic jet. It's sort of the "sports car" of pilot training aircraft. The aircraft seats the instructor and student in tandem, with the turbojet engines on each side of the fuselage at the wing roots. Its agile performance earned it the nickname "White Rocket." The US Navy and NASA also use T-38 variants. Training areas would include those similar to the T-37, with the added synthetic instrument trainer, the T-26.

■ AERONAUTICAL ORDERS: YOU ARE CLEAR TO MOVE ABOUT THE SKIES

I was officially authorized to fly when Aeronautical Order 181 was issued on 24 October 1967. It covered a period to 15 November 1968, so in effect, for the duration of my training class. I was eager to enter this training phase. After a few weeks, a core of academics was behind me, and I felt confident in moving forward with this basic knowledge. I experienced what I believed was excitement coupled with some anxiety; I witnessed my classmates experience the same emotions. In the back of our minds was the wash-out rate. Who would succumb to that?

It was day 1, Friday, 3 November, and my first flight lesson in the T-41. I did not get much sleep the night before since all I could think about was this first flight. I met with my IP early to review the goals for the training, complete a flight plan, check the weather, grab our flight publications, and proceed to the aircraft on the flight line.

We reviewed AF Form 781, which details the aircraft status and any previous flight issues. Then we met with the maintenance crew. The IP requested I step through the initial checklists that covered the aircraft internally and externally before engine start procedures. This would ensure the overall integrity of the aircraft, noting any leaks or damage, and suitability for flight.

Once in the cockpit, the instrumentation and controls I studied in the classroom and mockups were now in front of me. The left lower switch panel contained the master, aux-iliary fuel pump, strobe light, pitot heat, navigation light, landing/taxi light, and ignition switches. There were also knobs for the fuel strainer, manual primer, and fuel shutoff. Also on the left were a parking brake and several circuit breakers. On the right lower switch panel were the throttle, fuel mixture knob, cabin air knob, cabin heat knob, and flap switch.

The primary cockpit instrumentation was situated above these switch panels. Found there were a mic button on the two yokes that controlled the aircraft's attitude, a clock, an altimeter, airspeed indicator, turn and bank indicator, directional indica-tor, attitude indicator, VOR nav (a very high-frequency, omnidirectional short-range radio navigation system), transponder, magnetic compass, frequency placard, carbon monoxide detector, VHF (very high-frequency) radio, flap indicator, fuel flow indicator, fuel quantity indicator, tachometer, ammeter, suction gauge, oil temperature indicator, auxiliary mic jack, and trim tab.

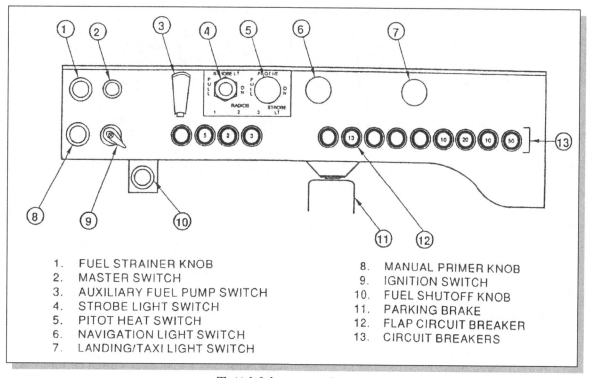

1. FUEL STRAINER KNOB
2. MASTER SWITCH
3. AUXILIARY FUEL PUMP SWITCH
4. STROBE LIGHT SWITCH
5. PITOT HEAT SWITCH
6. NAVIGATION LIGHT SWITCH
7. LANDING/TAXI LIGHT SWITCH

8. MANUAL PRIMER KNOB
9. IGNITION SWITCH
10. FUEL SHUTOFF KNOB
11. PARKING BRAKE
12. FLAP CIRCUIT BREAKER
13. CIRCUIT BREAKERS

T-41 left lower switch panel.

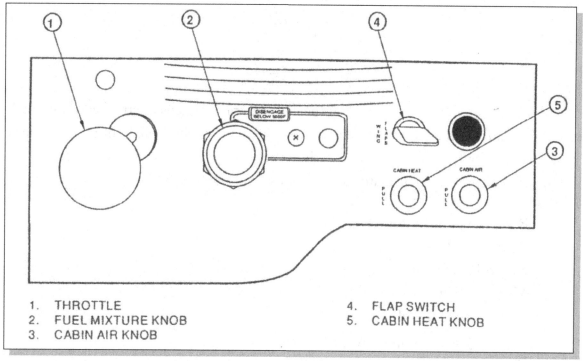

1. THROTTLE
2. FUEL MIXTURE KNOB
3. CABIN AIR KNOB

4. FLAP SWITCH
5. CABIN HEAT KNOB

T-41 right lower switch panel.

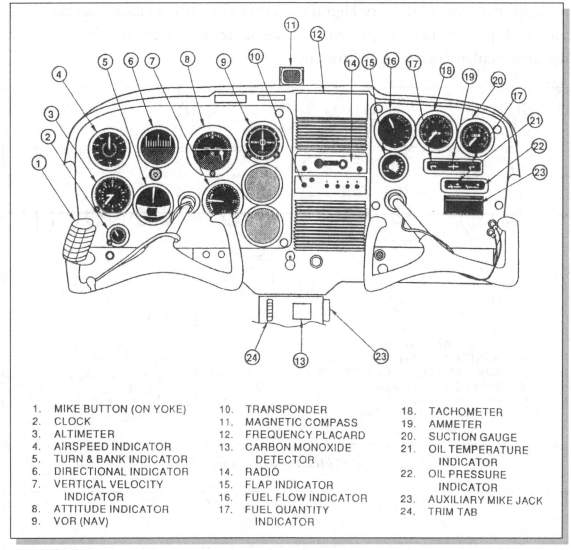

1. MIKE BUTTON (ON YOKE)	10. TRANSPONDER	18. TACHOMETER
2. CLOCK	11. MAGNETIC COMPASS	19. AMMETER
3. ALTIMETER	12. FREQUENCY PLACARD	20. SUCTION GAUGE
4. AIRSPEED INDICATOR	13. CARBON MONOXIDE DETECTOR	21. OIL TEMPERATURE INDICATOR
5. TURN & BANK INDICATOR	14. RADIO	22. OIL PRESSURE INDICATOR
6. DIRECTIONAL INDICATOR	15. FLAP INDICATOR	
7. VERTICAL VELOCITY INDICATOR	16. FUEL FLOW INDICATOR	23. AUXILIARY MIKE JACK
8. ATTITUDE INDICATOR	17. FUEL QUANTITY INDICATOR	24. TRIM TAB
9. VOR (NAV)		

T-41 cockpit forward view.

Our classroom sessions covered all the T-41 aircraft systems (instrumentation, fuel, oil, electrical/circuit breakers, engine, nose-wheel steering, brakes), lighting, and flight controls. We had to demonstrate a satisfactory understanding of all of them. Now seated in the cockpit, we initiated an interior inspection checklist:

- Required publications—on board
- Parking brake—set.
- Control lock—remove
- Master switch—off
- Ignition switch—off
- Auxiliary fuel pump switch—guarded
- Primer—locked

- Fuel shutoff knob—in
- Circuit breakers—in
- Carbon monoxide detector—check
- Trim—set at takeoff
- Master switch—on
- Fuel quantity—check (and agrees with Form 781)
- Lights and pitot heat—check
- Master switch—off
- Fuel strainer knob—check (pull out four seconds, push in)
- Loose articles—secure

We proceeded to the exterior inspection checklist:

- Tiedowns, gust locks, grounding wire, pitot tube cover—remove
- Left main landing gear section:
    - Chock—remove
    - Tire—check overall condition (cuts, blisters, wear)
    - Brake assembly—check thickness, security, leakage

- Left-wing section:
    - Flap—check
    - Aileron—check
    - Strobe navigation lights—check
    - Landing/taxi lights—check
    - Stall warning horn—check
    - Fuel vent—check
    - Pitot tube—check

- Engine section:
    - Oil quantity—check
    - Oil cap—secure
    - Fuel strainer knob—check
    - Access door—secure
    - Nose strut—check
    - Nose tire—check
    - Propeller—check for nicks, damage
    - Propeller seal plug—check for oil leakage
    - Nosewheel compartment—check for leakage

- Right-wing section:
  - Strobe/navigation lights—check
  - Aileron—check
  - Flap—check

- Right main landing gear section:
  - Chock—remove
  - Tire—check
  - Brake assembly—check

- Right Fuselage Section:
  - Static port—clear

- Tail section:
  - Trim tab alignment—check
  - Right elevator—check
  - Rudder—check
  - Rudder and elevator cables—check
  - Navigation light—check
  - Fuel caps—check
  - Left elevator—check

- Left fuselage section:
  - Static port—clear
  - Battery drain—check for leakage
  - Baggage doors—secure

Whether you are a novice or an experienced airman, flight safety cannot be overemphasized. It must be a top priority on every flight. Skipping steps or haphazardly racing through a checklist is a risk no pilot should take. Thoroughness and attention to detail enable you to have the best chance to complete your flight today and return to fly tomorrow. There are enough conditions that can contribute to flight hazards or life-threatening emergencies without adding to them because of a lack of discipline or procedure.

We were now ready to continue with the training session—engine start, taxiing, and takeoff. The IP directed me to continue with the checklist:

- Before starting the engine:
  - Parking brake—set
  - Seat—adjust and lock

- Seat belt and shoulder harness—fasten
- Heading indicator—cage
- Attitude indicator—cage
- Cockpit air and heat knobs—closed
- Flight controls—check for free and proper movement

- Starting engine:
  - Mixture—rich
  - Propeller—full increase
  - Master switch—on
  - Navigation lights—on
  - Auxiliary fuel pump switch—high
  - Throttle—set for eight to ten gallons per hour fuel flow
  - Auxiliary fuel pump switch—release
  - Throttle—idle, then in one-quarter to one-half inch
  - Clear the area around the aircraft 360 degrees—call, "Clear"
  - Auxiliary fuel pump switch—as required (off to low)
  - Ignition switch—start

There are several procedures and corrective actions to follow if the engine reacts to an excessively lean or rich fuel mixture or if the fuel line vapor locks (which is more apt to occur in hot weather with a hot engine).

- Before taxiing:
  - Radio—on
  - Transponder—standby
  - VOR—as required
  - Clock—set
  - Flight instruments—check
    - Altimeter—check and set
    - Airspeed indicator—check pointer for proper indication
    - Magnetic compass—check
    - Heading indicator—set and uncage
    - Attitude indicator—uncage
    - Vertical velocity—check pointer for proper indication

  - Flaps—check both sides for proper operation and indication
  - Radio—check
  - Parking brake—release

We were ready to taxi to the runway. I contacted Laughlin Tower via radio communications to request clearance to taxi. The tower gave us instructions to taxi to the appropriate takeoff runway dependent on wind direction; we would take off into the wind.

I can't remember our call sign, so I'll make one up. "Laughlin Tower, this is Bandit Zero Five; request permission to taxi," I stated.

Tower replied, "Bandit Zero Five, taxi runway three one left."

"Roger, Bandit Zero Five taxi runway three one left," was my response. Laughlin AFB has three runways oriented 130 degrees to the southeast and 180 degrees in the opposite direction to 310 degrees to the northwest.

As we started our taxiing, the IP checked the brakes by bringing the aircraft to a quick, complete stop. He followed this with quick minor turns left and right to check the turn and slip indicator needle and ball for proper indication. We were then underway. The IP demonstrated taxiing and gave the aircraft to me to taxi. There is always a positive handoff over the headset regarding who has control of the aircraft.

The IP said, "Take control."

I responded, with my hands on the yoke, "I have control." There was not much to it—steer and keep the power sufficient to go forward. So far, all was going according to plan without any concerns. Once near the end of the takeoff runway, the IP told me to request clearance for takeoff.

"Laughlin Tower, this is Bandit Zero Five. Request clearance for takeoff," I said.

"Roger, Bandit Zero Five. Taxi into position, and hold runway three one left," was the tower's reply. We lined up at the end of runway three one left, the shortest runway, on a heading of 310 degrees.

Less than thirty seconds later, the tower gave us takeoff clearance. "Bandit Zero Five cleared for takeoff runway three one left; climb and maintain five thousand feet; contact departure control at," were the tower's instructions. They gave us a VHF radio frequency to contact ATC departure control.

"Roger, Tower. Bandit Zero Five cleared for takeoff," I replied. The IP released the brakes, and we accelerated to fifty to sixty miles an hour. He raised the nose smoothly to takeoff attitude, maintained this attitude, and allowed the aircraft to fly off the ground as we reached between seventy and eighty miles an hour. Once safely airborne and at a minimum of eighty-five miles an hour, we raised the flaps. We then continued to climb at full power to five thousand feet at a constant speed of about ninety-five miles an hour. Although anxious, I thought, *This is cool,* as I watched our separation from the ground increase.

"Departure control, Bandit Zero Five heading three one zero, climbing to five thousand feet," was my call.

ATC gave us a vector for the training area and added a new altitude. "Climb and maintain seven thousand feet," was the instruction to us. At this point, we were only at about three thousand feet.

I responded, "Roger, Bandit Zero Five departing three thousand feet for seven thousand feet." This would be our training altitude unless we intended to do specific maneuvers that required a higher and safer altitude. The skies around southwestern Texas generally contained good weather and ample room for training in unpopulated areas.

During the pre-takeoff, takeoff, after-takeoff/climb, and level-off phases for this first flight, the IP had control and explained specific instrument readings to check, such as flaps up, throttle RPM, engine instrument indications, propeller RPM, and setting cruise fuel mixtures. When we reached our designated altitude, we reported to ATC again.

"Departure control, Bandit Zero Five, level seven thousand, heading," we repeated the heading they gave us. We were then cleared to the flight training area, which took a few minutes to reach. About fifteen minutes into the flight, my first attempt at handling the controls in the air would begin.

At first, the IP told me, "Maintain straight and level flight." An IP makes this look easy, but when I took control, the aircraft would climb slightly, so I pushed the yoke forward to bring it back to seven thousand feet. I also got off heading by a few degrees. I overcompensated for both and passed 7,000 feet on my way down to 6500+. The IP said this was normal with new guys and not to sweat it. After some practice, I felt I improved a bit.

We then progressed to simple maneuvers, including turning left and right while maintaining level flight. Once again, I overturned the number of degrees the IP gave me and could not maintain the exact altitude. So it was a series of execute, compensate, correct, and do it repeatedly for about fifteen minutes. I also practiced climbs and descents by a few hundred feet, and level-offs. This was all considerably basic, and I was beginning to get a better overall feel for the aircraft through these simple aerial maneuvers. However, at the same time, I was anxious and slightly queasy.

I didn't say anything to the IP, hoping it would pass. It didn't! As we progressed to tighter turns and more of a transition to a roller-coaster scenario, my nausea got worse. My stomach felt lousy, and my head was beginning to spin. I also did not respond very quickly to the IP when he spoke to me or asked questions. As this progressed over the next few minutes, I knew I needed to notify him that I felt sick. This guy was a professional; he had seen it all before and knew all the telltale signs. He was ready with the barf bag, which he handed me.

"Bill, I have control," he said.

I held off as long as I could, which was not very long. I used the bag to empty my stomach. The lesson was going downhill fast, and I sensed that disappointment was about to consume me. After a few minutes, the IP asked if I felt all right and if I thought I could continue. I said I would try, so we attempted to proceed with the training. I did not want to give up, especially on my first flight. But after a few minutes more, my stomach decided otherwise and delivered round 2. The IP again asked if I wanted to continue.

I told him, "I don't think I'm going to be very effective any further today."

We headed back to the airfield to land. The return flight was not wasted, however, as he continued to instruct me on approach and landing procedures using the checklists for each phase of the flight and making all the radio calls with approach control and the tower. I was able to observe rather than participate.

Once we got back to the student building, my IP completed a quick debrief and counseling session and explained that I would need to repeat this flight to achieve the objectives to progress to further flight lessons. He also indicated, with encouragement, that I was not the first student who experienced what I did and that others got through it. I heard him loud and clear. But it did not make me feel any better. I was upset with myself and disappointed with my performance.

I told Fran all the gory details of the day. She was very empathetic and tried to rebuild my self-confidence. But all I could think of was that I needed to do much better when I repeated the lesson. I had the weekend to pause before my next lesson on Monday, 6 November. I reviewed all the lesson material, and I tried to bolster my mental state much of the time. I could not think past that flight lesson or worry about any follow-on lesson objectives. All my attention was telling me, *Get through this!*

I learned that some of my fellow trainees had gone up for their first flights; some were scheduled for the next training day. Naturally, we shared our experiences, and to my surprise, a few others also used their barf bags. Strangely, this made me feel good! But I then realized that sharing a common unpleasant experience did not help any of us. *Why am I happy they got airsick? Just because I did? That makes no sense!* We all tried to remain positive; group therapy was a booster shot. But group therapy only goes so far, and performance was on an individual basis. In the aircraft, it's me and the IP. No one else.

Monday, 6 November came fast, and the aircraft, I, and a different IP were on the schedule for another lesson. All went like clockwork through the flight planning, checklists, taxi, takeoff, and simple aerial maneuvers. To fast-forward a bit, I completed a satisfactory amount of basic aerial tasks and extended my time effectively. But as we progressed to more difficult maneuvers, my stomach again reminded me it was taking over. This eventually led to barf bag number 2.

We finished the lesson in the same fashion as before. But in the debrief, my IP told me he thought I accomplished enough to move on to the next flight lesson. It was scheduled for 14 November. I had mixed emotions. I was glad I progressed a little but was unhappy with the rest. I updated Fran, who continued to encourage me. And with that, I fought to remain positive.

On a morning flight this time, the IP wanted to evaluate my ability to control the takeoff. So while I had control, he kept his hands at the ready in case I messed up. With a bit of weaving back and forth off centerline, and with his intermittent control, I managed to contribute to the takeoff. With more practice under my belt—and with no onset of nausea in the training area—I thought, *Hey, I am making progress.* But over time, it happened again, and we needed to cut the lesson short.

The IP instructed me to see the flight surgeon to determine if there was a cause for my airsickness that could be corrected. Perhaps I had an ear infection affecting my inner ear, an imbalance, or some other condition causing motion sickness. Treatment with medication was not a long-term remedy but might have helped in the short term to enable a better adaptation to the flight environment.

With the aid of some Bonine tablets for motion sickness provided by the flight surgeon, I advanced longer into that morning lesson than I had previously, which was a good sign. But it was about to change. In the latter part of the flight, I again experienced airsickness. The flight surgeon switched my medication, and I had a second flight that afternoon with the same results. Definitely not a good trend.

On the next flight lesson, Thursday, 16 November, the IP said he would demonstrate stalls and falls. It is vital to understand what leads to a stall to avoid it and how to recover if it does happen. We got clearance to climb to eight thousand feet, a comfortable altitude for this type of demonstration. The intent was for the IP to execute the maneuver first, followed by my execution and practice for several minutes.

At straight and level flight, the IP pulled back slightly on the yoke, which raised the aircraft's nose. He did not add any power, so the airspeed bled off until the aircraft became unstable and wobbled, causing the stall warning horn to blare. Ignoring any attempt to correct this, the nose rapidly dipped down, and we were quickly in a stall, facing the ground below as our airspeed increased.

This woke up my stomach as if it stretched its arms from a deep sleep, yawned, and said, *Oh, I'm falling out of the sky!* The IP recovered the aircraft as speed increased and returned to straight and level flight. I didn't say anything to indicate any change in my attention, so the IP gave me control as we climbed back to eight thousand feet. Once straight and level, he ordered me to execute the same maneuver. I pulled back on the yoke, the stall initiated, and we were in a fall as before. However, before I could completely recover the aircraft, I had to turn control over to the IP. I already had the barf bag he gave me before the flight.

Two more flight lessons were scheduled: Friday and Monday, 17 and 20 November, respectively. I felt I had made progress: I was able to complete all checklist items at the aircraft, taxi, take off on my own, approach the flight training area, and perform some maneuvers. These additional lessons allowed me to stretch my time airborne before I got airsick, but I continued to experience this dilemma and did not go through an entire flight lesson without the same result. I was falling behind the training schedule. When we returned for the debrief, the IP told me he would recommend a faculty board review of my flight performance.

■ AERONAUTICAL ORDERS: SECOND ROUND

Under other circumstances, such as a separate or slower track for training like slipping into a class behind the Class 69-04 schedule and limited medication to overcome motion sickness, this might have worked toward my completion of the T-41 phase. However, the AF does not consider that an option and stresses the need to accomplish specific goals within a given amount of time. It needed to maintain pilot production due to the Vietnam War requirements and ensure that only the most qualified pilot trainees advanced to the next training phase into specialized aircraft that serve AF operations. They had elimination standards, and I was a viable candidate to plus up the wash-out statistic.

As a result, Headquarters 3646th Pilot Training Wing at Laughlin issued Aeronautical Order 198, dated 21 November 1967, which stated, "2nd Lt William A. Cimino, Jr" (followed by my service number), "3645 Stu Sq, ATC, this base, is hereby suspended from flying status as a crew member effective 21 November 1967. Reason for suspension: Pending Faculty Board Action—Manifestations of Apprehension. Officer will report to…" I reported to Personnel IAW the AO instructions that followed.

On 27 November 1967, Special Order A-1205 contained the appointment of four officers—a board president, two additional voting members, and a nonvoting recorder to hear my specific case. The order also listed two other pilot trainees with their own appointed wing faculty board. The board was to convene at the call of the president.

At this point, I had completed thirty academic course hours, thirty-five hours in other training like PT and marksmanship, and five hours and forty-five minutes of airtime.

In the few days before the faculty board reviewed my case, I continued to attend class instructions. On Thursday, 30 November, I attended the board review. I entered the review room, stood before the board president, and saluted. "Sir, Lt. William Cimino reporting as ordered."

He told me to be seated as the members called up my records and read the IP comments for each flight lesson, highlighting what was achieved and what was not. They asked for my comments regarding training. In a nutshell, I expressed my appreciation for all the flight instruction, both classroom and inflight, and that I was disappointed in my performance in the air but felt I was making progress and would eventually get over the airsickness. I was sincere and didn't try to blow smoke at them.

They convened to review the seven flight lessons I had over thirteen days. Later, they called me back into the room to summarize their findings with me. They noted that I did make progress and did perform some of the contact flying requirements. However, the common underlying airsickness problem deterred my advancement in the T-41 phase.

The board president addressed me and stated the official board findings:

1. My recurring apprehension would preclude the successful completion of the UPT Program.
2. My difficulty was caused by apprehension toward either the aircraft or flying itself.
3. My deficiency was not the result of factors over which I had control.

He went on to state the board's recommendations to the training wing commander:

1. That I be eliminated from the present course of pilot training.
2. That I not be allowed to reenter the same course of training at a later date.
3. That I not be allowed to apply for further aircrew training.

The last recommendation would prevent me from applying to Undergraduate Navigator Training (UNT) and, in effect, would rule out any AF flying career. At that time, I did not fully realize the severity of the board review nor comprehend the rapid change in my status. I was in pilot training for thirty-eight days, far short of fifty-three weeks, and the last few weeks were a rough ride literally and figuratively.

My ATC Form 240, Summary Record of Pilot Training, contained these board findings and recommendations, as well as my complete training record at Laughlin AFB. The training wing commander approved the board findings and recommendations, but with two exceptions: That I be allowed to reenter the same course of training at a later date if I attained rated status. This basically meant that if I were to become rated through navigator training, I could reapply for pilot training. His second exception was that I be allowed to apply for further aircrew training.

So in effect, the wing commander opened the door for me to return to aircrew training. I jumped on that opportunity and applied for AF UNT. While I waited for a response from Air Training Command (ATC), I performed other assigned duties to use my time. I would review all the records that captured my deficient performance in UPT. The AF added another form to my records—AF Form 475, Training Report, dated 14 December 1967. It was a simple statement that said I did not complete UPT with a comment section that contained one line:

"Manifestations of Apprehension (not due to factors over which he had control)." "Manifestations of Apprehension." I hated that phrase!

Christmas 1967 came and went, and we drifted into the new year. We were approaching mid-January, and I still had not received a response to my UNT application. On 16 January, the Base Personnel Office contacted me. A message from ATC arrived dated that day.

Subject: Assignment to Navigator Training. The request for further aircrew training of 2nd Lt William A. Cimino [followed by my service number] is not favorably considered. This is in no way a reflection upon Lt Cimino's qualifications but is indicative of the keen competition. Report officer to HQ USAF for assignment.

This news put me in a tailspin (no pun intended).

■ PSYCHOLOGICAL IMPACT

My wash-out in UPT and the AF rejection for UNT was a one-two punch that enhanced my feelings of incompetence and added complexity to my mindset. While I never held with any certainty that the AF would be a significant long-term career in my life, I was certain my performance in UPT was not the way to start one. If I felt ineffective during the seven training flights I attempted, by comparison, I now felt completely inept. I questioned myself as the days transpired between my Faculty Board Review and the notice from HQ USAF. It was a period of isolation of sorts, not sharing experiences and progress with the other pilot trainees, not being a part of the group with similar goals. Rather, I had been cast aside to do minor, meaningless tasks while my future in the AF was on hold.

All the value I put into a possible rated aircrew position in the AF was addressed and rejected with the recent administrative actions. And even though the wing commander gave me a peek into achieving aircrew training, that was quickly eliminated. Everything was in a downhill mode and accelerating. My feelings were multifaceted: worthlessness, incompetence, insignificance, depression, ineffectiveness, unhappiness, failure, anger, irritability, sadness, loneliness, and embarrassment. All were competing for my attention.

Fran, no doubt, recognized all this and understood my feelings and reactions. She remained the one source of encouragement and support that enabled my journey through hardship. She pulled me up from my daily anxiety and intrusive worry. Without her, my recovery was uncertain. While AF personnel would take an active, helpful, and official role in finding a new career field, Fran filled the personal element that I desperately needed to focus forward. The only way I would get my UPT experience out of my head was to put it behind me—easier said than done, but necessary. So the process began with a search for a new AF role for 2nd Lt. William A. Cimino.

■ CHANGE IN SPECIALTY

The Personnel Office had a regimented process for assisting UPT washouts, so it was no wonder they were able to get me involved in a joint search effort for an appropriate career field. They covered many programs where I could receive training before an assignment in an operational AF organization. Training in any field is an absolute requirement, and you quickly learn that you *never* stop learning in the AF.

Over a few days, and after a comprehensive review of hundreds of career fields, I narrowed it down to two that appealed to me: intelligence and munitions. Although I understood there were no guarantees, I submitted my preferences. On 23 January 1968, an ATC message from USAF Military Personnel Center, Randolph AFB, TX, announced my next assignment to the 3430th Student Squadron at Lowry AFB in Colorado to attend course 30BR 4621A—Aerospace Munitions Officer training with a report date of 13 February 1968. The course would end in August, followed by a Nuclear Safety Officer course for several weeks terminating in late September.

I was happy not to end up with an assignment that was outside my interest. That would have only contributed to my despair. As I reviewed a summary of the course material and the location for the training, it ignited a spark that would enable me to see some brightness ahead, one in which I could apply a renewed effort. This would be the first of many PCS moves to come. Fran and I, and now a little someone growing inside her, would be headed north in the middle of winter.

A NEW CAREER PATH

■ LOWRY AFB, AURORA, COLORADO

After out-processing from Laughlin, settling with our renter in Del Rio, and some sad goodbyes with friends, we headed north through southwestern Texas to begin the 960-mile trip to Denver, Colorado, on an off-the-beaten-path, picking up route US 285. This trip was a bit more scenic than interstate highways to the east, taking us through eastern New Mexico, its capital, Santa Fe, and the southeastern portion of the Rockies.

In the Land of Enchantment, we marveled at sites along the way, including White Sands National Park and the Rio Grande Gorge Bridge. Once we entered Colorado, the Centennial State, our route continued along the east side of many of the 14,000-foot peaks of the Rockies, which were well-covered with snow and offered unparalleled views of these majestic mountains.

On arrival in the Mile High City, it was a night-and-day experience. And a welcome one. We left Del Rio, with a population of about twenty thousand, for a state capital of nearly one million. Fran and I found a suitable apartment in southeastern Denver, conveniently located in the suburb of Aurora, only a few miles from Lowry AFB, where I would attend training. Our spirit was upbeat as we learned all the attractions and sites this new location would offer. While I still needed to focus on coursework, it seemed from the outset that the challenges—and the anxiety—would be more manageable.

Our household goods arrived from Texas, and we settled in quickly as I prepared to begin the Aerospace Munitions Officer Course on 14 February 1968, Valentine's Day. One of the requirements for this course was normal color vision, which would become understandable as I learned all the distinct types of weaponry the AF had in its inventory or were in development. My class had eleven other second lieutenants in attendance, a small, tightly knit group ready to apply the Cooperate and Graduate methodology.

■ WEAPONS: CONVENTIONAL AND NUCLEAR

As one would expect with the Vietnam War in heightened conflict, the AF and other military services maintained a steady flow and inventory of munitions of all types—from handheld rifles for ground troops to conventional dumb bombs, those converted to precision-guided munitions (PGMs), including air-to-air missiles and air-to-ground missiles. Our training would include these and extend into offshoot technologies that take the PGMs to the next level with infrared and radar homing, heat-seeking, inertial guidance, and uplinked data utilization for ground and airborne targets.

Over the weeks, our class would learn about every characteristic of munition fuses: types, principles of operation, classification, function, reliability, and safety. Fuse types may be impact (or contact), timed, or proximity, each with different blast effects on their intended targets. Fuses may contain a small explosive charge to initiate the main charge or a firing pin (piston) to strike the detonator.

We would study a variety of conventional weapons, like the five-hundred-pound iron bombs carried by the Boeing B-52 Stratofortress, designed in the latter 1940s and first flown in the early-1950s. Otherwise known by troops as the BUFFs—Big Ugly Fat Fuckers, or when in the presence of the ladies, Big Ugly Fat Fellows—the B-52 could carry eighty-four internally and another twenty-four under the wings. Tactical aircraft, such as the Republic F-105 Thunderchief, could carry 12,000 pounds of ordnance—8,000 of it internally, or a combination of 750-pound iron bombs and M61 Vulcan cannon, rocket packs, and missiles. These were just a tiny sampling of the range of weaponry used by AF weapon systems.

Another interesting training segment was the air-to-air missiles (AAMs)—both short-range, called "within visual range" or "dogfight missiles," and medium- and long-range, which are called "beyond visual range" and rely on radar guidance, like active homing radar. AAMs typically contain either fragmentation warheads or continuous rod warheads to disable or destroy enemy aircraft. As we studied each weapon, associated fuse types, explosives, blast effects, delivery methods, storage, safety inspections, and a host of related topics, it gave us a comprehensive understanding and appreciation for the military value of the range of AF weaponry.

Nuclear weapons were in a class of their own. They needed to be treated differently due to the destructive power and political implications if they were mishandled or misused. A follow-on Nuclear Safety Officers Course would address the details of these procedures, the two-man rule, special inspections, and much more. However, the present course provided details on the types of nuclear weapons, both strategic and tactical, long-range (like ICBMs), and shorter-range air-launched payloads. We studied the blast effect of these powerful weapons, both from ground and above-ground blasts, by viewing film footage captured during testing in various locations in western US deserts or the Pacific.

The Munitions Course prepared AF officers for duty in operational organizations such as Strategic Air Command (SAC), where heavy bombers utilize the full range of conventional weapons or are configured with nuclear weapons if hostilities called for such escalation. Assignment of officers could also be in other commands, such as Tactical Air Command (TAC), where AF wing organizations would contain the fighter squadrons equipped with various fighter aircraft and associated weaponry.

As the weeks of class instruction and field activity continued from February through August, I, along with my classmates, wondered where we would be assigned. The anticipation grew, and there was a lot of chatter among us. It could be anywhere, globally, not only due to the war in Vietnam, but because the AF had a footprint in numerous theaters in Europe, the Pacific, South America, Alaska, East Asia, and anywhere in between. But I had an additional expectation that was far greater, one due to materialize in early July. It would be a new Cimino, either a he or a she. We did not know which but knew we would be happy either way with a healthy one, nonetheless.

■ OUR FAMILY GROWS

We didn't have much money, but we managed on the little savings we had, and my AF pay. We were saving for the baby, buying some clothes and necessary infant items each month. We put a crib on layaway, paying it down as we approached the big month. It's ridiculous, looking back now on what we spent on food each month for example. We tried to get by on about $20 a week for food and even pushed to bring it down to $15. Gas was around thirty-five cents a gallon. We never bought anything beyond our means. We established a practice of frugality with our finances. We might splurge for our upcoming first wedding anniversary on 24 June, just before the expected birth of our baby, so we looked forward to this celebratory time together before it would be three!

William Joseph Cimino, all five pounds, thirteen ounces of him, decided otherwise. He was born at Fitzsimons Army Hospital, only minutes from our apartment, at 4:09 p.m. on 3 June, so we had to share our first anniversary with the little guy. When Fran went into labor in the morning, I took her to the hospital, and the nurses quickly ushered me out of the hospital and said they would call me.

It was not common for fathers to be in the delivery room to observe the birth of a child, although a shift to enable this began in earnest in the sixties, just not at Fitzsimons! I wondered, *What do I do while I am waiting?* I decided I better get the crib delivered and put it together! When the delivery guy arrived, he wanted to help me assemble the crib. I didn't know who was more excited—me or him!

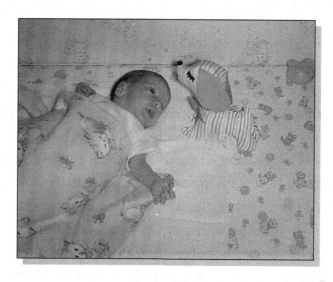

After little Bill was born, I received the all-clear to return to the hospital and no longer felt like I was in forbidden territory. I was able to hold the little bundle and feed him. He was so tiny; his legs reminded me of chicken legs; they were not much bigger. After about three days, I was able to take Fran and our precious addition home. I wondered, *Will I be able to concentrate on my coursework if little lungs keep us up every four hours or so!?*

Our little guy was eating well, gaining weight in the next few weeks, and all appeared normal. However, after about five to six weeks, he had difficulty holding down his formula. He would projectile vomit his food right after feeding. It did not take us long before we brought him to the doctor and heard the diagnosis: pyloric stenosis, or more technically, infantile hypertrophic pyloric stenosis (IHPS). It sounded awful and severe. We came to learn that this problem is common and affects babies between birth and six months.

The corrective treatment is surgery. Surgery! Our baby needed surgery! If left untreated, it could lead to dehydration and severe electrolyte abnormalities. It is a congenital disability, meaning a child is born with it, so the first form of treatment was to identify and correct any changes in body chemistry using blood tests and intravenous fluids. I cannot express how terrible it is to see your baby, only weeks old, all wrapped up in tubes, gauze, and bandages. But the definitive treatment for this condition is always surgery, called a pyloromyotomy, in which the doctor makes an incision to divide a thickened pylorus muscle and open the gastric outlet.

After surgery, tears came to our eyes when we saw him. But the doctor assured us he was OK. We brought him home after about a week, which seemed like an eternity. His condition improved rapidly, and our concern and fear diminished equally fast. We were so relieved and thankful that he was a happy little guy again.

■ NUCLEAR SAFETY

I was able to reestablish my focus on the munitions coursework with about four weeks remaining until the end of the training on 13 August. My student performance continued to go well as I developed a foundation of knowledge that would allow me to perform in an operational assignment where I could grow that expertise. I knew where that would happen. Earlier, on 2 July, I received Special Order AA-1184, which was a notification of my next assignment in the 18th Tactical Fighter Wing, PACAF, APO SF 96239. All an official way of saying my next duty station would be in Okinawa.

Before we departed from Denver, the AF assigned me to an additional three weeks of training at Lowry AFB in the Nuclear Safety Officer Course, with a graduation date of 24 September. I attended this class with twelve other officers. This training would supplement my learning from the munitions course and provide a more comprehensive knowledge base in the world of AF weaponry. At the end of the tunnel, the light began to appear. After months of training—some successful, some not—a shift to operations would occur.

Nuclear Safety Officer course, Lowry AFB, Colorado, September 1968.
I am sitting on the far right.

While conventional weapons require strict and safe procedures for storage, handling, loading, arming, and delivery, nuclear weapons are all of that and so much more. In the course, without disclosing classified information, I can attest to the variety of these weapon types—everything from strategic ICBMs, both land- and sea-based, to smaller and agile tactical weapons—from airborne platforms to land-mobile capabilities in locations around the globe.

Much of our training included mockups, viewing photos, film of test sites, detonations, and resultant damage. We came to understand the different results of an airburst versus a ground burst. We also learned about the time element in delivery and the differences between whether the target was fixed, as in the Cold War with the Soviet Union, where the movement of troops and equipment took days, or in a theater of operations, where tactical targets were more mobile and diverse.

The entire process of target identification and response to a particular threat has changed dramatically from that time in the late 1960s to today, where one of our significant threats comes from hypersonic weapons development in Russia and China. Hypersonic weapons can travel more than five times the speed of sound—Mach 5—and cover great distances in minutes. They are hard to stop due to their agility and ability to avoid detection and evade defensive countermeasures. The response time dwindles to minutes as opposed to hours or perhaps even days.

Nonetheless, handling nuclear weapons requires fail-safe procedures. To ensure that nuclear weapons are used only in the most severe situations, they must never be at risk of actions by a lone individual, a rogue aircrew, or the result of some psychological breakdown. Military personnel who have any connections with nuclear weapons are well screened and prepped. The "two-man rule," where no fewer than two personnel would ever be permitted to be in the presence of or to handle nuclear weapons would always apply. Every attempt to avoid a "broken arrow," a term used to describe incidents or accidents involving a nuclear weapon or component, such as radioactive contamination, seizure, theft, or loss, must be implemented. In declassified documentation, the Pentagon maintains that the United States has experienced thirty-two broken arrows.

Rigid procedures are required to validate a launch with specific coding that changes frequently. The president has the "nuclear football," carried by one of the rotating presidential military aides, whose work schedule is described by a top-secret rota (one from each of the service branches). A launch from fixed missile sites or sea-based submarines would require validation by way of codes beginning at the highest authority. Time is of the essence. No mistakes allowed!

By September 1968, I had two training certificates added to my records: Aerospace

Munitions Officer Course and Nuclear Safety Officer Course, a basic set of credentials to go and be effective somewhere. We prepared for a move once again, only this time, I needed to travel to Okinawa in advance of Fran and little Bill to ensure I could secure housing. The length of our separation would be unclear until I arrived there and learned about the housing status, so we put our interim plan into place.

6

OKINAWA

■ THE LONG ROAD TRIPS

My departure date for Okinawa was 15 October from Travis AFB in California. Once we had our household goods picked up in Colorado, we made our way eastward to New York. We took the most direct route using interstate highways to achieve the shortest travel time for this 1,800-mile trip. Not much sightseeing this time. We had to make good use of a little more than two weeks to travel home, get Fran and our four-month-old temporarily set up with Fran's parents until they could travel overseas, and for me to turn right around and travel from the East Coast to the West Coast to check our car at Travis AFB for its shipment before my flight over the Pacific. Naturally, I wanted to spend the maximum time possible with Fran and little Bill in New York before I departed, so I minimized travel time to spend more time with them.

The family visits to Long Island flew by. I did not want a moment to go by where I did not have Fran and little Bill by my side, but it was soon time to make the 2,900-mile trip westward. I completed it in four days! I departed Jamaica, New York, early on Friday, 11 October, and did not stop except for gas and to pick up some food, which I ate while driving. After traveling 1,011 miles the first day, I stopped at a motel late at night just west of Davenport, Iowa, to call home and get some rest. Early the next morning, I strapped the car to my butt and continued west.

The afternoon portion was a bit challenging as I made my way through endless cornfields in Nebraska. I terminated this eight-hundred-mile, thirteen-hour segment in Cheyenne, Wyoming, phoned home, and went to bed. On Sunday, my intended last day of this lonely trip and exhausted, I had to stop in Reno, Nevada, after driving 950 miles, hoping to stay at Stead AFB for the night. But I found that it was no longer operational, so I had no accommodations. I found a motel and crashed after another long day prone in the same position. On 14 October, I left early and passed through Sacramento on my way to Travis AFB, in Vacaville, California, about fifty miles northeast of San Francisco. It was an easy drive from Reno afforded by beautiful scenery, which rendered the miles of cornfields behind me as no contest.

As part of my reporting procedures, I checked in with the base services and obtained officer's quarters for the night before traveling overseas. I shared a room with a navy officer, who had a departure at 0230 hours, so while he slept, I wrote the first of many letters to Fran from a lounge in the building so as not to disturb him. I was able to keep the car until an hour before my flight the next day. It would take several days before the vessel loading would be completed because of the extensive amount of other cargo destined for points across the Pacific.

I stopped by the AF Finance Office to pick up my pay and prepare a money order to send home to Fran. I kept $75 for myself, plus a little extra for the trip. That would be enough until the next payday. The next day, after one final call home, I boarded the DC-8 United Airlines flight U271 for a 7:00 p.m. departure to Okinawa, over 6,300 miles away. There's a lot of ocean out there! My first stop was in Honolulu, and after a one-hour layover, we made our next stop on Wake Island, which looked like a tiny runway in the ocean. The islands along the way were few and far between and looked as if the sea could swallow them up. I arrived at Kadena AB at 4 p.m. on 16 October, eighteen hours after leaving the West Coast and crossing the International Date Line.

■ OKINAWA: HELLO, KADENA AIR BASE

Kadena AB →

Okinawa.
Photo: Courtesy of Robert L. Butterfield, retired AF colonel who served in Okinawa.

Landing in Okinawa provided an unforgettable sight. The island is situated about midway in a chain called the Ryukyu Islands, also known as the Nansei Islands, stretched southwest from Kyushu, the third-largest island of Japan, to Taiwan. Okinawa's landmass extends about sixty-seven miles long and varies in width from two to seventeen miles. Most of the population lived in the southern one-third of the island near Naha, its capital, the military bases, and surrounding areas to the north of the capital. The US Air Force, Army, and Marines all had and still maintain operations at facilities on the island.

Okinawa was the site of one of the bloodiest campaigns in the Pacific theater during World War II. The battle of Okinawa, a major battle with the largest amphibious landing in the Pacific War, code-named Operation Iceberg, took place between 1 April and 21 June 1945 and considered a vital precursor to a ground invasion of the Japanese home islands. It is considered the last major battle of World War II. It also resulted in the largest number of casualties, with over 100,000 Japanese casualties and

50,000 casualties for the Allies. The Americans were planning Operation Downfall, the invasion of the four great islands of Japan, but that never materialized.

Okinawa became a US territory after signing the peace treaty with Japan in 1951. US military troops and their families continued to be stationed on the island during the 1950s and '60s, increasing their presence on US military installations. The island has been a critical strategic location for the US Armed Forces since the battle of Okinawa and the end of World War II, and remained under American administration until 1972, when it reverted to Japan's control. Today, Okinawa currently hosts around 26,000 US military personnel, about half the total complement of the US Forces Japan, which spreads across thirty-two bases and forty-eight training sites.

Kadena AB remains one of the largest US military facilities in Okinawa. Several officers greeted me when I arrived there. Among them was Dave Drewry, who went through the munitions course with me at Lowry, and Major Milton, whom I would replace in the 18th TFW Wing Safety office. Milton would leave in a little over a week for Kirtland AFM in New Mexico to become the Chief of Safety. They had completed the paperwork for my room at the bachelor officer quarters—BOQ—for a monthly rate of $18, which included getting laundry and uniforms cleaned. I had everything I needed, including a bedroom, a small bathroom with a shower, a living area, and a small kitchen, but no phone or air conditioner. These were minor issues. The room fan was adequate, and there was a phone down the hall.

The next day, I immediately checked with base housing to get my name on the waiting list and learned it would take three to four months before my family could join me. I gathered as much information about what the base would provide, and I was happy with what I heard—furniture, appliances, all the essentials. Many of the officers and enlisted bought homes that were inspected by the Housing Committee and were able to get their families there quicker. They would then sell them for a little more or break even, allowing their net costs to be for utilities only. The average price of a private home there in 1968 was around $5,000. Fran and I considered doing this, but we elected not to jeopardize our budget, especially with my deferred college loan due for its first payment in August 1969.

I met my new barber for the first time. The Okinawan gentleman did a great job, and I tried to tip him after the seventy-five-cent haircut. Taxis on base were about twenty cents. I quickly learned that Okinawans get insulted if you tip them for any-thing—taxis, dinner, haircuts, anything! I also learned there are two options for phone calls. A regular phone call would cost between $9 and $12 for the first three minutes. Yikes, pretty steep! The second method was through the military communications called MARS—Military Auxiliary Radio System—on the base, where you would be charged from a Utah service area to the location you were calling. However, since it is over a military line, an amateur radio link, it must be somewhat formal to be switched back and forth to the active party. In other words, "Hi honey. Over. I love you. Over. How's the baby? Over" Ugh! I decided to call over a regular line so I could talk the way I wanted! Who wants some unknown monitoring of my amorous talk?

I ate a Kobe beef dinner for $2.25. Loved it. I tried Saki. Hated it! The local shops were great, such as the East & West Gift Shop on Moromi Main Street in Koza, Okinawa, with everything from jewelry, watches, kimonos, dolls, rattan furniture, batik art, shoji screens, wood furniture, and more. *Fran will love it here,* I thought.

While I rooted myself into my new job, I balanced that with learning as much as possible about Kadena AB and the surrounding environment so I could keep Fran informed. I told her about the gracious Okinawan people, the sites we could visit, the vast military social community, and activities. I tried to frame the next thirty months of our lives in Okinawa. We shared eighty-five letters between us while we were apart in addition to postcards and holiday cards. We still have them all!

18TH TFW

An AF combat wing has a specific functional designation and mission in combat, whether it is bombardment, fighter, strategic, tactical reconnaissance, airlift, air re-fueling, or missile. The 18th TFW has a long history going back to January 1927 and engaged in combat in the Pacific region under lower unit-level designations such as Pursuit Group, Fighter Group, and Fighter-Bomber Group. The organization moved to Kadena AB on 1 November 1954. After some reorganization and receiving several aircraft squadrons, the unit received the official designation as the 18th Tactical Fighter Wing on 1 July 1958.

The 15th Tactical Reconnaissance Squadron, located on Kadena Air Base, was attached to the 18th TFW in March 1960. The pilots of the 15th TRS operated the RF-101 Voodoo aircraft until receiving the RF-4C Phantom in 1967. In 1963, the 18th TFW converted from the F-100 Super Sabre to the F-105 Thunderchief aircraft, nicknamed the "Thud." The wing became involved in the Vietnam conflict late in 1964, deploying the 12th TFS. Some of the wing's fighter squadrons deployed to the combat zones but fell under the control of the 2nd Air Division and operated from Korat Air Base, Thailand. The 18th TFW received its first F-4C Phantom fighter aircraft in 1971.

When I arrived at Kadena, the wing had F-105, RF-4C, and EB-66 aircraft in their respective squadrons. A flying squadron typically consists of eighteen aircraft (this may vary) and aircrews under the leadership of a squadron commander, who reports up the chain to the deputy commander for operations (DCO), and ultimately to the wing commander, in my case, Colonel Monroe S. Sams, nicknamed "Sabre Sams." Sams flew in the F-105. I was introduced to him on my first day on the job, and he became one of my key relationships during my tour of duty.

■ WING SAFETY OFFICE

The Wing Safety Office, headed by the Chief of Safety, reported directly to the wing commander and is responsible for all safety programs, including flying safety, weapons safety, explosive safety, and unit ground safety. It was located in a controlled area on the flight line. When I arrived, there was no assigned Chief of Safety in our office. However, there were two flying safety officers—Major Nedbalek and Captain Thompson. Nedbalek functioned as the Chief of Safety while the personnel office searched for a permanent candidate.

I was responsible for the weapons, explosives, and ground safety programs. Later, a civilian took over the ground safety program's responsibility. My official job title was Wing Weapons Safety Officer, although my responsibilities extended across all weapons and explosives. My job required a captain's billet or higher. No one in the safety office knew much about the munitions field or its safety requirements, so I had a steep learning curve. I was told I had big shoes to fill with Maj. Milton's imminent departure. A sergeant provided administrative support.

Our day started with an early morning comprehensive briefing in the command post—the wing's nerve center—to Col. Sams. The command post had links to each squadron's operations per aircraft type and airfield facilities, like the base operations terminal and the control tower. Our regular workweek hours included a half-day on Saturday mornings.

While the training I received at Lowry was in-depth and applicable, it only prepped me so far for the operational environment I faced. While I got all the support I needed, I was really on my own to gain expertise in a combat-ready TFW. Since no one knew my job or could convey any munitions safety experience, I dove into regulations and AF manuals, familiarized myself with all pertinent organizations within the wing, worked long hours, and never once thought about my past short, and unpleasant experience in the AF. There was no time to dwell on any of that.

Although the wing had many supportive organizations under the commander, for my purposes and duties, the chain depicted here was my focus from top to bottom, with specific daily attention on all munitions and related programs within the wing.

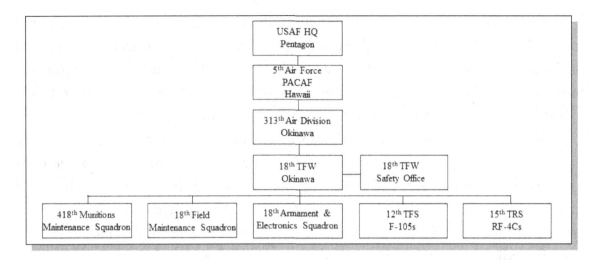

The wing also had a forward operating location (FOL) in Kwang-Ju, Korea, called the 18th TFW Tac Element. I would need to visit that location on a temporary duty (TDY) basis from time to time to ensure that good safety practices and policies remained intact there.

One week after I arrived at my new position, I learned the wing would get an integrated safety survey between 9 and 14 November from a deployed HQ USAF team from Norton AFB, California. This survey was a wing-wide comprehensive inspection of all safety procedures in all programs. There was no time to waste; much to learn and prepare. When it rains, it pours! No matter how new I was to the job, failing the survey was out of the question.

Maj. Allison, a weapons safety officer from 5th AF, Fuchu Air Station, Japan, provided needed help and guidance. The wing did very well during the survey. I began a steady positive trend in performance and expertise through an aggressive weapons safety program, ensuring compliance, conducting routine surveys, investigating mishaps, and advising the commander, resulting in a zero-accident rate for the wing. On the other hand, Strategic Air Command, also at Kadena AB, had a setback in their safety program on 19 November 1968.

■ SHARED AIRFIELD

The 4252nd Strategic Wing shared the airfield with the 18th TFW. Their facilities and B-52 Stratofortress aircraft were on the opposite side of the base, across the runways. Although the AF would not confirm it, it was believed the strategic bombers were flying Arc Light bombing missions over South Vietnam. On Tuesday morning, 19 November, at about 0415 hours., I was nearly knocked from my bed in the BOQ by a tremendous explosion. It was an awakening I will never forget.

A fully laden B-52 with 750-pound conventional bombs crashed just beyond the runway in a ditch just before Highway 16, outside the base. Unconfirmed reports said the bomber was halfway down the runway when one of the eight engines caught fire. Since it was not off the ground yet, the pilots executed an abort, but the aircraft was still at high speed and could not stop before the end of the runway.

The seven crew members aboard escaped the burning aircraft, and shortly after a series of explosions, the plane completely disintegrated. The only recognizable remnants were the landing gear and some engines. I witnessed the remaining debris later that day. I thought, *This is all that remains after that explosion!* Miraculously, five of the crew had minor injuries; the other two suffered severe burns as they all raced from the aircraft. Sadly, those two crewmen died as a result of their injuries.

Debris spread across two miles and inflicted damage to buildings. There were small fires and broken windows and some minor injuries to the local population. About two hundred Okinawan college students and riot police clashed near Kadena to protest the presence of the US military. Japanese government officials demanded that the B-52s be withdrawn from Okinawa. The bombers had been stationed there in late February 1968 and had a perfect flying safety record—until that day in November, their first mishap on the island.

Due to the extensive blast, it was necessary to conduct a complete inspection of all 18th TFW munitions storage and resources for any impacts or defects. Luckily, our storage igloos and munitions maintenance buildings were a few thousand feet away from the explosions, and not a single weapon sustained any damage. This was in no small way due to the protection provided by the massive fifteen-foot high by ten-foot wide, thousand-pound doors. Some doors, however, were pushed in as much as two feet by the blast shockwave. No wonder I nearly got thrown from my bed! The doors did their job.

Despite protests, the Buffs continued their missions. In letters Fran and I sent to each other, we included newspaper articles about the accident. Fran feared that escalating Japanese demands would impact a continued presence at bases in Okinawa, and perhaps even hers and little Bill's travel there. But that anxiety quickly diminished as all plans to rejoin our family remained on track.

■ TDYS TO KOREA

Before Fran and little Bill came to Okinawa, I completed two visits to our fighter element in Kwang Ju AB, in the southern area of South Korea. Due to its proximity to the Yellow Sea to the west and the East China Sea to the south, we called it "Kwang Ju by the Sea," although it was situated at about fifty feet mean sea level (MSL) and was surrounded by hills over several hundred feet. I left Okinawa on a C-130 cargo plane late on 25 November to perform a quick staff visit to familiarize myself with the operations and related safety programs there. I returned two days later, arriving at Naha AB at 1:30 a.m., where I got other transportation to my BOQ at Kadena. I quickly fell into bed. The next day, I celebrated Thanksgiving alone by having dinner at the Officer's Club (O'Club). The dinner was good and only cost $1.75, but it was not a great holiday. There were not too many others at the club, and eating alone was not a savored experience by any means. I missed my family.

Christmas came and went pretty much in the same fashion as Thanksgiving. A few days before Christmas, I worked long hours to complete a nomination for a safety award for the wing. I spent Christmas Eve with some BOQ friends but opted not to go to a wing Christmas party. I went to see a Bob Hope show at the Stillwell Field House instead with thousands of others. It was a good show that lifted my mood a little, but on Christmas Day, I found myself at the O'Club again, alone for dinner. This time at the cost of $2.25. My holidays desperately needed an injection of family.

My next trip to Korea, on 27 December, was a bit longer—five days. This time I traveled on a C-141 cargo plane (much bigger) to support a special mission requirement. The fighter aircraft of the 18th TFW had frequent deployments to South Korea to maintain an alert air defense posture there ever since, on 23 January 1968, North Korean patrol boats intercepted the USS *Pueblo*, a naval intelligence vessel engaged in routine intelligence gathering sixteen miles off the North Korean coast, in international waters. I would make periodic trips to Kwang Ju. We also had a presence at Osan AB further to the north, about forty miles south of Seoul, to complement the element at Kwang Ju and other aircraft assets under the 5th AF/313th Air Division's AOR in this part of the Pacific.

During the captivity of *Pueblo*'s crew, the North Koreans demanded that the crew sign false confessions. The crew famously raised their middle fingers at cameras and told the North Koreans it was the "Hawaiian good-luck sign." Once the North Koreans learned the truth, they punished the prisoners with beatings, cold temperatures, and sleep deprivation. According to reports, some of the *Pueblo* crew later filed lawsuits against the North Korean government. The remaining eighty-two crew members were eventually released on 23 December 1968, walking one by one across the so-called Bridge of No Return at Panmunjom to freedom in South Korea.

On this TDY, it was much colder. I shared an open room with a center-positioned kerosene heater that provided ample warmth for me and three other officers. Each bed consisted of a mattress placed directly on the planked wooden floor. There were similarly occupied rooms further down the hallway.

One night—I won't ever forget it—one of the officers let out a scream that almost did not sound human. In the darkness of night, and as he slept, a rat crawled across his chest. We had other roommates! I don't remember if anyone caught the rat, but I do know that none of us got any sleep that night. The enlisted troops stayed in "Tent City," with less-than-desirable conditions. I often wondered if they, too, had any four-legged visitors.

If the rat wasn't enough excitement, there was also a helicopter crash outside the base during that visit. Numerous locals quickly assembled at the dangerous crash site. I went along with another officer, USAF Security Police, the ROK Police, and Korean Army troops to secure the area. Just another day at the office—mitigate further mishaps and ensure safety.

I returned to Kadena and arrived at my BOQ room at 5:30 p.m. on New Year's Eve. I was exhausted from the trip and hit the hay in the early evening. And while others celebrated, I rang in New Year by spending time in dreamland, sawing a huge log. Fortunately, Col. Sams had a nice 18th TFW reception at the O'Club on New Year's Day. While that was a welcomed distraction from the work and travel routine, it was another chance to miss my family on a major holiday. *Damn, this sucks,* I thought more than once.

During my thirty-month tour of duty in Okinawa, I made five more TDY trips to Kwang Ju AB for similar safety staff visits and surveys; a tag-on trip to Fuchu AS, Japan, to attend a 5th Air Force Safety Conference; and a three-week TDY back to Lowry AFB, Colorado, to attend the Air-Launched Tactical Missiles Safety Officers course to enhance my knowledge and the wing program for missiles safety. During that course, our class took a field trip to Davis Monthan AFB in Tucson, Arizona, for a specialized part of the study. There were six officers in the class, including myself.

■ FAMILY ARRIVES

Back on 5 December, after routine checks with base housing for available housing off base and my status on the list, I learned that Fran and little Bill could travel to Okinawa in late January 1969. I was excited to write that news to Fran, and she now had to complete several tasks before travel could be authorized: contact Fort Hamilton in Brooklyn to arrange for a household goods shipment; contact Suffolk County AFB to arrange a port call (travel date from Travis AFB, California); and get medical clearances for herself and little Bill, including numerous immunizations. The doctor appointments were completed, and the movers picked up the household goods on 20 January 1969. Fran and little Bill would begin their 7,600-mile-long travel in a couple of days.

Our car arrived in early December, and I completed all registration paperwork and had the "Keystone of the Pacific" license plates mounted. Having our own transportation would make travel to and from the base and all points in the vicinity much easier. Early in January, I coordinated all arrangements to move Fran and little Bill into a house in Awase, a housing section about three miles southeast of Kadena AB. I contacted Family Services to arrange for all the furniture and appliances we would need. Not much longer now, and we would be together again!

The family felt sad that Fran and little Bill would be leaving to go overseas, but happy, naturally, that we would be together again. Grandma Costa, my maternal grandmother, wanted Fran to bring her freshly made Sicilian pizza to me, but reluctantly, Fran had to tell her, "Oh, Grandma, Bill would love to get your pizza, but we will be traveling for a very long time, and the pizza would spoil." Naturally, Grandma was very disappointed. When I heard that from Fran, I could almost taste Grandma's pizza; I wished there was some way to get it.

On 22 January 1969, Fran and the little traveler completed their flight across the States, departing from JFK on a 10 a.m. flight to San Francisco, arriving at 1 p.m. They made their way to the Greyhound Bus Terminal to catch a 2 p.m. bus to Travis AFB. They arrived there at 3:45 p.m. and assembled for a break in travel for the remainder of that day with other Okinawan-bound passengers for a flight that would depart the West Coast at 10 p.m. A long day so far, but it was far from over. Next step: Head further westward, and fly for an extended time! They took a similar route to what I took, not that there were many options. I had all the travel information and knew the arrival date and time. They could not arrive soon enough. I was ready for them!

I was waiting at the Kadena AB air terminal when I heard the flight arrival announcement. Since I had a security badge for work that allowed me to be on the flight line, I could go to the aircraft parking area in front of the terminal. Once the pilot cut the engines off, the terminal operators positioned a stairway to the aircraft door. I walked up to the base of those stairs; I was the only person there. The stairway had approximately twenty-five steps from the platform at the aircraft door to the ground.

The aircraft door opened, and it is hard to recall how many passengers departed before Fran and little Bill came into view because I was so excited to see them. My anticipation was through the roof. As they exited the plane, Fran, with little Bill in one arm and a big red bag in the other, began to scan the area from side to side rather than looking down to see me right there at the base of the steps. I called up, "Fran, Fran, I'm down here!" She heard me, looked down, and her "where-is-he-face," turned into the "there-he-is-face," accompanied by the most beautiful smile. Within a few seconds, we were all arms, hugs, and kisses! What a great moment, a moment we did not want to end! Little Bill was smiling too! I believe he finally realized all those pictures of me turned into a real person!

The house in Awase was an old WWII army quarters of cinder block construction with a tiled roof. It was a small house but very adequate for the three of us: three bedrooms, one bathroom, a kitchen, a small eating area, and a living room. We found that the water heater was not working properly, so we needed temporary accommodation while it was repaired. We went to a hotel that turned out to be bad—not comfortable and had roaches. So since I still had not checked out of my BOQ room, we spent a second night there, even though it was not authorized. When the maid came in the next day to clean and saw Fran and little Bill, we put our fingers to our lips and relayed, "Shhhh!" She giggled, smiled, and went about her chores.

The short BOQ stay went fine except for one slight deviation. I forgot to remind Fran that I had roommates—a tiny green gecko family that hung out in the shower. They were harmless, but you could not tell that from Fran's reaction when she saw the little monsters and heard their "kissing" sounds while she was taking a shower!

We finally made it to the Awase house and began to settle down as a family once again. Once we got past the incident where little Bill fell onto his head from a faulty highchair and hoped there would be no further hurdles, we saw the light ahead. We would spend the next two years here and wanted to make the most of it. And we did.

During our time in Awase, there was a family that did not want to ship their dog, a German shepherd named Heidi. We took her into our family. She was a beautiful, obedient dog, very protective of Fran and little Bill. The only problem was that Bill was allergic to Heidi's hair. After a few weeks, we realized this could not continue, so we decided to keep Heidi and give Bill up for adoption. No, hold on a second. It was the other way around. We kept little Bill and moved Heidi to a new home once again. We were incredibly sad to let her go.

Our family in Okinawa, 1969.

■ TYPHOON ALLEY

In the United States, we get hurricanes and storms that form east of the international date line and north of the equator. In East Asia, storms west of the dateline and north of the equator are called typhoons. These storms tend to form over the Pacific Ocean and move toward the coast of Asia. The island of Okinawa is in what is called "Typhoon Alley." Perhaps more than any other base, Kadena AB needs to consider these natural storms as a threat to aircraft and other resources and prepare for the timely evacuation of aircraft to a safe location as required. The islanders need to prepare for torrential rainfall and winds of more than one hundred miles per hour.

Typhoons occur during the monsoon season, which lasts from May to October, peaking in August and September. While mainland Japan may get only two or three typhoons each year, Okinawa may average seven to eight in the same period.

My next TDY to Korea was scheduled for mid-August to perform another safety survey for about five days. Typhoon Cora began to form on 12 August as a tropical depression after Typhoon Betty dissipated. The storm intensified into Tropical Storm Cora on 14 August and later into Typhoon Cora by 18 August. Over two days before the winds intensified, Kadena AB and Naha AB evacuated aircraft that could not be protected by any cover. I was on the last plane that departed Okinawa on 18 August, headed for Kwang Ju AB. Hopefully, there would be no rats this time!

There was a routine support plan for squadron personnel who evacuated the island with aircraft. Their families left on the island would receive necessary items, such as stored water, food, and other essentials to ride out the weather. For some reason, that support did not get to Fran and little Bill, so she was left to prepare and improvise on her own as conditions worsened.

The next two days were a frightening experience for her. The sounds outside the house and the impacts on the house were a constant, undiminishing reminder of the dangerous conditions. We had wooden shutters covering the windows, but the wind found a way to blow the shutters off. Fran wedged window coverings with furniture where she could in the bedrooms and moved little Bill and herself to the center of the living room for the duration of the storm. She stuffed towels under the entry door in an attempt to barricade any water from entering the house.

We heard that we should fill the bathtub with water in the event of a storm and water may become unavailable. The water stop in the tub did not hold the water, and it eventually drained out. Fran did have a five-gallon container of water as a small reserve. The electricity was out for two days. There was no running water, and with no phone, as if that would be operational in such a storm, she only had a three-inch square transistor radio for one-way communications with the outside world. It was a terrifying experience for her, especially on 19 August, at the height of the storm. But little Bill thought moving into the living room with Fran was a party.

The forecast for Typhoon Cora was not as severe as it turned out. It was much worse, with the winds approaching one hundred miles per hour and the rainfall reports ranging between ten to seventeen and a half inches in twenty-four hours. I was surprised the car didn't slide down the hill next to our house and fall over the cliff in our backyard!

Fran was prepared to give me high hell for being gone during the typhoon. However, when I approached the house, she came out and broke into, "Billlllllllllll," with open arms and tears to accompany her relief. *OK, no more TDYs when there is even a hint of a storm,* I thought. Overall, the damage was more psychological than physical, with only minor damage to the house. Fran had a picture taken of her lying under one of our flattened banana trees while little Bill helplessly stood next to her as a reminder of that lonely experience. She reminded me of it often.

■ KEY RELATIONSHIPS

During my assignment to the 18th TFW, Fran and I developed relationships that undeniably contributed in many ways: to my career, to our social life, to our world experience, and perhaps in ways we will not fully understand. We just know that we have unquestionable and upbeat lingering recall of many of them.

At Kadena, Dave Drewry was extremely helpful in getting me established on the base, driving me to pick up the car, spending time together around the holidays, and generally hanging together often, especially before Fran and little Bill arrived. I recently learned that Dave lives close to me here in northern Virginia, and we have connected again after fifty years!

Dave went through OTS as I did. When he arrived at Kadena AB, he was assigned to the 400th Munitions Maintenance Squadron (MMS), which provided support to the B-52 bombing in Vietnam from Kadena. Shortly afterward, he interviewed for a job in the 418th MMS as the Assistant Officer in Charge (OIC) of munitions, maintenance, and storage, with additional duty as the squadron unit reliability monitor. Dave completed a Nuclear Safety Course while TDY to Japan, which enhanced his munitions certifications.

The B-52 crash at Kadena inspired Dave to attend Explosive Ordnance Disposal (EOD) School when he returned to the States. Dave was one of the most resourceful guys I knew, always finding ways to take or create opportunities as needed. He later went on to assignments, including in Korat RTAFB, Thailand; the Nuclear Defense Agency in Washington DC; as the Director of Munitions, 5th AF, Yokota AFB, Japan; the Checkmate Program at HQ USAF (in the Pentagon); and Chief US Allied and Munitions Readiness Assessment for Logistics Readiness Command.

Dave completed PME through Air War College and retired as an AF lieutenant colonel in June 1988, when he established Drewry Home Inspections, Inc. He managed this successful business for twenty-five years, during which he conducted over 14,000 home inspections in northern Virginia!

When I first met Col. Sams, the wing commander, he welcomed me to the organization and told me what he expected from me in the Wing Safety Office. He knew about my training at Lowry but emphasized the need for a more robust munitions safety program. I was all in. As I threw myself into the job, I learned that he and his vice commander, Col. Rosenbaum, played handball. I had developed an interest in the game and played a few times with others on the enclosed courts at the base gym.

Handball is not played as extensively today as it was back then. The hard rubber ball is about the size of a golf ball. The courts vary from a single wall to a full court with four walls and a ceiling. The game can be between two players—a singles game; three players, each playing on their own; or four players, two to a team, making it a doubles game. In a long match, whoever first reaches twenty-one wins.

The players wear gloves on both hands, and the best ones learn to use both hands. Being ambidextrous is essential since the ball on return from the opponent can land on either side of you as it bounces directly off any wall or the ceiling, and only one bounce is allowed before you must return the ball.

It's easy to bruise your hands in the game when you are slapping with maximum speed and pinpoint accuracy. The trick to prevent bruising is to soak your hands in the hottest water you can stand for a few minutes. This increases the circulation in your hands and usually prevents bruising.

On one Saturday morning in early January 1969, I was in the office doing some work when Col. Rosenbaum stopped by and asked with a grin, "Why are you here? Shouldn't you be practicing?" Capt. Henderson and I had a doubles match scheduled with Sams and Rosenbaum later in the afternoon. Rosenbaum and I laughed, but Henderson and I had the last laugh before the day was done. We beat them! I played handball as often as I could and especially tried to match up with someone better. That is how you improve your game. I continued to challenge Col. Sams at handball during the year, which enabled us to get to know each other better.

It was only recently that I have come to fully appreciate who Col. Monroe Seabrook,

"Saber" Sams was through some research into his service before his position as wing commander. This story is worth telling, and it never came from him.

Sams was a sophomore at the University of Tampa when the War Department opened aviation cadets to men who had a year of college. He immediately enlisted and entered pilot training in early 1942, receiving his commission and pilot wings on 14 January 1943. In June of that year, he married Norma Elizabeth Evans. Sams was assigned to the 511th Squadron out of Walterboro, South Carolina, and deployed in the spring of 1944 to Christchurch, England.

After flying eighty combat missions over France in the P-47 fighter, he took a thirty-day leave back to the States. In October 1944, he returned to his unit, which transferred its operations to Saint-Dizier, in northeastern France. After his first deployment, first combat missions, and first child, Norma received a Western Union telegram in Tampa, Florida, dated December 7, 9:36 p.m.: "The Secretary of War desires me to express his deep regret that your husband Captain Monroe S. Sams has been reported missing in action since eighteen November over France. If further details or other information are received, you will be promptly notified."

His plane took on enemy flak and burst into flames while on a mission to strafe a German rail line. Sams regained control of his single-seat P-47 aircraft but had to bail out. He floated for twenty seconds before hitting the ground in an open field near Hassel, Germany. He was quickly surrounded by a mob who threatened him with pitchforks and axes. A German officer from the flak unit that shot him down arrived, pulled out his Luger, and insisted Sams be shot. This became known because a German history professor, Klaus Zimmer, documented all airmen of the Allied Forces who were shot down over northwest Germany in World War II.

A nephew of Sams and his wife were the first of his family members to visit the site where their uncle landed that fateful day in 1944. They heard what happened to him directly from Zimmer, who had interviewed an eyewitness to the incident, his mother-in-law. From a piece of perspective, D-Day was five months earlier, and Hitler was on his heels by the fall of 1944.

Sams family account:

The villagers ran toward Seabrook with pickaxes and spit on him, but in all honesty, the villagers saved his life. The military guy that ran up wanted to shoot Seabrook, but they stopped him. He then wanted to take Seabrook to the SS, but the villagers had recently found a group of murdered soldiers in the woods on the outskirts of the village, so they insisted that the local cop take Seabrook to the proper authorities, no doubt saving Seabrook's life.

Sams was fortunate to be saved by the German police officer named Lorenz, who thought a summary field execution was inhumane. Sams was taken to Saarbrucken and then to Wiesbaden, Germany, where the Luftwaffe interrogated him. Weeks later, he ended up at a POW camp, Stalag Luft 1, on the Bering Sea, fifty miles due south of Copenhagen, near the German coast. He remained a POW until May 1945, when the Soviets were about to liberate Luft 1. The German guards fled. Capt. Sams and another POW walked out of the camp and returned to service on 9 May. Norma was notified of his release, and his story hit his hometown, Tampa, newspaper.

Col. Sabre Sams and his wife went on to have five more children. He completed eighty-nine combat missions in World War II, flying P-47s, and over seventy missions flying F-84s and F-86s in the Korean War. He was the first wing commander to fly one hundred missions over North Vietnam in F-105s. I didn't realize it at the time, but I was playing handball with an incredible individual, a legend! I had a lot of respect for him then, and it has multiplied many times over.

Additional duties are assigned as needed and, as the name implies, are additive to one's primary duty assignment. There are many types of extra responsibilities, and officers may be assigned more than one. These may be for a short period—perhaps a few days—or over many weeks or months. One of the F-105 pilots from the 12th TFS was assigned additional duty as a flying safety officer in the Wing Safety Office. His name was Anthony Cameron Shine. Everyone called him Tony.

When I first met Tony, I immediately got a sense of his unforgettable character. He was a big guy with a deep and soothing voice and a firm handshake. But he had a gentle side that was quickly apparent. He had an ever-present smile that spread across his face and a twinkle in his eyes that conveyed not only friendliness but self-confidence and willingness to work together. I first mentioned Tony to Fran in a letter I wrote on 22 November, a week before Thanksgiving. Fran had sent me a batch of cookies, which I took to the office to share with others. That was a mistake! There were about five of us who devoured them in no time flat, including Dave and Tony. I let Fran know we needed more cookies!

As I worked with a very affable Safety Office staff, I learned a bit more about Tony's career to this point, and I gained a better grasp of his dedication to his craft and the inner being of his personality. He was a family man, married to Bonnie. They had two sons and a daughter—Anthony, Shannon, and Colleen. He was twenty-nine years of age and from Pleasantville, New York, north of NYC in Westchester County, not that far from my beginnings in Brooklyn. I am convinced there is something in the water there; you just know when you meet someone from your neck of the woods. We became instant friends, and it was no surprise that many others recognized the same inimitability of this man.

When Tony arrived at Kadena AB, he had already completed one hundred missions in Vietnam in the F-105 in some of the most dangerous air activity of the war. He was a master at his job, but getting to that point was not easy for Tony as he had to encounter and overcome severe challenges that went back to his childhood. Excerpts from *Overcoming Incredible Odds,* by Anthony, Colleen, Shannon, and Bonnie Shine tell an amazing story.

> As a young boy, his first love before flying was football, but at the age of 11, Tony became a victim of polio and was bedridden for many months. The days of running, blocking, and tackling were over. But, although physically weak and atrophied, Tony had an inner drive that enabled him to overcome a badly ravaged left hand that required muscle transplant surgeries to restore use of his thumb. The deterioration was such that he couldn't pick up or hold a pencil with either hand. Doctors explained the overall severity of the damage to Tony's muscles and stated he would be lucky to walk normally again, let alone play football.

Knowing Tony, I had no doubt. He was no quitter.

> He was devastated, but his self-determination, diligence with his physical therapy, and sheer mental application surprised his doctors. It took months of steady, hard work, but Tony learned to write again, only this time with both hands. He extended his recovery by learning to walk without a limp and trained for his high school football team. It was difficult.

But Tony was a "never-give-up" young man.

> Even though his left hand was impacted by the muscle transplant surgeries and remained smaller than his right, this condition could have disqualified Tony from AF pilot training.

It appears that in Tony's mind, this was not an obstacle. It was only another challenge he was determined to defeat.

> He used weights and handgrips that he carried in his coat pockets, and constantly exercised his left hand.

Tony made his way into the air force, and early in his career, became an instructor pilot.

> He led by word and example, always encouraging his students to work harder, to persevere to reach their goals. He drew on his personal experience and would use a special segment of the poem, "If" by Rudyard Kipling to get his message across to his students:
>
> > If you can force your heart and nerve and sinew to serve your turn long after they are gone, And so hold on when there is nothing in you except the will which says to them "Hold On"!

I often think of the many times I have heard someone tell another person, "Oh, you will never be able to do that!" Can you imagine someone saying that to Tony? His determination and self-discipline were incredible!

Tony was responsible for adding another great talent to our office in June 1969—Sheila Rockholt. Sheila's husband, Bob, was in the army, stationed at Torii Station Joint Service compound, just northwest of Kadena, in November 1968. Like Fran, Sheila had to wait to travel, arriving about the same time as Fran. Even though she had a civil service job in Arlington, Virginia, she had to retest for civil service status. Sheila had three interviews scheduled, but Tony called the personnel office and said, in no uncertain terms, that he wanted her for the Safety Office.

This was not the first time Sheila had come to Okinawa. When she and her brothers were young children, back in 1950, her father had enlisted in the army, completed OCS, and was eventually assigned to Okinawa as a captain. His family arrived in 1950, after a typhoon destroyed many homes on the island.

Sheila was this resolute, energetic, and upbeat lifeblood of the Safety Office and one of those rare individuals who maintained a connection with many of us long after our days in the 18th TFW. We have continued to exchange Christmas cards with her and Bob ever since. We know that each year, the first card we receive will be from them, and it will arrive the day after Thanksgiving without fail. In 2020, Fran and I hosted Sheila for a brief visit to our home. We hadn't seen her since the late 1990s, when we attended a memorial service. Her visit brought back many good memories and stories. We reviewed photo albums and shared the sadness of friends and loved ones no longer with us.

After Maj. Nedbalek departed, Maj. Doug Alexander became my supervisor. Doug was an EB-66 pilot; his primary job was as a flying safety officer in the Wing Safety Office, so we interacted daily. Doug was great to work with, and he provided significant mentorship and encouragement to me in pursuing my career progression. He was another family man I admired, like Tony. Doug's wife, Sharon, and their children added to our social network on the island, one that grew to the point we did not look forward to suddenly ending it with another assignment. But that is the nature of AF life—make new acquaintances, build relationships, say goodbye, and start the process all over again in a new location.

Capt. Denny Jarvi was another special officer and friend, a family man, and an F-105 pilot who worked in the Wing Operations and Training Office. We got to know Denny and his wife, Becky, and family well enough to entrust them with our son, little Bill, when Fran and I took a trip to Hong Kong later during my assignment. Denny was a soft-spoken individual and another guy I cannot ever remember not smiling. The image I have of him is truly crystal clear.

Before his assignment at Kadena, Denny was assigned to the 469th Tactical Fighter Squadron at Korat Royal Thai Air Base, Thailand. He flew one hundred missions over North Vietnam as an F-105D pilot from October 1967 to May 1968. During this time, he was one of nine F-105D pilots who flew on the Rolling Thunder mission, where he participated in a raid on the Paul Doumer highway and railroad bridge on 14 December 1967.

Denny spoke about that mission during a visit from President Johnson to Korat RTAB on 23 December 1967. Also in December 1967, Captain Jarvi was one of four F-105Ds who participated in a morning mission from Korat, striking the south end of the Hanoi Railroad Classification Yard. He was awarded the Third Oak Leaf Cluster to the Distinguished Flying Cross for these missions.

During the period of drafting this book, after over fifty years, I found Denny through an exhaustive search. We exchanged several emails. We spoke on 6 August 2021 and tried to cram in all the past years during our seventy-five-minute phone call. It was one of the highlights of writing this memoir.

Denny has dedicated much of his time to creating the Dennis W. Jarvi Aviation Collection, a comprehensive cache of flight manuals, handbooks, and pilot training manuals for aircraft, many of which he piloted. Other materials he submitted are books, drawings, lithographs, posters, and photos. The repository for his work is huge and located in the Special Collections and Archives, Paul Laurence Dunbar Library, Wright State University in Dayton, Ohio.

Denny is also a member of the Pioneers of Stealth, a group that worked on the low-observables programs from the early 1970s until the deployment of these systems. They are a mix of government and contractor personnel who span everything from engineering to finance to flight testing. They also worked to propose a memorial for the air force.

Maj. Dave Nichols came to the 18th TFW Safety Office as Chief of Safety in July 1970. His prior assignment was with the 357th TFS, 355th TFW, Takhli Royal Thai Air Force Base, Thailand, where he completed one hundred combat missions over North Vietnam in an F-105D. Before that, Dave completed F-105D training at McConnell Air Force Base, Wichita, Kansas, in January 1967. He started his AF career as a navigator. On graduation from Aviation Cadet Undergraduate Navigator Training in August 1955, he was assigned as a navigator flying Liftmasters with the 30th Air Transport Squadron, 1611th Air Transport Wing, at McGuire Air Force Base, New Jersey. He married Janice (Jan) Elaine Lesan in February 1958. Another great couple, he and Jan joined the Safety Office network.

Dave also became a mentor and fully supported my next career step after my position in the Wing Safety Office. Dave would become the 12th TFS Commander on 6 December 1971, after my departure in March of that year. He would progress beyond that prestigious position up to the rank of lieutenant general, with many vital responsibilities in the AF. I had the pleasure of meeting up with Dave later in my career, but for now, suffice it to say, he was a well-recognized talent with an ever-brightening future in the AF.

The individuals who served in the wing that Fran and I got to know and share our time with at Kadena were a family. In a sense, they provided a home away from home. We worked hard, and we played just as hard. I genuinely consider that assignment unique.

▪ LET'S FLY

Denny Jarvi offered to take me for a flight in the T-33 Shooting Star called *T-Bird*. AF pilots received training in this aircraft between 1953 and 1968. This was a subsonic American jet trainer produced by Lockheed that made its first flight in 1948. It was born from a need to transition pilots from propeller-driven aircraft to the new world of jets.

I didn't think twice about it and said I would love to do that. For some strange reason, the prospect did not conjure up the terrible experiences I had in UPT. I didn't think that was strange then, but as I reflect on it now, I can't account for not being even a little bit anxious. I think it was more about my state of mind. I was happy in my job, collaborating with great people, and interacting well with everyone, especially the pilots, and snapped at the opportunity to be airborne again. Everyone around me flew regularly. I heard the roar of jet engines daily. In fact, all day long. Flying was "in the air," for me, so to speak. It was not my job, but I was hearing and breathing it every day.

The AF has rules when it comes to flying. Even if you're going up in an AF aircraft as a passenger, you need specific training as a safety precaution. I completed the one-day minimum training requirement from life support personnel on 4 August 1969, after which I was tested, certified, and received a training certificate called Annual Aircrew Survival Training IAW PACAFR 50-22.

The flight experience with Denny was fantastic! My first flight with him was on 13 August 1969; we flew for ninety minutes. Though there were some clouds, it was mostly sunny skies above the island of Okinawa and the blue waters of the Pacific. While flying over the Ie-Shima range on an island off Okinawa, we got "tapped" by an F-102 interceptor and another T-33. They were using us as "targets." Denny quickly initiated some evasive maneuvers. He annotated his flight log with the date, time airborne, my name, and comments: "First AF flight without airsickness—he stayed with me during the chase." Denny knew of my experiences at UPT. His comments meant a lot. No barf bags necessary this time!

My second flight with Denny was on 25 August. Yeah, I wanted another flight since I enjoyed the first one so much! We flew for a little over two hours around the vicinity of Okinawa and neighboring islands, sightseeing and doing some simple maneuvers. He even let me fly the jet. No airsickness, no anxiety—just fun on a carefree afternoon! It was a perk of the job that was very satisfying and exhilarating. My interest in flying was somewhat revitalized, and word got around. Tony, Dave Nichols, Doug, Denny, and Col. Sams recognized my zeal and enjoyment from these flights. This provided me with a tremendous boost of confidence, and I am eternally grateful to Denny.

▪ HONG KONG

When I first arrived at Kadena, I learned that I could sign up for a free trip to Hong Kong. The list to go was long, which you would expect, and the anticipated wait was about fifteen months, so we could expect to go halfway through my assignment. There was no commitment to go if you signed up, so I figured, why not?

When our turn arrived, we asked Denny and Becky Jarvi if they would care for little Bill while we took the trip. They lived near us in Awase, They had a daughter, Elizabeth, who was nine months older than Bill, so he would have a little friend while we were gone.

We left Okinawa for Hong Kong on a C-29 twin reciprocating-engine cargo plane with seating for a few people. It was a noisy, five-hour flight but delivered us safely to our destination. While there, we saw numerous beautiful sites in Kowloon and Hong Kong Island. We ate at the famous Juno Revolving Restaurant, where we enjoyed an exquisite meal of Peking duck while viewing the city in the evening lights. The trip was well worth the wait, and with free transportation between Okinawa and Hong Kong, we scooped up that benefit without question.

When we arrived back in Okinawa and went to pick up little Bill, he was happy to see us but quickly reminded us that we were interrupting all the fun he was having with the Jarvi family, especially with his new friend, Elizabeth!

■ THE BEAT GOES ON

After the first few months on assignment, Fran and little Bill finally settled in, the tempo of the job steady, and feeling more comfortable in my role, I made progress in several areas. I was promoted to first lieutenant on 29 March 1969. This was a year and a half from my commissioning date and the normal progression. I received a little extra pay, but I was still low on the totem pole, considering the officers I worked with daily. No one ever made me feel inferior. On the contrary, they treated me with respect I genuinely appreciated. But I certainly knew my place and just aimed my focus on the job no one else could or would want to touch.

Over the next two years, there was significant progress and strengthening of the 18th TFW Safety Promotion Program and its status within the 5th AF. This was across the board in all safety disciplines—flying, ground, accident prevention, missiles, other weapons, and munitions overall, both at Kadena and the Tac Element in Korea. The Safety Office was running on all cylinders. Col. Sams was happy with our collective performance.

I can speak to the specific accomplishments in the disciplines that I controlled. One of my first duties was participating in base-wide ground and explosives safety programs since we were short of ground safety experts. In this capacity, I advised the Base Integrated Safety Council. I presented routine briefings to squadron pilots on weapons safety and the monthly bomb commander's course segments. As a result, the USAF Safety Survey Team and Armed Services Explosives Safety Board completed favorable survey reports for the base and the wing.

I found that the Wing Weapons/Explosives Accident Prevention Plan needed updating, so I did a complete revision of the plan to include a weapons information file for personnel on TDY at our Tac Element in Korea. I also conceived and wrote a comprehensive semi-annual Weapons Safety Training and Testing program for the wing. These proved to be effective, and the wing maintained a missile and other weapons zero-accident/incident rate.

My additional duties included being HQ squadron project officer for the Combined Federal Campaign to raise money for needy individuals and organizations. No one likes to ask others for contributions, and I was a bit apprehensive about the task. Still, I collected the second-highest per capita contribution in the wing among other project officers. I felt good about that, but I wanted to get back to my primary job!

I also had additional duty as wing disaster preparedness officer to develop and evaluate the wing's ability to respond to disasters and minimize the loss of life and combat resources. This duty was naturally entwined with so many other critical and expert resources on the base.

As I mentioned much earlier, training doesn't stop, and you can never have enough expertise. It was crucial to be present at all weapons-loading exercises to administer on-the-spot corrections and advice. My supervisor, Maj. Doug Alexander, recommended me for another short training course called the Air-Launched Tactical Missiles Safety Officer course to expand my weapons knowledge. I volunteered to attend this training and went TDY to Lowry AFB, Colorado, for the three-week course, conducted from 7–27 January 1970. It was a very comprehensive course on the latest missiles and technology. We even went on a field trip from Lowry to Davis Monthan AFB in Tucson, Arizona, for specialized training.

Air-Launched Tactical Missiles Safety Officer course, Lowry AFB, Colorado.
(Back row: second from left)

When I returned to Okinawa, I turned right around and went TDY again to Korea in early February, this time with Doug Alexander, for another safety staff visit in the colder climate. No worries. I was still chillin' from my trip to Colorado.

In spring 1970, which was a year out from reassignment, I gave more thought to where I would like to go. It is always a good idea to let the AF know your preferences. There is no guarantee they will comply, but it's in your best interest to attempt to steer your career as much as possible.

Since I had a couple of flights in the Tweet and all went well, I communicated my interests to Doug, Denny, Tony, and Col. Sams. They quickly concurred that I should apply to become a rated officer. Doug strongly recommended that I be accepted for flight training in his write-up for my six-month official performance report. I applied in May 1970 to be reinstated into pilot training. It was worth a shot. In a reply letter dated 25 May from the USAFMPC, my request was rejected. No big surprise there, especially since the faculty board findings at Laughlin AFB made it clear I could not return to UPT. So why did I apply?

In discussions with my supporting officers and friends, they were aware of my experience in UPT. I had given them a complete summary of that dark part of my career. Given the waiver by the training wing commander at Laughlin, they agreed I had a particularly good chance to be accepted for navigator training. The possibility for UPT was greater if I completed UNT because I would then have achieved the rated status required to reenter pilot training if I wanted to apply later.

In that same letter, it further stated, "Officer is approved for entry into undergraduate navigator training providing he is found medically qualified by the Surgeon, Headquarters Air Training Command." That was the good news portion of that letter. In June, a follow-up letter confirmed my qualification for flying training, and a letter in September assigned me to class 72-13 to begin in early May 1971. I was all set. I knew my next assignment well ahead of the end of my overseas tour.

Not that I ever stopped or slowed down in my current job, but knowing and being excited about navigator training allowed me to focus totally on greater performance. Maj. Dave Nichols came to the Wing Safety Office as the Chief of Safety in July. He also became one of my unwavering supporters. Col. Sams departed the 18th TFW in the summer of 1970. I missed this great leader, friend, and handball player. Col. Philip Howell Jr. replaced him as the wing commander.

On 29 September 1970, I was promoted to captain, three years from my commissioning. Again, this was the typical time frame to be promoted to this rank. Col. Howell became my advocate, and after my work in the wing in the second half of the year, he nominated me for the 5th Air Force Commander's Individual Weapons Safety

Award. He cited my chairmanship of the Kadena Weapons Safety Council, management and performance in safety surveys, staff visits, and inspections, safety education, and training—all rated outstanding.

Lt. Gen. Gordon M. Graham, Commander, 5th Air Force, sent a letter to Col. Howell on 2 February 1971 stating his great pleasure to announce my selection as the award recipient. I was happy for myself, knowing I achieved this recognition. But I was even more satisfied that I could do it for the 18th TFW. Col. Howell and Nichols, now a lieutenant colonel, each sent me a letter of congratulations. Dave Nichols also sent a separate letter to Fran acknowledging her support for me and that she should share in the award. Dave knew exactly the role Fran played in supporting me in my assignment, and she deserved that recognition.

The end of our time in Okinawa was approaching. It was a time for recollection and accountability.

▪ END OF TOUR

In October 1970, we moved from the Awase off-base house to on-base housing in a section called Sebille Manor. The house was much nicer and had central air and heating. We needed a minimum of six months remaining in Okinawa to qualify for the move, and we just made the cutoff with an expected rotation in April 1971. However, I did request a voluntary curtailment of one month to allow time to return to New York to visit family before traveling again to settle my family in our on-base house during my assignment for navigator training at Mather AFB, Sacramento, California, for which I had a reporting date of 6 May 1971. The curtailment was granted, and we would depart Okinawa in mid-March.

Our experience on this island extended well beyond my AF job. We quickly developed an appreciation for the Okinawans. They were amiable and congenial people. The young Okinawan women loved little Bill. *Everyone* there loved little Bill, and they made us feel welcome. We had a terrific social life there, with many parties and gatherings among the 18th TFW team. We enjoyed the trip to Hong Kong, being on bowling teams, and spending relaxing and enjoyable times on the beach at the Officer's Rest Center in Okuma, in northern Okinawa. The maximum speed limit at that time in Okinawa was thirty miles per hour, so we could leisurely take in the sites of the island as we traveled to the center. They provided individual family cabins right on the beach, barbecue grills, a small grocery store, a golf course, and other amenities.

While there, I decided to play golf, having never played before. I started with nine holes. I rented some golf clubs from the center and lined up at the first tee. The fairway for the first hole was straight. I had the driver lined up and took my first swing. Perfect! The ball traveled a long way right down the center of the fairway toward the first hole. I thought, *Wow! Golf is easy.* After that, it was all downhill, and I don't mean in ground elevation. I was so terrible, I didn't finish nine holes. I made up my mind right then and there: *I'll stick to handball!*

During our time in Okinawa, we visited many sites history made famous, including the Nakagusuku Castle ruins. Fran's mother even came to visit us. We took her to many shops and sites that would contribute to our memories for years to come.

The end of a tour of duty is a time for reflection. How can I sum up those two and a half years in the AF? I can define my experience in Okinawa as intense and meaningful work, personal professional growth, appreciation for the recognition, and a genuine sense of contribution. It is not difficult to capture the essence and benefits of my assignment in Okinawa, which go well beyond any personal benefits to me. I have also come to appreciate the mutual respect among fellow officers, enlisted, and civilians alike, and the teamwork that contributed immensely to the mission of the 18th TFW. Everyone's goal was to put the wing's best foot forward in its operations. I will always appreciate and be grateful to those individuals at Kadena who served as early role models and mentors through their dedication, actions, leadership, support, and loyalty.

■ A NEW MINDSET

As I look at the totality of my first assignment in a strategically located AF fighter wing and contrast that period of twenty-nine months against the rough start at UPT, I concluded that I achieved what I would characterize as a "soft redemption." After Laughlin AFB, I proceeded to get valuable training in the munitions field with enhanced training along the way, many opportunities, and challenges through tasking from my supervisors and commander. More important, I gained real-world operational experience that gave me a sense of accomplishment. My outlook was exceedingly optimistic, and I thought, *There is a lot of AF out there. I am ready for the next challenge. I'm ready for a shift in my career. Bring it on!*

RECOVERY: PHASE 1

■ MATHER AFB, SACRAMENTO, CALIFORNIA

We left Okinawa with mixed emotions—enveloped in sadness as we departed the core of friends that developed out of work relationships, shared goals and interests, and social activities, and with a view on the horizon as we looked forward to seeing and catching up with family after more than two years, and in anticipation of our next road trip across the United States.

We enjoyed making the rounds to visit our families in the NYC vicinity and on Long Island, hearing about them, showing them photos, and telling them our endless stories. All of this ended in a couple weeks as we prepared for our westbound trip. This time it would be much more enjoyable because we were together. We had sold the Corvair in Okinawa and picked up a new 1971 Chevy Nova in a "give-me-a-ticket" red. Our April trip went without incident, and we were anxious to get settled for the remainder of the year as we were Mather-bound.

Mather AFB has its origins in 1918 in an area called Mills Field, located about twelve miles southeast of Sacramento. The base was named after 2nd Lt. Carl Spencer Mather, a twenty-five-year-old army pilot killed in a midair collision while training at Ellington Field, Texas, on 30 January 1918. Mather had experience as a civilian flying instructor before he enlisted as an aviation cadet. He earned a reserve military aviation rating and promotion to first lieutenant but was killed ten days later.

Mather Field served as a base for primary flight training with an eight-week course for a maximum of three hundred students. When World War I ended in November

1918, the future operational status of Mather was unknown. Flight training activities eventually ended on 8 November 1919, and the field was closed in December of that year. However, the US House of Representatives appropriated funds for additional land at military camps, including Mather, to be part of a permanent military establishment.

During the interwar years, there was a series of closures and reactivations that led to Mather Field becoming the site for advanced navigator training in 1941. The Army Air Force Navigator School began operations on 2 August 1941.

In 1943, the Army Air Forces Training Command transferred the navigator school to Ellington Field near Houston, Texas. In 1944–45, Mather became a twin-engine advanced flying school and served as an aerial port of embarkation to the Pacific. Later, during the Cold War, Mather AFB became the sole aerial navigation training school for the USAF.

The 3535th Navigator Training Wing of the ATC was responsible for bombardier training beginning in 1946. It later transitioned to UNT, advanced navigator bombardier training, electronic warfare officer training, and weapon systems officer training after the closure of other navigator training bases. It was renamed the 323rd Flying Training Wing on 1 April 1973. The wing flew the Convair T-29 for navigator training until it was replaced in 1974 by the Boeing T-43A (Boeing 737-200) aircraft.

Mather AFB was decommissioned in September 1993 due to the 1988 Base Realignment and Closure (BRAC) Commission. Most of the base was turned over to Sacramento County. The current site includes Sacramento Mather Airport.

We arrived at Mather a few days before training would begin. Family housing provided an on-base house mere minutes from the training facilities. The base provided the usual services we were accustomed to from Kadena, but now we also had Sacramento and many other nearby sites within our reach. Not that I would have any real time to devote to these as I would have my head down, once again buried in the books.

■ CLASS OF 72-13

Our class consisted of about eighty students. Most were new to the AF and held the rank of second lieutenant, having been commissioned through OTS or the ROTC program. At the start of training, there were three first lieutenants and one captain—me. The first day of training, Friday, 7 May 1971, was an orientation. This provided a pause over the weekend to attempt to grasp the enormity and complexity of the subject matter for the next thirty-eight weeks. Graduation—Friday, 28 January 1972—seemed to be light-years away. There was a lot of ground *and air* to cover in that period.

The ranking officer in the class is designated as the class commander, and I was chosen. This had no particular benefit since I would need to complete the same training requirements as the rest of the class to achieve an aeronautical rating. It is merely a title, but the individual was responsible for any student concerns or interaction with training faculty that required class representation. I considered the role of class commander from a much different perspective, one that was more personal with the potential for success or disaster.

I had some AF experience with my previous training and an operational assignment. That was undoubtedly a leg up. I also had a couple of flights under my belt with Denny Jarvi in the T-33 and the support and encouragement of my fellow officers in the 18th TFW, all of which should contribute to the self-confidence I would need to be an effective leader in the class.

However, being the class commander meant a much deeper commitment on my part. It meant I had to be a role model for the other students, not just a title. I had to do well with the training. I wondered, *How would it look if I did poorly or failed?* I couldn't let that happen; I could not let UNT be "failure 2.0." As heard in the 1995 film *Apollo 13*, "Failure is not an option." Success in UNT would require my complete focus on academics, navigating on practice, and check rides, in team sports—the complete program. I was determined to have a different outcome in UNT than I did in UPT and to be worthy of the title of class commander. Even though I had been given that title, I felt obliged to earn it.

■ NAVIGATION: AN ART AND A SCIENCE

Navigation—getting from point A to point B and points beyond. It is as simple as that. Yet it is not so easily achieved when there are no reference points to indicate if you are on or off course. The complexity applies especially when you are at sea. Guessing does not get you to your destination.

As a student of navigation, I learned that the art of navigation goes back many centuries. The first Western civilization known to have developed the art of navigation at sea was the Phoenicians, about four thousand years ago (c. 2000 BCE). Phoenician sailors used primitive charts and observations of the sun and stars to determine direction.

Early navigational tools determined latitude based on celestial observations of the

North Star. They determined a ship's latitude at sea based on the angle of the star above the horizon. Another aid was the mariner's compass, an early form of the magnetic compass. Additionally, a chip log was used to determine a ship's speed. The chip log consisted of a line containing knots at regular intervals and weighted to drag in the water. It was let out over the stern as the ship was under way. A seaman would count the number of knots that went out over a specific period, and the ship's speed could then be calculated.

It was exciting to learn how navigation progressed over time. To determine longitude, the chronometer came into play. In 1764, British clockmaker John Harrison invented the seagoing chronometer. This invention was an important advance in marine navigation. In 1779, British naval officer and explorer Capt. James Cook used Harrison's chronometer to circumnavigate the globe. When he returned, his longitude calculations based on the chronometer proved to be correct within eight miles (thirteen kilometers). From the information gathered on his voyage, Cook completed many detailed charts of the world that completely changed the nature of navigation. In 1884, by international agreement, the prime meridian, located at 0° longitude, was established as the meridian passing through Greenwich, England.

In modern times, especially in the twentieth century, there were important advances to marine navigation with radio beacons, radar, the gyroscopic compass, and the global positioning system (GPS). Use of these devices and methods required an art to be effective and precise in early navigation. Most oceangoing vessels keep a sextant, a device designed to measure the angle between two points precisely and accurately, for celestial navigation onboard for use in case of an emergency.

The gyroscopic compass (or gyrocompass) was introduced in 1907. The primary benefit of the gyrocompass over a magnetic compass is that the gyro is unaffected by the earth's or the ship's magnetic field, and it always points to true north. The first practical radar (short for radio detection and ranging) system was produced in 1935. It was used to locate objects beyond the range of vision by projecting radio waves against them. This was, and still is, very useful on ships to locate other vessels and land when visibility is reduced.

The US navigation system known as long-range navigation (Loran) was developed between 1940 and 1943 and used pulsed radio transmissions from so-called master and slave stations to determine a ship's position. Loran's accuracy is measured in hundreds of meters but only has limited coverage.

The Global Positioning System (GPS) largely replaced the Loran in the late twentieth century. GPS uses the same time difference principle from separate signals as Loran, but the signals come from satellites. GPS accuracy can be measured in feet. The

GPS project was launched in the United States in 1973 to overcome the limitations of previous navigation systems, integrating ideas from several predecessors, including classified engineering design studies from the 1960s.

The US Department of Defense developed the GPS invented by Roger L. Easton, a scientist with a bachelor's degree in physics. However, as with many other inventions throughout history, there is a lack of consensus over who should be credited with its creation. At least four people have been acknowledged to be associated with the invention of this revolutionary technology.

The GPS initially used twenty-four satellites. Today, there are at least thirty-one. Three satellites provide two possible points for a position on earth. A fourth satellite provides a precise position.

■ COURSE OF STUDY

The AF defined the Undergraduate Navigator Training Course N-V6A-A as follows:

> Qualifies nonrated officers to perform duties and responsibilities of a navigator. Academic instruction in basic navigation procedures, map reading, celestial, pressure differential, grid, flight publications, weather, aviation physiology, and aircraft systems and equipment including radar, radio aids, Loran, consolan, doppler, and Astro trackers. Flight training in high/low altitude map reading and radar procedures; day/night celestial, grid, and overwater navigation; and use of combined aids on a typical navigation mission. Students receive approximately 231 hours of flight training in T-29 aircraft. Graduates are awarded the navigator rating (AFSC 1531) and are assigned to operational commands or are selected for further aircrew training in navigation bomb or electronic warfare.

The academic phase of training included 699 hours of prescribed instruction in addition to the 231 hours of prescribed flying training. The areas in both that were formally tested are indicated with a checkmark. The allocation of these hours spread across the academic and flying subject areas as depicted in my following training record:

Academic Training Phase	Prescribed Hours	Tested (✓)	Flying Training Phase in T-29C Aircraft	Prescribed Hours	Tested (✓)
			Undergraduate Navigator Training Course N-V6A-A		
Aviation Physiology	40.0	✓	Familiarization	6.0	
Aircraft and Navigation Equipment	57.0	✓	Dead Reckoning	18.0	
Aircraft Systems	22.0		Map Reading - High Level	18.0	✓
Navigation Procedures	46.0	✓	Radar - High Level	30.0	✓
Aural Code	10.0		Day Celestial	18.0	
Map Reading	21.0	✓	Night Celestial	24.0	✓
Radar Navigation	29.0	✓	Grid	18.0	
Day Celestial	44.0	✓	Overwater	32.5	✓
Night Celestial	45.0	✓	Radar/Map Reading - High/Low	24.0	
Grid Navigation	35.0	✓	Combined Aids	42.5	✓
Weather	22.0	✓			
Overwater Navigation	45.0	✓			
Operational Techniques	19.0				
Tactical Navigation	26.0				
Flight Publications	41.0	✓			
Electronic Warfare	16.0				
Integrated Navigation Systems	17.0				
Flight Mission Preparation, Briefing & Critique	164.0				
Total Hours	699.0			231.0	

In addition to academics and flying, there were 165 hours across several areas, including processing and indoctrination, officer career planning, physical training, and marksmanship.

Navigator instructors conducted classroom academics for each segment. This was supplemented by in-depth documentation to read and workbooks to complete. Dinners at home were a temporary break after long days in the classroom, only to jump right back into the subject matter late into the night. There was rarely any pause during this nonstop activity except, perhaps, for holidays, which would be an opportunity to catch up. We were on a train that had left the station and had only one stop: graduation in January 1972.

My focus and plan were to fully understand every element of every academic subject. I was confident that I understood the material and would do well on any testing in the classroom. I would also ensure I could pace myself through mock flights in preparation for flying training and flight navigation check rides.

I found the subject of navigation to be fascinating. Starting with the basic concept of dead reckoning, one would determine a new position using known or estimated speeds over elapsed time and course (heading). The expression originated from the use of the Dutchman's log, a buoyant object thrown overboard to determine the vessel's speed relative to the object, which was assumed to be dead in the water. The phrase "dead reckoning" dates from Elizabethan times (1605–1615).

A navigator's responsibility is always to be aware of the aircraft's position relative to the next destination point and the ground. A navigator must stay ahead of the aircraft to maintain course or ensure proper course corrections. Falling behind tends to compound the navigator's ability to reach the destination point successfully.

The various navigation methods—such as map reading, radar navigation, celestial—and associated navigation equipment contributed to most of the skill sets required to navigate well. For example, a comprehensive understanding of celestial bodies was paramount in celestial navigation, and it was not limited to the sun, moon, and planets. Still, it included fifty to sixty stars that we needed to identify in addition to what many might consider the most essential navigational star, Polaris, the North Star.

We didn't have GPS or computers in which to plug in data. We had maps, star charts, aircraft systems with radar scopes to identify blips, and sextants mounted in the ceiling of the aircraft fuselage to measure lines of position from celestial bodies. Handheld calculators and forms were used to complete complex calculations. All of these were used to determine where our position was relative to the ground over land and relative to a point with a latitude and longitude over water.

The navigator must make effective use of one or more navigational tools as necessary to determine position. There were many opportunities to make mistakes in mathematical calculations that could potentially place your position on a map many miles from your actual location. You could plot a position that was in the next state!

The T-29C aircraft, the "flying classroom," was used for navigator flying training. This modified Convair aircraft was an unpressurized version featuring fourteen navigation stations for students/instructors and one radio operator station. It was delivered to the USAF on 26 July 1951. Each navigation student had access to a map table, Loran scope, altimeter, and radio compass panel.

In the fuselage roof were four astrodomes that could allow sextants to be mounted, which students used to take sights from celestial bodies. There were also five drift meters used to determine the drift of an aircraft by visual sightings of points on the ground. The aircraft continued to provide navigation training until the T-43 replaced it; the T-29 was flown to the Strategic Air & Space Museum in July 1973, its final resting place.

■ COMPETITION

Cooperate and Graduate applied to UNT, just as it had in OTS, UPT, and munitions training. Everyone wanted to earn their navigator wings, and a spirit of discussion and exchange via study groups facilitated achievement toward that goal. However, in parallel with that cooperation, there was a fiercely competitive environment with specific awards on the line for best placement in several categories: the ATC Commander's Trophy for the student in the class with the highest overall grade; the Husik Memorial Trophy for the student with the highest grade in flying training, and the Outstanding Graduate Letter for students who ranked in the upper 10 percent of the class and had an average grade of 95 or above in both flying and academics.

The school administration would post computer printouts of class standings after each academic or flying exam with an overall grade, flying grade, and academic grade. It gave a very clear snapshot in time of who was at the top, the bottom, and everyone in between. If you can recall thin printer paper with hole-perforated left and right edges, that's what the computer output looked like.

The awards were valued achievements, so to eliminate any chance of ties in the grading, scoring was carried out to three decimal places—to the thousandths of a point! The difference in the award categories was often by just a few thousandths, so missing one correct answer on a test could make all the difference in student placement. The students on the upper part of the list were keen on gaining an advantageous edge throughout the program in pursuit of these awards.

After each exam or check ride, we anxiously awaited the results to see who was ahead. There was one first lieutenant who was in the race with me and others during the entire program. Somehow, his wife gained access to the results before we learned of them. She would state, "Cimino got one wrong on the test," followed by other information on grades for other individuals. This information quickly spread among the class. No one knew how she was able to acquire this information. Perhaps she knew someone in the administration office. As a result, I became known as "One-Wrong Cimino." The title was pretty accurate as I usually answered one test question incorrectly. In fact, the only academic test on which I scored 100 percent was on the day celestial segment. All the others were in the nineties.

In the flying evaluations for high-level map reading, night celestial, overwater, and combined aids, all my grades were above 97 percent, except for high-level radar navigation, which was above 99 percent. I diverted a disaster that could have impacted my flying average and overall grade. It was during the check ride for the night celestial phase of training. Our route was a five-hour flight originating from Mather, departing to the south toward Los Angeles, with a dogleg turn to the east just north of the city. It would proceed to the California-Arizona border at Lake Havasu City and the Colorado River. At that point, we would plot our course to return to Mather via the same route.

I had planned to use three stars to provide separate lines of positions (LOPs) which would intersect at close to 120 degrees apart to give me a fix. This fix is not crack cocaine or some other drug; it's a position on a chart, a position fix. This particular fix was the one I planned to plot just north of Los Angeles to determine the turning point to proceed eastward. It became slightly cloudy toward the end of this first leg south of Mather.

I was positioned at the sextant mounted on the ceiling next to my map table on the aircraft. I "shot" the first star; it takes about two minutes to get a good reading. I did the same for star number 2. However, as I turned the sextant to position for star number 3, sporadic clouds began to obscure a clear view of the star, and a sufficient reading was not possible. Having only two LOPs could throw off my chart plot. Your grade is determined by how close you can plot to the actual course, among many other factors, so I desperately needed that third LOP!

I quickly jumped down from the platform I was positioned on at the sextant location and looked out the aircraft window on one side. I saw nothing that would help. I switched to the other side and looked out. There it was! The moon was faintly visible through the clouds, so I took a two-minute shot, sat at my map table, and calculated the fix.

Celestial navigation using a sextant is a complex and involved process that requires a fair amount of mathematical calculations, corrections, references to tables, and knowledge of the heavens and the earth. There is no way around it. One can easily miscalculate during this tedious process, resulting in a bad position fix. Fortunately, I was able to use the LOP from the moon as the third component to determine an excellent position fix from which I could provide the instructor with an accurate turn point that was less than one minute ahead in the flight.

LOPs must also be adjusted for the Coriolis effect, which describes the pattern of deflection taken by objects not firmly connected to the ground as they travel long distances around the earth. All went according to plan before this excitement and for the remainder of the check ride. My actions secured a grade of 97.15 for this evaluation ride. I was still in the race for the top!

■ GRADUATION

The stage was set; the graduation ceremony began with all the pageantry the air force could muster. Fran sat in the audience along with the other wives and families of the students of Class 72-13. The wing commander and other officers gave their speeches, congratulations, and good wishes for successful careers. Students sat proudly in their impeccable uniforms, relieved after months of intense training. It was time to announce the award winners. Four of us received awards.

Four UNT outstanding graduates flanked by senior wing officers.

I completed my academic training with an overall score of 96.73 and flying training of 97.69. I completed the prescribed 231 hours of flight training with 202.9 hours.
The combined grades enabled me to receive all three awards as the student who placed
at the top of the class: the ATC Commander's Trophy, the Husik Memorial Trophy,
and an Outstanding Graduate Letter. All are documented on my summary record of
training. Three other students also received an Outstanding Graduate Letter.

Receiving the ATC Commander's Trophy.

Receiving the Husik Memorial Trophy.

During the months of training, some students washed out for various reasons. Out of an initial class of eighty students, fifty-nine graduated. Navigator training wasn't for everyone, and our class was no exception. I was over the moon with the results! Fran pinned on my navigator wings, and I received my certificate of aeronautical rating for UNT dated 28 January 1972. We partied hard that evening! It was time to celebrate—not to think about the past year, moving again, the next assignment, or anything else. Just celebrate!

My navigator wings.

Convair T-29 USAF Navigator "Flying Classroom"

UNT Class 72 - 13
Graduation: 28 January 1972
Captain W. Cimino - far left under aircraft nose

■ ASSIGNMENTS

According to placement in the class, each UNT graduate would choose the aircraft assignments available to our class. The list for our class included:

- Eleven to NBT—navigator bombardier training (pretraining for the B-52 aircraft at various locations)
- Eight to EWO—electronic warfare officer (pretraining for electronic warfare aircraft at multiple locations)
- One to the RF-4C (tactical reconnaissance training at Shaw AFB, South Carolina)
- One to the EB-66 (electronic warfare aircraft at Korat RTAFB, Thailand)
- Seven to the F-4 (fighter aircraft at Homestead AFB, Florida)
- Seven to the F-4 (fighter aircraft at Luke AFB, Arizona)
- Five to the C-130 (cargo aircraft: two to Ching Chuan Kang AB, Taiwan, and one each to Langley AFB, Virginia, Pope AFB, North Carolina, and Dyess AFB, Texas)
- Three to the AC-130 (gunship aircraft at Ubon RTAFB, Thailand)
- One to the EC-121 (early warning and control radar surveillance aircraft at McClellan, AFB, California)
- Twelve to the KC-135 (tanker aircraft: one each to Altus AFB, Oklahoma; Beale AFB, California; Dyess AFB, Texas; Ellsworth AFB, South Dakota; Fairchild AFB, Washington; Grand Forks AFB, North Dakota; Grissom AFB, Indiana; K. I. Sawyer AFB, Michigan; Loring AFB, Maine; Pease AFB, New Hampshire; Plattsburgh AFB, New York; and Wurtsmith AFB, Michigan)
- Three to the C-141 (cargo aircraft, various unrecorded locations)

Since I finished at the top of my class, I had the first choice of aircraft available. I selected the single RF-4C tactical reconnaissance aircraft for assignment at Shaw AFB in Sumter, South Carolina. Training would begin in early March, after I completed winter survival training and POW camp at Fairchild AFB in Washington during the first two weeks of February, and a four-day water survival training at Homestead AFB in Florida. Then to Sumter.

■ SELF-EVALUATION

It was important to assess the training I just completed and what it meant to me personally and professionally, as well as to the USAF. I call this point in my career "Recovery: Phase 1" for a very specific reason. The term automatically implies there is at least another recovery phase, something to follow.

I was extremely happy to have done well at UNT, not only with performance as a student of navigation, but as a representative of the class that allowed a bit of leadership. However, a broader perspective enabled me to contrast this training with my terrible experience at UPT. I felt I redeemed myself to some degree. But more introspection gnawed at me and suggested a more complete perspective was necessary.

Deeper self-evaluation allowed me to prevent being naive or overly boastful. I recognized full well that I did nothing to be of any value to the USAF at this point. The AF spent a good chunk of money on my training. Sure, I did well, but I had no operational navigation experience yet. The ROI—return on investment—to the AF up to this point from me as a rated officer had been zero! This would continue over the next few months in RF-4C training—ROI equals zero!

I earned my navigator wings—an aeronautical rating—with honor. But what was my worth to the AF? *How will I make this training—past, and future—pay off for the branch I serve?* "Recovery: Phase 2" must serve that purpose, or at a minimum, proceed toward that end. Otherwise, the AF invested in me to get nothing in return. My future service must contain the utility of the outstanding training I received. Then and only then would I provide benefits and value to the USAF as a rated officer.

RECOVERY: PHASE 2

■ WINTER SURVIVAL TRAINING/POW CAMP

After UNT graduation, I left Mather AFB for a thirteen-day TDY to attend the first of several survival training courses the AF requires of aircrew members. Men and women who are aircrew may find themselves in many different environments given the global reach of the armed services. Learning to survive in these settings is critical. The first of these would be in Washington, near Spokane at Fairchild AFB, in what Washington Irving described in his book *Salmagundi* as, "in the dead of winter, when nature is without charm." It was February, and it was cold!

The training taught fundamental skills that address bailing out over a wilderness area. The classroom portion of the training was in a comfortable, well-heated building, as you would expect. But that didn't last very long. We would apply our training in the field after we heard presentations on how to survive extended periods in winter conditions, where we would need to provide shelter, trap and prepare food, improvise needed tools and equipment, obtain and purify water, learn communication techniques, and render first aid.

Our class consisted of a few trainees and an instructor. We battled the elements for several days and nights, all while trying to evade a force of instructors set on capturing us. This is why the training was called SERE—survival, evasion, resistance, and escape. The POW camp addressed the resistance and escape components. A couple feet of snow were already on the ground, so making a shelter where we could ensure warmth and dryness had additional challenges.

Assuming we had ejected from an aircraft, we learned to use parts of our parachutes to serve as a lean-to (tent structure) for shelter. Light snow accumulated on the lean-to during our time in the field, but we constructed it at an angle to allow the snow to slide off. At night, we would strip down to our underwear and zip ourselves into thermal sleeping bags. Removal of any wet clothing and keeping our body heat trapped in the bag allowed sufficient warmth. We prepared the sleeping area in the lean-to by removing snow and adding layers of tree branches that offered a barrier from the damp ground.

To hone our navigational skills in the wilderness, we used compass readings and interpreted topographical maps. We mashed our way through the snow, brush, and forested areas to get to a rendezvous point. We did night treks with thirty-pound backpacks, wearing snowshoes as we proceeded through deep snow.

At one point, one of the trainees slipped off a fallen tree trunk that spanned across a depression. He went flying headfirst into several feet of snow, screaming all the way. Due to the heavy weight of the backpack and his weight and clothing, he could not maneuver to get free. So he remained there, upside down, with his feet kicking in the air. We quickly freed him. Cooperate and Graduate was alive and well. He was very grateful as he recovered normal breathing! This part of the training was exhausting but taught us what a real-life survival situation might be like.

Obtaining food was another challenge. We learned how to construct traps and snares to catch wildlife. I had a bit of hesitation after we caught some rabbits and had to prepare them for dinner. I was never one for hunting, even to this day; fishing is more my style. The snare would not necessarily kill them, so in that case, I was selected to perform the execution. It was inhumane for sure, but this was survival. It was either you or the rabbit. I clunked it across its head and proceeded to skin our meal.

As it turned out, cooked rabbit tasted very good, especially for tired and hungry troops. We sat around the campfire, absorbing warmth and smoke—lots of it. Smoke got into our clothing, our hair, everywhere. When I returned home, it took about a week of daily showering to eliminate the smell of smoke and remove the grit from my fingernails.

The POW training compound was at another location at Fairchild. This was the hardcore, intense training to experience the conditions where an aircrew member might need to evade and resist if taken prisoner. As the war in SEA continued, this training could prove to be invaluable. Previously, this training was conducted at Stead AFB in Nevada, in desert conditions. Those familiar with the training stated it was much more intense before the transition to Fairchild and that a student had died there. This unfortunate incident prompted some changes to the program.

If you had to go through this training, you would only want to do it once. Before being taken prisoners, we had to make our way through an obstacle course at night, crawling under barbed wire and crossing and climbing in and out of muddy pits—all while gunshots and explosions distracted us. This was extremely tiring, and we ended up being captured, hooded, separated from each other, shoved, and manhandled. I was no longer an officer in the USAF. I was a POW—not a real one, but real enough for training purposes as I would learn.

Isolated in a cell, alone, your mind can wander. You wonder what comes next. The anticipation is enough to cause self-doubt and worry. In the back of your mind is, *This is only training. Remember that!* But that didn't help much as I quickly faced a visit from some pretty scary dudes. They ordered me to strip and then did a *very* comprehensive strip search. They made insulting comments about my manhood, making every attempt to humiliate me. They laughed and pointed while I stood naked before them. Humiliation was a frequent psychological tool during this phase of training. There was no opportunity to sleep; I had to stand and remain awake in my cell. Guards came to check often, so there was not much chance I could get any rest.

One of the most challenging periods in this training came when they forced me into a small wooden box, twenty-four inches wide and about three feet high. I was about six feet in height at that time (now more like five feet, ten-and-a-half inches). I was in the box, crouched down—more like *squeezed* down—with the lid locked. There was no room to maneuver, and I was in total darkness. This was another attempt to break you. I can only imagine if I had developed any cramps or muscle spasms while in the box and had no way to find relief. I wondered, *How long will I be in this thing?* I decided to distract myself and focus on pleasant things, like my family, a calm beach, and happy occasions. This helped me pass the time, of which I had no sense.

After the box, the ogres took me to a room with nothing more than a small desk and a single hanging light bulb. They began their threats and torments as they banged on the table and got up close and personal. They knew I was married and had a son. "Your wife and child will never know what happened to you. You Americans are weak," they would shout close to my face. They went on and on. The Geneva Convention stated that I only had to give them my name, rank, and serial number. My simple answers in this regard only angered them. They said I was not a prisoner but a war criminal. This went on for long periods, always in an attempt to get more answers from me and wear me down.

When you didn't comply, more bad stuff followed. I was forced to chip the ice on the ground in the compound almost all night. It was freezing. I shivered in the cold, and a sharp pain ran through my spine. When they gave us any food, it was a tiny mixture of rice and something I could not easily identify. I was not able to eat much of it.

On the last morning of training, we were lined up at attention as the guards continued to harass us. They screamed at us and said we were despicable. They marched us around for a time; we were tired and sent in the direction of our cells. Only this time, as we turned, we saw the American flag being raised. The instructors then told us we were no longer prisoners but Americans. Free! The course was over! I was tired and hungry and very glad it ended.

I am so grateful for this training, and I have immense respect for all those Americans who had to endure POW status far worse than the mere exposure I had for a few days in a training environment. I have even greater respect for those who made the ultimate sacrifice through tragedy or while imprisoned under the harshest of circumstances.

Wiped out after winter survival training and POW camp.

■ WATER SURVIVAL TRAINING

The thought of all those MIA/POW personnel who had not been with their families for extended periods lingered in my mind. I was glad to be home on 14 February and see Fran and little Bill again at Mather AFB. I had missed Fran's birthday on the fifth, so we celebrated that. Our attention quickly turned to preparing for the movers who would come to pack our household goods and load the truck before heading eastward.

MANIFESTATIONS OF APPREHENSION

I was due to report to Shaw AFB by 7 March 1972 but needed to complete a four-day water survival training at Homestead AFB, Florida, en route to South Carolina.

The training consisted of classroom and field, or should I say ocean, components. In the event of a water landing without the aircraft—that is, an ejection over water—an aircrew member needs to know how to survive under various conditions: high winds that could drag the parachute and aircrew member resulting in drowning, being stuck under a parachute in the water, at sea in a raft for extended periods without food and drinkable water, in rough seas, in variable weather. The circumstances go on.

The classroom training was excellent, but we all wanted to get in the water to practice the skills we learned. We used the pools on base and a training area in Biscayne Bay, east of the base and south of Miami, for different parts of water survival training. They have very different characteristics and conditions, such as choppiness, buoyancy, visibility, and habitants—like sharks! The average depth of the bay was somewhere between five and one-half to ten feet, so while not very deep, you didn't need much to drown. We learned how to maneuver just before water entry and after contact with the water.

The instructors took us to the bay to simulate coming down from an aircraft ejection over water with a parachute. They attached a rope that could extend several hundred feet to our harnesses, which were worn over our flight suits. We had our flight boots on; our flight suits; survival vests with radios, small rations, some drinkable water, and other items; along with a one-man raft. All items you would normally have as part of your after-ejection survival gear.

We stood on a platform towed by a boat. The parachute fully deployed behind us as we were about to get towed upward. The instructors added power and steered the boat to extend the rope to its entire length. The boat would continue to pull us up until we were several hundred feet above the water.

Some trainees flopped right into the ocean at the outset. The instructors let them remain in the water for a while before they retrieved them to start the process all over again. As trainees successfully lifted from the boat, they would reach several hundred feet, and the instructors would signal them to release the tow rope. Trainees would then free fall with the chute above them. In effect, we had "ejected" and were now on our way to the ocean below.

Hitting the water properly is especially important. The tendency is to look down at the water, but that can be very deceptive. Without good references, it is challenging to determine exactly how high above the water you are. You must be ready to release the two harness clamps that hold your parachute so that you can be free from any entanglement. The training taught us to look out at the horizon, not down. When you hit the water, then, and only then, release the parachute.

As several of us observed this, I remember a trainee who did not use the horizon as his reference. He looked down and thought he was just a few feet above the water. He released his parachute and was now free-falling, screaming all the way as he fell from about thirty feet above the water. He hit bottom! Good thing the bay was shallow. We all had a good laugh at that one. He also did—after he recovered and stopped choking on the saltwater he swallowed. That was a perfect teaching moment!

One of the most challenging things to do once you hit the water is to maneuver into the one-man raft. You have all the flight gear on that I mentioned, which weighs you down. This can be further complicated by high winds and swells or choppy water. The proper method is to pull the raft under you as you inch your way into it while facing down. This could take considerable effort and tire you out quickly. Sometimes you get partly in only to slip out and need to try again.

Once in the raft, you must flip over from face down to face up and eventually move into a reclining position. Once you did that, the instructors added power to the boat, waved goodbye, and disappeared. You were on your own for several hours to learn what it means to have survived an overwater ejection and to be stranded in the ocean with no assurance that you would be picked up anytime soon.

If you landed in the water and the chute fell on top of you, you could easily drown as the weight of the wet chute forced you underwater. The survival technique was to find a main seam and pull it down from over your head toward your midsection until you reached the edge and could then be free of the chute. However, you always tried to retain the chute as it could provide the material needed for other aspects of survival. As I said before, training does not stop. It's all necessary and valuable. And one day, it just might save your life.

■ SHAW AFB, SUMTER, SOUTH CAROLINA

Water survival training ended on 5 March. We departed Homestead AFB for the last leg of our trip to Sumter. It was a one-day trip by car. Sumter is about one hour east of Columbia, the state capital and home to Shaw AFB. The base is located approximately 8.4 miles west-northwest of downtown Sumter.

The base is named in honor of World War 1 pilot 1st Lt. Ervin David Shaw. Shaw was one of the first Americans to fly combat missions in World War 1. A Sumter County native, he was assigned to the Royal Air Force 48 Squadron as a Royal Canadian Flying Corps member. He died after three enemy aircraft attacked his Bristol F.2B while returning from a reconnaissance mission on 9 July 1918. Shaw downed one of his attackers before he was killed.

In the early days of the Army Air Corps, Shaw Field conducted cadet flying training in the Air Corps Basic Flying School and later changed to advanced flying training. On 1 April 1945, the jurisdiction of Shaw Field was transferred to the AF.

For a brief time, Shaw Field also served as a POW camp. The first group of German prisoners arrived on 1 March 1945. Eventually, 175 of them lived in an encampment just off the main base and worked on farms in the area. They departed in the early months of 1946 to rebuild European cities and towns devastated during the war. Those prisoners were eventually repatriated to Germany around 1947. Some returned to the Shaw and Sumter area and obtained US citizenship.

From July 1946 until May 1947, Shaw was the home of the 414th and 415th Night Fighter Squadrons. They flew the P-61 Black Widow in Europe with the Ninth Air Force during World War 2 and were reassigned to the United States after the end of hostilities. The 414th was transferred to Caribbean Air Force at Rio Hato AB, Panama, in March 1947 to perform an air defense mission of the Panama Canal. The 415th was reassigned to Alaska Air Command at Adak Island, Alaska, in May 1947 to perform an air defense mission over the Aleutian Islands and the territorial waters of western Alaska.

On 1 April 1951, the 363rd Tactical Reconnaissance Wing transferred to Shaw from Langley AFB, Virginia. The wing eventually contained several operational recce squadrons and the 18th TRS, which conducted training to qualify pilots and navigators in the RF-4C. The navigators were called WSOs (pronounced whizz-ohs), meaning weapon systems officers. This was the general term for back seaters in the F-4 (fighter) and the RF-4C (recce bird), even though the RF-4C did not have weapons. Instead, it carried a suite of sensors to collect target intelligence and bomb-damage assessments.

Shaw was also home to Headquarters 9th AF, a major numbered AF organization that transferred from Pope AFB, North Carolina, on 1 September 1954. It maintained operational control over several tactical wings at various eastern-based locations.

▪ RF-4C AIRCREW TRAINING

My RF-4C training would begin on 8 March, so we quickly familiarized ourselves with Sumter. There wasn't much there; it was similar in scope to Del Rio, Texas, in many respects. Shaw had the usual services, and we had temporary base housing until our household goods showed up and were delivered to our assigned home on the base at Sycamore Street. We got used to the moving process with several moves in nearly five years of active duty. Getting quickly settled in our new home was routine, and we knew it would not be long before the end of the course on 21 August, when we would prepare for another move unless we were stationed at Shaw after training. That, however, was not likely to happen.

Class 72-3 had eight pilots and six WSOs. We would all go through the first phase of training together in the RF-4C familiarization course, an intense thirty-seven-hour fire-hose blast of classroom training focused on all the systems that make up the aircraft. In many respects, the RF version was similar to the fighter version, the F-4. The only significant difference was that the RF-4C fuselage had a more extended nose section to house various imagery sensors and a forward-looking radar.

The technical order (TO) 1F-4(R)C-1 is the bible for RF-4C aircrews. It contains nearly four hundred pages that describe the aircraft's various systems, normal procedures, emergency procedures, auxiliary equipment, operating limitations, flight characteristics, system operation, crew duties, all-weather operation, and performance data. We learned it from beginning to end.

The aircraft systems in the RF-4C were numerous. The major ones included: the engines (two General Electric J-79-15 turbojets with afterburner thrust up to 17,000 pounds each); the fuel system; hydraulic power supply system; pneumatic system; flight control system; boundary layer control system; electrical power supply system; communications; sensor equipment; and the ejection seat system.

The WSO sat in the rear cockpit (I call it "the WSO's office") with good visibility to the sides and rear but limited visibility forward due to the bulkhead between the WSO and the pilot. The rear cockpit contained many instruments, indicators, and controls similar to those of the pilot. The rear cockpit instrument panel included thirty such devices. The rear cockpit left console contained twenty-one devices; the rear cockpit right console contained another fifteen devices. The WSO's cockpit contained most of the electrical circuit breakers associated with various systems. The pilot had only seven circuit breakers in the front cockpit. The WSO had three circuit-breaker panels (depicted in 1, 2, and 3 below) containing a total of 230 circuit breakers.

The rough schematic below depicts the rear cockpit of the RF-4C. A complete depiction is in appendix D, "RF-4C WSO's Office Illustrations."

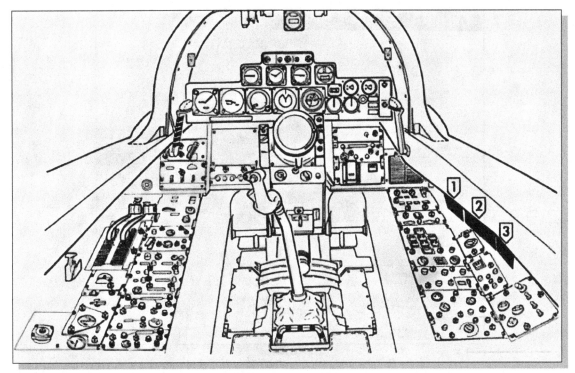

RF-4C rear cockpit.

The primary phase of training, which lasted through August, was the USAF Tactical Reconnaissance Training course. It included some common elements for both pilots and WSOs and specific elements for either pilots or WSOs. These elements would be in both academic subjects and flying training sorties. A sortie is defined as a mission for the flight, such as a night radar recce sortie or an air-to-air refueling sortie.

The WSO controlled all the cameras and sensors. Directly aft of the forward-looking radar in the nose of the aircraft were three camera stations: a forward oblique camera, a low-altitude panoramic camera (which swept horizon to horizon on each side of the aircraft and driven by ground speed for accuracy), and a high-altitude panoramic camera. A side-looking radar was mounted in the fuselage below the pilot's location, and an infrared reconnaissance sensor was mounted in the fuselage below the WSO's location. Photoflash cartridges could be ejected from the aft fuselage as needed flash for night imagery. The WSO controlled this. WSO training would include the use of all these systems.

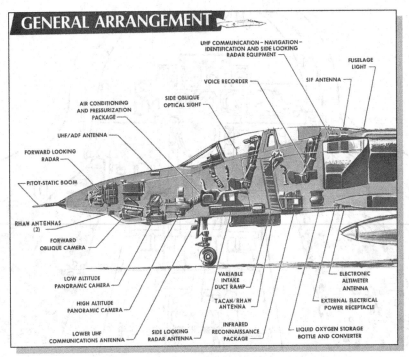

RF-4C forward section depicts the suite of sensors.

The altitude hypobaric chamber was another critical part of the training required due to the flight altitudes we could encounter. Since tactical reconnaissance is all about getting to the target area and quickly egressing without incident, most of our flight training would be at low altitudes and high speeds. However, there would be occasions when a mission objective would also include a collection of high-altitude imagery intelligence or high en route flights from one location to another. Although we would routinely wear an oxygen mask, a flight altitude above ten thousand feet and upwards toward forty thousand feet would demand wearing an oxygen mask. The altitude chamber provided critical, lifesaving information if our oxygen supply was in jeopardy.

The training simulates loss of cabin pressure and oxygen deprivation at various altitudes. We learned the hazards of high-altitude flight and the physiological effects of low barometric pressure, where hypoxia would begin. This is an insidious danger that could lead to unconsciousness.

The training crew would ask us to remove our oxygen masks to experience the onset of hypoxia. They asked us to answer simple questions or count backward from one hundred to enable us to recognize that mental confusion was a symptom. Another telltale sign of low oxygen in the blood is cyanosis, a bluish color to the skin. We were trained to look at the color of our skin below the fingernails to detect this condition.

Another valuable training device was the RF-4C simulator. It was an excellent mechanism to practice routine procedures for many types of training missions, but certainly for emergency procedures as well. If you crash in a simulator, you get to return another day to try it again! Simulator training also saves money and resources that would otherwise be dedicated to actual flights. Pilots and WSOs got many hours of simulator time in addition to actual flight training.

Flight training would begin with flight planning, assembling charts for the flight route, from takeoff to high-level en route navigation to an approved low-level training route, where four targets were assigned for collection. The low-level course would have a precise route marked with headings and initial points (IPs) to hack your watch, which would then allow you to calculate exactly how many seconds ahead the target would be as you approached at a given ground speed. During the flight, interaction and coordination between the pilot and WSO are critical. For example, as the aircraft approaches a target from an IP, communication must be clear.

Approaching the IP—which could be any identifiable ground feature, such as a bend in a river, a bridge, a structure, or a terrain shape— the WSO would alert the pilot to initiate the inbound leg to the target. Just before the IP, the WSO would call out, "Approaching IP; standby to hack your watch."

The pilot would respond, "Roger, standing by."

The WSO would respond, "Ready, ready … Hack." Both the pilot and WSO would zero out their stopwatches. They would know when they were above the target in a known time from the hack point. If any course adjustment was necessary, the WSO's responsibility was to give those instructions to the pilot before turning on the sensors. At low levels—five hundred feet above ground level (AGL), you could miss the target if you are off course even by a small amount.

Just before the target, the pilot would call out, "Cameras on."

The WSO would respond as he turned on the appropriate sensors, "Cameras on."

Seconds later, the pilot would call out, "Cameras off."

The WSO responds as he turns the sensors off, "Cameras off."

The mission would continue until all targets were acquired, followed by an exit from the low-level route, a climb to a cruise altitude to return to base (RTB) to initiate an approach and landing. Sometimes the pilot would practice several approaches and go-arounds before a final approach and landing. It could be a straight-in approach or a visual approach, which means you fly two thousand feet over the runway and then initiate a 180-degree turn, maintaining two thousand feet of altitude until you get back to parallel to the approach end of the landing runway. The pilot then does another 180-degree turn while descending toward and lining up with the landing runway. He puts the landing gear and flaps down, and we approach the runway at the proper landing speed.

The landing speed depends on gross aircraft weight, which can be calculated by the remaining fuel on board. Both the pilot and WSO do independent calculations and compare them to verify the proper approach and landing speed. After taxiing back to the parking location, final checklist items would be completed, write-ups in the TO 781 noting any discrepancies would be made, and the crew would proceed to the squadron to debrief the mission and review the film with the photo lab personnel.

Day and night training missions are a greater challenge when the WSO uses radar to guide navigation. Flight planning must show what the WSO expects to see on the radarscope while on a low-level flight, usually no lower than 1,500 feet AGL at high ground speed (GS). Our usual training GS was 420, or seven miles per minute. Some of these training flights were in the weather, which necessitated extreme safety measures.

These are just a few examples of the training that a WSO needs to complete. The breakout for the WSO training included four hundred hours of prescribed academic instruction and thirty-five flying training sorties in various areas of expertise. Four of the flying sorties were check rides. The training summary follows.

USAF Tactical Reconnaissance Training Course 132105F/N, RF-4C			
Academic Subject Title	Hours Completed	Flying Event Mission	Sorties Accomplished
General Reconnaissance Subjects	14.0	Transition Phase	
Inertial Navigation System	12.0	Day Transition	6
Forward Looking Radar	13.0	Air Refueling Phase	
Mission Preparation	4.0	AAR Day	1
RF-4C Cockpit Mock-up Lab	2.0	AAR Night	1
Optical Sensors	7.0	Reconnaissance Phase	
Infrared Sensor	6.0	Day Recce	13
Side Looking Radar	7.0	Night Recce	9
Sensor Aided Combat Systems	2.0	DCM Phase	
Testing and Critique	6.0	DCM	1
Field Training Detachment	36.0	Check Flights	4
RF-4C Simulator Training	26.0		
Simulator Briefing/Debriefing	12.0		
Squadron Specialized Training	35.0		
Intelligence Training	12.0		
Squadron Activities (Briefings, Debriefings, Safety, etc.)	180.0		
Flying Phase Briefings	26.0		
Total Hours	400.0	Total Sorties	35

Each academic area was graded either with a satisfactory (S), unsatisfactory (U), or a number grade. I achieved all satisfactory grades and scores of ninety-two to one hundred for the five other subjects. However, the flying portion did not start well for me. My instructor, Maj. Peter Dubay, was an excellent and personable officer. In the transition phase of the first few flights, I experienced airsickness. But this time, I was able to recover well enough during each flight. I wondered, *Not again. Why is this happening?* The environment in the RF-4C cockpit was undoubtedly different. Only this time, I dug deeper into my resolve to get through this recurring problem and persevered. I was not going to let manifestations of apprehension claim me as its victim again.

One of my favorite RF-4C subjects was the inertial navigation system provided by the Guidance and Control Systems Division of Litton Industries, Inc. This system was strictly an aid to navigation as RF-4C WSOs primarily relied on the disciplines of DR, map reading, and radar to demonstrate their abilities to navigate. The inertial navigator system continually determines the aircraft's position based on measurements made entirely within the aircraft itself using sensitive instruments called accelerometers, which detect and measure vehicle accelerations, and gyroscopes, which hold accelerometers in their proper orientations. It is only as good as the data you enter the system when parked at the airfield location and its alignment to heading, true north, and other factors.

Here are some of the photos taken during training when I took Fran and little Bill to the flight line to see the aircraft up close.

■ TEAMED WITH PASSION

After the pilots and WSOs completed their flying training with instructors, they were teamed up to flight plan, brief, and fly practice missions focused on acquiring four targets utilizing various sensors. After the flight, the aircrew debriefed the instructors on their missions and reviewed the photo intelligence products with the photo interpretation lab folks and the instructor.

I was most fortunate to be teamed with 1st Lt. Bob Morris. Bob had completed pilot training at Vance AFB in Enid, Oklahoma. I don't know how the pilot/WSO match-ups were made, but I was extremely grateful for the opportunity to train with Bob. I learned a little bit about his background when we met. He was from the Alabama Air National Guard and had an interest in medicine. I didn't know much more than that.

RF-4C Training Class 72-3. I am second from the left. Front row: Bob Morris is behind me and another friend, Russ Metzler, two to my left—front row.

We focused on our training and developed a great friendship—Fran and I with him and his wife, Peggy. We also quickly established great confidence in each other in the aircraft. I had complete trust in Bob's ability at the controls, and he trusted my ability to navigate, especially during night terrain-following radar missions. On our first flight together, no longer with instructors, we were cruising back to Shaw after acquiring targets on a low level. I recall Bob's words: "Bill, this is great."

"Yes, it is," I said as I relished the moment.

A typical target photo annotated with our names, aircraft number, and other information.

It was good to get a break from training now and then. Fran, little Bill, and I looked forward to going to Myrtle Beach occasionally; it was only two hours due east from Sumter. In the summer, Bob and Peggy joined us for a trip there one day on a weekend. It was a welcome pause to just soak up the sun and relax.

Our son Bill, helping Bob deflate a raft.

If I were to describe Bob's focus and motivation then, I could not do it justice because I did not know specifics of his earlier zeal and would only learn more when we spoke in August 2021 of his passion and the remarkable achievements he made since our training together. His life's work is a testimony to the heads-down focus I observed that set Bob apart from others. He had an indescribable concentration that seemed unique to me. He would apply this ability throughout his life, and many have benefited from his extensive, incredible work.

By way of background, Bob graduated in 1967 from Purdue University with a degree in physics with honors; he minored in premed. Even before that, he aspired to be an astronaut. Bob was influenced by his contact through his father's associations as director of administration of the Marshall Space Flight Center in Huntsville, Alabama, with the pioneering rocket scientist Dr. Werner von Braun. However, with the NASA cancellation of the Apollo manned spaceflight program, Bob switched to his "plan B."

Bob completed his degree at the University of Alabama Medical School and his internship at the Birmingham Hospitals/Department of Ophthalmology. Bob noted that when we landed on the moon in 1969, "we had not yet reached the back of the human eye." The quest to explore the eye's "inner space" was an opportunity he recognized and seized with passion. He pursued deep-eye surgery, training with the inventor of vitrectomy—eye surgery that treats various problems with the retina and vitreous—Dr.

Robert Machemer, at the Bascom Palmer Eye Institute. This was followed by a fellowship in ocular trauma in Cologne, Germany.

Bob returned to Alabama in 1980 as the first trained vitrectomy surgeon in the state. The rest is history as Bob completed decades of pioneering work in this area under the auspices of the Helen Keller Foundation for Research and Education, for which Bob currently serves as its president.

Robert E. Morris, MD, is a remarkable leader in his field of medicine. I could not begin to describe or enumerate the extraordinary achievements Bob had made in his life's work—everything from other prestigious positions he holds, memberships in his field, honors and awards, patents, national collaborative studies, and the scientific presentations and publications he has completed. Bob is a dedicated professional, and I especially respected that of him when we flew together. I truly believe we were a model of the foundation of mutual trust that aircrews *must* have to be effective.

■ "THE BILL CIMINO SONG" BY DICKIE— AND PINK SQUIRRELS

I walked into the squadron to begin flight planning for a low-level sortie that I would fly later that day. The flight-planning room had several large tables where aircrews would lay out their maps, draw their routes, and cut and glue them as appropriate for their recce mission. Several classes of aircrews were training simultaneously, so the crowd always included other airmen outside my class.

When I met with another WSO RF-4C trainee, Capt. Dick Bauer, it was a new experience that lit up the flight-planning area. When he met me and heard my name, he immediately broke into an on-the-spot rendition of "The Bill Cimino Song." He would belt out a few lines, singing my name repeatedly while holding the last letter "o" at length at the end. It sounded like an old Italian favorite! After the song, he would point to me and matter-of-factly say in a mild voice as he looked at others, "Bill Cimino." This would always get the same level of laughter, no matter how many times one heard it.

As he came to be known by all as Dickie, he quickly earned the reputation as one of the funniest and wittiest guys in our midst. He was always joking, singing, and drawing attention from everyone. He and his wife, Andrea, became good friends with Fran and me. Every so often, we would go to the Officer's Club, especially when we could listen to and dance to a band we liked there. Andrea would wear long, loose dresses to sneak the pink squirrels, which were hidden under her dress, to our table. These are not fluffy plush toys! Instead, they were alcoholic drinks made with vanilla ice cream, white crème de cacao liqueur, crème de noyaux liqueur, and some grated nutmeg. Think adult milkshake!

While in the club, it was always an unforgettable time when Dickie would grab the mic during a band break, and say or sing something. The "Bill Cimino Song" included. The whole base knew that song. Dickie was not shy by a long shot. He was a natural on the stage and could get away with anything because of his reputation for being willing to entertain when most others could or would not. Others would be reprimanded if they tried to duplicate some of what Dickie did. But Dickie was revered up and down the ranks.

When our training at Shaw approached completion, we planned to meet for a few days in Upstate New York since we would visit Fran's parents in Rhinebeck, New York, and Dickie and Andrea were going to a Bauer family lakeside home at White Lake—less than two hours by car from Rhinebeck.

While Fran's parents kept our son, Bill, now four years old, we stayed at the lake home for a couple days with Dickie and Andrea, Dickie's brother and wife, and another couple. We had a great time lakeside, and we consumed dozens of clams, beer, and gin and tonics—a dangerous combination. It was getting close to midnight when the women said they would go up to the house to retire for the evening. Sam escorted Fran to our bedroom and stayed with her for a while. *Who's Sam?* you may be wondering. He was the Bauer's dog—a friendly, loving, beautiful Afghan Hound that ensured Fran was safe.

The guys continued well into the morning—around 4 a.m.—with more beer, jokes, and stories as we sat by a campfire and gazed across the lake. It was a great time! Dickie's next assignment was in SEA, where he would fly on tactical reconnaissance missions. We weren't sure when, or if, we would see him and Andrea again, so it was a sad goodbye.

■ A SPECIAL VISIT

We returned to Myrtle Beach one weekend to visit Tony Shine and his family briefly. Tony had been assigned to Myrtle Beach AFB and had transitioned from F-105s in Okinawa to an A-7 aircraft squadron at Myrtle. Tony and Bonnie had a house right on the beach. We were sitting together, taking in the view, and catching up on the years since our time in Okinawa. Their sweet daughter, Colleen, nearly eight years of age at the time, came out with a tray of freshly baked cookies. She had this big smile, wavy blonde hair, and offered us the treat. I will never forget the conversation.

She asked, "Would you like some cookies?"

"Yes, thank you," we said.

She then turned to Tony and asked the same, "Would you like some cookies?"

"No, but thank you for asking so nicely," he said.

After a while, we said our goodbyes and departed, not knowing when we would see them again. This was the nature of military life—socializing, common purpose, good friendships, nice families, and farewells.

■ TRAINING SUMMARY

When training was over, Maj. Dubay signed off on my official RF-4C Summary of Training form:

Transition: "He was able to progress along with his contemporaries. Basic DR (dead reckoning) and knowledge of the systems was excellent."

Instrument: "Had a good understanding of instrument interpretation and basic procedures."

Formation: "N/A." (This only applied to pilots regarding formation flying.)

Reconnaissance: "No problem in this phase. His map reading and basic DR were excellent. His grasp of what a WSO can do to aid the pilot greatly added to his crew effectiveness."

Air Refueling: "No problems noted." (The WSO aids the pilot during air refueling.)

BFM/DCM (basic flight maneuvering/defensive combat maneuvering): "No problems noted." This was especially gratifying since the DCM phase included pulling up to about five Gs while the pilot put the aircraft through its flight limits in a mock chase by an "enemy" aircraft.

Other Remarks: "A very good student. His strong desire to complete the course enabled him to overcome a severe airsick problem."

The training included several areas associated with high-performance flight, as in DCM just described, and the potential for situations ranging from minor to deadly. Emergency procedures, effects of high altitude without oxygen, G-suit function, use of checklists and safety procedures all contributed to the basic knowledge necessary for effective and successful mission completion.

My airsickness issue was primarily due to increased g-forces. Once I adapted to that physical strain, I was over the hump. Part of the aircrew equipment for sustaining high g-forces while maneuvering in the aircraft is the G suit, sometimes called the anti-G suit. These are pant-like chaps with air bladders worn over the flight suit and inflated over areas of the body including the abdomen (abdominal aorta), front of each thigh, and the side of each calf. Cutouts allow for mobility at the knees and groin.

A hose that connects inside the cockpit is part of the suit. It pumps air into the bladders at a ratio aligned with the g-forces. The more Gs an aircrew pulls, the more air pressure is applied to the lower body. This provides a tightening pressure on the abdomen and around the legs and muscles that helps prevent blood from pooling in the lower extremities and helps to push it back up to the heart and brain. When you are sitting in the aircraft, or anywhere for that matter, you are experiencing an acceleration force of 1 G (gravity on earth). When you are flying straight and level, again you experience a force of 1 G. When an aircrew member pulls back on the stick, it does not matter if you are upright, tilted to either side with one wing pointed to the ground and the other to the heavens, or upside down, you will experience positive Gs. The harder the pull, the higher the g-force. If too many positive Gs are sustained for too long, you could eventually black out.

Most RF-4C training missions included pulling up to about four Gs (four times your body weight forced against the seat). In addition to the G suit, aircrews learned to perform a grunt during the high g-maneuver, tightening the abdomen and providing a counterforce. If g-forces increase further, complete vision loss will occur, though consciousness remains, to a point. These effects are due to a reduction of blood flow to the eyes before blood flow to the brain is lost; the extra pressure within the eye (intraocular pressure) counters the blood pressure.

Pulling high Gs for more than a few seconds becomes dangerous. The sequence quickly goes from impact to the body while flying to loss of peripheral vision—an actual narrowing of eyesight—to eventual blackout. If you black out and lose consciousness, it's game over!

If you experience negative g-forces, a simplified example would be like pushing the aircraft control stick forward. You become weightless in the cockpit, and blood pools in the other direction—to your eyes and brain. This is extremely uncomfortable, and anything over one negative G can be devastating.

Endless situations could lead to emergencies. The checklist, carried out by the pilot and WSO, addresses many of them. However, some require rapid reaction by the crew, and there is no time to flip through pages of a checklist to determine proper actions. For example, if a crew was accelerating down the runway for takeoff and it became necessary to abort, the pilot and WSO must be able to repeat and execute three things without hesitation or error:

Throttles—Idle
Chute—Deploy
Hook—Down

The parachute pops out behind the aircraft to assist in slowing down. The hook is mounted at the aircraft's tail and is lowered to catch an arresting cable strung across the runway. This enables the crew to stop the aircraft from going off the end of the runway.

This is one of several boldface procedures the crew must commit to memory. It was evaluated on written exams, flight checks, and in the RF-4C simulator. There is neither time nor excuse to screw this up. It must be perfect. Any deviation from the exact wording is a failure, and aircrews can be subject to grounding in an operational squadron. Fran remembers me sitting up in bed in the middle of the night during my RF-4C training, repeating some of these steps in my sleep as my rote memory consumed me.

The use of checklists is paramount. No crew member should ever rely on memory (except for bold face procedures) to complete the necessary steps for any phase of flying, or preparation for flying for that matter. Without getting into the vast number of steps it takes to prepare for takeoff, here is a short list of the areas the pilot and WSO must execute:

The pilot conducts the following:

Preflight Check: This is a review of Form 781, which gives aircraft status.

Before Exterior Inspection (front cockpit): This contains twenty-one steps conducted by the pilot.

Exterior Inspection: This contains twenty-two steps related to the nose area, forward fuselage, center fuselage and wing, and aft fuselage area.

Before Entering Front Cockpit: This contains five steps but includes twenty-five substeps related to the ejection seat alone.

Front Cockpit Interior Check: The pilot performs seventy-one checks.

Before Starting Engines: Five steps.

Starting Engines (this can be done by a pneumatic start or a cartridge start):

Pneumatic start—twenty-four steps.

Cartridge start—nineteen steps.

Before Taxiing (front cockpit): seventeen steps.

The WSO conducts the following:

Before Entering Rear Cockpit: This contains six steps but includes the same twenty-five substeps for the rear cockpit ejection seat as done by the pilot.

Before Electrical Power (rear cockpit): Twenty steps.

After Electrical Power (rear cockpit): Five steps, including substeps for gyro-compass alignment and heading memory alignment, and aligning the INS.

Rear Cockpit Interior Check: This contains thirty-seven steps.

Before Taxiing (rear cockpit): This contains eleven steps.

Once the crew completes all the above checklists, you are ready to taxi to the assigned take-off runway. At an area near the takeoff runway, the crew chief and his team will check for any hydraulic/oil/fuel leaks, wing surface movements initiated by the pilot, tires, and more—all while wearing ear protection since the engines are very loud even running at idle.

One final checklist procedure is completed—before takeoff—which includes thirty-two more steps.

You get the idea. Before an aircrew takes off, there is a lot to get done. This becomes routine as crews achieve and maintain proficiency. But I must emphasize again that nothing should be left to memory or shortcuts. Never be lax, never assume, and most important, never think you are so good that you can skip checklist items or safety measures. Absent-mindedness kills! Don't become a statistic.

Safety always. Don't leave home without it! One of the critical safety measures applied to night radar missions is determining ETC—emergency terrain clearance. This was especially important since many of our radar missions were in the approved low-level routes in the Smokey Mountains. We would train 500 feet above the ground in the daytime and at 420 or 480 ground speed (seven miles per minute or eight miles per minute, respectively).

We could see the ground and easily avoid it. However, at night, even though we were restricted to no lower than 1,500 feet above the ground, if you got disoriented, you could quickly find yourself at a dangerous altitude relative to the surrounding terrain. If you became confused or did not know your position, you executed a climb to ETC.

This was calculated ahead of time by starting with the highest terrain altitude in the area, rounding it up to the nearest one hundred feet, and then adding another thousand feet. For example, if the highest peak is 4,285 feet tall; round up to 4,300 feet and add another thousand. ETC would be 5,300 feet. I had to do this on a couple of occasions when night radar was severely impacted by weather (which, if dense enough, can show up on radar and be confused with terrain), and I could not determine our position.

No hesitation: "Climb to ETC 5300 *now!*" The WSO, the pilot, and the aircraft are one and must work together. They must always be in sync.

When you transition from training to tactical operations, as I would do in my next assignment, the concept of one collective asset—the aircraft, the pilot, and the WSO as a unit—becomes a move in the direction of ROI for the USAF. When you flight plan, prebrief, fly, execute the mission, and debrief, you build upon any mistakes, improve performance, learn the enemy—their aircraft, weapons, and capabilities—and how to counter them. You become *combat ready*. That is the next goal.

■ SELF-EVALUATION: UPDATED

I thoroughly enjoyed RF-4C training, even with a minor bumpy start. Completely satisfied with the results of my training, I believed my self-confidence as a rated officer stepped up a notch. There would be many opportunities to test that confidence in the future, but for now, all was good. Recovery phase 2 was a step in the right direction.

RF-4C; Tail "BA" designation is for aircraft at Bergstrom, AFB. That's where I'm headed!

I was qualified as a WSO in the RF-4C. Being qualified is far from being experienced, but it is the first necessary step to getting there. I received notification of my next assignment to the 91st Tactical Reconnaissance Squadron of the 67th Tactical Fighter Wing at Bergstrom AFB in Austin, Texas. Back to Texas again! It was time to apply all my aircrew training in an operational organization.

TACTICAL OPERATIONS

▪ BERGSTROM AFB, AUSTIN, TEXAS

I had a report date in late September 1972, which gave us ample time to travel to New York after my RF-4C training to visit our families and catch up with everyone. Little Bill was now four years old and much more interactive with all the relatives who could not get enough time with us, especially him. In mid-September, we departed once again with a leisurely trip to Austin and looked forward to our next adventure as we expected to be there for three to four years.

We purchased our first home, a new home—no previous owners. It was in northeast Austin, about thirteen miles from Bergstrom AFB. It had three bedrooms and a nice, fenced-in backyard with a patio. Several of our neighbors were also AF personnel. It was perfect for us.

Bergstrom was initially activated on 19 September 1942 as Del Valle Army Air Base. The US Army leased three thousand acres from Austin on land acquired from the Santiago Del Valle Grant. The Chisholm Trail ran through the tract. The name of the base was changed to Bergstrom Army Air Field on 3 March 1943, in honor of Austinite Capt. John August Earl Bergstrom, who was killed at Clark Field, Philippines, during one of the early Japanese bombings at the start of the war. Bergstrom was a member of the 19th Bombardment Group. The base was renamed Bergstrom Field on 11 November 1943 at the suggestion of then-Congressman Lyndon B. Johnson. It became Bergstrom Air Force Base in December 1948, coinciding with the creation of the AF as a separate service.

On 1 July 1966, the base was transferred to Tactical Air Command (TAC), one of several major commands in the AF, becoming home to the 12th Air Force and the 75th Tactical Reconnaissance Wing (TRW). The 12th was responsible for all TAC reconnaissance, fighter, and airlift operations west of the Mississippi River. On 15 July 1971, the 75th TRW was replaced by the 67th TRW. The base became the primary tactical reconnaissance base in the entire USAF. Four squadrons equipped with the RF-4C Phantom aircraft operated under the 67th: the 12th Tactical Reconnaissance Squadron (TRS), the 45th Tactical Reconnaissance Training Squadron (TRTS), the 62nd TRTS, and the 91st TRS.

A drawdown of USAF tactical reconnaissance, hastened by the end of the Cold War, saw the 45th TRTS and 62nd TRTS disband, followed by the 91st TRS. The 12TRS deployed its RF-4Cs to the Middle East in support of Operation Desert Shield/Desert Storm in 1991. Shortly after their return from the desert, the 12th and its parent 67th TRW were eventually disbanded.

In 1990, Bergstrom ended up on a list of seventy-five military facilities under review for closure by the post–Cold War Base Realignment and Closure Committee. On 30 September 1993, Bergstrom was officially closed, and a bond was raised for Austin-Bergstrom International Airport. Much of the former airbase, including buildings, trees, and structures, was demolished. There were a few exceptions, such as the circular Twelfth Air Force Headquarters building, which was converted into a hotel, and the original 12,250-foot runway. Air cargo operations began in June 1997, and passenger operations started in May 1999.

■ 91ST TRS

In September of 1972, I was assigned to the 91st TRS, one of the two recce squadrons that would have a dual-based role with overseas allied bases in the event of hostilities in eastern Europe. The 91st is where recce aircrew honed their craft to be effective in a combat environment. The squadron was equipped with eighteen RF-4C aircraft and its personnel totaling in the mid-fifties.

The squadron was led by Lt. Col. Lowell LeMay and his operations officer, Lt. Col. Bernard DeKeyser—who preferred to be called Deke. The squadron was organized with four flights, A-Flight through D-Flight. These are tactical sub-elements of the squadron. Each flight had a commander or a flight lead. Typically, a flight would consist of about ten aircrews of pilots and WSOs.

Other aircrews from the wing organizations—like wing training, wing standardization/evaluation, ops and training—needed to fly and maintain proficiency. They were designated as squadron-attached aircrew. Lastly, the squadron had a dedicated staff of four to five personnel from the Photo Processing Interpretation Facility (PPIF) to review and analyze the recce collection with the pilot and WSO after each sortie.

The 91st was a proud squadron of closely knit personnel, like many other squadrons. In an operational squadron, you develop a shared sense of mission and always strive to make your unit contribution the best possible. The 91st had an excellent reputation as tested in many operational assignments, operational readiness inspections (ORIs), simulated combat exercises, and, of course, in everyday training.

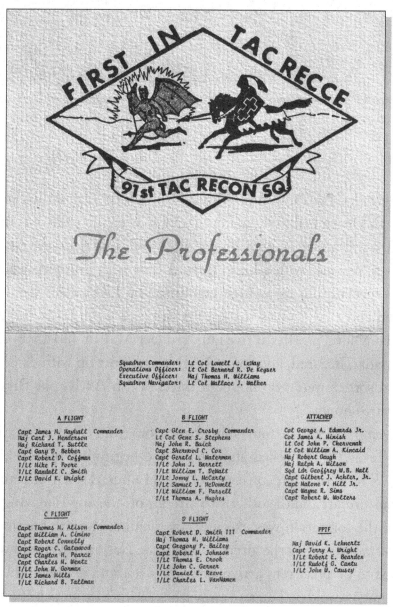

91st TRS squadron roster Christmas card in 1972.
Illustration by RF-4C WSO 1st Lt. Tom Crook.

Bergstrom RF–4C tactical reconnaissance aircraft over the southwestern United States.

◾ NEWBIE

I was in C-flight, led by Capt. Tom Alison. Tom was a very skilled pilot, and from October through December 1972, many of my recce sorties were with him. I had arrived at the 91st with a total of 66.8 hours of RF-4C time from my training at Shaw AFB, so I was a "newbie" with a lot to learn. I flew with Tom occasionally after the initial sorties, especially during an ORI conducted by Tactical Air Command (TAC).

We planned and flew various sorties, primarily in west Texas and New Mexico. They included low-level profiles at five hundred feet AGL at 480 knots GS (552 mph), day and night radar, infrared, and some AAR in conjunction with extended low-level flights. Typical sorties were two hours or fewer. With AAR, our flight time could extend above three hours.

On 4 November 1972, a four-ship formation from Bergstrom flew over the University of Texas (UT) packed stadium at the beginning of a Texas-Oklahoma football game. The formation consisted of a lead aircraft with one aircraft off one wing of the lead aircraft and the other two aircraft off the opposite wing of the leader. The timing of the formation was executed in conjunction with communications on the ground that would notify the aircrews when the National Anthem was underway.

Timing had to be precise to arrive over UT's stadium as the anthem concluded. Also, one wingman would pull up and away from the formation to indicate the missing man for the POW/MIA flyover. I was in that aircraft with Tom for the overflight and pulled up to about ten thousand feet using engine afterburners as the other three aircraft continued past the stadium.

Our execution and split-second timing were commended in a letter from the 12

AF commander, Maj. Gen. Blood, for our performance. While the job of tactical reconnaissance had many requirements, the intermittent perks like flyovers in a demonstration of patriotism helped convince us that we were doing something additional for our country. I participated in other four-ship flybys: in Abilene, Texas, for a Fourth of July 1973 celebration; in Dallas Texas for Memorial Day; and at the AF Academy in mid-July 1974. These were always fun to plan and execute.

■ COMBAT-READY CERTIFICATION

For the squadron to be combat-ready and deployable to engage in reconnaissance actions in a hostile environment, its aircrews must individually certify as being combat-ready. This process is comprehensive as it includes training, study, proficiency, testing, and evaluation. Then finally, the certification of pilots and WSOs with stamps of approval.

The flying training entailed a wide variety of recce sorties that would contribute to the proficiency of both pilot and WSO. AF regulations stipulated the minimum number of sorties in different categories that each crew member must accomplish in a given period. Proficiency requires training flights. When you fly often, it becomes a routine that enables you to complete your assignment with expertise and confidence. It's like getting up in the morning, brushing your teeth, taking a shower, and preparing for the day—only you do it with the utmost safety every time.

Since the RF-4C does not carry weapons, although it could be configured to carry tactical nuclear weapons and has the switch network to enable a delivery if hostilities ever got to that point, the aircrews must know the enemy's aircraft and weapons capabilities. This knowledge allows the recce crews to plan any countermeasures for these threats.

The best defense for the RF-4C is to evade these threats with speed and stealth. Since stealth technology in the 1970s was not as advanced as today's, stealth for the RF-4C meant "terrain masking." This made use of terrain features such as hills, mountains, and valleys to mask any direct line of sight by the enemy's aircraft or weaponry. Low and fast—haul your ass out of there! In the event of a lock-on by the enemy, whereby they would launch an air-to-air missile or a ground-launched threat such as a surface-to-air missile (SAM) or anti-aircraft artillery (AAA), we would study and practice certain flight-evasive maneuvers to overcome each of these threats.

The study of enemy resources, particularly Soviet assets, was paramount. We spent hours learning about their different aircraft, weapons, and capabilities. We would identify their aircraft by their simple outlines and shapes as well as up close and personal photos. We learned the enemy's weapon range and lethality and the best counteractions if necessary. We practiced specific exercises, like Red Flag out of Nellis AFB in Las Vegas, where we flew through the Caliente Range in the Nevada desert or over the ocean in specified practice areas.

Testing was not limited to in-flight; we also tested in written and verbal evaluations at the squadron level and from the prestigious flight-abled group from Standardization/ Evaluation (Stan/Eval). Pilots and WSOs of Stan/Eval (at both squadron and wing levels) were among the best of the best in their craft. They were specifically chosen to test others and were naturally subject to the same standards when they were tested. As at Shaw, some flight testing could be conducted in the RF-4C simulator.

The final step in becoming combat-ready involved meticulously planning a specific route with targets in a potentially hostile environment in eastern Europe. The route would be from our dual base in Aviano, Italy, and contain several targets for acquisition with several known threats along the route.

We were required to plan and brief our squadron commander, operations officer, and intelligence officer on the route, our understanding of the threats, threat counter-measures we would use to capture the targets, and specific communications and actions to evade and escape enemy territory in the event we were shot down or had to eject. This included our knowledge of selected areas for evasion (SAFE) or employing survival, evasion, resistance, and escape (SERE) techniques if needed.

Having achieved combat-ready status earlier, during the HQ TAC ORI in April 1973, I was selected to present a detailed combat-ready certification briefing to the inspection team and fly a sortie to obtain sensor coverage of challenging targets. The briefing was rated "outstanding" as Tom Alison and I acquired 100 percent coverage of the targets.

I flew with various pilots throughout my assignment at Bergstrom. Later, around the fall of 1973, I was teamed with Jim Mills to fly many sorties. Jim was a very skilled pilot. He entered the US Army and flew helicopters for four years. He left the army to finish college and applied to the airlines, but they were not hiring at that time.

Jim considered the navy's pilot training program, but they told Jim he had astigmatism, which could prevent him from entering training after he was in the navy. That was too risky for Jim, so he applied to the AF, went through OTS, as I had, and left there for AF pilot training at Laredo AFB in Texas. After RF-4C training, Jim transferred to the 91st TRS at Bergstrom.

After my assignment at Bergstrom, we lost touch, and many years would pass as I tried to find him. I checked LinkedIn, various veteran websites, Google, and more with no luck. I had been in touch with only one person, another WSO from the 91st, primarily through Christmas cards each year—Tom Crook and his wife, Pat.

I connected with Tom, and he informed me of a TAC Recce Roster—a fifty-page list of names and information with some addresses, phone numbers, and email addresses. I wasn't on it, and I noticed other recce aircrews I knew were not on it. But it did contain many pilots and WSOs, including Jim Mills. Many listings included wives, so Sheila Mills was also on the roster. I was able to reach Jim, and we spoke for over an hour, trying to cram in forty-seven years of our lives after Bergstrom.

Before I describe the many great times I had with Jim, I must emphasize his skill and expertise as a pilot and leader. Jim left Bergstrom to be an instructor at the instrument flight school at Randolph AFB. He then recertified in the RF-4C and went on an assignment at Alconbury Air Base in the United Kingdom for four years. Jim's superior piloting skills and knowledge quickly earned him a position in Stan/Eval (the best of the best) at HQ USAFE at Ramstein AB in Germany.

Jim then went to Eglin AFB, Florida, at the 4485th Test Squadron at the Tactical Air Warfare Center (TAWC), where he tested many aircraft and weapon systems. The test squadron only takes the best pilots to engage in their test activities. He eventually made his way back to Bergstrom, coming full circle, only to rapidly move from duties as wing safety officer to the 45th TRTS as their operations officer and, eventually, the commander of the 12th squadron. Jim led the deployment of his squadron, early in 1991 in Desert Storm, a military operation to expel occupying Iraqi forces from Kuwait, which Iraq had invaded and annexed months earlier.

After returning to Austin from the Middle East, Jim retired to Granger, Texas, where he and Sheila live on their multiacre farm. When we spoke, he sounded very happy as he looked forward to tending to his daily farm routine. He and Sheila had raised two boys, who were doing well. My conversation with him brought back so many good memories. I had missed his humor, his southern accent, and his friendship for many years. But that has now been restored.

My records indicate that I flew with Jim forty-four times while stationed with the 91st. The first was a local low-level sortie on 8 November 1973. Our last flight together was on 1 August 1974, when we flew two sorties during an "out and back"—one low-level sortie outbound and landing at another base, followed by an instrument sortie before landing back at Bergstrom. Those flights, every bit of flying we did together, were pure exuberance. My longest aircrew pairing with one pilot, Jim, was between 18 January and 7 April 1974, when we flew eighteen sorties in a row.

■ ORIS AND OODA LOOPS

As I mentioned earlier, I participated in ORIs, in which higher headquarters test the wings' and squadrons' capabilities to accomplish their reconnaissance missions. ORIs could be announced ahead of time, which would allow a period of preparation to ensure the best performance. Or they could be unannounced, where the inspection team would arrive at the base and kick off the inspection, which would last several days. Either way, we were expected not to only pass the inspection but to perform with excellent results.

The ORI sorties were on routine low-level routes. However, the inspection team selected the targets; some were very difficult to acquire just by the nature of the terrain in western Texas and New Mexico. During the ORI, crews may have to double-bang, which means they would need to plan, brief, fly, and debrief twice in one day. This scheduling was to simulate real-world hostilities with a multitude of targets to be acquired for intelligence and then passed on to fighter crews for target destruction. After the fighter strikes, recce crews could then be assigned to collect imagery for bomb damage assessment (BDA).

The RF-4C aircrews' job is essentially the first part of a process called the "OODA loop" developed by military strategists and Col. John Boyd of the USAF. Boyd applied the concept to the combat operations process. The OODA loop (observe, orient, decide, act) is a four-step approach to decision-making that focuses on using available information, target collection from recce sorties, putting it in context, and quickly making the most appropriate decision to strike or not.

For a little extra excitement, in part of one of the ORIs, aircrews had to wear chemical gear in addition to their flight suits and G-suits to simulate that we were in an environment of chemical warfare, where a weapon of mass destruction (WMD) was used. Even though the ORI was conducted in the spring, the addition of this gear added to the weight and discomfort felt in the cockpit. We would switch from gas masks to oxygen masks and back again. Body heat would collect inside the chem gear, drenching us in sweat. It was a relief to remove that chem gear after the flights, but we then had to also simulate decontamination after removing the protective clothing.

This was the life of an operational recce squadron—being well prepared for the real thing, to be of value, to be an ROI for all the training the AF provided. This was the daily routine for aircrews. Train, study, maintain proficiency, and be ready for deployment. We wouldn't fly every day but often during the weeks and months. On a day we didn't fly, we could get training in the simulator, brush up on tactical knowledge, or perform additional duties, which everyone had to some extent.

My additional duties included Squadron Chief of Safety Officer and Squadron Awards and Decorations Officer. These required a good knowledge of AF regulations in both areas, briefings to the squadron about safety measures, and written preparation for awards and citations for individuals, the squadron, and in some cases, the wing organization.

One narrative I wrote was for the Wing Outstanding Unit Award, and we received an outstanding rating for our squadron during a wing safety inspection, where I was commended by name. It wasn't just me; other officers did their additional duties with pride and success. This collective effort is what makes a squadron work together, everyone pulling their weight with additional responsibilities as well as their primary aircrew duties.

Our squadron occasionally flew a frag in support of the EPA in its effort to detect pollution violations. These included sorties over rivers near industrial areas to capture photos and other sensor evidence, as well as other overflights to monitor similar activity that violated EPA guidelines. I wrote and submitted an award for our squadron's contribution to the EPA's goals. I found out during my next assignment that the 91st TRS received the award. The squadron commander and his wife attended a ceremony in Washington DC to accept it.

Additionally, Col. Sauls selected me to escort several general officers on a base tour. OK, this one is not so elegant, but as "queen for a day," I did my job, earning gratitude from the senior officers. During my assignment at Bergstrom, with some good experience under my belt, I was recommended and completed training to be a squadron instructor WSO. This step confirmed the added value that I could now provide to our squadron WSOs, and it was another bit of confidence that my role was growing more meaningful.

The AF always emphasized advanced education, civilian and military, which would be a critical element in the competitive environment for promotion. I began an MBA program at UT, taking one course at a time to work toward an advanced degree. While in Austin, I took four classes and maintained straight As. This was much better than I had ever done at St. John's University. Whatever it was, it was working; I was firing on all cylinders! I guess I just learned how to apply myself better and be more self-motivated.

▪ TDYS

During the two years I was assigned to the 91st, TDY assignments applied to everyone, and we all participated in them whether they were one day or several. This required that we pack an overnight bag, which included clothing and personal articles to take for the trip. The baggage could be stored in the aircraft's extended nose section and around the three-bay sensor suite. We had flexible bags that could be molded to fit.

The flight assignments varied widely for photo-reconnaissance support for other military customers and commercial customers who asked for AF assistance. Other TDYs tasked our squadron resources for participation in joint military exercises, testing, or aircraft delivery and pickup for a major overhaul and periodic maintenance at special AF facilities. It also included the deployment of aircraft overseas. My records show that I went on thirteen TDYs while stationed in the 91st TRS.

In June 1973, Gary Bebber and I, and Tom Crook with his pilot, Woody Cox, were among several 91st TRS aircrews designated to fly as refueling spares for another recce unit at Bergstrom, the 12th TRS, which was tasked to participate in a JCS coordinated, US Commander in Chief, Europe (USCINCEUR)-sponsored exercise at Alconbury Royal Air Base in the United Kingdom. This exercise enabled our aircrews to engage in simulated war operations with other allied forces. We went through the entire deployment prep, including wearing "poopy suits" (protective outer garments) in the event we went down in the cold Atlantic. We were part of the formation up to the first refueling over water. If all the 12th aircraft were "healthy," we would RTB at Bergstrom. That's exactly what happened. We logged 3.7 hours of flight time but never made it to Alconbury as the other aircraft proceeded without problems.

In mid-August 1973, our entire squadron participated in Coronet Organ IX, an air combat training exercise organized at Nellis AFB, in Nevada, and hosted on the Nevada Test and Training Range, the USAF's premier military training area with more than 12,000 square miles of airspace and 2.9 million acres of land in the southern portion of the state.

While there, I flew in four simulated combat sorties with different pilots through the desert areas of the range in a clockwise route around Area 51, which is situated within the test range. We were forbidden to overfly this protected and highly classified section of land and could be grounded if we violated its airspace. No one wanted that!

The range simulated enemy threats like ground-launched surface-to-air simulated missiles called "Smokey SAMs," small rockets used to simulate a SAM launch. The name comes from the white smoke that trails from the rocket after launch. The pilots had to react to that smoke and perform threat reactions and evasive maneuvers. The Smokey SAMs are constructed from paper and plastic foam, allowing a safe way to practice threat reactions. It helps pilots practice the maneuvers they will need to avoid getting shot down during combat without the threat of any real danger to the aircraft or aircrew.

I was crewed with Tom Alison in a four-ship formation flight to Nellis AFB, Nevada, for another TDY. After leveling off at our cruise altitude, we were in west Texas en route and conducted our routine ops checks for oxygen and fuel levels, circuit breakers, and other indications. All appeared normal at that time. As we made our way through eastern New Mexico, our next ops check revealed that our fuel levels were lower by a few hundred pounds than the other three aircraft. This was not a big concern at this point since aircraft could have minor variations in fuel readings.

After another fifteen minutes, we initiated another ops check. This time, our fuel readings differed by a wider margin, so we ran through some checklist items to ensure all other indications were normal. They were. We notified the other aircrews that we might have a fuel leak problem, so we would all be thinking of actions that may be necessary if the situation worsened.

Now, positioned in central New Mexico, we assessed the need to divert to other bases. We had Cannon AFB behind us in eastern New Mexico, Holloman AFB in the south-central part of the state, and Kirtland AFB in the central part of the state. Ahead, in Arizona, we had Luke AFB and Davis Monthan AFB in the south-central area. With many options, we decided to monitor the fuel status closely as we also computed the nearest divert base while en route.

Though the fuel depletion continued, we were still not in an emergency status. We notified the ARTCC that we had a fuel problem and asked them to pass that information to Nellis AFB approach control and tower. We calculated the fuel needed and the range to Nellis. We determined a point in western Arizona to begin a letdown to a lower altitude and an optimum glide distance to conserve fuel.

Before too long, we were committed to Nellis, descending and conserving as much fuel as possible with our glide slope. If you cut power to the RF-4C, the bird will drop like a rock, so we needed to keep the throttles set at the proper position to maintain flight while attempting to conserve fuel. After we were handed off to approach control, we notified them we needed priority in landing. They indicated there were several other aircraft in the pattern to land. At that point, we declared an emergency, which ensured *we* would get priority.

Approach control immediately gave us a new radio frequency and handed us over to Nellis tower; they permitted us to land with a visual approach behind an F-111 that was about to touchdown on the runway. A visual approach involves flying directly over the runway lengthwise at two thousand feet above the ground and initiating a 180-degree turn back to the approach end, making a final 180-degree turn to line up on the runway as we descended and put the gear and flaps down.

We landed without incident. But if we had to go around—not touch down but terminate the landing and initiate another visual approach and landing, it would have consumed more fuel (approximately five hundred pounds) for the acceleration and climb back to two thousand feet to complete another approach and landing. Luckily, we did not need to do that; it was determined after we landed that we may not have had enough fuel to execute that maneuver. That was a close call due to a leak in one of the main fuselage fuel tanks.

My co-WSO and good friend, Tom Crook, had a similar incident after flying with his pilot, Bobby Johnson, on a low level in West Texas. They completed the mission and flew some high-level recce before returning to Bergstrom. Before they could land, another aircraft had an emergency and had to take the barrier on the runway with its hook down, similar to a naval carrier landing. This incident caused the runway to be closed.

Tom and Bobby were approaching minimum fuel. Tom did some calculations to determine how long they could remain in a holding pattern while the aircraft was cleared from the runway. They eventually declared an emergency and were vectored to land at Kelly AFB in San Antonio with very little fuel remaining.

This is just another example of the value of the WSO in a fighter-type aircraft, and in this case, Tom's expertise. The WSO does a lot more than plan and navigate a recce or a fighter mission, turn sensors on and off, or assist the pilot in target strikes. The WSO and pilot work as a team. And there is no doubt that Tom was an experienced and dependable guy to have in the back seat! He was another set of eyes and ears and another source for solutions to problems that emerged on the fly (no pun intended).

During one of our TDYs to Nellis AFB, we ended one mission in the practice range with a four-ship join-up to fly down Death Valley in California. We flew at a low ground speed of about three hundred knots to casually take in the terrific view. We let down gradually to watch our altimeters register below zero mean sea level (MSL) since the lowest point there (and in all of North America) is 282 feet below sea level.

Bobby Johnson, our flight lead, came over the radio: "See guys, just like in the movies!" It was a *cool* thing to see and do in a *hot* spot! Saw nothing but an inhospitable desert! Tom Crook was in Bobby's back seat for this joyride and recalls that shortly after that, low-level passes through the Death Valley National Monument area were restricted due to noise damage. Damage to what, I don't know. Snakes maybe? More recently, flights are permitted but with minimum-level restrictions. We may have been one of the last to fly the "Death Valley Very Low-Level route!"

■ THE NEW MATH: 3 + 1 = JOEY

At this point in my career, we were not alone as several of our peers were expecting additions to their families. We did not know if Fran would deliver a boy or a girl but hoped for a healthy baby in either case. St. David's Hospital in Austin was the center of attention on 10 and 11 September 1973. This was significant as it was in the second state capital our children could call their place of birth: Bill in Denver, and now Joey in Austin. The fact that it was a state capital would grow in significance later.

The wife of one of the pilots in the 91st TRS worked at St. David's. Sue Bebber and her husband, Gary, were our friends, and we socialized with them occasionally. Sue was a nurse there and about to complete her shift that day. But when she learned we had arrived at the hospital, she asked if she could stay and assist in the delivery room.

This was also the first time I was allowed to be there for the delivery. No one told me to go home and wait for a phone call *this* time. We arrived at the hospital around 9:00 p.m. on 10 September, and Joey was born at 1:19 a.m., Tuesday, 11 September 1973, weighing seven pounds thirteen ounces, measuring twenty-one inches, and making a lot of noise.

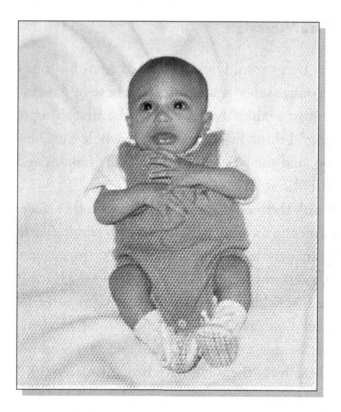

We brought little Joey home after a couple of days, and his big brother, Bill, was very excited to see him. He looked after his baby brother and cared for him: holding him, feeding him a bottle, and just hangin' with him.

As 11 September took on a new significance much later in our country's history, where we would share the sadness of that day remembering the three thousand or so lives lost, we could counter the tragedy of that date with the celebration of another birthday in our family, adding a bit of happiness. Our home in Austin contained a little more life and a lot more joy.

■ WORK HARD, LAUGH HARDER

The daily routine in a recce squadron was to strive for the best tactical reconnaissance capability possible. It required the utmost skill, safety, dedication, and responsibility from the entire team. It was serious business. Given that, no one ever said it had to be boring, and there was no lack of fun, kidding around, laughter, and hilariousness. We all made sure of that, and this element was part of the motivation to go to work every day to share a joke, to hear the next story, to tease your fellow aircrew, and build upon an essential part of a legacy that would become one's AF career.

Each of us in the 91st had many fun times and stories to tell. I have chosen to share a few and have given each an appropriate title.

Dickie Returns—More Nonsense

After my first year at Bergstrom, Dickie returned from his tour in SEA and was assigned to another reconnaissance squadron at the base in Austin. It was great to link up with him and Andrea again. And, of course, the first thing out of his mouth was the "Bill Cimino Song." I think he practiced it the whole time he was in Thailand! He sang other songs, too, and the lyrics were always silly hokum and made the audience laugh! His autoschediastic ability was unique!

We would meet with them on occasion, but not too often since we were in different squadrons. Still, the times we did meet were always memorable, like the visit to Copeland's, a well-known BBQ joint outside of Austin, where Dickie managed to get the attention of this jammed-packed, loud crowd with his crazy antics—which I will not describe!

We lost touch with Dickie and Andrea a few years after I left for my next assignment until a quick rendezvous at the Pentagon later, when Fran and I were in the building, and Dickie snuck up behind Fran and surprised her. Since then, I have desperately tried to search for them but have been unsuccessful. Wherever Dickie is, he is making someone laugh—I'm certain!

Mint Up My Nose

Jim Mills and I arrived at the squadron one midafternoon since we had to plan and fly a night low-level training sortie. We completed our planning, gluing map sections together, tracing and marking our route with checkpoints and targets, filing the flight plan with the FAA, and checking the weather before heading to the Officer's Club to have dinner.

We had a nice unrushed dinner and were on our way out to the parking lot, passing through a covered section of the club from the main building to the lot. As we walked and talked, I opened the wrapping from a chocolate mint that was provided with the meal. I had just inserted the mint in my mouth when Jim looked up and noticed an electrical outlet in the passageway ceiling with nothing connected to it. Usually, you see an outlet on a wall a few inches above the floor.

"What the heck is that doing up there?" Jim asked as he pointed.

Do you ever remember drinking milk when you were a kid, and someone made you laugh? You would pass milk through your nose, gasping for breath. That's what happened to me as it just struck me, not so much what he said, but *how* he said it! I couldn't get the mint flavor out of my nose all night. We just kept laughing about it. When we got back to the squadron, Jim took great pleasure in telling everyone about it.

"Hey, Cimino passed a mint through his nose," he would shout out.

I was teased about this for months. Even during our flight that evening, I would tell him, "Jim, standby to hack your watch. Damn, this mint is still in my nose. It won't go away!"

"Mint Up His Nose Cimino." That was me for a while.

When I recently contacted Jim by text after losing touch with each other for forty-seven years, we planned to talk by phone. During the call, it was a great reunion as we caught up on our lives. I jokingly mentioned that I could still feel the mint in my nose. He laughed and apologized! We both relived that story and laughed just as hard as we did back then.

Kicked Out of the Olympia Brewery

In late March to early April 1974, three aircrews and their aircraft supported a TDY at McChord AFB, south of Tacoma and Seattle in Washington State, where we would serve as targets for the Airborne Warning and Control System (AWACS), the NATO E-3A, a modified Boeing 707 equipped with long-range radar and passive sensors. The aircraft serves as an eye in the sky to detect aircraft, ships, vehicles, missiles, and other projectiles at long ranges and performs command and control in the battlespace.

Using our RF-4C aircraft as targets, the AWACS could calibrate its radar system. They were in the early days of refining the systems onboard. The three aircrews included our ops officer, Deke DeKeyser (pilot) and Sam McDowell (WSO); Tom Alison and Tom Crook; and Jim Mills and me.

When we arrived at McChord, the weather was adverse, but we planned to fly on several sorties in that environment anyway. A few days it was so bad we stood down and had to find something to pass the time. We decided to do some sightseeing in nearby Tumwater and tour the Old Olympia Brewery. The six of us showed up there with a healthy supply of bags of pretzels and other snacks to go with the free beer. I took a great photo of the other five guys as they gave an Italian gesture (not the bad one) and held a beer. After the third time through the tour, the management asked us to leave the premises. We managed to sober up before we had to fly, of course!

Left to right: Tom Alison, Jim Mills, Sam McDowell, Tom Crook, and Deke DeKeyser.

Pilot Afraid of Heights

Wait a minute, a pilot afraid of heights? How is that possible? It went like this. We were on the same TDY up at McChord, and during our time there, we had to stand down another day due to the weather. *Is the weather here always like this?* I wondered. We made our way to the Seattle Space Needle, a 605-foot-tall spire, and waited our turn to enter the elevator to the top observation deck. Not that we would be able to see very far with the crappy weather.

Our turn came. As the doors to the elevator opened, we, as in five of us, approached to enter. But Deke held back. "Are you coming?" we asked him.

"No, you guys go ahead," he said.

"No. C'mon," we said.

He looked nervous, and we finally learned he didn't like heights. We all asked him how he could not like heights when he flew a fighter-type aircraft. He stated that it was different. Unsatisfied with his answer, we convinced him to go up with us. He entered the elevator, and we went to the top. But he didn't look away from one elevator wall and didn't go anywhere near the glass of the observation deck.

We learned very quickly not to tease him too much about this. After all, he was our operations officer. We learned to be nice. It turns out this was not as uncommon as one would think. There were other pilots with the same acrophobia, and there is nothing in the rulebooks that says a pilot can't be afraid of heights. The bottom line is Deke was a damn good pilot, and that's all that mattered.

Port—Left, Starboard—Right

Jim Mills and I, ready to depart on a TDY to McChord AFB.

This is the third story connected with the McChord TDY trip. We flew tracks over both land and ocean in adverse weather, which required extreme precision navigation and communications with the AWACS bird. On our first task, Jim Mills and I were vectored by departure control from McChord AFB to an altitude and westerly heading past the West Coast and out over the Pacific. As we approached our last assigned altitude, they handed us over to Seattle's Air Route Traffic Control Center (ARTCC), one of about twenty across the United States. Seattle Center gave us final instructions with a higher altitude and heading that continued west.

We then would be handed off to the AWACS aircrew on a specially assigned UHF radio frequency so they could conduct the calibration of their radar system. I made up the call signs since I don't remember them, but I do remember how the communication between us played out.

Their first call was to ensure good communication: "Tango 01, this AWACS Central, how do you read?"

Jim responded, "AWACS Central, this is Tango 01—got you five-by-five, over." Five-by-five is just a confirmation that means, "I understand you perfectly," or as some would say, "loud and clear." Once we made contact, said our good evenings, and asked how they were doing, we stood by for their vector instructions of headings and altitudes.

"Tango 01, this is AWACS Central, turn port to one-niner-five degrees." Jim and I did not key the mic button to respond immediately but did key our intercom for communications just between us.

"Jim, what's this port business?" I asked. We knew they meant to turn left but didn't understand why they were using seamen's terms. We quickly discussed how to respond.

"Roger AWACS Central, Tango 01 turning *left* to one-niner-five degrees," Jim responded (with a bit of emphasis on *left).* No reaction.

After about a minute on this heading, AWACS Central gave us another heading: "Tango 01, AWACS Central, come *starboard* to two-three-zero degrees." Jim and I got on our hot mic again.

"What's with the starboard already?" I asked Jim. "Maybe they feel obligated to use *port* and *starboard* because we're over the ocean?" It was a rhetorical question.

Jim responded, "Roger, AWACS Central. Tango 01 coming *right* to two-three-zero degrees." This time with a little more emphasis on *right.* Still no reaction.

A few more minutes passed before we received a new vector. "Tango 01, this is AWACS Central; come *right* to three-zero-zero degrees." Jim and I got on our intercom again and quickly exchanged some laughter and discussed how to reply. We figured they finally got the hint.

"Copy that AWACs Central. Tango 01 coming *starboard* to three-zero-zero degrees," Jim responded. We waited for any reaction.

A few seconds later, the AWACS crew keyed their mic, and we heard a roar of laughter from them. Everyone enjoyed the mission that continued in this fashion for the rest of the exercise. Jim and I couldn't wait to tell this story to our buddies back at McChord. Fun in the night sky, in the weather, over the Pacific.

Hey, Wake Up!

In April 1973, John Ganley, one of the pilots from the 91st TRS, and I were assigned to deliver an RF-4C aircraft, serial number 69-365, to Zweibrucken AB in Germany. Another aircrew, Krieg and Rogers, would deliver aircraft 69-0367. We would be in a four-ship formation with two F-4Cs (fighters) from the 1st TFW at MacDill AFB, Florida. This involved a deployment out of MacDill AFB, near Tampa as the departing point for the overseas flight. Deployments over the ocean demand a detailed briefing on normal and emergency procedures and require numerous inflight refuelings off a KC-135 tanker aircraft en route. John and I departed Bergstrom on 10 April and arrived at MacDill 1.7 hours later.

We spent the next day at MacDill with the fighter and tanker crews going over the plans for the aircraft ferry flight. Our first destination would be Torrejón AB in Spain. From there, we would have a one-day layover before departing for Germany.

This was my first ocean crossing in the RF-4C, so John and I went over everything carefully. We discussed taking flight control breaks by shifting aircraft control back and forth about every twenty minutes to give each other time to relax while cruising across the ocean at an optimum cruise speed of about 300 knots indicated airspeed (IAS) and at high altitude—somewhere above thirty thousand feet MSL.

We departed MacDill on 12 April after a final check of the en route weather and final flight briefing with the other aircrews. I was excited about this different mission and looked forward to the experience. We headed east, reached our cruising altitude, and passed over Bermuda as the East Coast of the United States became more distant.

Once we initiated our routine ops checks for oxygen levels, fuel, circuit breakers, and other instrument readings and switch positions, we slowly separated and increased our distance among the aircraft for better comfort, but we stayed within visible range of each other. We were underway, and John and I had already switched control several times. It can get boring on a long flight, and this one would tally up to 7.8 hours in the cockpit.

We were midway to our destination. We were on the lead's right wing, out several hundred feet—a comfortable separation distance. We were in the middle of the Atlantic, and John asked if I was ready to take control so he could give his neck a break from being constantly cocked to the left to keep an eye on the lead aircraft. I said sure, and I had control with a slight shake of the control stick. This was an added positive indication of aircraft control transfer, in addition to the verbal response.

Twenty minutes went by, and I was now ready to hand off control to John so I could take a break. I keyed my mic: "John, you ready to take the stick?" No reply. I called out again—nothing! I realized John had dozed off, which is easy to do. You're not watching a movie or going to the lavatory on this flight! You are stuck there in the cockpit for the long haul. I decided to try something else.

Most WSOs carry a flexible metal device about twenty inches long with a button at one end. When depressed, prongs open at the other end. This is useful if you ever drop anything in the cockpit. You couldn't reach the floor without it because your parachute harness is attached to your ejection seat, and you can only bend forward a short distance. The retriever worked very well if needed. While holding the control stick in my right hand, I extended the retriever with my left hand past the left side of the instrument bulkhead in front of me to gently tap John's helmet with the prongs. The distance between us was just close enough for me to do that.

A few taps with, "John, hey, wake up."

He was a bit startled. I think he said, "Are we there yet?" No, he didn't say that. I just added that for effect since you probably recall someone asking that same question on long road trips in a car. John took control. I made sure I didn't nod off, or I would have never heard the end of it. The rest of the mission was uneventful after completing four to five air refuelings before we let down into Spain. I can't recall the exact number. I would come to learn that John had more surprises up his sleeve!

Embarrassment at Torrejón AB, Spain

We remained at Torrejón AB on 13 April and prepared for the final leg of the trip. We would depart the next day, 14 April, for Zwi. This leg of the trip would only take two hours of flight time. Another day, another flight. We had completed all our checklist items and requested permission to taxi to the runway, and Torrejón tower gave us clearance to proceed.

We were about halfway to the runway, completing our taxi checklist, when I noticed that John was drifting us a bit toward one edge of the taxiway. *He couldn't possibly be asleep again, could he?* I wondered. No, he wasn't sleeping because he responded to me when I asked, "John, aren't we too close to the edge of the taxiway?"

"No, we're OK," he said. Within about thirty seconds later, our left main tire met with one of the taxi lights, which extended up from the ground by about a foot.

Boom! That was the sound as the air in our left main depleted, and the aircraft slowly tilted to the left. John gradually slowed the taxi to a complete stop. I sat there. Correction—*we* sat there at an angle in our mighty jet with a flat tire. I paused for a moment before making any comment.

"John, this is embarrassing," I said quietly.

He whimpered with a comment I could barely hear. "I know," he said.

We called for assistance and ended up shutting down the engines on the taxiway. The maintenance crew came out to change our tire while we sat there in the aircraft, our tails between our legs. When all was done, about an hour later, we cranked up the engines, continued to taxi, and proceeded to the end of the runway. John did not deviate from the exact centerline of the taxiway by even an inch.

I mentioned to John before takeoff, "John, I don't think we should ever come back here." The silence was deafening.

Gangster in Italy

In late January 1974, Jim Mills and I had TDY orders for an orientation visit to our dual base Aviano in northeastern Italy. This was part of the war planning that would enable us to operate from the NATO base were we ever deployed there. Our visit would also include a stop at the NATO 5th Allied Tactical Air Force (ATAF) HQ in Vicenza, Italy, about 150 kilometers (93 miles) from Aviano.

We took military airlift command (MAC) flights to make our way there. We first traveled to Loring AFB in Maine, where we caught a tanker (KC-135) flight to Torrejón AB, Spain. Yes, back at Torrejón, but this time not with John Ganley! Our travel included a military hop from there to Aviano, but we missed a connecting flight to Italy due to delays.

We checked the available military flight schedule, and we could only connect in a few days. So we had time to kill in Torrejón, and especially in nearby Madrid! Jim and I were in a hotel and somehow got linked up with another aircrew in an arrangement where the bedrooms were satellite rooms off a central living area. We shared the living area, and before long, we had lined up all the bottles across the room from all the wine we consumed.

We found out that dinner started later than we were accustomed to, so we sought a restaurant in Madrid for a late dinner. Then suddenly, the place turned into a dance floor with music and everyone dancing, so we joined in the festivities. We tried to blend in with the crowd—me and Jim with his Alabama accent! The music suddenly stopped, and they held a raffle, giving away shirts and other items. What a crazy night!

It was a good thing I had a hotel card with its address on it. We were pretty smashed from all the wine. I gave the business card from our hotel to a cab driver and asked him to take us there. I believe we slept all the way to the hotel and, once there, well into the morning.

We finally got on board a connecting C-130 to Aviano. We had a few days to go over war plans and get an airbase orientation before taking a day at the 5th ATAF. Of course, Jim and I wanted to get the Italian dining experience, so we ate at places like Orsini's Ristorante, where we had too many courses to count. We ate for three hours at the cost of about five dollars each, and that included all the wine and freshly baked bread you could consume. Unforgettable!

When we arrived at the 5ᵗʰ ATAF, the guard asked for our military ID cards. They would hold them until we departed. They took Jim's and then mine. Suddenly, the guard started to shout out something to the other guards. Of course, it was in Italian, but he was eyeing me up and down as the other guards approached. Jim and I didn't know what was happening, but we did know it didn't appear to be anything good, or friendly for that matter.

After the storminess settled down, and we got some interpretation going, we learned there was a very notorious gangster in Italy with the name "Cimino." Just my luck they would associate me with the thug! After all was calm, we went about our business for the day. As we left the HQ, we thanked the staff there. I emphatically snatched my ID card from the guard, giving him a cold stare. As we departed for Aviano, I said, "He's not me! Capisce?"

What was supposed to be a few days in Italy turned out to be a couple of weeks in Europe with some exciting stories to tell. I made sure I brought some gifts home to Fran so that she wouldn't focus solely on how long I was gone!

Hand Gestures

Before Jim and I left for Italy, Fran contacted her pen pal from high school years, Maura Tochet, who lived in Lido di Venezia. Her mother was Italian; her father was French. Fran met Maura when she joined her mother on a teachers' tour of Europe, which naturally included Italy. They maintained contact several times a year, especially for birthdays, Easter, and Christmas. Since Jim and I would be on TDY in Italy, Fran helped to arrange a lunchtime meeting for us with Maura while we visited Venice.

Getting to the rendezvous point, without either of us speaking any decent Italian, and especially with Jim's Alabama accent, was a challenge. Still, miraculously, the numerous gestures from a friendly Venetian, and our nodding accompanied by, "Grazie, grazie," resulted in a successful meeting. As we approached each other on the designated street. Maura whistled at us to get our attention. Undoubtedly, we stood out like sore thumbs!

It was a short but pleasant visit. Maura's English was very good. We took her to lunch, and she helped us shop for gifts to bring home. It was good to have a native Venetian with us—someone who spoke the language and was able to secure some good deals for us with local merchants. In later years, when I made the family tribute video for my parents, I studied a bit further about Italian hand gestures. I'm convinced they can carry on complete conversations using their hands and no words!

We kept in touch with Maura through 2017, after which we never heard from her again. We feared the worst but could never verify what happened to her. Fran, especially, lost a lifelong friend.

Swindle and Crook, Your Friendly Car Dealership

This one is quick to the punch! In addition to my good friend Tom Crook, we had another aircrew member who joined the 91st TRS—John Swindle. It didn't take long before someone coined the phrase for a fictitious car dealership. Go to "Swindle and Crook, the car dealership you can trust!" We also applied the name to a law firm! Anything for a laugh!

■ A FRIEND IS MISSING

We last met with our friend Tony Shine and his family during the summer of 1972, when we took a quick trip to Myrtle Beach from Shaw AFB in Sumter during my RF-4C training. In the fall of that year, Tony departed Myrtle Beach AFB for his second tour in Vietnam. Having served his first tour as an F-105 fighter pilot, Tony was now a combat-ready pilot in the A-7, a subsonic, light-attack aircraft.

He was a committed AF officer and fighter pilot who took pride in serving our country, as did his entire family. His father, George, was a USAF reserve lieutenant colonel. And Tony's siblings—his younger brothers, Alexander and Jonathan, and sister, Sarah—served in the army. Earlier, Alexander was wounded during his service in Vietnam but was able to come home. During Tony's first tour in Vietnam, in 1970, Jonathan was killed that October in an area northeast of Saigon called the "Iron Triangle." Tony took on the heavy and solemn responsibility to escort his brother's body home for a proper ceremony and burial at West Point.

Sheila Rockholt, our former secretary at the 18th TFW Safety Office in Okinawa, has maintained good contact with us through the years. At some point, in early 1973, Doug Alexander notified Sheila that Tony was on MIA status. She, in turn, notified Fran and me, and others.

Tony went missing on 2 December 1972, when he was on a reconnaissance and escort mission in North Vietnam, near the Laotian border. He radioed his wingman from the cockpit of his A-7D aircraft that he was descending through heavy cloud cover to get a better look at a North Vietnamese supply convoy along a ten-mile stretch of road called Highway 7. The wingman never heard from Tony again.

Ten minutes had passed when the wingman tried to radio Tony. There was no answer. There was no parachute observed or emergency signal that would have indicated an aircraft ejection or call for help. Airborne Command and Control directed an extensive two-day air search. Rescue teams reported a fire on the ground but no aircraft wreckage. This was devastating news to Tony's family, his co-fighter pilots, and many friends. Fran and I shared their anguish and, like them, held out hope that Tony was okay and would be found and return home.

The uncertainty of a loved one's status takes priority and remains central in one's thoughts. Everything else diminishes in importance. Tony was declared MIA that day. Bonnie Shine and her family wanted answers, and they spent years searching for any information. Their story is one of many years of fortitude, persistence, determination, and courage.

■ NO ORDINARY DAY—NO ORDINARY WEEK

In early June 1974, Fran and the boys took a trip to New York to visit family. Fran's parents lived in Rhinebeck, near Poughkeepsie and just east of the Hudson River. Since they stayed there for a few days, my parents and siblings Rob and Geri came from Long Island to visit them. They had a good visit and eventually returned to Texas.

Thursday, 27 June 1974, started as an ordinary day. I didn't fly that day but did other tasks in the squadron. I arrived home before dinner and spent the evening with Fran, Bill, and Joey as usual. After a few hours, we got the boys to bed, and Fran and I finally turned in around 11 p.m.

We had just fallen asleep when the phone rang. Fran answered the call. It was my brother, Rob. Fran said, "Hello."

Rob replied with two words: "Dad died." We were stunned for a moment, not immediately absorbing this terrible news.

I spoke with my brother, younger by ten years, to learn what happened. I knew my father had rheumatic fever as a young child and, as a result, had a damaged heart. He had encountered several congestive heart failures in his forties, but now, at age fifty, his heart gave up.

William D. Cimino
1923–1974

Fran and I decided it would be best for her to stay with our young boys in Austin. I went home for the funeral and to help Mom as much as possible. I went to the funeral home in Hicksville and planned Dad's funeral. We had the funeral home viewing and a funeral Mass at my mom's church, Our Lady of Mercy. The burial was at the Saint Charles Cemetery in Farmingdale. The family was in shock. Dad was the oldest of seven children and would have turned fifty-one on 30 September. His mother and all his siblings were still alive.

While I was in New York, Fran received a call from the squadron. They tried to contact me about a new assignment. Fran called me while I was in Long Island to tell me about the assignment to Thailand. We hadn't expected this; we thought we would be at Bergstrom another year or two. And this certainly wasn't the best time to get this news. In Thailand, the assignment was to an RF-4C squadron, the 14th TRS in the 432nd TFW at Udorn RTAFB. My report date was in late July. How quickly routines and life change! One day, one week, and a lot was different.

■ GET READY TO TRAVEL

After nearly two weeks on Long Island, I returned home to Fran and our sons to focus my attention on plans for them while I would be overseas on a remote tour for up to a year. Disruption was thriving in the Cimino family as we all navigated our ways through bad news and uncertainty. Due to my father's death, I requested a one-month delay in reporting to my new assignment in Thailand. The AF granted the delay and processed PCS orders for my report date of NLT 30 September 1974.

Fran and I discussed several options regarding where she, Bill, and Joey would live while I was away. We concluded the minimal impact would be to remain in our house in Austin. There would be no need to sell or rent our house, pack up and move our household goods, and settle somewhere else. Our home was in a good neighborhood with friends, some of whom were in the AF. And most important, Fran felt safe there.

One AF family, the Abells—Charlie and Vera—were two doors down the street. They had several children. Among them was Tina, who occasionally babysat for us, and KC mowed our lawn. They were a great family, and as time passed, they would prove to be an essential part of strong support to Fran in Texas while I was overseas.

I returned to the 91st TRS to complete my assignment there, flying ten more times between 8 July and 1 August. The movers came to pick up my hold baggage, which would be just a few boxes of clothes. I wouldn't need much more than that, plus my carry-on items when traveling. My departure date was adjusted to the first week in September, just a few days before Joey's first birthday.

■ A NEW ASSIGNMENT

I logged 365.2 hours of RF-4C flight time in 194 flight sorties while at the 91st for a total of 432 hours, including my training at Shaw. My final flight at Bergstrom was on 1 August 1974 with my buddy Jim Mills. I was certified as combat-ready and was prepared to join the squadron aircrews of the 14th TRS in northern Thailand, a few miles from the Laotian border. The war in Vietnam was winding down, but there were enemy actions and infiltrations on the ground as troops moved from the north into South Vietnam and Cambodia. I was confident that my training and operational experience prepared me for any role I would need to support.

Leaving my family for any length of time was tough, and leaving many friends and good times would also prove to be difficult as it was at the end of other assignments. Another WSO, Russ Metzler (we called him "Russie Babes"), who went through RF-4C training with me at Shaw AFB, would join me. The process of building relationships and trust with fellow aircrews would begin all over again. The reality of AF life was in motion as I prepared to cross the international date line again and head a bit more west—this time to SEA.

SOUTHEAST ASIA

■ UDORN RTAFB, UDON THANI, THAILAND

My assignment was in the northern section of Thailand, about fifty miles south of Vientiane, Laos, at Udorn Royal Thai Air Force Base in the 14th TRS—the only recce squadron remaining at Udorn.

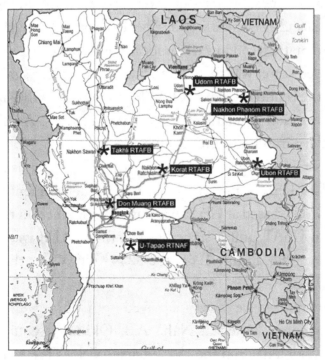

AF bases in Thailand.

Photo: Courtesy of Slide Player Presentation: The Far East Air Force by Jonathan Perkins.

The town of Udon Thani was right outside the main gate to the base. The base was established in the 1950s. The civil war inside Laos and fears of it spreading into Thailand led the Thai government to allow the United States to covertly use five Thai bases beginning in 1961 for the air defense of Thailand, and to fly reconnaissance flights over Laos. Udorn was one of those bases.

Under Thailand's "gentleman's agreement" with the United States, RTAF bases used by the USAF were considered RTAF bases and were commanded by Thai officers. Thai air police controlled access to the bases, along with USAF security police, who assisted them in base defense using sentry dogs, observation towers, and machine-gun emplacements. The USAF forces at Udorn were under the command of the US Pacific Air Forces (PACAF) 13th AF.

Udorn RTAFB was the Asian headquarters for Air America, a US passenger and cargo airline covertly owned and operated by the CIA. It provided essential resources for the war in Laos and elsewhere. Its predecessor, Civil Air Transport (CAT), started operations from Udorn on 11 September 1955 with three C-46s delivering food and emergency aid into Indochina. CAT had flown more than two hundred missions to twenty-five reception areas by the end of September, delivering a thousand tons of emergency food. Conducted smoothly and efficiently, this airdrop relief operation marked the beginning of CAT's, and later, Air America's support of US assistance programs in Laos.

Air America's roles were supportive of covert and overt situations related to hostilities in Southeast Asia and elsewhere worldwide. They provided buffers and solutions to problems the United States faced in various locations. Operations were focused in Laos as part of the so-called secret war the United States carried out against the Pathet Lao forces operating in the country. Udorn RTAFB also served as the site of Headquarters 333, the Thai organization in charge of their forces in Laos. Air America continued operations from Udorn into Laos until 3 June 1974.

The AF and other services grew at Udorn during the 1960s, as the war in Vietnam escalated with the first USAF unit, a communications detachment from the 1st Mobile Communications Group, based at Clark Air Base, Philippines, in the summer of 1964. The first permanent USAF unit assigned at Udorn RTAFB was the 333rd Air Base Squadron in October 1964. In July 1965, the 6234th TFW was the only tactical wing in Thailand.

Squadrons known to have been deployed to Udorn were the 45th Tactical Reconnaissance Squadron, based at Naha AB, Okinawa, equipped with RF-101 Voodoos (pre-RF-4C aircraft), and the 555th (Triple-Nickle) Tactical Fighter Squadron, also based at Naha AB, equipped with the F-4C fighter aircraft.

The 432nd TRW was activated on 18 September 1966. It was the most diversified unit of its size in the USAF with squadrons of fighters, reconnaissance, and special operations. In 1972, tactical fighter strength was augmented at Udorn by deployed TAC continental US-based squadrons in response to the North Vietnamese Easter offensive. During Operation Linebacker, between May and October 1972, the 432nd TRW had seven F-4 squadrons assigned or attached, and the 14th TRS with RF-4Cs made it the largest wing in the USAF. The 14th TRS was assigned at Udorn from 28 October 1967 to 30 June 1975.

With the signing of the Paris Peace Accords on 27 January 1973, most of the F-4 squadrons that participated in the 1972 campaigns returned to their home stations. The numbers of USAF personnel and aircraft at Udorn were reduced. Toward the end of my assignment at Udorn, the squadrons had dwindled to two fighter squadrons and one recce squadron—the 14th TRS.

It ceased combat operations in Vietnam in January, Laos in February, and Cambodia in August 1973. The wing remained in Southeast Asia to perform reconnaissance missions, called combat support, and routine training to retain combat proficiency, changing designations from reconnaissance to fighter wing in November 1974 while I was there.

By 1975, relations between Washington and Bangkok had deteriorated. The Royal Thai government wanted the USAF out of Thailand by the end of the year. "Palace Lightning" was the plan under which the USAF would withdraw its aircraft and personnel from Thailand.

The last remaining fighter squadron, the 13th TFS, and the 14th TRS were inactivated in June 1975. The 423rd TFW was inactivated on 23 December 1975. The last USAF personnel departed Udorn in January 1976, and Udorn RTAFB was turned over to Thai authorities. It is currently operated by the Royal Thai Air Force with aircraft from the 2nd Air Division based there.

I arrived at Udorn on Tuesday, 3 September 1974 at 1000 hours. I was only there a few days before I went TDY to Clark AB in the Philippines for a four-day jungle survival school course—more training and new survival techniques unique to the SEA environment. My friend and co-WSO, Russ Metzler, would join me. Bergstrom AFB screwed up and did not include jungle survival on our orders. Otherwise, we would have gone there en route to Udorn.

14th TRS hooch.

I had a few days to in-process at Udorn and get my living quarters at one of the 14th Squadron's "hooches" (sometimes spelled "hootches"), simple wooden buildings that housed several rooms with bathroom facilities in a shared central part of each building. Hooches were built off the ground by a few steps to separate them from the constant ground moisture and minimize the bugs and other creatures that might invade one's room. The arrangement did not prevent that too well.

My hooch was directly across the street from the officers' club and within walking distance to other facilities—gym, church, base exchange, bank, outdoor movie theater, and other services. The base was split in two, with living quarters and support facilities on one side, and all operational organizations—such as wing headquarters, squadrons, base support, and aircraft—on the opposite side. There was frequent bus transportation from one side to the other. Since I would not receive my hold baggage that contained the items I packed from home in Austin for possibly up to six weeks, moving in took a matter of minutes. I had what I needed for the time being.

I fired off a couple of letters to Fran to let her know I arrived safely and that I was headed to Clark. I also let her know that I planned to continue my professional military education (PME), the first of which was Squadron Officers School (SOS) that I had begun at Bergstrom. When I return from Clark AB, I would begin the process of in-theater indoctrination, including briefings and flying, which would commence in later September.

▪ IT'S A JUNGLE OUT THERE

I left Udorn on Saturday, 7 September. Classes were scheduled to start on Monday. Clark AB was a large AFB, second only to Eglin AFB in Florida. Despite that, I had to lodge off-base during training. The survival training was excellent. It included a thorough presentation of the jungle conditions in Thailand, Cambodia, and Vietnam, where our squadron flew specific sorties and supported special missions.

The survival training addressed situations in which aircrews were subject to such an environment in the event of an aircraft ejection due to hostile attack or aircraft problems. Even with the Paris Peace Accords, we understood hostile actions were a real possibility with Vietcong troops, officially known as the National Liberation Front of South Vietnam, operating in South Vietnam and Cambodia under the direction of North Vietnam.

In the classroom, the first part of the training consisted of familiarization with the flora (vegetation) and fauna (wildlife) in the area. We learned how to search the dense jungle for abundant natural food and water—from rooted plants (vegetable-type food), insects, and snakes—to using bamboo shoots to tap certain trees for pure water. We also learned how to test any food and to always wash any scent of food from our hands and faces to not attract predators. There were creatures out there that also must survive! Our survival vests would only contain a small supply of food and water, so knowing how to endure was essential.

Another part of the training focused on the extensive types of booby traps used by the Vietcong to injure or kill unsuspecting soldiers. This, of course, would apply if you survived ejection and were able to successfully free yourself from a tree after you descended in your parachute. So the school covered techniques for removing yourself from treetops and methods to detect, or more important, avoid the traps.

The actual training application was in a large area of jungle in the rolling hills and valleys where we would need to execute the evasion portion of SERE—survival, evasion, resistance, escape. Local men, called "Negritos," were indigenous. They were usually around five feet tall, wore nothing more than shirts and loincloths, and barefooted. They supported the instructor training uniquely. Instructors would turn us loose in the jungle area, which covered several square miles, and we needed to evade capture by the men as we worked our way to a rendezvous point.

Jungle training area: "Find Me."

Negrito, part of the survival training team.

Each student had two chits, coupons similar to ticket stubs. If a Negrito found you, you would give him one of the chits as a reward for his success. It would allow him to claim a large bag of rice for his effort. It would also indicate to you that you failed to evade. He was an experienced hunter. Survival trainees usually have some survival experience, as I had with two previous courses, but not in the jungle, the Negrito's backyard.

After being caught once, you had one chit left, so you could try to evade again, working your way to the destination. If you got caught again, no big problem. You had the second chit to reward the guy. But you had better turn yourself over to him this time. If you tried to evade again and got caught, that was not good! You would have no chit to reward the guy with the big Bolo knife he was swinging through the jungle to find you. These guys don't work for nothing!

We were on our own and had a one-hour head start. We did not travel in pairs or groups as instructors dropped us off in different sections of the jungle. I was making my way through a valley—two steep hills on either side—when I heard a Negrito *whooping* through the jungle behind me by some number of yards. I estimated fifty to seventy-five. They yelled *Whoop, whoop* as they swung their Bolo knives. I guess that was kind of a way to say, "I'm coming. Try to hide."

I decided I needed to get off my current path; he was probably tracking me with great skill. I made a ninety-degree turn and made my way up a steep hill covered with thick vegetation. I was careful to move slowly enough to turn and move the foliage back so as not to reveal a path. Once I had climbed up about thirty feet, I lay on my back on the terrain and covered myself with the vegetation. Bugs were everywhere. I heard him go ahead of me, so I felt good at having evaded him. However, while I lay there, before I thought it was safe to emerge, from the corner of my eye I saw something move.

It stopped. I turned my head a bit and saw what it was—a big, and I mean *big* spider! The body was nearly the size of my fist, with legs to match. It traveled from my right to left, stopping for a few seconds on the vegetation just a few inches right over my face! *How the hell long is that thing gonna be here?* I dared not move, so I had to wait a little longer. The creepy thing kept going. I got out of there after making sure no other guy swinging a Bolo was waiting for me somewhere.

I made it to the rendezvous point and still had two chits. Most of the guys did well, but a few were there with their tails between their legs, having provided enough rice for several men to feed their families for weeks. We lingered with the group, including the Negrito men, for a while. As this training segment ended, everyone wore smiles, and more so after some of the trainees, including myself, bought Bolo knives from the Negrito craftsmen. I recall paying about three dollars for it. I still have it to remind me of that excellent training experience. I just hoped I would never have to use it!

■ 14TH TRS: BUNNY SQUADRON

I returned from Clark AB on Saturday, 14 September, and after waiting two and a half hours to call Fran via the MARS, I was able to get through. It was great to connect by phone since we had last spoken in Austin before I left there. I wrote a letter to Fran and a separate one to Bill that evening.

I was ready to learn about the local flying area, the rules of flight in this foreign but friendly country, and support missions over South Vietnam and Cambodia. The sorties in Thailand would focus on maintaining proficiency, while missions in South Vietnam and Cambodia were termed "combat support." These missions would include specific targets compiled by intelligence as well as support to special operations.

The 14th TRS "Bunnies" have a long history that began in June 1942, during WWII. A narrative of that history, written by an unknown author, is in appendix E.

I quickly learned that the average RF-4C time for the twenty-eight WSOs in the squadron when I arrived there was 269 hours. With 432 hours logged in the cockpit, I immediately became one of the more-experienced WSOs in the squadron. In fact, there were only three other squadron WSOs with more time than I had. Even the squadron navigator, a lieutenant colonel who was leaving for Bergstrom in November, had less time. I thought I would have to go through the newbie process again, as I did at Bergstrom, but that was not the case this time.

The squadron commander, Lt. Col. Harlow, asked me what duties I would prefer in the squadron. I told him I wanted to get involved with Stan/Eval, become an RF-4C instructor WSO (IWSO), and work in training or life support. As a refresher, Stan/Eval is an elite group of the best aircrew members. They administer the check rides for other aircrews through written and oral testing and in-flight chase check rides.

Life support is a section in the squadron that cares for all the gear necessary for flight sorties in SEA—G suits, helmets, survival vests, parachutes, small arms weapons—and also conducts training aimed at aircrew survival.

He told me he was certain I would become an IWSO before Christmas. But that changed, and he immediately put me on a fast track. The first phase was to complete my theater indoctrination (TI) flights (TI-1, TI-2, and so on) and check out. This was usually about six or seven flights, including day and night sorties in Thailand along designated routes. An IWSO check flight would occur after three IWSO flights (IWSO-1, -2, and -3) demonstrating instructor capabilities. Both these checks have traditionally been done separately.

I began my TI rides on 24 September and completed them on 7 October. I flew my IWSO flights for the next three days, 8–10 October. The operations officer, Lt. Col. Gibson, told me that I would get both my local area TI check ride and IWSO check ride in one flight evaluation the next day, 11 October, and that they had never combined these two check rides before.

On the first TI-1 flight, I did a poor job. I could not get my act together. I had not flown since my last flight with Jim Mills at Bergstrom, on 1 August. I felt like I was behind the aircraft and could not keep up. Additionally, I was not accustomed to all the extra equipment that made me feel like I weighed three hundred pounds: a very heavy survival vest that contained two survival radios, a first aid kit, a compass, flares, a few rations, and other survival equipment. The WSO must stay ahead of the aircraft to anticipate turns and sensor operation, among other things. I thought, *This is not a good way to start as an experienced WSO!*

Ready to rock 'n' roll.

Two days later, I flew TI-2 and was quickly back in the groove. The squadron commander told me on 3 October that I was under consideration for a squadron Stan/ Eval flight examiner (SEFE) job but must do well on the check rides first. All flights after TI-1 went great and were rated as excellent. I checked out in both TI and IWSO on the eleventh, as scheduled, with Capt. Mitch Mitchell as my pilot. I would be sorry to see Mitch leave; he was due to rotate back to the States in December.

A wing Stan/Eval aircrew chased us for the evaluation. The evaluation crew also rated me on flight preparation, briefing the mission, and two written and oral tests for the local TI and the IWSO portions. I missed one of twenty questions, so "One-Wrong Cimino" was alive and well! I raced through the checkout program and felt the rhythm of aircrew duties once again. In mid-October, I flew with the squadron commander on a weather recce exercise with my upgrades behind me. We rose at 0200 hours to arrive at the squadron to prepare for a very early takeoff. Always good to fly with the boss, no matter what time of day!

My role was established in the squadron very quickly, and my below-average performance on my T-1 flight was way behind me in the rearview mirror. I heard from others that the operations officer had told them I would become a SEFE, so during my IWSO flights, I began to study for the test portion for that envious position. I also prepared to take my next SOS test. Even though I was in an operational squadron in SEA, studying for something was always in play. As an IWSO, my primary job was to fly with new pilots for their local TI rides throughout Thailand. I completed SOS in March 1975.

On Tuesday, 29 October, I got a call from Lt. Col. Hughes at wing Stan/Eval. He wanted to interview me for a position at wing headquarters. He would also interview two of my friends stationed with me in the 91st TRS at Bergstrom, who were now also in the 14th TRS—Jay Barrett and Russie Babes (Metzler). They, too, came to Udorn with above-average flight times in the RF-4C and were excellent WSOs.

The next day, 30 October, my 29th birthday, the squadron commander told me I was selected and that the others may move to wing Stan/Eval at a later date. By the end of October, I had flown nineteen times, all in Thailand, and was focused on my new role as a wing SEFE. There was a bit of drama associated with this new selection, however.

Lt. Col. Gibson was TDY when I received a thumbs-up from Lt. Col. Hughes about my transfer to the wing Stan/Eval position. When Gibson returned, he was upset about several issues, my move to the wing being one of them. It had nothing to do with my performance or qualifications since he had been supportive all the way. But given the status of activities in SEA and the associated drawdown of the wing's squadrons, he wanted to eliminate the wing slot and keep me in the squadron.

He had a decisive say since the squadron commander, Lt. Col. Harlow, was scheduled to return to the United States; Gibson would become the 14th TRS squadron commander on 21 November. He convinced Col. David Smith, the wing deputy commander for operations, and it was done. I would remain at the squadron level.

As I contemplated Gibson's perspective, it did not take me long to become flattered by the fact that both he and Hughes wanted me. Additionally, Gibson's rationale made sense, and it would allow me to do the same SEFE job at the squadron and hang out more frequently with my buddies there. Overall, it worked out for the best.

In one of his last duties at the 14th, Lt. Col. Harlow wanted me to fly with him on a TDY to Utapao AB, Thailand. I appreciated that he put confidence in me for the associated mission. As things go and sometimes do not, I came down with the flu and was grounded from flying for a couple days, so I could not go with him.

I had my SEFE upgrade check ride on 18 November. All went very well as Capt. Lord, in a chase aircraft with him, evaluated me on how I evaluated another aircrew. Since I attained both IWSO and SEFE status, I was also considered a supervisor.

On 19 November, we had a party for Harlow at one of the rooms in the hooch—lots of booze and drinking for our departing commander. We celebrated with him, wished him well, and internally, I was celebrating my new role in the squadron. I had devoted many hours of study, preparation, and practice to achieving valuable squadron ratings. And the hard work paid off. Nothing comes easy, and while some people can achieve their goals with less effort, I knew that certainly did not apply to me.

As IWSO, I conducted rear cockpit training on some equipment, including radar and LORAN. There were always some new techniques to learn regarding these systems, and it always proved beneficial to share knowledge among us. I also had the distinct pleasure of evaluating both Jay and Russie Babes for their IWSO upgrades. We made a good team!

During my first month in Thailand, we heard rumors of a possible rollback, an early return to the States given the activities in SEA were drawing to a close. I began a discussion with Fran, primarily through letters, about a follow-on assignment and preferences of locations. It was possible to return to Austin with an assignment at Bergstrom. There would be minimal impact since we had the house there and would not need to move. We did not want to return to Shaw AFB in South Carolina, but that was always a possibility as well. Other considerations were in Europe, either in the United Kingdom or Germany since there were RF-4C squadrons in both locations.

So as early in my tour in SEA as it was, it was not too early to get my preferences on official communications to the AF. AF Form 90, Officer Career Objective Statement, served that purpose, and I decided to complete it, as well as make plans to visit the

Military Personnel Center in San Antonio, Texas, when I hoped to return home on leave in spring 1975. San Antonio was not far from Austin, and it would be worth a trip to talk to someone face-to-face.

My preferred next duty was as a WSO in various aircraft, the RF-4C and F-111 among them. I highlighted supplemental duties as an aerospace research flight test officer and a special development engineer. I listed my ultimate career goal with a duty preference in AF Systems Command after an AFIT (Air Force Institute of Technology) tour, where I could then be considered for an assignment at one of System Command's test centers. A recent course was open to navigators at Edwards AFB, California, where they conduct flight tests on various aircraft.

I had considered an assignment in the SR-71 (Black Bird), SAC's strategic reconnaissance aircraft that flew as high as 80,000 feet at speeds up to Mach 3 (basically three times the speed of sound) with primary surveillance missions over China and the then-USSR. Tom Alison ended up as one of their pilots when he left the 91st at Bergstrom, but Tom was fortunate because most SR-71 aircrews were homegrown from within SAC. They did not take TAC pilots into the program very often. Besides, I did not have anywhere near the total flight time hours needed to qualify. I quickly focused elsewhere.

Tom went on to do well with the SR-71. His high-altitude flight suit with his name tag is in a glass-enclosed display a few feet from the SR-71 housed in the Smithsonian National Air and Space Museum annex called the Stephen F. Udvar-Hazy Center, near the Washington Dulles International Airport in the Chantilly area of Fairfax County, Virginia. Anytime I go to the museum with others, I always show them that display and add, "I flew many times with that guy!"

In the 14th, we conducted flight operations seven days a week with limited hours on Sundays. Daily, I focused on the sorties within Thailand to maintain proficiency or evaluate other aircrews. Even though Thailand was our host country, remote areas could be detrimental and require evasive actions if one had to eject for any reason. Through intelligence, we noted SAFE areas and contacts if we found ourselves on the ground. We carried full survival gear and some weapons—a .38-caliber pistol and a survival knife with a five-inch blade. Not much, but something. And we flew "sanitized"—no ID, no name tags, no family photos, no rings or jewelry of any kind.

I used to load the pistol chamber with five rounds and leave the first one empty. My thought was if I was ever captured and someone took my gun to use against me, the first trigger pull would be nothing, and perhaps I would have a chance to react and defend myself. Maybe it was wishful thinking or nonsense, but hey, any option toward survival would be worth trying. The knife was in a leather sheath strapped to my right calf, hidden under my flight suit.

The topography in Thailand is characterized by mountain ranges, karstic plateaus, and rolling hills of low to medium relief, with lowlands between. The mountainous ridge elevation reaches over eight hundred meters ASL, karstic plateaus are developed between three hundred and five hundred ASL, and the lowlands are at about a hundred meters ASL. In the karstic plateaus and mountains, springs, caves, and dry streambeds exist—many places for friend or foe to hide.

Having the added security of a personal weapon was important to the aircrews. One day, however, that all changed. In late October, one of the aircrew members accidentally fired off a round in the personnel equipment room, where we suited up for flights. The squadron commander was in the room at the time, among others! We were fortunate no one was injured or killed! In addition to a severe reprimand that was absolutely justified for the individual, the whole squadron was prevented from taking a weapon on routine flights within Thailand. The aircrews were not happy about this. We would, however, only be permitted to carry them on combat support missions. This is what can happen when one guy is not careful to follow safety procedures and screws up!

My neck hurts! Not so much now, but it did back when my pilot and I pulled 8.3 Gs twice in one training sortie. We were flying a routine but challenging day, visual, low-level route in a very flat region of Thailand—much of it soaked rice fields with no good reference points. We had the usual four targets to acquire on film. We had no problem with the first two as we maintained course and flew directly over the targets.

The third target was a tiny structure the size of a small shed. As we flew the course at 540 knots GS (nine miles per minute) at five hundred feet AGL, we constantly communicated to confirm our position and visually pick up the target. We confirmed that we had our initial point (IP) in sight and hacked our watches as we flew over it. We then knew we would have about thirty seconds to reach the target. But we did not see it.

Shortly after the IP, I called out, "Standing by for cameras on; time to target twenty seconds."

The pilot responded, "Copy that. I don't have the target yet."

I called out again, "Time to target ten seconds."

Suddenly, he says, "Ah, target at 10 o'clock, standby for cameras on," as he snap-rolled the aircraft left. Our right wing pointed skyward, and the left wing pointed to the ground and pulled 8.3 Gs to make the tight turn toward the target.

My response, as I grunted through the G maneuver and with my peripheral vision narrowing to a small "soda straw" view forward, was, "Standing by. Cameras on."

The groundspeed in this high-G maneuver bleeds off very rapidly, so my attention, in addition to camera operation, was focused on four main things: the ground, the groundspeed indicator, the G meter, and my pilot.

He rolled out just seconds before the target as he increased the aircraft groundspeed from about 250 knots back to 540 as we approached it from an approximate forty-five-degree angle from our course moments ago. We were off course but about to fly directly over the target from this new angle.

My response was, "Standing by," as my full peripheral vision (and his) was restored.

Just a few remaining seconds before the target, he called, "Cameras on."

I responded, "Cameras on," as I watched the camera film indicators counting down to confirm camera operation.

"Cameras off," he said.

"Roger. Cameras off."

We were now considerably off our planned route and needed to turn right to get back on course to pursue the fourth target. We didn't do this gradually. No, not at all. We pulled another 8.3 Gs to return to course. More grunts, more narrow vision, and more of me—and him—feeling the effects of 8.3 times our normal body weight against our cockpit ejection seats. This entire sequence happened in under fifteen seconds.

We acquired our fourth target and headed back to Udorn. When we landed and taxied back to our parking location, we were both happy we acquired the targets but were physically spent. Even though the high Gs only lasted a few seconds, they were very demanding on the body. The worst part of this mission was about to come, however.

Since we flew with three external fuel tanks, one under each wing and one center-line under the fuselage, aircrews were restricted in training flights to a limit of six Gs to avoid unnecessary strain on the tanks or the struts that attached them to the aircraft. The crew chief, who has responsibility for the aircraft's maintenance status, was not happy that we put the aircraft through such flight performance parameters, and rightly so. He took immense pride in maintaining the best operational aircraft possible for the aircrews. So we had to listen to him for a few minutes and restore our appreciation for his role and dedication to the mission. And I must add, these men did a magnificent and commendable job on the flight line every day under brutal conditions.

He found out about the high Gs in two ways: First, we had to disclose this to him verbally and in our sortie write-up on TO Form 781. And second, by looking at the G meter in the nose wheel well. There are three G meters in the RF-4C. One in each cockpit indicates Gs as they increase to the highest level pulled and then return to zero. However, the meter in the nose wheel well pegs at the highest level pulled and remains there for the crew chief to review postflight. He then resets it to zero before the next flight.

My neck hurt since my head pressed against it at 8.3 times its normal weight. I learned later that two of the seven vertebrae in my cervical spine were pushed slightly out of alignment due to this excessive g-force and pressed against my spinal cord, causing chronic neck pain. This continued to be an issue for me on different levels, but not enough to cause me any great concern.

Looking way ahead, when I took my final physical before I retired from the AF, the flight surgeon told me I could have my cervical spine corrected and gave me two options: via neck surgery, either from the front of the throat (where the surgeon pushes everything to the side to get to the affected vertebrae) or via the back of the neck; or Tylenol. When I saw illustrations for the procedures for surgery, I made my choice. No contest! I chose Tylenol. And fortunately, my neck pain gradually dissipated to a tolerable level.

In mid-October, I was given a squadron additional duty as the publications officer to maintain updated flight publications. An RF-4C pilot from the squadron was also assigned as this was an extensive task. As we worked together, we bonded very well. Guy Munder and I had a lot in common, and our attitudes on everything and everyone were in sync. No wonder we got along so well! Our personality traits were so similar that we could be considered twins. Guy would become one of my closest and trusted friends at Udorn.

14th TRS aircrews.
Guy Munder to my right as we stood at the front end of the left-wing fuel tank.

Guy and I standing proud!

My additional duties were not limited to the 14th TRS. In January 1975, I was assigned as the wing flight manual control officer, which required that I maintain all the flight publications for the recce and fighter squadrons. Not the most envious of duties, but one that needed attention and detail. After several months, I convinced senior officers that I should not be responsible for the fighter squadrons' publications. Their files were a real mess. I was happy to dump that additional duty.

■ LIFE AT UDORN

While my role and responsibilities in the squadron and the wing multiplied over the first few months, I adapted to the new way of life on this remote tour far from home. My goal from the outset was to keep myself busy, both on and off the job, and race through this assignment to get back home to my family. So let me describe myriad subjects relative to life at Udorn.

My hold baggage, which had most of my clothes and personal articles, finally arrived one month after checking in at Udorn. I received them on 4 October, and they were in decent shape. There was nothing in that shipment of high value anyway.

I spent a portion of my time working through the Squadron Officer School course, taking periodic tests and moving through the sections toward completion. My scores were high, and I would be happy to get this essential credential in my records. Completing AF professional military education was one of many factors contributing to a higher success rate for promotion.

I learned that every squadron had its own "party suit," which was a requirement, not by any written regulation, but certainly by peer pressure. You wouldn't want to be at a party and stick out like a sore thumb without your party suit! *Where do I get my party suit?* I wondered. There was one place that every aircrew member at Udorn went to get theirs fitted and ordered. You went to see Brother Amarjit Singh Vasir, better known as "The Thief," at The Maharajah Clothiers in Udon Thani.

Squadron party suit.

Based on a design from Col. Victor N. Cabas, former wing commander, 432nd TRW, Brother Amarjit produced the prototype party suit, which was hung in the Officer's Club at Udorn.

Brother Amarjit had quite a business going right outside the main gate, making the suits and patches—name, rank, squadron patches that stuck on with Velcro for everyone at Udorn. During the peak years of the war, it was said that he had as many as eighty to a hundred seamstresses working to produce the party suits. A party suit cost fifteen dollars and took three to four days for delivery. Our squadron party suit was a one-piece maroon garment with short sleeves, flared pants, white inserts at the bottom, and a zipper up the front.

I maintained a consistent physical exercise program by running, swimming, working with weights, and playing football, racquetball, or handball. We had a good squadron football team with no losses and several wins. But one of our crew members had a severe injury that grounded him for several months. I didn't want that to happen to me, so I dropped off the football team. I did play handball and racquetball frequently, and one player, Lt. Col. Rivello, made the game even more fun because we called him Col. Spaghetti or Ravioli. He loved it!

My weight was coming down rapidly, not only due to the exercise, but because of the lack of excessive snacks or between-meal eating. I had a small refrigerator in my room but didn't keep much food there. I was 197 pounds when I arrived in Thailand; I strived for a goal of 175. By Christmas, I was down to 178. I was still on a downward trend as the months came and went.

Entertainment consisted of the occasional party to celebrate a "Sawadee" (pronounced sah wah dee), or sometimes spelled "Sawasdee." Both expressions could be used to say, "Hello," or, "Goodbye." We usually held a Sawadee party to say goodbye to a squadron or wing member. Party suits would be on full display, and there was no shortage of food and drink. Some parties got out of control with food fights, rolls and other items flying everywhere.

During one party at the Officer's Club, we were giving a general officer a traditional sendoff when a roll came flying from somewhere. In fact, at my first meal at the Officer's Club, lunch, I sat at our squadron table with a few others having just met them. I asked someone to pass a roll from the other end of the table, and he threw it at me. *OK, so this is how it's going to be here!* I decided.

Getting back to the party, it didn't take long before an array of rolls crisscrossed the crowd. Our squadron commander was sitting next to the general when he observed an entire steak hit the general in the neck. (I think it was medium-rare!) Our commander's eyes widened. He looked around, ready to reprimand the culprit. You could almost see the steam coming out of his ears! But before he could do anything, the general picked up the nearest food item and entered the battle. It went downhill from there! The party continued. The rolls—and steak—were replenished. Grown men, having fun, far from home and civilization!

I usually had my meals at one of several places on the base: the Officer's Club or the Thai restaurants on the base. The prices for dinner were under $1.25 to $1.50 at that time, and once each month, there was a free membership night at the Officer's Club, where you could get a free meal. It wasn't great, but hey, it was free!

I went to a party where the host roasted this huge pig all day. Someone who tasted yelled out, "Bad pig!" And after I had just taken a bite, I confirmed exactly what I heard. I spat it out and left after a short while. Some of the other squadron guys ate more of the pig and got very sick. I rarely ate off base, or went off base, for that matter, other than to do a little shopping for Fran and the boys.

I would buy Fran some lovely custom-made jewelry at Bill's Jewelry Store and later at Seng's, outside the main gate. I handpicked the gemstones and had the jeweler make the settings in gold or white gold. For protection during shipment, I wrapped the jewelry in tennis ball cans, which I enclosed in a box to send home. Fran loved each unique gift and still has all the jewelry I bought for her in Thailand. She, in turn, sent me items I needed. Our base exchange store at Udorn was very sparse. It lacked many items, so I had to rely on Fran to send specific things to me. I didn't need much and managed to get by without too much help.

We also had an outdoor theater. It was not very big but was another diversion from the work routine. I saw some good movies there—*Walking Tall, Dirty Harry, The Harrod Experiment*, and, *Thunderbolt and Lightfoot*. The last one was written and directed by my first cousin once removed, Michael Cimino (my dad's first cousin), among others. The only problem was when the theater was open during the evening, we also had flight operations. So we had to strain at times to hear the sound from the movies over the roar of the jet aircraft on takeoffs. Just a minor annoyance! I also read a few books, including *Jaws* and *Breakheart Pass*.

I kept my hair short, well within the AF regulations. The barbershop was in the Officer's Club, right across the street from me. Roll out of bed and get a haircut. It was that easy. Haircuts were seventy-five cents—not too steep. I could handle that.

Along with the other squadron members, I employed local Thai help to do my laundry. Jeannie, this sweet Thai lady, cleaned my room, made the bed, did my laundry, and shined my flight boots for a few Thai baht (currency) each week, which would amount to $11US/month.

Jeannie and her daughter.

Jeannie also provided maid service to my neighbor next door. I estimated she was in her forties. She had a teenage daughter, although I do not recall her telling me her name. Jeannie was a pleasant woman who always worked with a smile and had my boots ready at my door. She would knock on the door to hand me my clothes. After she washed the laundry, she ironed everything, and I mean everything: my flight suits, my shirts, pants, socks, underwear, and even my jockstrap. Yes, I never saw my jockstrap look so perfect, folded and pressed!

I tried to call Fran as often as possible using the MARS service. But would often wait for up to several hours before my turn came up, only to find we had a terrible connection. Persistence paid off, however, and when we did get a good connection, it was great to hear each other and catch up on everything going on at both ends of the world. I occasionally snuck in a call via the squadron autovan phone service, which was primarily for official business. Everyone took their turn at that!

It was tough being away from family during the holidays. But we tried to make the best of it. Thanksgiving came and went with no considerable fanfare. I had turkey dinner at the Officer's Club. We had a barbecue outside the hooches on Christmas Eve—burgers, hot dogs, and beer. Some of the squadron's enlisted troops dressed up as Santa Claus and reindeer for the little children there; some of the aircrews had their wives and young kids there to live in Thailand while they were assigned at Udorn.

Jeannie gave her clients a watermelon and carved pineapple for Christmas. She also gave me a tie pin. I thought that was extremely sweet from someone who did not make a lot of money. Some of the guys gave her cash; I gave her a box of candy. She genuinely appreciated anything she received. Jay Barrett and I went to midnight Mass, and I slept late Christmas morning. On Christmas Day, I had a two-dollar buffet dinner at the Officer's Club. I flew the day after Christmas. Back to work!

One of the annual traditions in Thailand was the Water Festival (called Songkran). This occurs for a few days in mid-April, typically between 13 and 15 April, but could extend for a week. The water stands as a symbol for the cleansing of body and spirit. It is also supposed to rinse away the sins and bad luck from the past year. To prepare for this, it is best to be in a swimsuit. Or if in work clothes, wrap your money or any other items you hope to keep dry in plastic. Songkran entails throwing a massive amount of water around, and more specifically, at each other.

You could not get from point A to point B without getting completely soaked. If you rode a bus to the squadron, the windows would be open due to the heat, and people would throw buckets full of water at the bus as it made its way down the street. Even in the Officer's Club, I remember the half-inch standing water on the floor near the bar. It is all done in wholesome fun, but you had to realize and accept there was no way to stay dry! Water was lurking everywhere, even where you least expected it!

I coordinated a thirty-day leave with Fran around the Easter holiday, when Bill would be off from school. There were "Young Tiger" flights (KC-135 tankers) I could take from Utapao RTAFB, Thailand to March AFB in California, followed by a connection to Texas from there.

We all knew life was both routine and temporary at Udorn. Do your job, stay fit and healthy, complete some educational requirements, socialize, have fun, laugh, keep in touch with home, plan for the future, and ultimately, get home safely. Many of us shared photos and stories of our families. This helped to stay connected to home in a group fashion. It was a common goal as we also worked together as a team.

▪ EVERY SQUADRON HAS AT LEAST ONE

We had a few pilot and WSO misfits. Some pilots had big egos and always talked about how good they were in the aircraft. They would also say, "If you're not a pilot, you ain't ..." Use your imagination for the last word of that ridiculous statement! The good aircrew members, and there were many, did not talk about it; they demonstrated how good they were through their commendable actions and professional abilities. The WSOs and pilots knew how to separate the wheat from the chaff. Capabilities are one thing, but idiotic behavior is something else.

There was one WSO who just annoyed everyone, not the least of whom was me.

Not only did I share everyone's opinion about this guy, but I also had to share a room with him in the hooch for a time. That was pure agony.

I won't use his real name, and since I have four stories to tell, I have named him Lt. Quattro. In my 28 October letter to Fran, I mentioned that "my roommate is a real ass," and that I got along with most of the guys at Udorn, but, "this idiot is in a class by himself." I learned that he had several roommates before me, and they all moved to other rooms when that became possible. The guy was inconsiderate, sloppy, noisy, lacked common sense, talked to himself (a lot), and thought the AF owed him everything. And he was a loner. I never saw him hang with anyone. Gee, I wonder why!

In a way, it was sad. I reminded myself that he was there in SEA to serve our country, and to his credit, he graduated from navigator training and RF-4C training. But that becomes a fleeting thought when you observe all the nutty things he constantly did. You revert and focus on his most distinguishing characteristic—he's an idiot!

Film Depletion

Lt. Quattro and his pilot were scheduled for a training sortie. After planning the flight to acquire four targets, they proceeded to the aircraft, completed the checklist items, and were taxiing to the end of the runway for takeoff clearance. The WSO went through several more checklist items during taxiing, including checking the camera operation. He turns the three cameras (forward-looking, low-panoramic, and high-altitude) to the on position and observes that the film counters decrease. This indicates the cameras are operational. The WSO must then immediately turn the cameras off before completing the taxi checklist.

Right after Lt. Quattro turned the cameras on, he got distracted. Maybe he was having a conversation with himself. Who knows? He didn't realize the cameras remained on until they had gone through the last checks at the end of the runway, with the crew chiefs, for any fuel, oil, hydraulic fluid leaks, and other checks before taking a takeoff position. He told the pilot that they were out of film. I can imagine what the pilot thought! Thank goodness it was a training sortie and not a combat support mission. They flew the route nonetheless to get the training completed.

When the crew returned to Udorn and went through the normal process of debriefing the flight, the photo-processing personnel showed Lt. Quattro all the beautiful hundreds of feet of expensive Eastman Kodak photos of the aircraft's nose gear and concrete taxiway he took. It was meant to be a teaching moment. I'm not sure it sank in!

Nude Sunbathing

There was a deck on top of the hooches where you could gather to socialize or catch some rays. Most of us did that from time to time. The weather in northern Thailand was mild with little rain and much sunshine through the fall and winter, until the monsoons and rain began in March. You bring up a towel, lie down, and get some sun. It was that simple.

Not for Lt. Quattro! He decided he would go au naturel but took it a step further. He constructed an elaborate array of aluminum foil that surrounded his entire body to deflect the sun's rays in the hope of getting that perfectly balanced tan. He did this often. We got to the point that we didn't want to see this anymore when we went up top for some sunshine. We found a few buckets, filled them with iced water, snuck up the stairway, and let him have it! Another example of grown men, perhaps very bored, in need of some entertainment! Needless to say, he didn't go nude anymore!

Gecko in a Pickle Jar

I love this one! One day, Lt. Quattro walked into our room with a large pickle jar. Inside the pickle jar was a giant gecko, about eight or nine inches long. I asked, "What is that gecko doing in there?"

One of the senior wing officers was departing Udorn for his next assignment, and many of us would celebrate his service and send him off in the usual celebratory fashion. Quattro had this brilliant idea that the gecko would be a great gift! He said, "I am going to present this to our guest of honor at the Sawadee party tonight!"

Oh, I'm sure he will be thrilled! I mused.

Quattro proceeded to open the jar lid and poke a bent coat hanger into the jar in an unsuccessful attempt to remove the gecko. I thought he was just provoking it in some way and his foofaraw caused me to ask, "Why are you doing that?" He said he wanted to get the gecko out so he could put some stones and grass in the bottom of the jar. *Did he think the gecko would enjoy that environment much better than a bare jar?*

I said, "Just use your hands. You won't get him out with a coat hanger!" Of course, he never thought to turn the jar upside down and shake the little guy out.

He replied, "No! He'll bite."

I said, "Geckos don't bite. Just stick your hand in there."

He hesitated and asked, "Are you sure?"

With all seriousness, I said, "Yes, I'm sure. I know they don't bite."

He seemed happy to hear this. He put the coat hanger down and stuck his hand in the jar. At that point, the gecko latched onto the soft skin of his hand between his thumb and forefinger and would not let go.

Quattro screamed as he waved his hand to try to disengage with the gecko, who was clearly out for revenge. It apparently bit down hard as Quattro's screaming continued. Quattro then screamed at me. "I thought you said they didn't bite!"

With a grin, I simply replied, "I lied!" It felt good to side with the gecko on this one.

Light Bulbs

This one is even better. It's my favorite! Our rooms at Udorn were simple. When you entered, you were in one section with some seating, a table, a fridge, and nothing else. From there, you entered a room further back that had two beds and lockers. There is no door to the bedroom area, just a hanging cloth to offer some sense of decoration.

I had a long day and got into bed early, around 9:30 p.m. I turned all the lights off. Lt. Quattro was out somewhere, doing something crazy; I was sure. Suddenly, he entered from the outside and turned on the lights. My hopes of falling asleep were impeded. After a few seconds of hearing him talk to himself, I hoped he would realize I was in bed and turn the lights off. No such luck. In fact, after about a minute of mumbling, he left the room. I thought, *OK, why didn't numbnuts turn the lights off? Maybe he'll be right back.*

No such luck again. After a few minutes, I got up from the bed and turned the lights off. Back in bed, I covered myself and cozied up for a nice restful night. He came back a few minutes later, and as he flipped the lights on again, he said, loud enough for me to hear him, "What the?" That's all he said, no more, no less, just, "What the?" Like he was perplexed! I'm sure he was perplexed!

My anger intensified. I was about to get up and tell him to keep the lights off when he quickly left the room again and did not turn the lights off. *I'm gonna kill this guy!* Same routine. I got up, turned the lights off, and went back to bed. A few minutes later, he returned and said the same thing to himself as before. He did not display any sense that maybe *I* turned the lights off, not the fairy godmother! He didn't say anything that indicated he would just be a few minutes and turn the lights off. No, nothing like that!

Before I disclose my remedy for this, I want to relate a similar story that involved a legendary actor, Steve McQueen. After McQueen established himself as a bankable movie star, he purchased a mansion in Malibu, California. His next-door neighbor, Keith Moon, drummer of the famous English rock band The Who, lived the partying lifestyle of many rock stars. Particularly annoying to the actor was that the drummer always left his bathroom light on, the light that faced McQueen's bedroom window, affecting his sleep.

You see where this is going.

McQueen asked Moon numerous times to be mindful of turning off the bathroom light, but Moon continued to ignore his pleas. McQueen grabbed a shotgun one night, leaned out the window, and shot the light out. Problem solved!

Now back to Udorn, to the hooches, to my room, and to my own "Keith Moon." I didn't have a shotgun. If I did, I might have used it! While he was gone, I rose from my bed once again, went into the other room, and removed the light bulbs. In fact, I removed all the light bulbs everywhere in the room, including the bed area, and hid them under my bed. He returned and flipped the switch several times with the same, "What the," coming from his mouth.

I got up, stormed toward him, and said, "I am trying to get some sleep, and you keep going in and out of the room, leaving the lights on, when anyone would realize that *I* turned them off!" He just looked at me.

I continued, "I have *all* the bulbs. You can't have them back until you show some consideration!" The expression on his face told me that maybe he grasped this. Or maybe not. Nonetheless, I did not replace the bulbs for several days. This was in October, and I did not move to another room until mid-December, when Mitch Mitchell rotated back to the States. His roommate had his family in Thailand and lived off the base, so I finally had a room to myself when I took Mitch's room. Until then, I conducted several more teachable moments for Lt. Quattro. There were plenty of opportunities for that!

■ LET'S GET BILL HOME

This is a complex story with many moving parts, any one of which could have impacted my visit home to Austin. All along, Fran and I discussed by letter and over the phone when the best time would be for me to come home for a thirty-day leave. We targeted the end of March since Easter would be on the twenty-sixth, and I could start my visit with Bill's spring break from school.

There was a deployment of RF-4Es (retrofitted RF-4Cs) that crews from the States would deliver to Japan. The aircrews would then come to Udorn to deploy five of our RF-4Cs to Shaw AFB in South Carolina. A pilot from the 14th TRS, Henry Johnson, and I were selected to be an airborne spare for the deployment back to the States. I had flown with Henry several times, two of which were in combat support missions, so we knew each other fairly well.

As the spare, we would take off with the state-bound crews for the first leg of the deployment, which was to Guam—about a six-hour flight with three inflight refuelings. We would fly to the first refueling point, and if any of the other aircraft dropped out of the deployment for any reason, we would continue to Guam. From there, Henry and I would continue to the next leg of the deployment to Hickam AFB, Hawaii. The next legs of the trip were to George AFB, California, then to Bergstrom AFB, Texas (where I could see Fran and the boys overnight), and finally to Shaw AFB for the last leg of the trip. Then I would go back to Austin for leave.

The crews ferrying the RF-4Es got to Hawaii from the States but encountered several maintenance problems that would delay their delivery to Japan. After much coordination, the AF decided to leave the RF-4Es at Hickam for the necessary repairs and directed the aircrews to Udorn to deploy the RF-4Cs to Shaw AFB. They would send other aircrews to Hickam to deliver the RF-4Es to Japan when the aircraft were ready.

The stateside crews showed up at Udorn in early February 1975. Henry and I were still tagged as the spare if needed past the first inflight refueling point. Now all along, my buddies in the 14th TRS knew how much I wanted to get home to see my family. We all often talked about that mutual desire. But they went above and beyond.

We decided to invite the aircrews from the States to a party on 4 February, the night before the deployment. Henry and I went very light on the alcohol since we had regulation restrictions regarding alcohol consumption by a given number of hours before a flight. For the most part, they were cautious with the booze, but we focused on the weakest link, and one WSO was going a little too far. We found out the next day that it wasn't a hangover that grounded him; he had become sick with flu symptoms. Since they flew as a team, both the pilot and WSO were grounded. Perfect—I'm in!

On Fran's birthday, 5 February, Henry and I took off with the other four RF-4C aircrews headed for Guam and arrived after our 5.8-hour flight. I notified Fran I was on my way home! We had a one-day layover in Guam and departed for Hickam AFB on 7 February. After four air refuelings and a 6.9-hour flight, we arrived in Hawaii. I thought, *This is great. I'll be home soon!*

Not so fast! As we taxied into position at Hickam and cut the engines, who came running toward the aircraft? The WSO who was left "very sick" back at Udorn. He immediately traveled from Thailand to Hawaii and, with the day layover we had in Guam, recovered from whatever ailment he had. He was back on flying status. Crap!

He informed us that he would be authorized to fly as Henry's back seater from Hawaii to the States to complete the deployment. I'm not sure why his pilot did not show up. Not the news I wanted to hear. My TDY status was now effectively over unless I returned to Udorn. I had to quickly determine what I would do next. I could go on leave and fly commercially to Austin from Hawaii, or I could return to Udorn to complete my TDY and continue with my plan to go on leave in late March.

Another thought came to mind. What about the tankers, the KC-135s that accompanied the RF-4Cs across the ocean for refueling? Perhaps I could get a ride on that to some destination in the States. That turned out to be the perfect solution. I spoke to the KC-135 aircraft commander, and he was more than willing to take me on as an "aircrew passenger" for the trip back to Little Rock AFB, Arkansas. Once there, I could easily get a short commercial flight to Austin, Texas.

We departed Hawaii on 9 February. Now I was in the deployment, only this time from the vantage point of the tanker, not the RF-4C. I had fun watching the refuelings from the boom operator's position in the rear of the tanker. He even let me operate the boom that connects with the RF-4C for refueling. In the prone position, I connected the refueling boom with Henry's aircraft and was providing him a fuel offload when he said, "I have to add a little power here, falling back a little."

He didn't know I was operating the refueling boom. I replied, "Not a problem, Henry. That's just me on the boom. Too much backward pressure?"

He said … On second thought, I won't tell you what he said, but we did laugh about it a bit. I quickly turned the boom operation back to the expert.

My view from the KC-135 tanker of Henry, ready to hook up for air-to-air refueling.

We arrived at Little Rock AFB too late for me to connect commercially to Austin. The tanker squadron commander, a lieutenant colonel, came out to meet his crew.

They, in turn, introduced me to him. He learned how I deployed to Hawaii and needed a ride to Texas. He was most accommodating and courteous. He took me to his office to use his phone to check on flights to Austin. When I told him I could only get a flight out the next day, he said, "Well, let's get you set up in the BOQ for tonight, and we'll get you to the airport tomorrow!"

What a great guy! He drove me to the BOQ and arranged for my transport to the airport the next day. I thanked him but thought to ask, "How often do you fly out to Hickam? Could I possibly get a hop back there to return on TDY status?"

He said I could fly on one of what he called, "my birds." He gave me a schedule, and I determined the day I would return from Austin to Little Rock AFB in mid-March to catch a ride again on a KC-135. This could not have worked out much better. I was grateful for all the support from my buddies in the 14th TRS and my aircrew friends in the KC-135s.

When I arrived home in Austin, it was a very happy reunion. I looked a bit different, weighing 169 pounds. Fran had lost some weight too, not that she needed it. After a month at home, it was tough to leave again. I think Bill understood that I needed to go back, but Joey, at eighteen months old, was confused. He must have wondered, *Why is Daddy going away again?*

I arrived back at Udorn on 14 March. The guys asked how my leave was. I responded with one word: "Terrific!" My first flight after taking leave was with my friend Guy Munder on 17 March, in what I described in a letter to Fran as flying in the "forbidden land." This was my fourteenth combat support mission, and I was glad I was teamed with someone I immensely respected and trusted.

I'd fly with Guy Munder anytime, anywhere!
Photos: Courtesy of Guy Munder

■ IN-THEATER COMBAT SUPPORT

My time in the 14th TRS (September 1974–July 1975) was during a phase that lasted two and a half years and was termed the "Final Draw Down and Surveillance Phase," which began after Operation Linebacker II (18–22 December 1972) and continued through the collapse of Cambodia, South Vietnam, and finally ended with the SS *Mayaguez* incident (12–15 May 1975).

The squadron ops desk was the communications hub to the aircrews and the wing command post, which was staffed by several officers and enlisted men. This command center had communications with the base tower, fire and rescue, the supervisor of flying (SOF), and other base services via phone—some open, some secure—and radio links to other bases and their resources. It would monitor the flight activity for all squadrons with representatives from each squadron. Most aircrews, including myself, occasionally pulled duty for several hours in the wing command post.

At the ops desk, we would see the list of daily aircraft sorties, with aircraft serial numbers and airfield parking location, names of the crew—pilot and WSO—and the aircraft call sign. The 14th TRS had the call sign Atlanta with a number designation for each sortie, such as Atlanta 45, Atlanta 06, and so on. Specific call sign numbers were assigned to the upper echelon of aircrew members, such as the wing commander and the deputy commander for operations.

Combat support missions included specific targets provided by intelligence sources to the 14th TRS. They were in both Cambodia and South Vietnam and had a connection to Vietcong activity that was becoming more prevalent there and would lead to each country's seizure. It also included reconnaissance overflight, reporting, and sensor coverage of specific sites for two primary operations associated with civilians and government personnel evacuation.

While the air war in Vietnam was virtually over, the ground activity continued to pose a serious threat to both South Vietnam and Cambodia. I kept many articles from the *Pacific Stars and Stripes* and underlined key sentences. I sometimes made some notation of my flights in the margins. These stories described ground skirmishes, communist advancements from the north, and incidents leading up to Phnom Penh and Saigon evacuations.

The Vietcong approach to Cambodia's capital, Phnom Penh, resulted in the increased isolation of that major city, even though the United States stepped up resupply efforts. Our reconnaissance flights over all approaches to the capital became essential in estimating the conditions on the ground. Conditions worsened rapidly, causing the rebels to limit flying to and from Pochentong airport, which shortly later closed all flights due to constant rocket attacks.

I flew a reconnaissance mission on 22 January 1975 to image several highways that led into the capital city. Two days later, 24 January 1975, I flew another mission seven thousand feet over Pochentong and seven areas around the airport to gather photo intelligence. The Mekong River became more essential as a means to deliver critical supplies to the capital. A short time later, I would fly another mission to cover supply routes along the river south of the capital.

I participated in twenty-one combat support sorties between 6 November 1974 and 5 May 1975. Each of these was a single-ship sortie (meaning one aircraft) assigned for the mission. The targets were varied and required a full array of aircraft sensors. They were all during daylight hours; some were in inclement weather. I present a few of the more memorable episodes.

In full combat support gear.

Alone, Unarmed, and Unafraid

The role of the RF-4C and its aircrew has a powerful story that I held off telling until now. It is more germane to the SEA theater of operations than RF-4C training at Shaw AFB or operational training and certification to become combat-ready in the 91st TRS at Bergstrom AFB.

Our training at both locations exposed us to a special training story, *Alone, Unarmed, and Unafraid*—a thirty-nine-minute video filmed on location in SEA during the height of the war in Vietnam. Robert Stack, the actor who starred in *The Untouchables*

(1959–1963), narrated the film. He traveled to SEA to speak with recce aircrews and came to understand the tactical reconnaissance mission. The story naturally belongs here.

This video well defines the recce mission. The RF-4C aircrews are *alone*; there is no fighter escort or support against enemy threats. They are *unarmed*; there is no aircraft armament or countermeasure other than speed and terrain masking to negotiate or dodge the enemy. As for *unafraid*, I don't recall any crew member, me included, who didn't use his training to counter or face a stressful situation in the air. I firmly believe that the more you rely on your training, the less likely you are to be subject to second thoughts and perhaps find yourself in a situation where you *do* become scared.

One of the senior officers in the film, who just returned from a recce mission, simply described the tactical reconnaissance role in a hostile environment. He said, "Fighters go, Boom, Boom; RF-4Cs go Click, Click." And I would like to add to that: "Then you haul your ass out of there!"

Use Your Training

One situation to best describe this occurred in Cambodia, when my pilot and I had several targets near Phnom Penh. There was intelligence of significant Vietcong occupation and movement that needed updated sensor coverage that included imagery from both camera and infrared systems. We departed Udorn and headed south to the Thai-Cambodian border, where we hooked up with a KC-135 tanker to top off our jet fuel before letting down into Cambodia.

RF-4C AAR off a KC-135 tanker.

We initiated radio silence as we entered and descended into Cambodian airspace. We continued in a southeasterly direction, crossing over the ancient temple, Angkor Wat, and a section of Tonlé Sap, a freshwater lake south of the temple. We obtained imagery of the assigned pinpoint targets at a low level, and at a GS of 540 knots without incident. We then proceeded to a stretch of the Mekong River southeast of the capital, where we needed to take side-looking coverage of a forty-eight-kilometer section (about thirty miles) of road parallel to the river in the Kandal Province.

Angkor Wat, my RF–4C photo.

Due to Cambodian T-28 flight operations in the same area, we needed to maintain a safe separation. They were instructed to fly no higher than 3,800 feet AGL. We were instructed to fly no lower than 4,500 feet AGL. Just before reaching our IP, we both observed a T-28 rapidly cross directly under us from the 11 o'clock position to the 5 o'clock position. It was fast—an instant! If we had occupied the same altitude, we would have collided. But since we both followed the rules, we had a safe separation.

Shortly after that thrill, we quickly obtained a very visible IP along the river and hacked our watches. Within a few seconds, we approached the target area, and I turned on the infrared camera. We were about 75 percent finished when we heard a series of beeps in our headsets at a constant rate called PRF (pulse repetition frequency)—*beep . . . . . beep . . . . . beep . . . . . beep.*

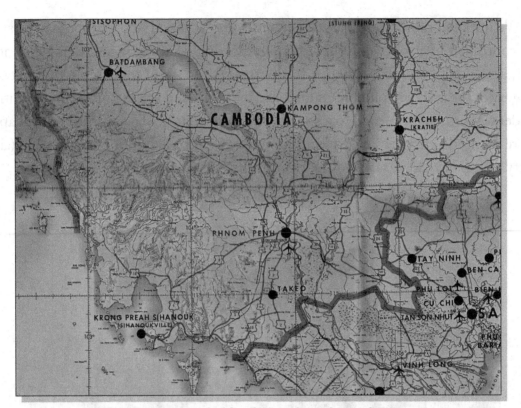

Phnom Penh, capital of Cambodia, photo of my cockpit map.

A visual cue accompanied this aural indication on our RHAW (radar homing and warning) scope. At the center of the scope is the position of our aircraft relative to the clock positions surrounding it. A thin line emanated from our rear quadrant at about the 7 o'clock position to the scope center. The pilot and I interpreted the combination of aural tone and visual indication as a potential threat coming from behind us and slightly to our left. We monitored this as we approached the end of our infrared coverage.

The indication meant we were being observed by some acquisition system or radar, most likely from the ground. The intensity of both the line on the scope and the tone in the headset increased as the scope line of sight became heavier, and the beeps in our headsets became more frequent—*beep … beep … beep … beep*. This told us that whatever was tracking us was moving from one phase to the next, from mere observation to pre-lock-on/prior launch. We were nearly at the end of our infrared coverage when the final indications caused us to take immediate and drastic action.

The beeps now merged into one long solid tone, no longer spaced with silence between the beeps—*beeeeeeeeep!* The line of the RHAW scope indicated that a SAM was in launch mode. The pilot immediately executed a series of S turns, where I could look behind the aircraft to acquire the missile visually.

SA-2 (S-75 Dvina).
Photo: Courtesy of Creative Commons, license: Share Alike 4.0 International,
https://commons.wikipedia.org/wiki/File:S-75_Dvina.jpg.

The SA-2s and SA-3s Russian-built aircraft weapons were the sizes of telephone poles. The S-75 Dvina missiles utilized command guidance using either Fan Song or Spoon Rest radar systems for tracking and launch. Their range could extend to forty-five kilometers (twenty-eight miles), and they packed a fragmentation warhead of up to 430 pounds. They had a lethal radius of sixty-five meters (213 feet) at lower altitudes.

These SAMs can be detected visually without too much difficulty. The training and practice we had in specially designated areas in the States taught us how to evade such missiles using a high-G maneuver tactic. Once you visually acquire the missile, if you try to outrun it, you will get shot down, or at the very least, take on some heavy aircraft damage. But the SA-2s and 3s could not out-turn the RF-4C or other fighter-type aircraft. The best countermeasure was to acquire the missile visually, wait until it was within a few seconds of impact, and then execute a high-G turn into the missile's path. This would enable the aircrew to outmaneuver the missile by going in the opposite direction before impact. The missile could not match the aircraft's change in direction or catch up.

This is a simplified version of the evolution of countermeasures fighter-type aircraft employed throughout the war in SEA as SAM capabilities and associated weaponry improved. In parallel, the fighters developed electronic countermeasures (ECMs) and flight maneuvers like those used by RF-4C aircrews.

As we made several S turns, we did not pick up the threat but continued to get the aural and visual indications at full strength. We had to take some other action. After the pilot rolled the aircraft downward and pushed the throttles forward and into the afterburner detents, he snapped, "I'm gonna hit the deck."

"Roger. Still don't see anything," I stated.

We were on the deck in a few seconds, flying fifty feet above the Mekong River in full afterburner, going over one thousand knots (1,150 mph). As the pilot continued to bank from side to side, we still had no visual indication of anything except all the people we blew out of their boats on the river due to breaking the sound barrier. The shock wave from our aircraft did its thing!

Mekong River near Phnom Penh.
Photo: Courtesy of Skye Bajoul, Trek Earth.

The headset tone and the scope indications disappeared. We throttled back and climbed out, heading northwest for the most direct route back to Udorn. Using engine afterburners consumes four times the average fuel flow, so you cannot sustain an exceedingly high ground speed for very long. Typical fuel consumption at a low level and at high speed (540 knots) is 150 pounds per minute. Engine afterburner consumes four times that—six hundred pounds per minute! We arrived back at Udorn after 2.8 hours of flight time, provided an in-depth briefing to intelligence and the aircrews, and acquired all our target coverage.

Alone, unarmed, and with no time to be afraid. It is when you think about the mission after you get back to your room at the day's end that you might feel otherwise. It was always best to just focus on your next mission and plan accordingly. Trust your training!

"I Will Ground You"

It's one thing to exercise all your planning, preparation, briefing, and training for such missions to ensure the best chance for its success. It's another to go through those steps and ignore them or deliberately put them in jeopardy. This happened on another combat support mission in Cambodia. We had the usual four targets; all of them required pinpoint coverage. The pilot I flew with on this mission had a bit of an ego issue that I was aware of, as word gets around about the aircrews that prefer to talk about how great they are rather than demonstrate their abilities.

For our last assigned target, which again was in the vicinity of the Cambodian capital, we were required to fly low level at high speed for specific camera coverage. All was going well for the first three targets, but for some reason, the pilot, who will remain nameless, decided it would be a great idea to try a different tactic to acquire the last target.

He said, "Bill, let's get this last target using a pop-up to about ten thousand feet, visually acquire it, and dive in for the coverage."

I was stunned for a moment by this intentional change in procedure. I was an IWSO and certified Stan/Eval member. I said something like, "No, we are not doing that. We planned and briefed the procedure, and we need to stick to the plan."

He insisted, "C'mon, it'll be fun. No problem."

I came back this time more forcefully: "Why would you put us at risk at such an altitude where some threat could pick us up? We would be much more vulnerable. If you do that, I will make sure you are grounded once we return to Udorn." I hated to have to say that as we were engaged in a mission in hostile territory, but it was necessary. Penalties could result in a much worse situation than just a grounding.

I had every authority to do that as a SEFE, and I would have. He backed off. We acquired the last target and returned to Udorn. After our briefings with intelligence and the photo interpreters, the pilot and I had a private discussion where I emphasized how angry I was that we even had that encounter in the aircraft, especially in a combat environment that day. We kept it to ourselves. I never heard of any problem from him after that, although I put out some feelers without disclosing why. Life went on. I found out later this pilot went home on leave to get divorced.

Crushed Cookies

When the pilot and WSO don't work as a team, as was possible in this last episode, your life becomes increasingly threatened. There is no need for that. So when a real emergency happens, you can appreciate the crew putting their heads together to mitigate or eliminate any risk.

On another day, 20 December, it was to visit our friends to the south again, acquire more intelligence, and log another combat support sortie when our flight rapidly deteriorated with several simultaneous malfunctions. This occurred in southern Thailand, on our way to an air refueling rendezvous before flying into Cambodia. Capt. Harris and I were crewed together for this mission. At this point, he had about seven hundred hours of RF-4C time; I had four hundred thirty-one hours.

We had a major power distribution electrical bus failure indicated by several obvious signs—fifteen electrical circuit breakers popped in the rear cockpit, we lost our UHF and VHF radio communications, we lost all navigation equipment except for the whiskey compass (magnetic), and we lost generators. Both AC and DC electrical power were affected. We also had some fuel transfer problems. It was a serious condition, and we needed to act fast! While the pilot focused on flying with limited electrical power, I pulled out one of my two survival radios and made a call on UHF guard channel 243.0 (for military operations). This frequency is often used for emergencies.

"This is Atlanta two-three on guard; request immediate assistance," I called out. This alerted several key response elements, including our wing command post and squadron operations at Udorn.

Fortunately, we had visual flight conditions and could see major geographical features on the ground and match them to our maps. One prominent feature was the Mun River, which we knew was directly west of Ubon Ratchathani, Thailand, and Ubon RTAFB. The base was eighty-five miles to our east. After running through our checklist to address this emergency and coordinate with our home operations, a joint decision to land at Ubon became clear. We knew we would not make it back to Udorn, and we needed to notify the closest airbase.

After a series of communications and handoffs by our command post and squadron at Udorn, and by us over the survival radio, we eventually got connected with Ubon approach control, declared an emergency, and landed there without incident. Their operations were in a drawdown phase, and there were no maintenance assets on the base that could address our aircraft problem. The operations and ground support at Ubon were great as they became fully engaged in our recovery effort.

The pilot and I would return to Udorn via the C-130 military transport aircraft that made the rounds daily to all bases in Thailand. We would be able to catch a ride back to Udorn later that same day. The next day, our wing would send a maintenance crew to Ubon with aircraft parts and supplies to make the aircraft airworthy again. Another crew would return to Ubon via the C-130 to recover the aircraft once it was ready to fly again and return to Udorn. Later, Harris and I, and our ops support at Udorn were commended for our actions in this emergency.

After we got something to eat, we waited at base operations for the C-130; we were in our flight gear—flight suits, G suits, survival vests, and weapons, with small flight bags for our helmets, checklists, maps, and so on. It was turning into a long day, and we wanted to get back to Udorn. We knew the C-130 ride would noisily make its way to a few stops before we arrived at our base; it was certainly not the fastest either.

Finally, we were aboard, the only passengers except for the aircraft's crew—two pilots and a loadmaster. We took off from Ubon, seated in web seating on one side of the aircraft, facing several cargo pallets cinched down to prevent movement. We settled back, anticipating a nap to pass the time until we landed at Udorn.

We were leveling off at some cruise altitude when the loadmaster (an enlisted troop) had finished his checklist, whatever that entailed, and came toward us. He stopped at the pallet of cargo directly in front of us and proceeded to climb to the top of the bags, stomping on them as he made his way to the top, about five feet above us. He stopped and then lay down on the pile to prepare for a nap. I was furious!

I called out to him, "Hey, come down from there," with all the anger I could transfer to my facial expression. He came down with a bit of concern showing. I asked, "What are you doing up there?"

He replied, "I was just going to get some sleep before the next stop."

I pulled out my .38 caliber weapon and waved it at him. "I should shoot you!" His eyes grew wide. I got in his face. "Now I know why the cookies my wife sends me are always crushed and in crumbs! Because you go stomping all over the mail!" He was motionless.

I told him never to do that again, and if I got crushed cookies again, I would come for him, that I had his name. He disappeared out of sight. I probably should not have pulled the weapon, but hey, crushed cookies deserved drastic measures. My pilot observed all this, did not intervene, yawned, and continued his sleep. I think he was just amused.

Operation Eagle Pull: Phnom Penh Evacuation

Air War over South Vietnam, 1968–1975, by Bernard C. Nalty, gives an excellent account of the falls of Cambodia and South Vietnam to the Vietcong in the spring of 1975. I provide top-level coverage to emphasize the role that the 14th TRS had in the final days' operations. Needless to say, there were numerous military resources focused on the activities surrounding these events with oversight from the US State Department and the executive branch.

The flaws in the Cambodian military structure, the American B-52 bombing halt in 1973, and the determination of the Khmer Rouge sealed the doom of the Khmer Republic. On 1 April 1975, after the Khmer Rouge captured Neak Luong, a commercial town sixty-one kilometers (thirty-eight miles) southeast of Phnom Penh, Lon Nol, a Cambodian general and prime minister, fled the country. Within five days, only fifty embassy staff members remained in Phnom Penh.

AF and marine units made final preparations to carry out Operation Eagle Pull. On 3 April, at the request of Ambassador John Gunther Deane, an AF HH-53 flew the combat element of a marine security force to the embassy grounds in Phnom Penh. Enemy troops had already entered the suburbs of the capital when Ambassador Deane, on 10 April, requested that the operation begin two days later.

Operation Eagle Pull was one of several US Advisory Group, 7th AF-directed combat missions. The 7th Airborne Command and Control Squadron at Udorn provided the C-130 airborne battlefield command and control center for the overall direction of the operation.

The role of the 14th TRS was to fly reconnaissance and weather surveillance at and around the extraction point for the evacuation of Phnom Penh on 12 April 1975 and provide inflight reports. I was selected as the lead WSO for this two-aircraft mission, which provided real-time reports that initiated the evacuation. Our call sign was Spear Lead. The airborne command post in orbit over northwest Cambodia was Cricket.

The first helicopter launched at 0615 hours, immediately after my reports to higher authorities while airborne. Captain Head was the pilot I flew with to support this operation. We briefed the mission with the second crew at 0130 hours that Saturday to take off at 0515 hours and landed back at Udorn at 0715.

That day, an HH-53 landed an AF control team, and marine CH-53s brought the remainder of the security force and carried out 276 passengers, including Ambassador

Deane. As the extraction was nearly complete, rockets began exploding at the soccer field that served as the landing zone as the last two AF helicopters took off. Both HH-53s sustained damage from Khmer Rouge machine guns, and the one that carried the marines was vibrating badly throughout the flight to Ubon AB, Thailand, where the two helicopters landed safely.

In my letter dated 19 April, I sent Fran an article from the *Pacific Stars and Stripes* newspaper, dated 17 April 1975: "Gayler Hails Services' Teamwork in Eagle Pull." The article described a "perfect example of joint operations," as it applied to the evacuation of personnel from the Cambodian capital city. Admiral Noel Gayler was the US Pacific commander in chief who directed the operation.

I also sent another article to Fran from the same newspaper on 20 April 1975: "Phnom Penh the Beautiful." The article had a photo of the view of the city beside the Mekong River that personnel would have seen as they evacuated in what the article described as "one of Southeast Asia's most beautiful cities where 600,000 people lived a uniquely relaxed existence among tree-shaded streets and graceful French-style buildings."

The article described the terrible conditions that evolved—two million refugees, homeless people in shacks that sprung up everywhere, wounded and emaciated children filling every bed in the city's hospitals; the list went on. In my letter, I expressed my deep frustration with how all the effort in SEA was going down the drain. I was not only frustrated, I was also outraged as I let my opinions fly. And today, Afghanistan! Why do we do this to ourselves? Why do we invest so much in losing and maiming so many?

With the accelerated plunge of the Khmer Republic into oblivion, the threat to South Vietnam intensified.

Operation Frequent Wind: Saigon Evacuation

Right after Eagle Pull, I was selected to be the first WSO flight commander in the wing at Udorn in May 1975. Our squadron commander, Lt. Col. Gibson, had a small group he called his "hardcore" to his trailer for a steak dinner. At that dinner, he announced I would take over D-flight with five pilots and four WSOs under my supervision.

Traditionally, flight commanders were pilots. It was documented in the Udorn *Easy Flyer* newspaper, 20 June 1975 issue, stating, "Weapons Officer, 1st flight leader. Captain William A. Cimino of the 14th Tactical Reconnaissance Squadron (TRS) is the first weapon systems officer (WSO) to become a flight commander in the 432nd Tactical Fighter Wing."

Weapons officer
1st flight leader

Capt. William A. Cimino of the 14th Tactical Reconnaissance Squadron (TRS) is the first weapons systems officer (WSO) to become a flight commander in the 432nd Tactical Fighter Wing.

Traditionally, the position of flight commander has been exclusively held by pilots. Air Force policy was recently changed, however, opening the position to any officer.

Captain Cimino, who arrived here last August, took over B Flight of the 14th TRS May 27. He supervises four pilots and five WSOs in the flight.

Three months after his arrival here, the captain was upgraded to instructor WSO and standardization-evaluation flight examiner for the squadron. He has 625 flying hours in the McDonnell-Douglas RF-4 Phantom II aircraft.

A graduate of St. John's University in New York City, Captain Cimino entered the Air Force in July 1967. He holds a bachelor of science degree in mathematics and has earned 12 hours towards a masters degree in business.

The captain's hometown is Rhineback, N.Y. He and his wife, Fran, have two sons, Bill, 7; and Joey, 2. He enjoys paddleball and handball.

Whereas US aid to South Vietnam declined, the Hanoi regime could deliver cargo to the battlefield in greater volume than ever before. Once the threat of aerial attack subsided, the North Vietnamese began extending the Ho Chi Minh Trail to the Mekong Delta. They delivered supplies with caravans of more than two hundred vehicles that rolled by day and night.

South Vietnam president Nguyễn Văn Thiệu, knew there would be no dramatic infusion of material aid from the United States. He revised any plans to defend the northern provinces that were still under Saigon's control. Instead of launching an orderly withdrawal, Thiệu succeeded only in creating doubt followed by panic as troops and civilians sought the dubious safety of the southernmost provinces. The United States sent cargos of military equipment to the embattled country, and rather than return empty, the C-5A aircraft provided evacuations as needed.

As conditions around Saigon became desperate, AF and marine helicopters prepared to join the cargo planes that were pressed into service. The evacuation of Saigon, Operation Frequent Wind, used both transports and helicopters in conjunction with ships. During the entire month of April 1975, there were numerous evacuation flights and fighting on the ground around Saigon and the closest Republic of Vietnam air force facility, Tan Son Nhut Air Base, with US Army, USAF, US Navy, and US Marine units there.

As the evacuations by air continued, there were also evacuations of personnel, civilians and military, and equipment made to Côn Sơn Island, in the South China Sea, about 147 miles due south of Saigon. In early May, the 14th TRS received an assignment to obtain imagery of the entire island. However, there were severe restrictions on how we would be able to obtain the coverage. With the fall of Cambodia and South Vietnam, we were not permitted to overfly either country. This included Côn Sơn Island.

Capt. Campbell and I were assigned to this mission. It would require a flight south through Thailand with air refueling over the Gulf of Thailand to avoid overflight of Cambodia. We would then proceed around Cambodia to the island located in the South China Sea to get the imagery coverage. We planned the mission on Saturday, 3 May, and were scheduled to fly on Sunday. But the weather was terrible and not conducive to flight or sufficient imagery coverage. Campbell and I were on alert status for a go once the weather broke.

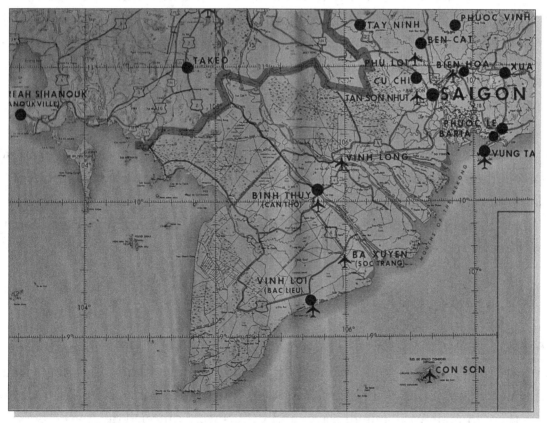

Target area, Con Son Island, south of Saigon in the South China Sea.
Photo of my cockpit map.

I got a knock on my hooch door early on Monday, 5 May, with a short message: "You're a go!" Since we could not overfly the island and needed to be three nautical miles off the coast, it required out-of-the-ordinary planning to get complete island imagery coverage. It was not a simple matter of flying over the target and turning the cameras on. I had to calculate several passes that would require intervalometer settings for the cameras. These are manual inputs for the camera operation that force them to operate differently than usual.

In addition, the pilot would need to fly with the aircraft banked at a constant angle, without turning or changing its heading. The only way to do that is to kick in rudder adjustments to enable the aircraft to fly straight while maintaining a banked attitude off the island's coasts. When you fly in this manner, you feel like you are flying sideways! It's a weird feeling in the cockpit, but it works.

I was particularly proud of this mission, not only for myself, but also for the skill that Capt. Campbell demonstrated. We both received commendations for this mission. Mine included the notation:

> The mission was extremely difficult in that it required complete island photography while avoiding overflight and proximity by three nautical miles. It required a complete utility of piloting and navigational skills and modified systems operations. Precise mission planning and aircraft parameter computation resulted in excellent photo coverage of the island.

We departed the island area after about twenty-five minutes to return via the same route inbound. But due to lack of fuel, we only made it to Utapao Air Base, eighty-seven miles southeast of Bangkok. That sortie took 4.1 hours. We refueled and took off for Udorn the same day, and flew another hour to RTB through very heavy thunderstorms. At times, passing through heavy weather, I could not see the end of our aircraft's wingtips! That was the last, and twenty-first combat support sortie I flew in SEA.

■ USS *MAYAGUEZ*, 12–15 MAY 1975

After my mission in support of Operation Frequent Wind, I flew three, day, visual low-level routes that week in Thailand before Guy Munder and I, and others would head out to Pattaya Beach, Thailand, for a well-earned three-day CTO. We had plans to go there in mid-April, but all leaves and CTOs were canceled due to the activities in Cambodia. We got on the C-130 that left on the afternoon of 11 May, thinking we were now in the home stretch with time to relax a bit.

After a stop in Bangkok, we landed at Utapao AB, then took a forty-minute cab ride to Pattaya after dinner. We arrived at our hotel, The Joint US Military Advisory Group (JUSMAG) Recreation Center. It had a pool, a nice restaurant, and other facilities; the cost was three dollars per night.

On 12 May, we went to the beach, did some water skiing, and walked through Pattaya village. We ended the day with an Italian dinner at La Gratta's. Our dinner, plus tip, was five dollars each. We arranged for a Thai guide to take us to various places on 13 May to do different activities, like snorkeling, water skiing, fishing (an army lieutenant colonel joined us), and excursions to nearby islands. I recall the total fee for his services for the day was four dollars each. We gave him the fish we caught so he could cook them for his family. He was all smiles! It was a pleasant diversion from work.

Our friendly Thai guide for the day.

On 14 May 1975, we took a cab from Pattaya Beach to Utapao to catch the C-130 back to Udorn. The cab ran out of gas a mile from the base's main gate, so we hopped on a *baht* bus for the nickel ride to the gate. It was a great CTO; we spent less than fifty dollars each for the entire trip. As soon as we arrived back at Udorn, we were told we would be on alert due to the seizure of the US merchant ship *Mayaguez* by Cambodian navy gunboats, which set off an international incident two days earlier. The thirty-man crew of the *Mayaguez* was taken hostage, supposedly in international waters, by communist government forces in the country.

The fighters were ready, our recce crews were prepared, and our first task was to ascertain the location of the ship's crew. I was scheduled for a recce mission and then off several times since the situation was so fluid. As it turned out, I did not fly any of the sorties for the recce coverage of the ship and surrounding environs. Still, our aircrews who did participate got excellent photo coverage that contributed to the intelligence of the situation.

The incident occurred from 12–15 May 1975, less than a month after the Khmer Rouge took control of Phnom Penh, ousting the United States–backed Khmer Republic. After the Khmer Rouge seized the US merchant vessel SS *Mayaguez* in a disputed maritime area, the United States mounted a hastily prepared rescue operation. US Marines recaptured the ship and attacked the island of Koh Tang, where it was believed the crew was held as hostages.

Encountering stronger-than-expected defenses on Koh Tang, three USAF helicopters were destroyed during the initial assault. The marines fought a desperate day-long battle with the Khmer Rouge before being evacuated. The *Mayaguez*'s crew was released unharmed by the Khmer Rouge shortly after the attack on Koh Tang began. It was the last battle of the Vietnam War. The last names on the Vietnam Veterans Memorial are the Americans who were killed, including three marines left behind on Koh Tang after the battle and subsequently executed by the Khmer Rouge.

One of the best accounts I have found regarding this incident was covered in *Air War over South Vietnam, 1968–1975*, by Bernard C. Nalty, a reference I mentioned earlier. Chapter 24, "Recapturing Mayaguez: An Epilogue," provides a detailed description of the seizure and its resulting activities.

■ NEW ASSIGNMENT: RAF ALCONBURY

Several months before departing Udorn, I worked to secure my next assignment. I communicated with the Consolidated Base Personnel Office (CBPO) at Udorn and the MPC in San Antonio, Texas. While I was home for leave in February/March, I made a trip to MPC to talk face-to-face with assignment personnel there. All indications pointed to a follow-on assignment at an RF-4C squadron at Zweibrucken Air Base in Germany. Everything official I read stated my assignment would be at Alconbury, and when I contacted assignment personnel about this discrepancy, they told me it would be changed to "Zwi." I received confirmation of this several times.

My friends at Udorn, pilots Guy Munder and Bill Bowman, were excited that we were all going to Europe, and we often talked about getting together. Bill Bowman told me in mid-March that he would go to Zweibrucken Air Base; Guy would go to Alconbury.

On 10 April, CBPO notified me of a 9 April message that changed my assignment from Zweibrucken to Alconbury. In part, it stated that due to current developments, an increase in WSO extensions at the base in Germany, and the changes in date of estimated return from overseas (DEROS) in Alconbury, which effectively meant more WSOs would leave there earlier, would require filling those positions. A bit upsetting, but as Fran and I discussed, the overall housing and cost of living would be better in the United Kingdom, so we set our minds on going there.

On 15 April, I received a letter from the 1st TRS squadron commander at Alconbury, Lt. Col. Karges, who welcomed me. He looked forward to meeting me and assigned John Miller as my sponsor. John knew me and had requested to be my sponsor. I wrote back to Karges on 19 April, thanking him for his letter and saying that I looked forward to serving there in the 1st TRS.

■ PRE-DEPARTURE FROM SEA

During the April–May timeframe, and with all the special missions associated with the fall of both Cambodia and South Vietnam, we continued to get rumors of a rollback in our assignment at Udorn. This meant we would return home earlier than the usual one-year remote tour of duty there. In conjunction with that, we also heard that we would probably deploy our aircraft back to the States. Much of this was in classified communications that I had access to but could not disclose to Fran or anyone else not authorized for such information.

Maj. John Heide, one of the senior officers in our squadron, kept our aircrews up to date on all incoming data, which came in bits and pieces. But eventually, it became clear with greater detail. Before long, we knew exactly when we would depart Udorn. My letters to Fran contained numerous changes that focused on when we should sell our house, arrange for our household shipments, when we could make the house available to the buyer, travel plans, family visits, medical requirements, concurrent travel, and our port call to depart the United States for the United Kingdom.

It was a roller coaster for several months, especially in May and June. It wasn't before 12 June that I could tell Fran I would be coming home early, and 25 June that I could tell her the destination for our aircraft deployment was at Bergstrom AFB in Austin. We were both happy about that!

John Heide was a good friend; we played paddleball together. He would become the last 14th TRS squadron commander before we all departed Udorn. John was great to work with as he could be professional while introducing a bit of humor in everything we did. He would lead our deployment back to the States.

With an end of tour (EOT) for the entire squadron, there was no shortage of parties and celebrations. I planned the final Sawadee party for our squadron. Lt. Col. Gibson was ready to rotate to his next assignment in June. In May, he held a steak dinner for his hardcore team in his trailer, and as I mentioned earlier, that's when he announced I was now a squadron flight commander.

We had a Sawadee party for our wing vice commander. It seemed like we had a party every night as operations at Udorn tapered down. While in Thailand, most of the guys in the 14th had nicknames, and while we sometimes used them at work, we most assuredly did at the parties. Names like "Rump Fairy," "Bullrider," "Knothead," and, "Mess Kit." Mine was "Godfather." Go figure!

Our Brother Amarjit, "The Thief," had done so well with his business making party suits and other clothing items that he wanted to thank us. He held a dinner at a local Thai restaurant and supplied us with much food and drink. When I had him make clothes for Fran, like her jeans, he would tell me that he hoped his sister—meaning Fran—liked them so that she would order more!

The parties were a welcomed outlet as we were all getting frustrated at Udorn in the final months there. The political environment, the downfall of Cambodia and South Vietnam, and with the heat reaching into the low 100s in the morning hours, we all wanted out of there. Many of my letters to Fran at this point stated how much I hated it there and could not wait to return home.

After my last combat support mission in South Vietnam on 5 May, our aircrews continued to fly local proficiency sorties during the remainder of May and June. We suspected all along that we would have been able to return home earlier than the deployment of our aircraft, now scheduled for early July, had it not been for the *Mayaguez* incident, which only contributed to extending the drama in SEA.

Our wing deputy commander for operations, Col. McAdoo, was making the rounds among the squadrons at Udorn to fly with aircrews from each. Lt. Col. Gibson, our squadron commander, selected me to fly with McAdoo as his WSO in a two-ship formation sortie led by my friend Guy Munder.

The takeoff was in formation, side by side, down the runway. Once airborne, we maintained formation until we split into separate low-level sorties for target acquisition. Colonel McAdoo and I acquired our targets and joined up with Guy and his WSO for an RTB. As I said earlier, it is always good to fly with the boss.

My last local sortie was a low-level in Thailand on 20 June 1975 with Captain Tim Peppe. We had flown together once before. All flying at Udorn stopped on 21 June. In June, the remaining time was to prepare for the deployment of all eighteen aircraft from Udorn to Bergstrom AFB, Texas—back home! We would make the trip in three legs: Udorn to Anderson AFB, Guam; Anderson to Hickam AFB, Hawaii; and finally, Hickam to Bergstrom AFB, Texas. We would have KC-135 tanker support that would deploy with us on all three legs as we would require numerous in-flight refuelings en route.

■ TIME TO GO HOME

Deployments require in-depth planning and briefing in terms of aircraft leads, in-flight operational procedures, emergency contingencies, and weather conditions en route at a minimum. I had aircraft ferry experience from my trip across the Atlantic with John Ganley and my most recent trip to Hawaii with Henry Johnson before getting stampeded by the sick WSO we left behind at Udorn.

Guy Munder and I, ready to go home.
Our names and the ground crew's names are on the aircraft.

The deployment schedule was 7 July to Guam, 10 July to Hawaii, and 12 July to Texas. We would drop back a day as we crossed the international date line. Deployments are very dull. You take off in pairs. Two aircraft (total first wave of six aircraft), join up in formation, climb and arrive at your cruise altitude, and then separate at a more comfortable distance of several hundred yards from each other, complete an ops check, fly at about three hundred knots IAS to ensure you consume fuel most efficiently, and drill holes through the sky until the first refueling. Each aircraft takes on fuel from the tanker in turn and then falls back to drilling more holes in the sky. More ops checks along the way to ensure everyone is A-OK and there are no concerns.

The second wave of six aircraft takes off thirty minutes after the first wave; the third wave of six aircraft takes off thirty minutes after the second wave. Ultimately, you have all eighteen RF-4Cs flying that are separated by these three waves, each thirty minutes apart. Our flights through each of these three segments were noneventful (thankfully). The leg to Guam took 7.4 hours and several aerial refuelings. The portion to Hawaii took 7.5 hours with several aerial refuelings. The last segment requires a bit more description as it contains my famous "piddle pack" story.

Our personal baggage is stored in the aircraft's nose; maintenance personnel removed the cameras to allow more room for baggage. Besides our checklists, the only things we bring into the cockpit are a box lunch, a water thermos, and two piddle packs. Piddle packs are small, sealable, reinforced, plastic bags that can be used to urinate if needed. They can then be sealed off to prevent leakage. Can't have a leak in the cockpit—no pun intended!

On the last leg of our deployment, Guy and I were designated as a ground spare aircraft for the first two waves of six aircraft from Hickam AFB to the US mainland. That meant that if one of the aircraft in the first wave dropped out for aircraft problems, we would take its place. If all six got off the ground, we would standby and be the spare for the second wave—the same deal. If both waves before us got off the ground, we would be in the third wave of six aircraft to depart the Aloha State.

This required that we start engines along with the first wave and sit with engines idling until they got airborne. We would continue to be idle until the second wave got airborne. Everyone in the first two waves got airborne with no problems, so we waited another thirty minutes before taking off with the third wave. This meant that Guy and I were in the cockpit one and a half hours before we even took off!

During this time, over the headset, Guy said to me, "Bill, I have to take a leak already!" *Why is he sharing this information with me?* I wondered.

I responded, "OK." In my mind, I calculated that he had one piddle pack left for the rest of the trip! *Hopefully, he won't need more than that.* What more could I or would I say?

We finally took off on that beautiful Saturday morning, 12 July, and climbed out from Hickam with a gorgeous view of Waikiki Beach and Diamond Head out to the left side as we headed east over the Pacific. In the distance, we saw the majority of the beautiful Hawaiian Island chain ahead of us. Before long, we only observed the vast ocean in every direction.

We settled in at our cruising altitude somewhere above thirty thousand feet and continued to our first in-flight refueling. All went well, and we resumed the spread-out flight configuration as we looked forward to meeting our loved ones soon! It didn't take long. Then Guy called out, "Bill."

"Yes."

"Have you used any piddle packs yet?"

"No, why?"

"I have to use my other piddle pack already," he stated with angst.

"You are drinking too much water. Don't drink so much water!"

He gave me control of the aircraft so he could take care of business.

As we proceeded through a couple more refuelings and were less than one hour from the US West Coast, Guy asked again if I had used any piddle packs yet. I responded with a long, "Nooooo. Why?"

He said he needed to go again and asked if he could borrow one of mine. *Borrow? Does he intend to give it back to me after he fills it?* "OK, here it comes on the left." I extended it from the rear cockpit as he reached back while keeping the aircraft in place with his right hand on the control stick. I added with some emphasis, "Don't drink any more water!"

He replied, "Roger that," but I didn't feel convinced.

We completed our final aerial refueling right over the west coast. The tanker would peel off to the north to land at Fairchild AFB, in Washington. We would proceed across the southwest through California, Arizona, New Mexico, and finally Texas. As we got within one hour of landing at Bergstrom, the weather deteriorated, and we would soon need to tighten up the formation to maintain visibility of each other.

Just before that, I received an additional request. One I prayed I would not hear.

"Bill, I hate to ask you this. Did you use your last piddle pack?"

I don't remember exactly what I said, but we were going on close to nine hours now in the cockpit, and I felt I might need the piddle pack at any minute. "No. Why?" As if I didn't know.

Hey, Guy is my friend. We flew combat support sorties together, exchanged family stories, and got along great while at Udorn. *Why jeopardize all that now?* So I reluctantly gave him my last piddle pack. He now had something close to four gallons of urine in the front cockpit. I wondered where he put it all.

We landed at Bergstrom and taxied to a remote section of the airbase, where buses would pick us up and transport us to our anxiously waiting families outside the Officer's Club. Bill Bowman was on a bus before me, and when he exited the bus, he saw Fran with our two sons, Bill and Joey. He recognized her and said, "Bill will be on the next bus."

Fran asked me later, "How did he know who I was, what I looked like?" I explained to her that the few of us who hung out together would share family stories and photos, so it was no surprise that Bill could quickly identify her.

When I got off the bus and saw Fran holding Joey with our son, Bill, beside her, I gave them hugs and kisses. But I had to add, "I'll be right back. I need to go to the restroom in the club!" I was about to explode after 8.6 hours in the cockpit (1.5 hours on the ground in Hawaii as a spare and 7.1 hours en route to Texas). The worst was on the bus headed for our reunion, where I knew a bathroom was nearby.

Everything after that was a blur. I don't even remember saying goodbye to my friends as I was so focused on my family. I suppose I thought I would see them soon in Europe. But Guy reminded me in a recent phone call that we did talk a while before leaving that reunion at Bergstrom.

I had finally contacted Bill Bowman after years of searching. We spoke briefly in February 2022, and it was great to catch up with him. Bill retired from the AF in late 1991, after assignments at Zweibrucken AB, Germany (twice); the Pentagon; and Bergstrom AFB, Texas. He flew for UPS for fifteen years and last worked towing AF Academy cadets in their soaring program. He finally retired in 2019.

After years of trying to contact Guy Munder, I finally found him with some recent search engines. I had sent a letter, but he did not respond right away; he and his wife, Maria, were traveling. We connected by phone in October 2021, nearly forty-seven years after we parted at Bergstrom AFB after delivering the RF-4Cs from Thailand. It was so great to finally hear his voice again!

Guy proceeded on to many assignments that enhanced his career, and the AF benefited from his work ethic and expertise. He went to RAF Alconbury in the United Kingdom. After a short while, the squadron of RF-4Cs was deactivated, which enabled him to remain in theater and acquire a staff position at HQ USAFE at Ramstein AB, Germany. After that, the AF wanted to send Guy to Shaw or Bergstrom AFB as an instructor pilot. Guy enjoyed the recce mission, but his heart was in fighters.

With the aid of a friend at Alconbury, a colonel who was the wing commander there, Guy was able to complete F-111 training and eventually ended up at RAF Lakenheath in the United Kingdom from 1979 to 1982 as Assistant Chief, Stan/Eval (the best of the best), and Mission Director for all aircraft related exercises. Guy returned to the States and took a job offered by Terry Schwalier, chief of recce assignments at Randolph AFB, Texas. We both knew Terry since he was assigned in the 14th TRS at Udorn with us. I had flown with Terry there a couple of times. Terry contacted Guy as he was attending ACSC and agreed to take the job of managing the Colonel's group assignments for two and a half years.

Guy's latest career assignment was at Myrtle Beach AFB, South Carolina, in the A-10 aircraft from 1986 to 1989. He retired from the AF in July 1989, after twenty years of service. As a civilian, he flew for US Air and retired in 2003. I always knew Guy's talent as a pilot, and his level-headed approach and interaction with others would allow him to advance in anything he chose to do. Guy was in a class by himself—a professional, a unique friend, and a confidant with whom I was so fortunate to share our experience in SEA. We remain in touch as we easily picked up from our days at Udorn. What a great guy (no pun intended)!

■ WHAT I LEARNED WHILE IN THAILAND

The wing at Udorn, and in particular the 14th TRS, supported intelligence operations through reconnaissance missions in SEA and ended with specific special joint missions Operation Eagle Pull, the evacuation of US personnel from Phnom Penh, Cambodia, on 12 April 1975, and Operation Frequent Wind, the evacuation of US and South Vietnamese personnel from Saigon on 29 April 1975.

From 12–15 May 1975, the wing played a significant role in locating the SS *Mayaguez* and in the joint military operations associated with recovering that US commercial vessel and its crew from the Cambodians. Unfortunately, we lost a significant number of marines on the ground before that incident was over, which is considered the last battle of the war in SEA.

The 14th TRS was deactivated on 30 June 1975. The wing would eventually be relieved of all operational commitments on 30 November 1975 and inactivated at Udorn RTAFB on 23 December 1975.

After this assignment, as I did in the past, I attempted to ascertain my value, my ROI to the AF. I finally felt that I had served a purpose, utilizing all the training I had received, and that my role there at Udorn was important for the unit I served and for me.

I completed 105 sorties, including twenty-one combat support missions, with a total flight time with the 14th TRS of 211.1 hours. This time included my three flights from Udorn to the States which took twenty-two hours to return. My overall RF-4C time at this point was 643.1 hours. I felt a genuine feeling of confidence and expertise in my roles as an RF-4C WSO, IWSO, SEFE, a flight commander, and a supervisor. And I looked forward to the next adventure.

However, I needed to put my service in SEA in the proper perspective. There is a wide disparity between the areas I flew over, the missions I completed in what was officially described as "hostile air defense environments," and the extremely hostile conditions that existed in the mid-to-late 1960s and early 1970s.

Through intelligence, it was certain that there were hostile forces on the ground in both Cambodia and South Vietnam while I was there, as witnessed in the eventual seizure of those countries. Aircraft that flew to cover the *Mayaguez* incident were exposed to gunfire. But the severity of the danger for other aircrews who flew their one hundred missions at an earlier period, like the fighter pilots I knew—Sabre Sams, Tony Shine, Dave Nichols, Denny Jarvi, and many more—was significantly greater. Many did not come home. And those who ended up in the Hanoi Hilton as POWs or went MIA, and those who sacrificed their lives, deserve the highest recognition.

With that reality aside, I had learned so much more during this assignment that needs recognition, and I believe it is also very important personally. As I read all the letters I wrote to Fran and her letters to me during our time separated by the job and the miles, I came to understand just how much we needed each other. Fran was a devoted wife and mother, and she endured so many challenges at home that I could only hope to help with my letters and occasional phone calls. But I often felt helpless and frustrated.

She dealt with long-term health issues with our son Joey and his ear infections and surgery for tubes in his ears. As young as he was, Bill helped her with Joey. She had to maintain the household and all that goes with it. She was many miles from her family, but fortunately, supportive AF families were nearby.

Many of our letters addressed finances and how we could manage my income. I lived on a budget ranging from $125 to $150 a month while in Thailand. We worked everything out, but not without constant coordination and strict compliance by both of us. Fran managed all that very well at home.

I witnessed several heartbreaking stories that involved our aircrews in the 14th TRS. One lieutenant received a letter from his wife stating, "You better come home now so the three of us can work this out." This was a total shock to him, and he promptly went home to try to save his marriage.

I already mentioned one pilot I flew with who went home on leave to get divorced. I knew of another aircrew member who was married and contracted syphilis locally. He was grounded from flying for a couple months. And there were stories like this in other squadrons too. It sometimes reminded me of the Wild West, where things could get out of hand. Only we were in SEA.

I learned just how lucky I was to have Fran as my wife. Our letters always expressed how much we loved each other. I looked forward to her letters every day. The mail plane did not always arrive for various reasons, which made all of us at Udorn a bit angry. The letters were a lifeline. There is no doubt the assignment in Thailand was a building block for our relationship and made it even stronger.

■ UNCERTAINTY IS CERTAIN

In the early history of our country, Benjamin Franklin said, "Our new Constitution is now established, everything seems to promise it will be durable; but, in this world, nothing is certain except death and taxes."

Much more recently, someone said, "There are now three things in life you can't avoid. Death, taxes, and software updates."

I would like to add a fourth element to that: PCS assignments! We sold our house in Austin and traveled to New York to catch up with our family again. My hold baggage from Udorn, which wasn't much, was on its way to the United Kingdom via the slowest method of transportation possible. Of that I was certain. Our major household goods from Austin went into storage; other household items (hold baggage) that would be needed immediately were on a truck destined for deportation from the East Coast to our next location in the United Kingdom.

While home in New York visiting family, we attended my sister's wedding on 2 August 1975. My sister requested I walk her down the aisle since our dad had passed away in 1974. I had always said I would be there if I could but could not commit due to all the activities that unfolded in SEA and my uncertain schedule. Fran's brother, Vince, was getting married that same day in Texas.

While in New York, I received a call that my assignment had changed—again! Due to a reduction of forces at Alconbury, the squadron I was assigned to was closing. So along with getting home to catch up with my wife and kids, selling the house, moving from Austin, traveling to New York, catching up with our families, and attending a wedding, we had to adjust to this news.

The first thing we thought of was that our hold baggage from Austin was scheduled for shipment to the United Kingdom. We needed to stop that ASAP! We finally contacted the appropriate AF agencies to divert our goods from being loaded on a ship that would cross the Atlantic. They were scheduled within a few days to be loaded. We were lucky to catch that in time. Whew!

My new assignment—back to Mather AFB, California, to be a navigator instructor. We would cross the country by car once again!

MULTICHALLENGES

■ RETURN TO MATHER AFB

My official PCS orders were issued in May 1975 and assigned me to a consecutive overseas tour in the United Kingdom. It was now a worthless piece of paper. Instead of reporting in August to the 1st TRS of the 10th TRW at RAF Alconbury, I was rerouted to Mather AFB by a message from AFMPC dated 28 July. I received this change while in New York to visit family, attend my sister's wedding, and prepare for our trip east, not west. My RF-4C flying and associated duties ended abruptly. At least for now.

Our new home would be an on-base house minutes from work. We were knowledgeable about the base and its services from my previous assignment there for UNT back in 1971–1972. We also liked the surrounding area, including Sacramento, the mountains, and the coast.

The jolt in the assignment changes dissipated as we crossed the country again from east to west. Our arrival in this familiar area was beginning to offer a level of calm and excitement. Maybe now we would have more opportunities to appreciate what was outside the base, especially since we expected to be here for several years. We knew one thing for sure when we arrived in California—the boys did not want to get into or anywhere near the car anymore. There had been too many long days sitting there, and they had enough of that!

In an ordinary move associated with a PCS, you would expect to get any hold baggage first. A reminder: This is the minimum amount of personal items you may need immediately or quickly after you arrive at a new base. My hold baggage from Udorn in Thailand went to the United Kingdom first since my assignment change was not in effect yet. I received the hold baggage last. The household goods diverted from a shipment to the United Kingdom arrived after our temporary storage items were delivered. These were all in the wrong order, but at least they all made it to the correct destination!

I was assigned to the 452nd Flying Training Squadron of the 323rd Flying Training Wing of Air Training Command. The squadron commander's wife, Pam Remsen, welcomed us almost immediately on arrival. UNT had the usual rolling class starts with hundreds of students in various phases of pursuing their navigator wings. I would now need to shift my focus from flying in a high-performance tactical aircraft to training new officers in the classroom and a new navigator training aircraft, the T-43. The T-29C, "Flying Classroom" aircraft I trained in during my UNT, was now obsolete!

■ T-43 AIRCRAFT

On 27 May 1971, the AF ordered nineteen T-43s, a modified version of the Boeing 737-200, as a replacement for the USAF's aging fleet of Convair T-29 navigation trainers as part of the UNT system.

The "Gator"—Boeing T-43 navigator training aircraft.
Photo: Courtesy of Adrian Pingstone, Wikimedia Commons; license—released to the public domain.

The Boeing T-43 was used by the AF for training navigators, now known as USAF combat systems officers (CSOs). Informally referred to as the Gator (an abbreviation of "navigator") and Flying Classroom, nineteen of these aircraft were delivered to the ATC at Mather AFB, California between 1973 and 1974. Two additional aircraft were delivered to the Colorado Air National Guard at Buckley Air Base (later Buckley Space Force Base) and Peterson AFB, Colorado in direct support of cadet air navigation training at the nearby USAF Academy.

From its entry into service in 1974 until the mid-1990s, the AF used T-43As for all USAF UNT. Starting in the mid-1990s, the AF used T-43As for USAF Undergraduate Navigator/CSO training except for those USAF navigators/CSOs slated for the F-15E and B-1B aircrafts.

In 1976, with the US Navy's retirement of its T-29 aircraft and deactivation of its associated training squadron TWENTY-NINE (VT-29) at NAS Corpus Christi, Texas, those student naval flight officers destined for land-based naval aircraft began training in USAF T-43s at Mather AFB under a program known by USAF as Interservice Undergraduate Navigator Training (IUNT) and by the US Navy as the NAV pipeline for training student naval flight officers slated for eventual assignment to land-based naval aircraft.

Externally, the T-43 differs from civilian aircraft by having more antennas and fewer windows. The T-43A had stations on board for twelve navigator students, six navigator instructors, a pilot, and a copilot. The student training compartment was equipped with avionics gear used in modern operational aircraft.

The aircraft had considerably more training capacity than the one it replaced. The plane included search and weather radar, VHF omnidirectional range (VOR) and tactical air navigation system (TACAN) avionics systems, LORAN-C, inertial navigation system, radar altimeter, and all required VHF, UHF, and HF radio communications equipment. Students used five periscopic sextant stations spaced along the length of the training compartment for celestial navigation training. However, with the advent of GPS, student navigators were no longer taught celestial navigation or LORAN.

Inside each T-43A training compartment were two minimum-proficiency, two maximum-proficiency, and twelve student navigator stations. Two stations form a console, and instructors could move their seats to the consoles and sit beside students for individual instruction. The large cabin allowed easy access to seating and storage yet reduced the distance between student stations and instructor positions.

Learning how to navigate onboard the T-43.
Photo: *Courtesy of David W. Roberts, AF.mil, Defense Media Activity—*
San Antonio; license—released to the public domain.

When the 323rd FTW was deactivated, and Mather AFB was closed by the Base Realignment and Closure (BRAC) action in 1993, most T-43s transferred to the 12th Flying Training Wing (FTW) at Air Education and Training Command at Randolph AFB, Texas. The 12th FTW assumed the specialized undergraduate navigator training (SUNT) role. In contrast, the US Navy's training air wing SIX (TRAWING 6), a naval ATC organization at NAS Pensacola, Florida, assumed a role in training those USAF student navigators slated for eventual assignment to the F-111, EF-111, F-15E, and B-1B aircraft.

■ NAVIGATOR INSTRUCTOR CHECKOUT AND DUTIES

I began classroom instructor training in Class 76-06 on 2 September 1975. The training was a thirteen-week course with academics from day 1. My flight instructor training started with a 4.9-hour flight on 9 October 1975. I completed thirteen instructional flights with navigation-focused areas such as over water, night celestial, radar, grid, and dead reckoning. I had an initial check ride on 22 October, and my final instructor check ride was a 5.1-hour flight on 4 December 1975.

Shortly after I began my instructor training, I received a regular commission from the AF after eight years of active-duty status as a reserve officer commissioned from OTS. The reserve commission is considered a probationary period when reserve officers could be separated from the service if there was a reduction in force (RIF)—for example, in peacetime—and could only serve twenty years. The regular commissioned status offered a higher rate of tenure based on rank. The AF eliminated the distinction between active-duty regular and reserve officers on 1 May 2005.

The academic phase of instructor training included 234 hours of instruction and flying training. There was formal evaluation in all areas with scores as satisfactory (S) or unsatisfactory (U). The allocation of these hours spread across the academic and flying subject areas as depicted below for my training:

ATC Instructor Training (Navigator) Course B-V7D-A						
Academic Training Phase	Prescribed Hours	Grade	Flight Phase Qualification	Aircraft	Flight Hours	Grade
Instrument Systems Development	14.5	S	Flight Qualification (UNT)	T-43	68.7	QUAL
Psychology of Learning	10.5	S				
Communications	7.0	S				
Methods and Techniques	9.0	S				
Evaluation and Measurement	9.0	S				
Practice Teaching Academics	42.0	S				
Review and Reteach	4.0	S				
Initial Qualification (T-43)	75.0	S				
Instructor Qualification (T-43)	63.0	S				
Total Hours	234.0	S			68.7	

Having upgraded to a qualified instructor in minimum time, I was now ready to instruct new navigator students in the art and skill of navigation in the classroom and in a new training aircraft and administer the academic and flying exams. There would be periodic instructor check rides that I would need to satisfy to maintain proficiency.

Once qualified as a squadron instructor, I was also selected for several other roles with specific responsibilities: squadron assistant flight commander, class section adviser, and faculty board member. I supervised and monitored over fifty instructors and students—the instructors in their abilities to teach academics and administer instructions while airborne, and the students in their progress toward achieving their UNT wings. It was great to be on the other side of UNT, teaching rather than learning.

The squadron had to meet higher headquarter standards for its instruction to students. The 452nd FTS received an excellent rating from the ATC IG and wing Stan/Eval inspections. In April 1978, I received a certificate of master instructor in flying training for completing nine hundred hours of instruction to UNT students.

I focused on the students' low-level and tactical navigation instruction, both in the classroom and in the air. I was fond of these navigational techniques, especially from the RF-4C, where I spent a good amount of my flight time in that same environment, only much faster and lower in altitude. These instructional flights were also shorter in duration than other training sorties, which enabled me to better balance my time among various instructional roles and management tasks as I spent time in the air, time in the classroom, and time at my desk.

As I moved from assistant flight commander to flight commander, I supervised several navigator instructors, evaluated them on their OERs, and advised them as needed for career enhancement.

My friend and fellow WSO for the RF-4C at Bergstrom AFB, Tom Crook, and I went through the UNT instructor training together at Mather. He and his wife, Pat, and kids were familiar faces, and we continued our friendship with them. Pat surprised Tom and me with a cake she made to celebrate our completion of the training.

"Enough pictures already. Let's eat!"

When I became a flight commander, Tom and his assistant built out a section of the squadron so I could have an office to myself. Tom was one of those resourceful guys who just found ways to get things done. He was a do-it-yourself individual who was talented in so many ways, including being an outstanding navigation instructor.

As a faculty board member, I heard cases involving student performance that was below standards or for possible elimination from UNT—kind of what I faced on the other end of a faculty board when I went before them at UPT—my first assignment after OTS. The shoe was now on the other foot!

Additional duties came fast. You can never elude these. Some are fun, and some are pure agony. But all must get done.

I became the wing's Additional Duty Career Advancement Program (ADCAP) manager. I thoroughly enjoyed this one because it allowed me to help junior officers broaden their careers and enhance their value to the AF. I spent a considerable amount of time on this, especially publicizing the program at commander's calls; through the base bulletin, *Wing Tips*; and through individual contacts. I managed fourteen ADCAP officer programs. The positive feedback from these officers was very gratifying.

As the squadron curriculum project officer for physical training, I suggested changes to the UNT physical training program to improve physical conditioning and to make it more responsive to student needs and desires.

Within the first couple of months at Mather, recognition for my previous service in SEA arrived. In early July, while at Udorn AB, John Heide had written me up for an AF commendation medal as recommended and endorsed by Col. McAdoo, who had become the wing vice commander there. I received this with the first Oak Leaf Cluster since I had received this medal previously in my career. Our squadron commander, Lt. Col. Remsen, pinned this on me and the air medal for the combat support missions I had flown in SEA.

I had established my place at Mather—instructing, managing, advising, supervising, and participating where needed for our squadron. It would not be long before the AF introduced a new element to UNT at Mather AFB. Traditionally, all the UNT students were men and would go to various aircraft training once they achieved their navigator wings. Those follow-on assignments could be located at home in the States or overseas in potentially hostile areas. At that time, women were typically not assigned to combat flying roles.

The AF began to open more opportunities to women. Over the years, women would demonstrate the skills that would enable them to fly many diverse types of aircraft, including fighters, or become navigators. History was about to happen at Mather AFB. The AF would include women in UNT.

■ FIRST WOMEN NAVIGATOR STUDENTS

A quick look at the history of women in the AF will lead to an appreciation for the timeline of AF firsts for women. March is Women's History Month. A February 2006 publication from Travis AFB, California, recognized women's many contributions while serving our military. The following list highlights those achievements up to the introduction of women into UNT and their graduation as navigators:

- 12 June 1948: Congress passes the Women's Armed Services Integration Act, establishing women in the AF.
- 8 July 1948: Esther Blake becomes the first woman to enlist in the AF.
- 1968: The first AF woman is sworn into the Air National Guard with the passage of Public Law 90-130, which allows it to enlist women.

- 5 May 1970: Air Force Reserve Officer Training Corps (AFROTC) expands to include women after test programs at Ohio State, Drake, East Carolina, and Auburn Universities prove successful in 1969.
- 2 March 1971: The USAF introduces a policy permitting women who become pregnant to remain on active duty or to return within twelve months of discharge.
- 17 March 1971: Jane Leslie Holley becomes the first woman commissioned through the AFROTC program. She graduated from Auburn University, Alabama.
- 18 March 1971: Captain Marcelite C. Jordon becomes the first woman aircraft maintenance officer after completing the aircraft maintenance officer school.
- 7 April 1971: 2nd Lieutenant Suzanne M. Ocobock becomes the first woman civil engineer in the AF and is assigned to Kelly AFB, Texas.
- 16 July 1971: Jeanne M. Holm, director of Women in the Air Force, becomes the first woman promoted to brigadier general.
- 29 September 1976: The first two groups of women pilot candidates enter undergraduate pilot training at Williams AFB, Arizona.
- 10 March 1977: The first women navigator candidates report to Mather AFB, California to begin UNT.
- 2 May 1977: 1st Lt. Christine E. Schott becomes the first woman undergraduate pilot training student to solo in the T-38 Talon.
- 2 September 1977: The first class of women pilots graduates at Williams AFB.
- 12 October 1977: The first class of five USAF women navigators graduates, with three of the five assigned to MAC aircrews.

The 1970s were a turning point for military women due to greater equality and opportunity through legislation and a change in how American women saw themselves, their roles, and their potential in the USAF.

In 1975, then-Air Force Chief of Staff Gen. David C. Jones, announced the launch of a test program that would enable women to enter pilot and navigator training. In March 1977, the first six women attended UNT at Mather AFB. They would complete the thirty-one-week course at Mather and be assigned to noncombat aircraft, such as cargo carriers, after graduation on 12 October 1977. The women were part of a larger group that would be assigned to pilot training, the first group of ten starting at Williams AFB in Arizona.

Almost a full year ahead, articles appeared in major newspapers across the country that women would enter UNT. They described the process where the women would be chosen by AF selection boards at the AF Military Personnel Center at Randolph AFB in Texas.

The first group of women who entered UNT was assigned to another section in my squadron. This was a new endeavor by the AF, and it had no lack of attention from all levels of management in the wing, our squadron, and the local press, including TV coverage and news media across the country.

First three, left to right: Bettye Jo "BJ" Payne, Florence "Flo" Parker, Margaret "Maggie" Stanek. Next three, left to right: Mary Kay "MK" Higgins, Ramona McCall, Elizabeth "Liz" Koch. Photo: Courtesy of DVIDS—Defense Visual Information Distribution Service. Photo is taken from a screenshot of a video commemorating the first women in UNT, Airman 1st Class Rome Bowermaster, Mathew Hester, Kailey Viator, 26 February 2022.

There were periodic interviews with the women as well as with their instructors and supervisors. The women held their own and did well in training. However, one trainee, Maggie Stanek, fell back in training due to a parasailing accident. She ended up in my section to continue training. Some of the men navigator trainees considered the women unnecessary competition for aircraft they might have wanted since the women, at that time, could not be assigned to fighters, and would be assigned to other aircraft types.

My response to that was simple. "You're still competing with *someone* in the class. It doesn't matter if it's male or female. Study your butts off to place near the top of the class and ensure your best chances of getting your choice of aircraft. Stop whining!" I spoke from experience from my UNT years before, when I studied *my* butt off to place at the top of *my* class!

Several videos were created to celebrate overcoming gender and racial barriers in the USAF exactly forty-five years since the first female class of navigators began their training. Several of the first six women in UNT relate their experiences in these videos, which are available on the DVIDS—Defense Visual Information Distribution Service website. They set a high bar for women in the AF that deserves honor and praise.

ADVANCEMENT IN EDUCATION

As I assessed my career to this point, and with some stability in my assignment at Mather, I decided it was a suitable time to pursue a master's degree. Having an advanced degree would contribute to my chances of promotion. I had begun an MBA in Austin, at the University of Texas, when I was at Bergstrom AFB. But that was interrupted by the tour to Thailand.

One of the programs that interested me was the systems management program offered by the University of Southern California (USC), located in Los Angeles. USC was one of the world's leading research universities. USC managed the university's Institute of Safety and Systems Management program. The instructors would come up from LA and teach at Mather, making it even more convenient.

The program began at USC in 1963 and was designed for the graduate education needs of students who are employed by large organizations, such as the military, government, and multinational and domestic corporations. The program content was multidisciplinary, involving core subjects in systems management, human factors, and systems technology. The program included two electives that, when added to the core courses, would add up to thirty-six credits.

I started the program in June 1976. The challenge for me was to carve out time from my existing heavy schedule and responsibilities to devote to the program to complete the twelve courses, each worth three credits. I could only manage one course at a time, so I calculated that I could complete the program in two years if I took back-to-back classes and included the summer semesters.

I also initiated the intermediate military PME, Air Command and Staff College, by correspondence during this assignment. Still, I would not complete this until later, especially with the increased demand for my time devoted to my master's degree.

A TWO-YEAR ROUTINE

I knew I needed to be even more organized now with my commitment to completing the master's program while I did my primary job and additional duties. While these were important to me, I also had the most important job of all—being a husband and father. So given twenty-four hours in a day, how would I accomplish all of that?

As far as I am concerned, getting started on any significant project or assignment is the most formidable challenge. Once you get into the rhythm of the schedule, you can operate on autopilot, so to speak, and navigate your way through the plan. It is still challenging work, but you get accustomed to it and keep going. It becomes part of what you do day in and day out.

I took classes twice a week, usually on Tuesdays and Thursdays. Those days were the most rigorous because I had to adjust to the routine that included flying early to instruct students, which included pre-flight briefings; a quick breakfast; flying the training sortie, which could last between four and five hours; debriefing the students; lunch; classroom instruction and office work; home for dinner; attend the USC course; back home to study; lights out! To squeeze all that in I had to get up at about 0330 hours, head over to the squadron, and begin the schedule I just described.

Having the USC instructors teach in the same building where I worked each day made it convenient. But it also made me feel I lived there more than I lived at home. In reality, I did just that, so getting home was a welcome relief.

I had a couple of friends who were with me in the program—Gregg Hughes and Norris Nering. We teamed up for some of the coursework that required term papers. We each contributed equally as no one slouched in our responsibilities to do our parts. With that shared commitment, we worked very well together. We met on weekends to catch up on any writing assignments or to do a group study. We were always in a catch-up mode, but we seemed to thrive on it, especially since we liked the subject material. Our grades for the papers were excellent and reflected the hard work we each contributed.

Fran and I have maintained a connection with Gregg and his wife, Janet, through the years, primarily at Christmastime, as we share stories of our families and work. I had a brief discussion with Gregg on 4 November 2021.

By July 1978, after two years, I had completed eleven of the twelve courses needed for my degree. And I only lacked one elective to complete the program.

The daily rhythm left little time for other activities, but there is always a means to an end. It was traditional to engage in some formal activity with each UNT class of students, such as the dining-in, where military members gathered for an evening of camaraderie in their mess dress, the tuxedo of the military.

I stand with some of my UNT students, future AF navigators.

■ THE FAMILY SIDE AT MATHER

Fran and I did our best to balance our social life with work. That social life extended into a relationship with UNT students, some of whom were married. The squadron and squadron sections would have the occasional picnic or party to get to know the students and their families, and friends. Special holidays, like Christmas and Independence Day, always had a social function attached to them.

Similarly, we had our group of close friends at Mather, where we would get together. On Memorial Day, we were invited to a BBQ at another instructor's house on base. Before we headed off to the party with our contribution to the feast, I wanted to mow my lawn quickly. I was always safety conscious with everything I did, especially having that drilled into me as an aircrew member. However, somehow safety was not utmost in my mind this time. Big mistake!

I was almost in a slow jog as I cut the lawn. Just as I took a step forward with my right foot, the lawnmower's front wheels hit a rut, and the back end of the mower popped up a couple inches off the ground due to the forward momentum. Just enough for my foot to enter the danger zone of the spinning blade. The cutting blade rotates clockwise, so as my foot entered the blade's spin zone, the blade just missed my small toes and hit my big toe squarely enough to knock my foot to the left. The lawnmower stopped by the impact with my toe!

I stood there stunned for a moment. *Did I just do what I think I did?* Right after that, though, the pain set in big time. I casually limped to the front door and sat on a chair. I calmly called for Fran, and she came to the door.

I quietly asked, "Could you please bring me a towel and a large glass of cold water?"

She looked at me and then at my foot, still in my sneaker, with a gash on one side with blood. "Oh, my God!"

I was reluctant to remove my sneaker. I did not know if I would find little toes in there that were no longer attached to my foot. My only thought was how much it hurt. Fortunately, all was intact, and I only needed a few stitches for my big toe. Fran called on a neighbor and asked if he could take me to the base hospital. Got the stitches done. Let's get to the BBQ. What a dumbbell I was to do that. Speed "kills" in more ways than one!

Folsom Lake was nearby. It was a great recreational area for picnicking, boating, and waterskiing. We decided to purchase a ski boat, a seventeen-foot Cobalt with a 150hp MerCruiser engine and a trailer. We had fun with neighbors, fellow instructors, and students on the occasional picnic lunch and waterskiing. What could be better?

In the summer of 1976, Fran was about six months pregnant and due to deliver child number three in late October. So she was the flag-bearer on the boat while I pulled skiers all over the lake. No skiing for her! Today, Folsom Lake is sadly a mere fraction of what it was when we were there. The boat slips are on dry land with the lake in the distance—a long way in the distance—a sign of the terrible drought conditions in the West!

While we were in New York after I returned from Thailand, we had encouraged my mother to visit us in California once we got settled there. She came in July 1976, in time for us to celebrate her fifty-second birthday on 20 July. We took her out on the boat at Folsom and toured San Francisco with views of the Golden Gate Bridge, Fisherman's Wharf, local wineries, and other attractions. It was a great visit, and Mom had a great time with us.

A few months later, on 23 October 1976, Fran was out shopping with her mother, who was visiting from New York. She told her mother the baby was coming, and they quickly returned home. It was around dinnertime that Saturday when Fran told me it was time to go to the hospital. The base hospital was not far. We arrived there at 7 p.m., and our seven-pound daughter, Jean Marie Cimino, came into the world with only a mild whimper at 7:57 p.m. I barely had time to get my scrubs and mask on to go to the delivery room for miracle number three! This little girl had two older brothers anxious to see the baby, not yet knowing if it was a boy or a girl.

Joey had told Fran that he wanted a sister. Fran told him she would do the best she could. She *did*, and Joey happily joined his brother as they now had a baby sister.

Our family life at Mather was chock-full of activity with a new baby in the family. Joey was happy that he had a sister, but that didn't prevent him from developing relationships with other little girls in the neighborhood. Nope, didn't want to miss any of that!

Father Andrews was one of the AF chaplains at Mather. He gave Bill his first Holy Communion and also baptized Jeannie. We got a two-for-one deal, so to speak while we lived at the base! Father Andrews was one of our favorites in the church community.

Bill was always interested in baseball, so he joined a Little League team on base. When Fran's parents came to visit us at Mather, Bill promised his grandmother that he would hit a home run for her. We all grinned and thought that was cute. But we cheered more loudly than anyone else at the ball field when he *did* hit a homerun. Holy cow! Surprised us.

We loved the Mather AFB community. Like many AFBs, it was a great place to have a young family, engage with many friends with their young children, and enjoy the environment in and near Sacramento.

Our young family, Christmas 1976.

Later in December 1976, a couple of weeks before Christmas, my mother became ill and was admitted to the hospital. We stayed connected daily with my brother and sister to follow her health condition. She was in the hospital through the holidays, and it appeared that she would go home sometime in early January 1977. However, she sustained heart failure, and her condition worsened.

The day after, Friday, 7 January, we heard the news, and I flew to JFK Airport in New York City and proceeded directly to the hospital. When I went into the room to see Mom, she was sitting up, alert, smiling, and happy to see me. My brother and sister were already there. I spoke with Mom for a while and showed her photos of Jeannie, just born in October. Mom had not seen Jeannie in person, so the pictures were the next best thing she could hold. We spent time talking, and my assessment of Mom was that she didn't appear to be that ill.

We remained with her the entire weekend and witnessed a very rapid decline in her health. In a couple days, her health crashed. She had advanced cancer, and no remedy would save her. At one point, while we were still able to speak with each other, she said, "I'm ready."

Mom's faith was always strong. She knew the end was near and accepted that peacefully. At about 4 p.m. on Sunday, 9 January 1977, Mom took her last breath. I left the hospital and immediately went to the funeral home in Hicksville to arrange her funeral. Mom was only fifty-two years old. Dad was only fifty when he passed away in 1974. Now they are at eternal rest together in the same cemetery on Long Island.

My plane ride back to California was quiet and pensive. I stared out the window and recalled many memories of my parents. It was difficult to accept they were gone, especially at such a young age. But reality is relentless, and it is what it is—in happy ways and sad ones.

Josephine N. Cimino
1924–1977

■ GUESS WHAT?

Whenever I asked Fran, "Guess what?" she knew we were going somewhere, we were moving again. We expected to remain at Mather AFB for four years, but it was only three when, in May 1978, I received notification of my next assignment. I do not know how I was selected for the Air Force Exchange Program. Perhaps it was due to my experience as an instructor (RF-4C IWSO, navigator instructor). I was chosen for the exchange program with the Canadian Forces. The assignment was at Canadian Forces Base (CFB), Winnipeg, in Manitoba.

Fran reacted as she always does, although this time somewhat reluctantly. "I'm packing my bags."

When I told Fran we were going to Canada, she reacted with some enthusiasm as she asked, "Where are we going—Ottawa, Montreal, Vancouver?"

"No, Winnipeg."

She was not sure exactly where that was. I said, "It's in Manitoba, just north of North Dakota." I notified her by phone, so I didn't see her expression, but I was pretty sure her facial expression changed dramatically.

As usual, questions started to flow: "What is it like there? What about the schools, health care? Where will we live? What's the weather like?" And many others. Ah, the weather! That would be a whole new ballgame for us. So with great anticipation and some apprehension, we settled on the reality we were moving again, even though we were perfectly happy at Mather.

In the first year at CFB Winnipeg, I would be in a comprehensive academic course, so one of my immediate concerns was completing my master's program since I needed one elective to satisfy the requirements for thirty-six credits. I produced a possible solution.

When I took four courses in an MBA program at UT in Austin while stationed at Bergstrom AFB, I received an A for each. I wrote to USC and explained my new assignment and circumstances. I requested they consider one of the courses I completed at UT as the missing elective. They reviewed the four courses and selected one that would be the best fit as an elective for the master's degree in systems management. I received my advanced degree on 2 September 1978. Now, on to the next academic challenge. Never stop learning!

The three-year tour I just completed was another case of how many balls one can juggle in the air at one time—multichallenges, including upgrading to a navigator instructor (teaching and flying), faculty board member, managing a squadron section, additional duties, women in UNT with all the attention that received, and educational advancement. Routines and changes to routines. That is one very accurate characterization of military life. Take it or leave it!

CANADIAN FORCES: A DIFFERENT MILITARY

Official family photo submitted for the Officer Exchange Program.

CANADIAN FORCES BASE, WINNIPEG

In early July 1978, we left the warm climate of California and headed northeast, stopping at some of the most beautiful sites in the United States, especially Yellowstone National Park. We traveled with two vehicles—our GMC van and an orange Subaru that reminded us of a pumpkin on wheels. When you opened the hood to the engine area, you could see the ground—just the basics made this little car very dependable, especially in any weather. Fran would drive the van with Bill and Joey; I had Jeannie as my companion for the trip in the pumpkin.

Canada is the second-largest country in landmass. Russia is larger by about 71 percent. The United States and Canada share the world's longest international border, 5,525 miles with 120 land ports of entry. And our bilateral relationship is one of the closest and most extensive. Ten provinces and Canada's three territories extend from the Atlantic to the Pacific and northward to the Arctic Ocean.

We were headed to Winnipeg, the capital city of the province of Manitoba, directly north of the North Dakota-Minnesota state border. When we moved there, the population of Canada roughly equaled that of California, around twenty-four million. Today, Canada's population is close to thirty-eight million. Despite the vast territory, more than 90 percent of Canadians live within 150 miles of the US border.

One thought that crossed our minds was, *Ah, another capital. Could that mean another child?* Since Bill was born in Denver, Joey in Austin, and Jeannie in Sacramento, we had our concerns!

The Canadian Armed Forces (or Canadian Forces) is the unified military of Canada, comprising sea, land, and air elements referred to as the Royal Canadian Navy, Canadian Army, and the Royal Canadian Air Force, respectively. Currently, the forces contain about 68,000 regular members and 27,000 reserve members. The air force component has 14,500 regular members, 2,600 reserve members, and a 2,500-member civilian force.

The Canadian Armed Forces train their airmen to become navigators in what used to be the Canadian Forces Air Navigation School (CFANS) at CFB, Winnipeg. This was their equivalent to the USAF UNT program. The components of the CFANS were the aerospace squadron, the senior air navigator course (SANC), and the electronic warfare operations course (EWOC). My three-year assignment was in the aerospace squadron, although I had official connections to all components of the CFANS during my term as an exchange officer. The training has migrated over time, and today, it is currently managed at the RCAF W/C William G. Barker, VC Aerospace College, 17 Wing, CFB, Winnipeg.

The central office for the USAF Exchange Officer Program with the Canadian Forces was located in Ottawa, Ontario, Canada, and led by Lt. Col. J. Harry Stow III. Col. Stow supervised about forty USAF exchange officers spread across Canada in distinct assignments in Canadian military units. There were five USAF officers at CFB, Winnipeg, each with different duties. The USAF also hosted Canadian officers in various assignment locations in the United States.

It goes without saying that I wanted to do a good job in Canada, personally and professionally. This assignment carried a greater responsibility. As a USAF exchange officer and as a citizen of the United States, I represented the USAF *and* my country. In every sense of the word, I was an ambassador of the United States, not from the US State Department, but the US military, and I strove to represent it as well as possible.

Fran and I would quickly learn that most Canadians fell into two categories, with only a few in the middle ground. There are those Canadians who loved the United States, embraced our presence there, and made us feel at home with their hospitality, support, and friendly engagement. Others would look for any reason to criticize or discredit Americans. By "Americans," I mean citizens of the United States, even though Canadians who live in North America are not usually considered Americans as we are. This was the case for a good portion of my assignment in Canada. But it seemed to wane in our last year there as acceptance outgrew the comparative nature of some Canadians.

▪ WE BOUGHT A HOUSE: WE SETTLED IN

Our first task was to acquire a place to live. We decided to purchase a house in Winnipeg. We bought a one-story house with a finished basement and a single garage built by a company called Quality Homes. They lived up to their name as the house was extremely well insulated for the harsh winters we would endure. For the next three years, our home was located at 275 Carriage Road, five kilometers from CFB Winnipeg (about three miles for us Americans). The Canadians use the metric system, so I felt inclined to use that (for now). Nonetheless, it was very convenient to work, and commuting was never a problem.

We were fortunate to have good neighbors. Next door lived John and Rita Lee, Asian Canadians born in India. How's that for diversity? They had two young boys close to Joey's and Jeannie's ages, Andrew and Ryan. They proved to be great neighbors, and we socialized and celebrated with them on many occasions. I even went fishing with John at times.

Our next concern was school for Bill and Joey, now ten and nearly five, respectively. Jeannie was under two years old. We enrolled them in the local public school during our first year there, and then moved them to St. Charles Catholic School, located on the west end of Winnipeg, about six kilometers (less than four miles) by bus.

Due to my assignment in Canada, we fell under the NATO Partnership for Peace (PFP) Status of Forces Agreement (SOFA), originally signed in 1951, and which provides the basis for the legal status of the military, US civilian employees, and dependents who are stationed on orders in NATO-partner countries. Under this agreement, we had access to free socialized health care, including hospitalization and dental services. Other agreements, such as the Reciprocal Health Care Agreement (RHCA), also provided similar services for DoD and civilians working in partner nations. We received excellent health care throughout our time in Winnipeg.

■ THE CANADIANS: A DIFFERENT BREED

You immediately learn several things when you arrive and meld into life in Canada. They are officially a bilingual country—English and French for the majority. Almost every sentence ends in "eh," as in, "We had a good game of hockey today, eh?" I found myself saying "eh" before too long, just like the Canadians, with a bit of inflection in the word to give it character.

Speaking of hockey, I am convinced Canadians can play hockey before they can walk. I think they were born with ice skates and a hockey stick, or at least received them as gifts at age one! They seem to live on ice skates. I've seen the youngest kids manage the ice with ease and make it look as natural as breathing. It looked like they could be in the Olympics too!

I found the Canadian Forces' work ethic very different from the US military. It was much more relaxed, and except for the course I was about to begin, the hours were shorter. The Canadians were much more inclined to have a gin and tonic with lunch, but I never witnessed this to any excess during duty hours. After duty hours, that was another story. (More on that later.) But it must be stated that the Canadian officers I came to know and interfaced with, both on staff and my classmates, were devoted military servants.

They were also competitive, and I suspect for several reasons. They wanted to ensure I saw them as a dedicated collective force for Canada, even though the numbers varied widely and certainly in proportion to their population, which was roughly 7 percent of the US population. The other reason was the individual pride I witnessed in each officer. I never saw anyone slack off in their jobs. I found them to be intelligent, witty, and funny.

Perhaps my description of the Canadians I came to know had similar traits to Americans. But they certainly have their own identity and are proud of it.

■ AEROSPACE SYSTEMS COURSE

The Aerospace Systems Course (ASC) has no USAF equivalent. The forty-four-week course prepares selected officers for duties requiring broad background knowledge of aerospace operational requirements and a practical appreciation of systems concepts and applications. It provides postgraduate training, which enables officers to fill assignments associated with the definition of operational requirements and time acquisition, analysis, and evaluation of aerospace systems.

The course is one of the most advanced operational/technical courses conducted by the Canadian Forces in the Aerospace Squadron of their Air Navigation School at CFB, Winnipeg. The Canadians conduct the course once a year, and the course number designates how many years the course has been conducted. I was in ASC 31 from September 1978 to July 1979 with sixteen Canadian military officers, each unique and talented in his way.

When I arrived there, Maj. Jimmie Boone, the current USAF exchange officer at CFB, Winnipeg, was my sponsor. He remained on the Aerospace Squadron staff for most of the time I went through the course. I would replace him and assume his staff position in the squadron after completing the course.

Colonel Allingham (now deceased) awards the AFCM, 2nd Oak Leaf Cluster to me

Shortly after I arrived at CFB, Winnipeg, I received an AF commendation medal, 2nd Oak Leaf Cluster, for my instructor navigator work at Mather AFB. The CFB, Winnipeg base commander, Col. Allingham, presented the medal to me as I was about to begin the ASC. I was on the Major's promotion list, and just before the end of the course, I was promoted on 31 July 1979. All my Canadian classmates were captains. It was an excellent way to start this assignment: a medal and on the Major's promotion list. Now I just needed to stop gloating, buckle down, and do a good job in the ASC.

I found the course to be one of the most challenging, not only due to the wide variety of topics, but the depth of each. The math and statistics courses within the math and applied science sector contained fourteen subjects. Physics, communications theory, aerodynamics, electronics, human factors, and computer programming made up the remainder of this sector with thirty additional subjects.

The systems studies sector contained radar systems, computer systems, electro-optical systems, weapon systems, communications systems, navigation and guidance systems, electronic warfare systems, and display systems—comprised of nearly the same number of subjects as math and applied sciences.

The operations and staff duties sector contained research, development, test and evaluation, operational factors, and staff duties—thirteen areas of study. A comprehensive list of all courses for the sectors is provided in appendices A2A through A2C.

Travel to the aerospace industry, military units, and other agencies of the United States, Canada, and the United Kingdom was an essential element of the course. During the course year, we completed several trips to gain the necessary exposure to the specific focus of study assigned for the class by Lt. Col. Rowlatt, the commandant of the CFANS. A comprehensive list of all travel locations for ASC 31 is listed in appendix A2D.

The thesis title for ASC 31's class project was "A Study of Canadian Forces Requirements for VTOL Aircraft—1980 to 2000." This required extensive analysis and assessment of state-of-the-art VTOL technology and its application in forecasting Canadian VTOL requirements. The report would be classified as secret.

VTOL represents vertical takeoff and landing aircraft. We would dive into the technology for VTOL from every perspective—R&D, manufacturing, command, operational and training establishments, testing, and all avionics. The list was endless, and the visits to VTOL-related facilities were important additions to classroom instruction.

One of our many industry visits took us to Sikorsky Aircraft in Connecticut. United Technologies owned it until they sold the Sikorsky Aircraft business to Lockheed

Martin Corporation in 2015. The company was established by the famed aviator Igor Sikorsky in 1923 and was among the first companies to manufacture helicopters for civilian and military use. We met with Sikorsky's eldest son, Sergei, who joined United Technologies in 1951 and retired in 1992. It was fascinating to hear about his father's pioneering directly from him.

The Aerospace Squadron staff included the commander, Maj. Noel Funge; a USAF exchange officer, Maj. Jimmie Boone; and a British exchange officer designated as the squadron standards officer, Maj. Gary Barber. A host of Canadian officers, ranked from captains to majors, were instructors for the ASC. The British and the Canadians use the *Oxford Dictionary* extensively, so that was a bit of an adjustment for me. I used to tease Gary Barber and ask, "If you use the *Oxford Dictionary*, why isn't your name spelled 'Barbre?'" Most others would laugh at that. He would just smirk!

We had course classes every day during the week, except when we would travel or break up the academic day with sports. You guessed it—hockey. We played floor hockey on wooden courts in a gym, not on the ice. Some of us also liked to run for exercise, so we had a good level of competition running from CFB Winnipeg to points in the city and back for a distance of about six miles. Maj. Funge was a short guy by comparison to others, but he was fast as a rabbit. He usually led the pack.

Significant elements of the course were reports and technical writing. Each student had a specific part of the course paper to research and write. My contribution focused on the electro-optical sensors and special devices necessary for effective VTOL aircraft operation in low-level light and adverse weather conditions. The title of my report was "Sensors for Tactical VTOL Aircraft." My paper was classified as confidential. My operational knowledge of tactical aircraft environments and sensor systems from past assignments certainly helped enforce my interest in my written contribution.

I quickly adapted to the Canadian writing style. My thirty-four-page report addressed the potential threat of NATO-Soviet/Warsaw Pact Forces in Europe with a severe and complex environment characterized by impressive threats, adverse weather conditions, and various terrain features. Tactical VTOL aircraft must be able to operate day and night with extended stand-off and nap-of-the-earth (NOE) capability in any weather.

I wrote about the theatre of operations: the threat, the mode of operations, and sensor performance criteria; electro-optical system technology: lasers, forward-looking infrared (FLIR), low-light-level TV (LLLTV), helmet-mounted sights, and night-vision devices; sensor studies for VTOL operations: low-level night operations programme and standoff target acquisition systems; modern sensor systems' application in advanced attack helicopter (AAH-64); target acquisition designation system/pilot night-vision system; and future sensor system requirements.

I delivered my portion of the course paper on 22 March 1979, along with others who completed their segments. The CFANS commandant congratulated us on the submission. It had been a long year so far, with still a few months to go to course completion. All class members were required to submit technical reports for an industry we visited throughout the course. I prepared and presented written reports for visits to the Hughes Aircraft Company in California and the visit to Smith Industries Limited in London, United Kingdom.

The pace and intensity of the ASC were demanding, but we found ways to relieve the stress by maintaining a high level of comedy. We would always find ways to inject humor, as everyone wanted to be the funniest guy in the room. We kept a log of what we called the ASC 31 *Course Mutterings* to which we each contributed; we were its authors. They were witty and funny; some required a bit of thought to understand fully. Some didn't make sense at all. They weren't supposed to make sense, just make us laugh. Here are a few examples:

Our squadron commander, Maj. Funge, was relatively short in height. Someone remarked that he was on the promotion to lieutenant colonel list by saying, "Maj. Funge is on the Canadian Forces shortlist."

Since the ASC was difficult, the instructors would try to encourage us by saying that it would be downhill after Christmas. I commented, "I knew all along it wouldn't be downhill after Christmas. There are no hills in Winnipeg." I would also comment that if you stood on a brick, you could see Calgary, Alberta, two provinces to the west.

In our electronics class, Capt. Ted Benson wrote and said, "I don't like electronics because it hertz." By hertz, I don't mean Hertz Rent-A-Car. The hertz Ted mentioned refers to a measurement of one cycle per second to measure the frequency of vibrations and waves, such as sound and electromagnetic waves. If that "hurts" your head, I'm sorry. I did not intend to hurt you over hertz!

In a discussion of navigation, Capt. Grant Luke said, "Coriolis effect is a spinoff." We decided to give honor to this one and called it a "Lukism." As I learned in UNT, the Coriolis effect is a force acting perpendicular to the direction of motion and the axis of rotation. It occurs due to the earth's rotation and the fact that the atmosphere and oceans are not "connected" to the solid part of our planet. All right, sorry. Too much on that!

In relation to the comprehensiveness of the course, we selected "Alfie." You know the opening line: "What's it all about, Alfie?"

When we discussed optics, I mentioned they were like the ones I had in my camera, which was a Mamiya Sekor I bought in Okinawa. But I called it my "Mama Mia" camera.

I had one more to share. It was when we were traveling to LA. My classmates would tease me about the smog there. I said, "You're just jealous you don't have the industry to manufacture this stuff!"

When one of the classmates asked an instructor to explain a point he misunderstood, the instructor said, "I will say it again, only louder."

One of our classmates told us he had to see the base surgeon on Saturday, and the surgeon was unhappy he had to come in on the weekend. Our classmate said, "If you get sick, make sure it's on a weekday!"

Capt. Don Timperon, one of our instructors, occasionally talked extremely fast in our Electronics Theory class. Capt. Grant Luke commented, "Whenever Don speeds up, take notes fast. It will be on the exam."

Capt. Al Steele told one of the instructors, "I know what you are saying, but it's wrong!" I tend to believe that Al was right. He was one bright dude.

While visiting Hughes Aircraft Company in California, USAF Maj. Jimmie Boone told the Canadians, "You Canadians are looking more and more like Americans every day."

This was the classroom and travel atmosphere during the grueling year—learn, but make it fun. We did just that! And now, a couple of stories to sum up my experience with my Canadian classmates from ASC 31.

How Many Black Russians Can You Drink?

We were on our third TDY trip, this time to tour several industry and military facilities in the United States. We arrived at Eglin AFB in Florida at 1930 hours on Friday, 30 March 1979. We had the weekend to take a pause from the trip before assembling on Monday morning to meet the ranking USAF general from Eglin. We ate at the Eglin Officer's Club on Sunday evening and remained there for drinks afterward.

My classmates asked what I liked to drink—as if they didn't know by now. I told them I liked Black Russians—vodka and Kahlúa over ice in an old-fashioned glass. I went to the bar and ordered my drink, unaware of what my crazy Canadian friends were planning. When I returned, one of them said he never had a Black

Russian and asked if he could taste it. I said, "Sure," and passed the glass to him. He took a sip.

"Mmmm, not bad," he said as he made a motion to return it to me. Just as I was about to retrieve it, another classmate grabbed it and took a sip. After that, it went through all the remaining Canadians and was finally returned to me—empty!

I was about to go back to the bar when one of them said, "Bill, we're sorry. We'll get you another one." I didn't realize that they snuck over to the bartender and ordered a Black Russian for me—only it was another one from each Canadian classmate. So I had sixteen Black Russians placed before me.

They all said in unison, "Drink up, eh!" It took me a while, but I *did* finish them, and as we closed the bar at Eglin AFB, like my international buddies, I was three sheets to the wind! We had to be up early to meet the USAF general. I spent most of Sunday night and the wee hours of Monday morning hugging the porcelain throne. Once I finished that, I was as good as gold and slept like a baby.

Monday morning, I felt great. I knew from experience that once I hurl, I feel normal again! I made my way to the large auditorium to await the call to attention to greet our Eglin AFB host. My Canadian classmates arrived, though some staggered in. Our accompanying Canadian general officer and other Canadian staff from CFB, Winnipeg quickly joined. We were ready for the general. Well, most of us were!

As the USAF general approached the room, his aide called the room to attention: "A-tennn-tion!" Most of us snapped up from our seats and stood at attention. A few of the hangovers slowly managed to rise to a standing position; a few couldn't get up at all.

The visiting Canadian general and staff were very embarrassed, but they didn't realize that our USAF general had seen this all before. He laughed and said something like, "Gentleman, I heard you closed the bar last night at our Officer's Club. I'm glad you're having a good time. Welcome to Eglin AFB!" We quickly put that episode in the past, although I heard some stern counseling happened after we got back to Winnipeg.

The American Scored a Goal

As I mentioned, we would play floor hockey in the base gym. We looked forward to the competition and stress release. It was great to slam the puck around, but more fun slamming an opponent with the hockey stick, although it was not intentional (I think). The Canadians pride themselves on their ability to play this sport and felt an obligation to teach me the finer points of playing the game and scoring a goal.

One day, our classes ended in the early afternoon, and we looked forward to a good game before we left for home. The match was intense. The American—me—was dying to get a goal. I played my heart out, and finally, I scored. "Goal!" I shouted. The opposing team looked stunned for a bit. I could just imagine them thinking, *How could this happen?*

One guy started it when he shouted, "The American scored a goal!" Then another shouted the same thing. Seconds later, they all repeated this announcement, louder each time, seemingly to the entire base. I could only smile and soak up some of the glory. But I had paid a price.

When I arrived home after the game, as I went to greet Fran, she looked at me in horror and asked, "What happened?"

I said, "What?"

She said, "You have blood all over your T-shirt. What happened?"

I smiled. "Oh, we just played floor hockey, and I scored a goal!"

Fran started to inspect me—my face and head, my arms. She must have wondered, *Where did all that blood come from?* She could not unsee it, especially since I was wearing a *white* T-shirt!

I said, "Don't worry. I'm not the only one bleeding today!" As if that would make her feel any better. Just to wrap this up, it was worth a little blood to show those Canadians I could score one for the team, and for the Americans.

Crud

This is one of the RCAF's favorite games, especially since it originated in Canada and is a tradition. It has been adopted by many AFs worldwide as something to do on TGIF night or whenever the opportunity presents itself.

Crud is a team game played on a billiard or snooker table with a cue ball and a striped ball. No other equipment is necessary except for a pen and paper to keep track of the individuals' participation in the game. Teams consist of any number of people, equally divided into two teams. One referee is usually required.

The game's objective is to win prizes from your opponent. For Canadians, this means free drinks. To do this, you must *kill* all your opponents three times. The game runs by placing the cue ball on one end of the table and the striped ball on the other end. The first person up to "throw" the cue ball is known as the server. They have three chances to strike the ball. If they miss all three times, they inflict a "kill" on themselves, and the next person in the rotation becomes the server. However, if the server hits the ball, and the ball moves at least six inches, then the receiver—the first person in order from the other team—becomes the server and must retrieve the cue ball and shoot it at the striped ball.

Then, if the ball is successfully struck, the second person from the first team must now retrieve the cue ball, becoming the server, and this continues. You must hit the striped ball before it stops spinning/moving or you lose a life. Got this so far? It is imperative to respect the table rules. You may only shoot from the ends of the tables. Anytime you shoot the cue ball, the midline of your body must not pass the corner ends of the pool table. If this happens, either the referee or spectators will yell, "Foul," or some other word that will get your attention. You then lose a life. Still with me here? A team wins when everyone on the opposite team has been killed three times. Throughout my three-year assignment in Canada, I—and Fran—have played this game many times. It was a ton of fun!

I suggest that if you become interested in playing crud, read all the rules, take a trip to Canada, and have at it. You will easily notice where crud is played. Any pool table with a worn-out rug traced around it is a popular crud table. They are everywhere!

My Van Is Stuck

When we arrived in Canada in the summer of 1978, we had no idea how cold it gets there in the winter. My sponsor gave us general information about the winters, and we prepared with the proper clothing and especially engine-block heaters for our two vehicles. A block-heater is a simple device that plugs into an engine port and warms up antifreeze, oil, and internal engine components before you start the vehicle. OK, that is one indication of just how cold it gets.

The CFANS had a special function at their Officer's Mess (Officer's Club) around Christmas. The officers would wear their formal military uniforms—mess dress adorned with rank and medals—and their wives would wear their best formal attire. We drove to the club in our 1978 GMC van, which was basically a bread box on wheels. Even though we had snow tires mounted and the regular tires positioned in the rear area to provide extra weight for better traction, the vehicle did not perform well in snow and ice.

I dropped Fran off at the club entrance and then proceeded to find a parking spot. The parking lot was covered in bumpy ice ruts. I got stuck and couldn't park the van properly. No traction—wheels spinning! I went into the club to find my Canadian classmates to ask if they could push the van to a parking slot. They had all been there, already had several drinks, and jumped at my request, ready to help.

They were ready to follow me but did not put their coats on. So I remarked, "Hey, it's cold out there. Better get your coats!"

They all said, in effect, that they didn't need "any stinkin' coats!" When I say it was cold, let me expand that a bit. It turned out that the winter of 1978 was the second-coldest winter in Canada in the century. The temperature that evening was minus seventy-five degrees Fahrenheit! The Canadians use the Celsius scale for temperature. At −40 degrees, Celsius and Fahrenheit are equal. At −75 degrees F, C is −59.4.

My Canadian friends came outside without coats like it was a walk in the park. They helped me move my van, and we got back to the business of celebrating in the club. They were nuts!

I kept track. It never went above freezing from mid-November 1978 to mid-March 1979. The coldest temperatures would range from minus twenty to minus forty degrees through the winter. Believe me, it was hard to smile when your face was that cold! It didn't snow that much in Winnipeg, at least when we were there. Any snow that fell was there for the duration. I would shovel it to one side of the driveway, and the wind would blow it back. I just shoveled the same snow all winter!

You get accustomed to the winter to some degree (no pun intended). After our experience in Canada, we would answer any question about how the weather was there by saying, "Winnipeg has two seasons, winter and July 15!"

ASC 31 Class: I am in the back row, far left. The rest are my crazy Canadian officer friends.

■ TEACHING AND ASC DEVELOPMENT OFFICER

And so it went on like this day in and day out. There was no lack of humor, a funny story, or a friendly insult that was thrown around so we could laugh a bit while we worked our butts off. It helped keep our class together with a common goal of reaching July 1979. For my Canadian classmates, it would mean moving on to their next assignments at R&D centers, test facilities, to work with industry, or some other location where they could apply what they learned.

ASC Graduation - July 1979

For me, as a graduate of ASC 31 on 4 July and a new USAF major (promoted on 31 July), I would join the Aerospace Squadron and become part of its staff. I instructed over forty Canadian students across the Aerospace Systems course, the Senior Air Navigator course, and the Electronic Warfare Operations course for each of the following two years. I selected the subjects I liked to teach: electro-optics, weapons systems, and human factors engineering.

In September 1980, I completed the eleven-day Canadian Air Command Electronic Warfare course of the CFANS. Using this training as a main project seminar director for the new ASC conducted from 1979–1980, I supervised and guided members' technical research to thoroughly aid in their comprehension of electronic warfare.

The Canadian commanders—the Aerospace Squadron commander and the CFANS commander, indicated to Lt. Col. Stow that I was selected for a prestigious job as the ASC course development officer. The ASC had never had a complete formal document to capture all course subject content, application to overall course objectives, time allocation, technical merit, and course flow.

Before I left CFB, Winnipeg, I completed that assignment. I also completed the training plans for the Staff Air Navigation course and wrote several comprehensive studies on USAF navigation, which were instrumental in formulating CF policy in their navigation school. I also introduced a plan to integrate systems management studies into ASC based on my graduate work and a degree from USC. I proposed a fifteen-hour program of systems management principles and techniques, which was critically needed in the ASC. The plan was approved. The senior Canadian officers at CFB, Winnipeg valued the totality of this work very highly.

Some of my other responsibilities in the squadron included managing the squadron budget and coordinating logistical support for part of the course travel to industry and military facilities. I volunteered to plan a CFANS trip to the USAF Academy in Colorado Springs, Colorado, in February 1980. All went very well.

Lt. Col. Stow selected me among several exchange officers to represent the US Armed Forces with the American consul general in Winnipeg during Canadian National Remembrance Day ceremonies by placing a wreath to commemorate victims of previous wars. After the formalities, the consul general invited a group, including Fran and me, to his home for wine and cheese. A little bit of Napa Valley atmosphere, eh! This privilege to participate in the ceremony boosted my intention to be the best ambassador of the United States possible.

While at CFB, Winnipeg, I also completed the mid-level USAF PME, Air Command and Staff College by correspondence. This was another vital credential for any officer's records to be seriously considered for promotion. There are several more that I could take in the future. I had my eye on the AF Air War College, a senior-level program that I would fit into my schedule in a few years.

I appreciated the level and range of responsibility the Canadian commanders entrusted to me. I never considered myself the smartest whip in the room, but the one thing I *was* good at was being organized, and they recognized that as they added more tasks to my job jar. That is probably the most important factor that enabled me to address multiple tasks. I never learned to juggle balls in the air, but I can multitask with the best of them.

■ SPECIFIC ACHIEVEMENTS

A summary of my contribution as a USAF exchange officer for the CF is captured below:

Duty Title: DOD/Joint Activity Canadian Forces Aerospace Squadron Course Development Officer
Resume of Major Activities
Prepared and drafted amendments and published Course Training Standards (CTS)s and Plans (CTPs)
Developed a Course Review Plan for ASC and SANC
Organized and chaired an annual Course Review Meeting with the Squadron Commander, Chief Instructor, Standards Officer, and Course Directors
Supervised all planning and arranged all logistical support for ASC and SANC tours
Prepared annual forecasts and quarterly revisions of the Aerospace Squadron budget
Organized and coordinated the curriculum and obtained speakers for the annual Air Command Electronic Warfare Course
Presented Electro-Optical Electronic Warfare instruction to Air Command Electronic Warfare Course
Drafted and wrote the CFANS Report of the Air Command Electronic Warfare Course to Air Command Headquarters
Assisted in the establishment of a permanent Air Command Electronic Warfare Course in the Air Defense Group, CFB North Bay, Ontario; enabled the 414th Electronic Warfare Squadron, Air Defence Group at North Bay to construct a two-week course in a short time
Consultant to the Aerospace Squadron commander to aid him in the preparation of CF staff officer annual performance reports
Consultant to Special Projects Officer of CFANS Navigator Squadron to study navigator training/manning problems within the CF; my graduate program papers contained in-depth analysis of USAF issues which helped overcome problems in forecast changes and requirements
Reorganized and updated Electro-Optical (EO) Systems and Weapon Systems with current technology
Provided counseling and instruction to members of the ASC for preparation of written and audio-visual presentations
Provided guidance to several members of the ASC for their written visit reports from tours of aerospace/military facilities
Briefed CF navigation students in USAF history and organization, aircraft, and navigator utilization
Member of the CFANS Unit Fund Committee

However, life in Canada was more than a job. It was family in a new country, and Fran and I determined how best to experience it.

◼ LIFE IN CANADA

We adapted to the customs, the weather, and the lingo too, eh! We socialized with several married Canadian classmates from ASC 31 and courses after that. There were also special staff members and their wives who embraced our visit to their country with open arms and support.

One instructor, Tom Bailey, and his wife, Sharon, were always happy to engage—meet socially, get us involved in cross-country skiing, and curling. Their children had fun with ours. We bought some cross-country skis—still have them. We learned to trek our way through some beautiful, quiet trails, and if we wanted a hill—we did find one—we would ski down the banks of the Assiniboine River (pronounced, uh-sin-uh-boin) that ran through Winnipeg to join up with the Red River. You would end up on the river, which was frozen over by feet, not inches. It was great exercise and built stamina.

We tried curling a couple of times, but that required real skill. Curling is a sport in which players slide stones on a sheet of ice toward a target area split into four concentric circles. The curling stone is dense polished granite, with each one weighing between 17.2 to 19.1 kilograms (or thirty-eight to forty-two pounds). It has become an Olympic and Paralympic winter sport with medals in women's, men's, mixed doubles, and mixed wheelchair teams. We watched a bit of curling in the recent Olympic Games in Beijing. We preferred cross-country skiing!

We took an occasional trip to Grand Forks AFB in Grand Forks, North Dakota, just to get away and sample some familiar AFB environment for a change. We missed the usual services, like the commissary and base exchange, although we never really lacked anything we needed while in Winnipeg. One episode really surprised us. I had purchased some AF uniform items while at the base.

When we crossed into Canada, the border control officer asked if we had purchased anything in the United States and if we had anything to declare. I mentioned that I had some items that I was required to wear in the AF. He told me I had to pay a customs tax on it! Whoa—wait a minute here! I challenged that in my most diplomatic tone possible as I explained that I lived in Winnipeg and was assigned as a USAF exchange officer at CFB, Winnipeg, and they were required uniforms. It took a while, but he finally acquiesced.

One afternoon, Fran called me while I was working at the squadron. It was getting close to leaving for home. She said three words that caused me to pause.

"Joey is missing."

I asked, "What do you mean, Joey is missing?"

"He's gone! I can't find him anywhere."

"Did you look in the basement, outside, everywhere?" I prepared to leave the squadron building in haste.

"Yes. I'm checking with the neighbors," Fran said.

He was found safe and sound before I arrived home, which was only a few minutes after Fran called me. My eyes scanned the streets as I approached the house. Now, at age seven, Joey decided he needed some Life Savers candy. He put on his coat, grabbed some change from somewhere, and proceeded to a nearby neighborhood store to buy his candy. He had been there before with adults, so he knew where to go. He was spotted in an alley not far from our house on his way back, enjoying his candy. We didn't scold him too much; we just hugged him and told him not to do that again.

I maintained a regular exercise program and ran at least one hour each time for about an eight-mile distance. I heard about the Second Annual Manitoba Marathon scheduled for 15 June 1980. I never ran a marathon but decided I wanted to tackle that challenge. On a few runs, I would try some stretch goals beyond my usual eight miles and found I could achieve that. But I was usually exhausted afterward.

Our son Bill turned twelve years old on 3 June and decided he also wanted to run in the event, so we trained together as often as possible. He did pretty well as he ran with me, usually going the distance of eight miles. We decided to try for our best times in this race, which started and ended at the University of Manitoba Stadium, and knew we would split up. I kept up a pace of seven-and-a-half minutes per mile for roughly half the marathon. After that, I fell back in my pace, feeling the strain but never stopped running. After three hours, fifty-seven minutes, and ten seconds, I finished, placing 1,016 out of over 2,300 who finished.

Bill ran an amazing twenty-one miles without stopping before he walked about four more miles. He then finished by jogging the remaining 1.2 miles to cross the finish line in 5 hours, 49 minutes, and 49.4 seconds! Our times were posted in the 1980 *Results Book*. I was very proud of him. We made it, although my knees hurt so bad, I had to kneel on a bag of ice for a while, which seemed to help. We both slept very well that night!

Fran and I went to the movies with several Canadian couples to see *The Deer Hunter*, cowritten, produced, and directed by Michael Cimino, my first cousin once removed (my dad's first cousin). As we sat in the theater and the movie began, key names came up, including Michael Cimino. Our Canadian friends then stood up, shouting to the entire theater, "He's here! Cimino is right here," as they pointed to me. They kept repeating this louder and louder!

I told them, "Stop, stop that! sit down! I am not Michael Cimino!"

We all had a good laugh, of course, but that's just one example of Canadian spontaneity. Like the Black Russian drinks at Eglin AFB, you never knew what was coming! The movie went on to win five awards, including best Picture in 1979, and Michael won an Oscar for best Director. My favorite actor is Robert De Niro, who starred in the film.

USAF Exchange Officer's Conference
Ottawa, Ontario, Canada - May 1981

There was another family activity that was connected to my official duty assignment. Each year, the AF Exchange Office in Ottawa, Ontario, Canada, conducted an exchange conference. All exchange officers and their families were invited to attend. Fran and I, with our children, attended the three-day conference in May 1981. It was an excellent opportunity to meet the other exchange officers and their families from across Canada, share our specific assignment duties and experiences, and spend time seeing the sites in Ottawa. In May, it was still jacket weather, but it allowed for comfortable touring in the city.

■ FINAL REPORT

Each USAF exchange officer must submit a final report to the Exchange Office IAW AF regulations. In advance of my next assignment back in the United States, I submitted my report in May 1981 for the period 5 August 1978 through 26 July 1981. The report also went to the commandant of CFANS at CFB, Winnipeg, Canadian Air Command at CFB, Winnipeg, and Canada's National Defence Headquarters in Ottawa.

The report contained a résumé of my job assignment, which mirrors the specific achievements I have already addressed with greater detail. I also included the section, "Differences between USAF and Host Services Doctrines, Operating Practices, and Concepts," which described the subtle differences between the USAF and CF. While the CF graduates of the ASC would go directly to duties at R&D centers, test centers, and NORAD positions, the USAF is more specialized in its training through the use of the AF Institute of Technology (AFIT) and various university programs to provide trained officers for selected positions within AF Systems Command.

My report also included, "Main Problems Faced by the HOST Service within the Officer's Occupational Area," which addressed the occasional disparity of CF exchange officers at Mather AFB, usually a major. Suppose the USAF exchange officer at CFB, Winnipeg was below a major. In that case, he or she could be underutilized due to the RAF exchange officer, usually a squadron leader who is immediately designated a senior staff position as standards officer. It was important to ensure that the USAF exchange officer was a major, in my opinion.

My last report sections addressed "Benefits Derived from the Exchange Tour," education gained from the free-world aerospace industry and invaluable career-broadening of allied military missions and capabilities. "Additional Comments Considered Appropriate" focused on facilities, climate, resident status in Canada, SOFA interpretations, and medical care. I felt that future USAF exchange officers should know about these areas before arriving at their assignments—and not afterward, as I had.

■ HOUSE HUNTING TRIP, JUNE 1981

In March 1980, I submitted my Officer Career Objective Statement, AF Form 90, which outlined my preferences for my assignment objectives after my tour in Canada. I listed air operations officer and navigator WSO as my position at various locations—Eglin AFB, Florida; Cannon AFB, New Mexico; Bergstrom AFB, Texas; and the United Kingdom and Germany. I listed my secondary preference for a faculty member assignment at the USAF Academy in Colorado Springs, Colorado. My longer-range goal was as a squadron commander at Mather AFB, California.

I submitted these preferences with the expressed knowledge that they were consistent with AF's current and near-term needs and my commitment to return to flying duty. However, I attempted to leverage my systems management training, a degree from USC, and ASC completion and work during my exchange assignment for other positions.

The AF decided to send me back to requalify in the RF-4C at Shaw AFB in South Carolina. Of all places to return to that role, Shaw was the least of my and Fran's preferences because of the location, the size of Sumter, and the surrounding communities. But it would turn out to be a great tour in every aspect—professionally and socially.

I requested a permissive TDY trip to Sumter to look for a house. This was not a trip where the AF would reimburse expenses, but it did allow up to seven days, including travel time, to search for our new residence. Our next home, at 933 Shadow Trail, was on the west end of Sumter, South Carolina, and only nine miles from Shaw AFB. It was a single-level home in a nice neighborhood with a large backyard. How long we would live there, only God and the USAF knew.

■ THE NEED FOR SPEED

About halfway through my first year with the Canadians while in the ASC 31, I earned my senior navigator wings, which are awarded after seven years of rated time. Since I earned my basic navigator wings on 27 January 1972 at Mather AFB, 28 January 1979 was the effective date for my upgraded wings. I was thinking, *I never flew with these wings. Perhaps I need to go back to flying again to earn them properly, not just by sitting behind a desk and letting the time go by.*

My senior navigator wings.

The action thriller movie *Need for Speed* came out in 2014. In 1994, the movie *Speed*, starring Keanu Reeves, was released. Tom Cruise, as Pete "Maverick" Mitchell in the 1986 movie *Top Gun*, said, "I feel the need … the need for speed!" A few years earlier, in 1981, I didn't say anything about speed. I just felt it growing from within—to get back to the cockpit—back to low-level, high-speed flight, back to flying operations. That's the need I experienced.

While I did not obtain the precise career path choices I submitted on my "dream sheet," I did gain an assignment that would utilize my flying experience to broaden my utility within the 363rd Tactical Fighter Wing at Shaw AFB. The wing was about to undergo significant changes, and I would become immersed in them. Now, wearing my senior navigator wings would be justified!

RETURN TO OPERATIONS

■ RETURN TO SHAW AFB, SOUTH CAROLINA

Having sold our house in Winnipeg, which was routine and with no snags, we departed after a few days in a hotel to complete any final obligations in Canada. We had visited family in the summer of 1980, so we did not include a drive to New York this time before heading off to Shaw AFB in South Carolina.

Our last trip home took us through the upper-middle states as we made our way back to New York. We recalled our visit to Lake Itasca in Minnesota at the primary source of the Mississippi River; in Bemidji, where we did some canoeing; and traveled across northern Wisconsin into Michigan to cross the five-mile Mackinac (pronounced Mac-in-naw) Bridge that connected the upper and lower peninsulas of the Wolverine State, or if you prefer, the Great Lakes State—either one works.

But this time, we traveled south, passing through the Dakotas. We stopped at Offutt AFB, Omaha, Nebraska, to see some friends. We heard that Father Andrews was assigned there, and since we knew him from Mather, we made sure to stop by the base chapel for a visit. It was great to see him again.

Our visit with Lt. Col. Andrews, Catholic base chaplain at Offutt AFB, August 1981.

I was due to report to Shaw AFB by 30 September 1981, with early reporting authorized. We arrived there early in the month, which helped get the kids established in school at the beginning of the academic year. Since we acquired a house based on my permissive TDY from Winnipeg in June, we knew where we would live and were very familiar with the surrounding area. Not much had changed since I went through the initial RF-4C training in 1972.

◾ REQUALIFICATION: RF-4C

My initial assignment at Shaw was in the 33rd Tactical Reconnaissance Training Squadron (TRTS) of the 363rd Tactical Fighter Wing. I would only be assigned to the squadron until my check ride, after which I would transfer to my official duty in the wing. While assigned to the wing staff, I was attached to the 16th TRS for flying.

It had been six years since my last flight in an RF-4C, where I had accumulated 643.1 hours in the aircraft. While I did not need to repeat the entire course that I took for initial training, I did need to requalify by completing academic and flying training requirements. I began an eight-week classroom course called Tactical Reconnaissance Aircrew Training on 15 September 1981. This refresher included 112 hours of academics, flight simulations, and specialized training. I completed the academic course on 12 November 1981.

I began the flying sorties on 9 October and completed twenty-nine hours of flight training by 21 December, when I passed my requalification check ride. The flights leading up to the check ride included a good mix of day and night radar sorties and cross-country trips. During that training phase, I had the pleasure of flying a day radar sortie on 19 October and a practice check ride on 11 December with John Heide, former and final 14th TRS commander at Udorn AB, Thailand. It allowed us to catch up with our careers since we parted on arrival at Bergstrom AFB, Texas, where we completed the deployment of RF-4C aircraft from SEA in July 1975.

My AF Form 475 training report indicated completion of all requirements and noted a discrepancy-free check flight. It further recommended I should be upgraded to an IWSO immediately. Naturally, my experience as an IWSO didn't hurt. I completed a nine-week refresher course for the RF-4C from 5 January to 2 March 1982, which was focused more specifically on instruction and testing that I would administer as an IWSO and Stan/Eval qualified crewmember. More training certificates to file away. Training: it never stops!

■ A WING IN TRANSITION

When I arrived at Shaw AFB for the first time in 1972 to train in the RF-4C, the primary organization was the 363rd Tactical Reconnaissance Wing with a tenure from 1951 to 1993. It was a wing with reconnaissance squadrons, some for training and some for operations. The wing converted to the 363rd Tactical Fighter Wing as it acquired more fighter aircraft and was one of the first units dispatched to Operation Desert Shield, in which the military responded to check the expected advance of Iraq into Saudi Arabia following the invasion of Kuwait. And now, even more transitioning would begin with the advanced F-16 Fighting Falcon phasing into the wing.

The F-16 Fighting Falcon.
Photo: Courtesy of DVIDS—Defense Visual Information Distribution
Service, TSgt. Wes Wright, 23 February 2017.

This was a period of adjustment as aircraft repositioning and personnel reassignments were in motion. It required an unusual assumption of duties within the deputy commander for operations (DCOs) organizations, especially in the divisions for stan/eval and operations and training. As a result, this created opportunities to acquire some key responsibilities for wing operations. I was fortunate to be in the right place at the right time, especially with my experience as a combat-ready IWSO and SEFE.

■ WING STAN/EVAL

I was assigned as a wing/base stan/eval flight examiner for the RF-4C and as assistant chief, Wing Stan/Eval Division on 22 December, the day after my check ride. I had full responsibility for the operation of the division in the absence of the chief. Part of my duties included maintenance and quality control of the flight crew information file, AF forms related to flight operations, flight evaluation guides, and publications. I also maintained the flight check fragging systems, which allocated targets and parameters for all wing check rides.

Controlling all check-ride paperwork for the wing required extensive coordination with numerous agencies to ensure deadlines were met to maintain proficiency among the aircrews in all categories of flight sorties. I also had oversight of the wing's conversion to a new automated flight management system with the implementation of a small computer program. Ah, the world of computers on our doorstep!

Shortly after my Wing Stan/Eval assignment, the TAC IG performed its management effectiveness inspection (MEI), a measuring device of individual aircrew evaluations and collective trend analysis programs. The MEI report aims to accurately assess the Stan/Eval functions' capability to measure the quality of output of the unit training programs. The goal was to maintain a high degree of proficiency among the aircrews and trend away from incidents or serious accidents. Our division received an excellent rating.

During my second year at Shaw, I was moved up to the chief, Wing Stan/Eval Division responsible for its management and all wing aircrew flying evaluation programs, supplemental evaluations, and trend analysis data. Usually, the chief was a pilot, but in the interim period, before an F-16 pilot would become the division chief, I had the privilege of representing the wing deputy commander for operations in that role. I was honored to be entrusted to lead that office of expert aircrew flight examiners.

I also was the wing project officer for the TAC's g-force tolerance test conducted in our fighter wing. And I was selected to serve as the wing's Joint Exercise Solid Shield 1983 mission director and reconnaissance mission director during ORIs.

■ WING TRAINING

After a permanent chief of Stan/Eval came on board during my second year at this assignment, I took over responsibility for wing/base chief, Wing Training Division, another essential organization under the DCO. My office had responsibility for aircrew ground, continuation, and specialized flight training accomplishments for three combat-ready squadrons and other prominent wing programs, such as supervisor of flying (SOF), runway supervisory officer (RSO), annual instrument refresher course (AIRC), life support, and F-16/RF-4C simulator training. I would also function as a critical adviser to the DCO on wing aircrew resource management and the base flight records section.

During my assignment in the Wing Training Division, I received a handwritten note dated 23 September 1982 from Col. Daniel, congratulating me on my selection for promotion to lieutenant colonel. Even though this would not take effect until months later, when my promotion number came up, it was satisfying to know I made the list.

As previous acquaintances and friends cross paths in the AF from time to time, it was great to have Russ Metzler (Russie Babes) working within the division. We had been through several assignments together after we went through the same class for initial RF-4C training at Shaw AFB in 1972, were at the 91st TRS at Bergstrom AFB, Texas, and the 14th TRS at Udorn AB, Thailand. Russ was my right-hand man for the life support section when he took over that role in the spring of 1983.

Russ managed the life support staff, consisting of a master sergeant, a staff sergeant, and a sergeant. All had significant experience in the life support field. Since the wing now had two fighter-type aircraft—the RF-4C and the F-16—Russ managed and conducted the ejection seat training for both: the Martin-Baker seat for the RF-4C, and the ACES II seat for the F-16.

He also managed and conducted the annual water survival training for all aircrews on equipment and procedures to support aircrew survival in case of ejection over water. He performed periodic inspections of squadron life support equipment in the F-16 and RF-4C squadrons.

Another critical part of training pertained to the evasion of aircrews who might find themselves in hostile territory after an aircraft ejection. Russ planned, coordinated, and conducted periodic evasion exercises to prepare aircrews for this environment and thereby enable the best chances for their rescue and safe return.

I also depended on Russ to write, update, and maintain training syllabi to support all aspects of life support training for the 363rd Tactical Fighter Wing.

Captain Russ Metzler.
Photo: Courtesy of Russ Metzler.

Russ was the perfect guy for the job, which demanded a dedicated focus on key components that contributed to aircrew safety. Did I mention that training never stops? You can never have enough training. And the one thing to never forget—always use your training—may save your life!

Russ not only went through Jungle Survival School at Clark AB in the Philippines with me, he also completed a special survival school in the swamps of Georgia at the direction of our Wing DCO, Col. George Forster. While he was reluctant to go (who wouldn't be), Russ came back more qualified than anyone.

Russ entered the AF in the fall of 1970 and completed twenty-two years of service after several RF-4C assignments stateside, in Thailand and in Germany. Later in his career, he was assigned at Kirtland AFB, New Mexico, to the Air Force Operational Test and Evaluation Center (AFOTEC), for eight years. This is a choice assignment for experienced airmen to evaluate the capability of systems to meet warfighter needs by planning, executing, and reporting independent operational assessments. Given his extensive experience in tactical reconnaissance, Russ focused on advanced reconnaissance vehicles. He retired in the summer of 1992.

In October 2021, I was able to contact Russ after many years. It was great to catch up with each other. After the AF, Russ went into the plumbing business for sixteen years and retired (again) in the fall of 2008. I was honored to have Russ work side by side with me.

◾ OTHER DUTIES

Each day of flight operations, the Wing DCO designates his representative to act as the supervisor of flying (SOF). The SOF is a highly trained aircrew member entrusted to perform specific duties related to flight operations. The SOF has access to the SOF truck, an AF vehicle equipped with radio communications to the base tower, the aircraft squadrons, the wing command post, and emergency resources such as the base hospital, firefighters, and other emergency response teams.

During my assignment at Shaw AFB, I was the designated SOF on a routine basis. Before any aircraft takeoffs, the SOF begins the day inspecting the runways for any foreign object debris (FOD) that may be hazardous. This could be anything from items that may have blown onto the runway, something that separated from an aircraft previously, or even a dead animal. The SOF's responsibility is to make a thorough inspection and report the inspection as "complete" to the base tower before they would authorize any takeoff clearances for the aircrews.

After the runway inspection, the SOF spends time in the base tower, monitoring the flight activity for the day—all takeoffs and landings. If there is an emergency at any level, the SOF helps coordinate the proper elements to render aid to the aircrew as needed. While I had a full grasp of all RF-4C aircraft systems and potential hazards/emergencies through my training and experience, I had almost no knowledge of the F-16.

One time when I was on SOF duty, an F-16 had a severe emergency involving hydrazine, a colorless liquid that feeds the electrical systems and the emergency power unit (EPU) as part of a backup system on the aircraft. The F-16 is a "fly-by-wire" (FBW) aircraft. The FBW is a system that replaces the conventional manual flight controls of a plane with an electronic interface. The movements of flight controls are converted to electronic signals transmitted by wires, and flight control computers determine how to move the actuators at each control surface to provide the ordered response in flight.

When activated, the EPU provides emergency power for the electric jets system in case of an electrical failure. In case of a flameout, emergency power generated by the EPU is designed to give pilots the time they need to land the aircraft safely. Hydrazine can be extremely dangerous to the pilot and ground crews. After a brief communications exchange with the airborne F-16 pilot, I coordinated a handoff to the pilot's squadron and wing command post while in the tower. The pilot remained in constant communication with all of us during some tense moments before he landed and was assisted by emergency response teams on the ground. Just a little excitement on an otherwise typical day of flying!

Another duty that was an absolute pleasure was the Operation Air Force Program, a six-week orientation program for sixteen AFA cadets. I briefed and trained a team of unit project officers who assisted me in the program. The cadets will be a welcomed group if you ever want to meet some of the most eager and willing young potential AF officers. They are full of questions and soak up everything they can learn. Their motivation is what makes interaction fun.

Besides my wing staff jobs and related programs, I had my share of flight sorties to maintain proficiency, to participate in wing exercises, and perform flight readiness inspections. I did not have extensive TDYs during my assignment at Shaw, but the few I had were memorable.

My first TDY while on this assignment was during my initial requalification phase in October 1981. Lt. Col. McKim and I flew cross country from Shaw AFB to Andrews AFB, Maryland, on my birthday, 30 October. The next day, we flew a short aircraft handling characteristics (AHC) mission in an appropriately designated airspace over the Atlantic before proceeding to Charleston AFB, South Carolina, to refuel. This sortie profile is a requirement for the pilot, but WSOs also learn specific aircraft characteristics while under abnormal flight attitudes for the aircraft. We departed Charleston AFB and returned to Shaw later that day.

In July 1982, I flew with Tom Hughes on cross-country flights over three days with low-level sorties en route. Our trip included a landing at Eglin AFB in Florida, followed by another low-level before landing at Randolph AFB in Texas. The next day we departed Randolph and landed at Navy Dallas Air Station in Texas after another low-level flight. On our final day, we made our way back to Shaw after another training sortie. Landing at different military installations offered a good variety of training.

My final TDY in the RF-4C was during two weeks in August/September 1982 for another visit to engage in Red Flag exercises out of Nellis AFB in Nevada, where we could fly in a simulated combat threat zone. I had been there when I was assigned to the 91st TRS at Bergstrom AFB in Austin.

On this trip, I flew five sorties with Dick Schwinn in the desolate areas in western Nevada, evading smokey SAMs while going after our targets. Bobby Neese and I flew an air combat training (ACT) sortie with some high-profile maneuvering on one of the days there. On our last day, 5 September, I flew from Nellis AFB to Kelly AFB, Texas, with Dick Schwinn. After lunch and refueling, I swapped pilots with another WSO and returned to Shaw AFB with Lt. Col. Penney in the front seat. During this trip, I logged 10.9 hours.

Other than TDYs, I flew in support of other activities. In November 1981, Dick Rouse and I flew an "out-and-back" to Warner Robins AFB in Georgia to pick up some aircraft parts at their supply facility. We stored them around the camera bays in the nose of the aircraft. As before, we usually don't merely fly from point A to point B without getting some training benefit en route. So we tackled a couple of low-level sorties that day before we returned to Shaw.

Based on prior coordination, on 24 February 1982, Gary Cooke and I met up for a DACT engagement off the East Coast, over the Atlantic, in designated airspace with an F-4E out of Seymour Johnson AFB, North Carolina. DACT—dissimilar air combat training—where the F-4E was the aggressor, and we needed to employ countermeasures to evade its attack.

It's good practice and experience with other fighter-type aircraft, although the F-4 and the RF-4 are similar in many respects. The training was about twenty minutes of rock 'n' roll in the sky—lots of g-forces, dives, climbs, use of engine afterburner—all to evade the aggressor's ability to lock on us as a target. No contribution from my stomach, but I always seem to lose about four pounds of sweat on these sorties! It's very physical.

In October 1982, I flew in two sorties, one with Jim Bortz and the other with Al Johnson, supporting an exercise called Sea Owl. In June 1983, I flew six sorties with Tony Orr in a wing ORI between 2 and 5 June. On two days, Tony and I "double-banged"—flew two sorties in one day on two different days. You get the targets assigned by the inspectors, plan and brief the plan, return, and debrief the mission. Then repeat the process all over again on the same day. It amounts to a long and tiring day, but needless to say, it's gratifying when you acquire all the targets on film, which we did on all our assigned sorties!

On 1 February 1983, I called Fran's brother, Vince. He was the deputy base commander at Myrtle Beach AFB in South Carolina. I asked if he was available for lunch and that I would plan a low-level training sortie out of Shaw and land at Myrtle to refuel before flying another training sortie before landing back at Shaw. He said he was available and would pick me up on the flight line.

After landing at Myrtle Beach AFB, my pilot, Dave Brett, taxied into our parking spot. I saw Vince drive up in his staff car just as we cut power to the engines. He had radio communications with the tower, so he knew exactly where we would park the aircraft. I exited the cockpit, gave him a salute (after all, he outranked me; he was a lieutenant colonel), and we headed to the Officer's Club for lunch—he in his uniform of the day, and me in my flight suit. I left my G suit at the aircraft. Dave said he would stay with the aircraft during refueling.

We had a nice lunch and conversation before he drove me back to the aircraft, now refueled, to see me off. It was good to see each other at our respective jobs. We would always talk about one of our favorite subjects: handball. Vince was an excellent handball player, and whenever we had the opportunity to have a few days of family visits, we would reserve the court for some games.

In all the years Vince and I challenged one another in the court, I think I only beat him once. *One time!* And we played a lot of games. The same thing happened when we converted to racquetball. He always had the edge over me. I know one thing for sure: Playing opposite him made my game better, but never better enough to win against him.

After takeoff, we requested a low-level clearance from departure control to fly at five hundred feet AGL, parallel to Myrtle Beach but over the ocean, where we saw a few people walking along the surf on the sand and waving. We rocked our wings in reply. No one was in the water. Remember, this was February.

In my experience flying with some of the best pilots in the RF-4C, we had never needed to make an approach-end barrier landing. This method of landing is only used for emergencies, when there is doubt regarding the integrity of the aircraft's landing gear, among other concerns. A cable spun across the runway surface is one of several types of aircraft-arresting systems that stop an aircraft's forward momentum in a landing or aborted takeoff.

One day, as we made our approach to the runway at the end of a local low-level training sortie and return to Shaw, the pilot moved the handle to put the gear down. We could hear the gear extending and could feel its effect on the aircraft's attitude in the air. But the pilot did not get a "nose gear down" indication in the cockpit. He notified approach control and coordinated another approach after he cycled the gear up and got a good indication the gear was up.

Approach control vectored us around for another approach and landing. But again, indicators showed that the nose gear was not completely extended and locked. We did a flyby past the base tower so they could look through binoculars to verify if the gear was down. They communicated that it appeared to be down, but we still had no proper indication in the cockpit. Therefore, to be on the safe side, we coordinated an approach-end barrier landing.

We went through the checklist, part of which required us to lower the hook mounted at the rear of the aircraft and lock our harnesses so that when we engaged the cable at the approach end of the runway, our bodies would not be thrust violently forward. In this situation, as your approach the runway at speeds varying well over one hundred knots, you come to a complete stop in a few seconds. All worked well. Our nose gear did not collapse. A ground crew helped disengage us from the barrier, and we taxied back to our parking position. The maintenance crew would determine why the indicators did not sync with the actual nose gear configuration. Another thrill in the RF-4C. Another bit of experience.

Thrills are appreciated more when all your training pays off, you follow procedures, your support ground crew and standby emergency personnel are at the ready to assist, and you chalk each thrill up to experience. Things can go wrong. But on this day, they went right!

My last flight in the RF-4C was on 15 September 1983, with Capt. Dave Greggs. Dave had been recently assigned to Shaw. We planned a route survey on IR-002, one of our low-level training routes in the Smokey Mountains, which straddle the border between North Carolina and Tennessee. Several peaks in the area are over six thousand feet above MSL. The highest elevations along this route were at Inadu Knob, at 5,925 feet, and Old Black, at 6,370 feet along the Appalachian Trail on the North Carolina-Tennessee border.

During my training, I had flown this route when I first qualified in the RF-4C in 1972. While at Shaw for this assignment, I flew on this route about ten times, according to my records. The terrain varies by a few thousand feet as we routinely fly the course at 500 feet AGL during the day and 1,500 feet AGL at night, at 480 knots GS.

My last recorded RF-4C flight, with Captain David Greggs, on 15 September 1983.

■ LIFE IN SUMTER

Now that we were in Sumter, South Carolina, again, this time with three children, not just Bill, we had one in high school, and the younger two were in elementary school. This was a new dynamic in our family's social life focused primarily on sports and church activities and interactions with other families with similar interests.

Bill started eighth grade in Sumter and soon became involved with baseball and a confirmation class that prepared him for that sacrament in our church. In the next two years, he transitioned from a short time with soccer to the Sumter High School football team as a kicker. It was the thing to do on Friday night in Sumter! Think *Friday Night Lights.*

Joe started third grade in our first year back in Sumter and participated in basketball, baseball, and the Confraternity of Christian Doctrine (CCD) classes at church. Our youngest, Jeannie, started kindergarten. When she turned seven, she was also in CCD and received her first Holy Communion. She also loved being in Brownies and dance class. This kid wanted to do everything!

Fran and I joined other parents whose children were in Bill's confirmation class and complemented their learning with trips and projects. Joe and Jeannie both loved hanging out with the older crowd—Bill's friends—and did not want to miss out on any of the fun that group created.

There were two Catholic churches in town, St. Anne's and St. Jude's. We usually attended St. Anne's. One of the priests from St. Jude's, Father Tony Rigoli, said a mass at St. Anne's one Sunday, and we loved his sermon and his ability to communicate, sometimes through song and his guitar!

Father Tony is an Oblate priest belonging to the Missionary Oblates of Mary Immaculate (O.M.I.). Through the church activities, which became part of our lives, we got to know Father Tony very well. On one occasion, Fran and Father Tony took the high school CCD class to the beach, packed in our van, Joe and Jeannie included. Fran also devoted time to other church-related activities. Our relationship with Father Tony is one of the best that has resulted from my assignment there this second time.

We usually maintain contact with Father Tony through Christmas cards, but also on other occasions from time to time. He characterizes his experience in Sumter as a blessing in many respects. He grew up in an Italian and Catholic neighborhood he calls "an Italian ghetto." He had never been in the South and feared that he would be accepted as a Yankee first, followed by a priest in the Bible Belt.

His fears quickly turned to feelings of warmth and welcome in Sumter. He made many friends, one of which was a local rabbi. Father Tony's love of the Sumter community and Shaw AFB was returned to him many times over. In his own words, he said, "My relationship with Shaw AFB was truly a blessing. They named me Auxiliary Chaplain, and the many friendships that developed I will always treasure … I am always grateful that I was blessed with eight years in this wonderful church and City. I must say I left part of my heart in Sumter, SC."

Father Tony at a parish event.   *Kids loved it when he sang with them.*
Photos: Courtesy of Father Tony Rigoli.

Father Tony is presently the pastor of Our Lady of Guadalupe Church & International Shrine of St. Jude in New Orleans, Louisiana. He has been there for many years and has helped the local population through so much hardship and devastation resulting from intense hurricanes. When we think of priests, we naturally think of this gentle and devoted man who has given his life for the welfare of others.

▪ "I WANT YOU TO BECOME AN EXPERT IN TENCAP"

In June 1983, Col. Ronald Knecht called me from HQ USAF at the Pentagon. Ron was the chief of the Space Operations Division, office symbol AF/XOSO. He reported directly to Maj. Gen. John Storrie, the director of Space, office symbol, AF/XOS. I will never forget Ron's words.

After he introduced himself, he said, "I want you to become an expert in TENCAP."

I replied, "OK, sir. What is TENCAP?" I had never heard of it. In the back of my mind, I wondered, *Am I about to have another tour of duty cut short?* I was at Shaw for nearly two years, and things were going great. I was on the wing staff, regularly flying on proficiency sorties and administering check rides. We had a good social life. Fran and I and the kids were happy there.

Ron explained that his division was responsible for developing concepts, procedures, and techniques for improving national satellite support of military operations.
TENCAP stands for Tactical Exploitation of National Space Program Capabilities—a
mouthful! He said he selected me because of my experience in tactical air operations.
I'm not the only USAF officer with those qualifications, but I was honored that he
chose me.

This would mean another move for the family. I discussed this with Fran, and
since I would not need to report until 30 September, we decided that I would move
to the northern Virginia area, rent an apartment, and look for a house before moving
the entire family from Sumter. The kids would finish their school year, and we would
relocate in June 1984. At least the drive between northern Virginia and Sumter was
manageable for any visits we would make.

My experience at Shaw was about as good as it gets for an RF-4C WSO. I flew in
128 sorties during my two-year assignment—various day and night radar scenarios,
visual reconnaissance, day and night AARs, and a host of exercise support, readiness
inspections, and special missions. I had the opportunity to manage wing-level divisions
and was rewarded with endorsements by the commander of the 9th Air Force at Shaw
on my officer effectiveness reports. The higher the endorsements, the better!

My last RF-4C sortie with Captain Dave Greggs, which lasted 1.8 hours, contributed to my career total RF-4C flight time of 846.2 hours and my total RF-4C sorties
at 462. My total flying time was 1480.5 hours which included UNT student, the 91st
TRS, the 14th TRS, UNT instructor navigator, and instructor in the 16th TRS. Since
I now had an assignment to the Pentagon, it was unknown if I would ever fly again
for the AF. At least for now, as it is often said, I would "fly a desk."

AF TENCAP: SPACE OPERATIONS

▪ THE PENTAGON

It was September 1983. The kids were back in school in Sumter to start the new academic year. I arranged to rent a tiny, one-room apartment close to the Pentagon for the next ten months, until Fran and the kids moved to Virginia. I packed the van to the limit with everything I needed, including a single bed. The trip from Sumter, South Carolina, to 1200 South Courthouse Road in Arlington, Virginia, was 444 miles and took about six and a half hours to complete.

I rolled up to the apartment building late at night and used the service elevator to make several trips to bring my car's contents up to apartment number 627, on the sixth floor. I was exhausted. The first thing I did was prepare the bed to collapse for the night at around 11 p.m. Setting up the room could wait until the next day.

I chose the apartment location specifically for its convenience to the Pentagon. As the crow flies, it was one and a half miles away, and I would split commuting by bus or walking. The elevation at my apartment was 197 feet; the Pentagon was at 30 feet, so the pace to work was an easy, gentle, downhill walk, most of the way along Columbia Pike. Coming back, the hike up this steady slight incline helped to keep me in shape.

The Pentagon is the Department of Defense (DoD) headquarters, the successor agency to the National Military Establishment created by the National Security Act of 1947. The Pentagon's three occupant groups—military, civilians, and contractors—contribute to the planning and execution of the defense of our country. It is one of the world's largest and most recognizable office buildings. It is twice the size of the Merchandise Mart in Chicago and has three times the floor space of the Empire State Building in New York City.

Construction on the Pentagon, originally known as Arlington Farms, began on 11 September 1941, precisely sixty years before the 9/11 attacks, on a plot of land that was once part of the grand estate of Confederate Gen. Robert E. Lee. The land was confiscated during the Civil War. The Pentagon was conceived at the request of Brig. Gen. Brehon B. Somervell, chief of the Construction Division of the Office of the Quartermaster General.

The original purpose of the Pentagon was to provide a temporary solution to the War Department's critical shortage of space. Post-WWII plans were to recycle the Pentagon into hospital, office, or warehouse space. Construction was completed on 15 January 1943, just sixteen months after it began, and it remains the largest office building in the world.

Learning my new job would be one challenge. Learning how to navigate the Pentagon requires a learning curve all its own. The Pentagon spans a gross area of about 6.34 million square feet (about thirty-four acres). This building includes five floors plus a basement and a partial mezzanine, reaching a total height of about seventy-one feet.

The Pentagon.
Photo: Courtesy of DVIDS—Defense Visual Information Distribution
Service, SSgt. Brittany Chase, 11 May 2021.

The halls of the Pentagon are five concentric pentagonal rings intersected by ten corridors for a total walking distance of about 17.5 miles. Despite the Pentagon's massive size, the average time to walk between two points is only about seven minutes. In the center of the Pentagon is the five-acre area known as the Center Courtyard. There was a café in the center of the courtyard that we jokingly called the Ground-Zero Café, suggesting the Pentagon would surely be a prime target for Russia, with ground zero being the aim point for one (or more) of their ICBMs.

The office for Space Operations, with the office symbol AF/XOSO, was located in the basement, along with many other functional divisions for the operations side of the HQ AF staff and other agencies. When someone asked where our office was, we would respond, "In the basement, near the purple water fountain." If they didn't know where that was, we would recommend they go to the basement and ask someone where the purple water fountain was, which would get them within a few feet of our office door.

Photo: Courtesy of Oriana Pawlyk, journalist.

Once I had my badge, I had access to the Pentagon and specific offices within the building. The building contained restaurants, a barbershop, a bank (Pentagon Federal Credit Union), access to the Metro (bus and rail), and other conveniences.

▪ TENCAP

AF Space Operations conducted several programs with a total staff of between eight and ten officers under the direction of Col. Ron Knecht. The office reported to the Director of Space, Maj. Gen. John Storrie. His Directorate fell under the AF Deputy

Chief of Staff (DCS) for Plans and Operations. The Assistant DCS for Plans and Operations was my former boss at Kadena AB, Okinawa, Dave Nichols, now a major general. A year later, Dave became the DCS and was promoted to lieutenant general.

TENCAP was one of the programs in Space Operations and was congressionally mandated to the DoD in 1977. The program's purpose was to exploit the current and future potential of existing national, commercial, and civil space systems and national air-breathing systems and to provide these capabilities to the warfighter as rapidly as possible.

TENCAP provides commanders with situational awareness and decision-making assistance while also providing intelligence preparation for the battlefield, targeting assistance, and threat location/avoidance tools to the tactical warfighter. TENCAP uses a rapid-prototyping capability to conduct operational concept demonstrations with prototypes in the field within a short period.

The original charter contained three major thrust areas: exploit existing national systems (for example, satellites and remote sensing) for the benefit of the tactical war-fighter; educate the warfighter about national system capabilities through training, exercise participation, and wargames; and influence the development of future national systems to better meet the needs of the warfighter by advocating warfighter requirements to designers early in the design process for new systems.

Three primary officers in Space Operations focused on the TENCAP program: Maj. Chris Caravello, Maj. Denny Haynes, and me. We worked very well together. Our official title was Headquarters Air Force (HAF) Space Operations Officer.

Responsibilities focused on developing concepts, procedures, and techniques for improving national satellite support of military operations. I was very familiar with tactical reconnaissance through my operational assignments in the RF-4C. However, a vastly broader scope required that I develop expertise in national reconnaissance and surveillance systems linked to strategic and tactical airborne systems and USAF tactical operations.

The job included planning and conducting special tests and military exercises in various theater operations. This activity required interfacing with Air Staff (USAF) Major Commands (MAJCOMs), Office of the Joint Chiefs of Staff (OJCS), Office of the Secretary of Defense (OSD), national agencies, and contractor personnel at management and technical levels.

The collectiveness of this job was a whole new world for me. The learning curve was steep and multifaceted. It was not limited to the "who's who" in these upper-organizational echelons. It included the "how" relative to interrelationships, budget allocations, cross-organizational priorities, and exposure to politics. After all, the Pentagon is within the Capital Beltway surrounding Washington, DC.

I had to learn how Air Staff functioned, how satellites operated, and how to correlate weapons' functions and reconnaissance needs. I also had a budget of over a half million dollars to manage contracted efforts from various defense contractor organizations.

Like many of the offices within the Pentagon, Space Operations also contained a sensitive compartmented information facility (SCIF) within its space because we handled highly classified material regularly. The SCIF was a secure room with associated procedures for entry and exit and shielded from any external audio- or electronic-sensing devices. No phones or other devices, like the old pagers, were permitted. They needed to be checked by security while using the SCIF and were returned when leaving.

During my years in tactical operations, I had a top-secret clearance, which enabled me to access intelligence as needed to do my job as an RF-4C WSO. This job required a higher clearance level due to the exposure to sensitive program information and the interaction among many diverse military and defense contractor organizations. Therefore, I received clearance to the TS/SCI level after a thorough security clearance and polygraph exam.

Later, at the Pentagon, when the job required a more specific focus on an individual program, I obtained an additional clearance, a special access program (SAP). In the US federal government, security protocols provide highly classified information with safeguards and access restrictions that exceed those for regular (collateral) classified information. SAPs can range from so-called black projects to routine, but especially to sensitive operations.

SAP clearance is given only to those who need to know the information to carry out their programs responsibly and lasts only for as long as required. The clearance may end, but the responsibility to protect the information is paramount and binding as long as it remains classified. You safeguard that information to your grave unless there are clear official indications that it has been declassified.

During my initial few months at the Pentagon, I focused on gaining expertise in TENCAP. However, I balanced my time among work, exercise, seeing some of the sites in the DC area, and looking for the best affordable neighborhood in the northern Virginia area with nearby schools—both elementary and high school. Bill had started his sophomore year at Sumter High.

Every few weeks, I would plan to work earlier on a Friday and leave around 3:30 p.m. for Sumter to visit Fran and the kids for the weekend. On the return side, I would depart around 6 p.m. on Sunday to arrive back at my apartment by 1:00 a.m. Right to bed as I had to leave for work in six hours!

On one fall trip home, during football season, as I got within radio range of a

Sumter High School football game while traveling on I-95 South, I tuned up the game. As I said before, it was like *Friday Night Lights*, with my attention focused on the last few minutes of the game. Sumter was behind, and time was running out. Our son Bill was the kicker for the team. The coach called for Bill to try for a field goal. The entire team, including "Big Willie," who often carried Bill to the coach at practices, was focused for the play. Tense moments. I was all ears!

The local newspaper the next day posted something like, "Bill Cimino, Sumter High School kicker: The biggest little man on the team." Bill had kicked the winning field goal. I went crazy in the car that night! The next day, the newspaper photo showed his teammates carrying him on their shoulders. The irony of it all is that the "biggest little man" was, in fact, the smallest guy on the team! I couldn't wait to see him and offer congratulations!

Fran came to the DC area to attend my promotion to lieutenant colonel on 1 December 1983 in the Pentagon. Major General John Storrie officiated at the ceremony and promoted me. Fran participated once again by pinning my new rank on one shoulder as the general pinned the other. That was on a Thursday, so we took a long weekend together. We visited some of the famous sites in DC and checked out some potential neighborhoods for our next family move. She took the van back to Virginia and left me with our other car.

Maj. Gen. John Storrie and Fran at my promotion ceremony to lieutenant colonel.
Photos: Courtesy of Maj. Gen. John Storrie.

The distance between Sumter, South Carolina, and northern Virginia certainly did not prevent me from being home for holidays as I had been so constrained in Okinawa and Thailand. I took advantage of the leave I had built up to be home for a few days over Thanksgiving, Christmas, and the New Year.

WEDNESDAY, 4 JANUARY 1984

The Pentagon is a complex communications hub where news, good and bad, travels fast. Sadly, 4 January 1984 will remain in my mind due to my connection with two airmen: pilot David Greggs and WSO Scott Miller, an RF-4C crew from Shaw AFB. They were near the end of their low-level photo reconnaissance mission in the Smokey Mountains when they crashed south of Cosby, Tennessee. They were on the same route I flew on my last mission before leaving Shaw AFB for my assignment at the Pentagon. I flew that route with David on 15 September 1983. Scott was one of my navigator students when I was a navigator instructor at Mather AFB.

They crashed in the early evening as their aircraft almost cleared Inadu Knob, a 5,925-foot mountain near the Appalachian Trail, near Old Black Mountain, at 6,370 feet. It was unknown if they were executing a climb to ETC due to disorientation or other problems. I never heard the accident board's findings on the crash. I later read that they could not determine the exact cause of the accident. ETC would have been 7,400 feet AGL.

Scott, thirty-two, from Irving, Texas, was a bachelor. David, twenty-eight, from Montgomery, Alabama, had a wife and one son. Larry Arrendale, a duty officer with the FAA in Atlanta said there was no indication of trouble before air traffic controllers lost radio contact with the jet at 7:12 p.m. Wednesday.

But Estelle Jenkins, who lives in the town of Cosby, about five miles from the crash site, said the jet flew low over her house before it crashed, and it sounded like it was in trouble. "We were watching TV, and I heard it fly over, and … I knew there was something wrong with that plane," she said. "And then … it sounded like something burst."

About thirty-five park rangers, Civil Air Patrol volunteers, and AF personnel searched on foot and horseback for about eight hours Thursday before finding the wreckage. The Air National Guard contributed a helicopter and fixed-wing plane for the search, and the Tennessee Highway Patrol brought in a helicopter.

The loss of any airman is tragic. It can happen for various reasons while flying any type of aircraft. Sometimes we learn the cause of the accident; other times, we don't. This tragedy was a bit more personal since I knew David and Scott. They were young men serving their country, and that alone deserves my admiration and respect.

SATELLITE IMAGERY AND THE NRO

Important note: I must emphasize that this entire section has information relative to satellites and their capabilities that can be readily found on the internet. However, to be cautious, I avoid any specific details suggested by these sources and only illustrate their utility relative to the TENCAP program. It undoubtedly provides intelligence in many forms and at multiple levels—commercial and government—county, state, federal, the intelligence community, and the DoD.

While you can overwhelm yourself with information from the internet on US satellite programs, types, agencies, contractors, capabilities, and more, much of what is declassified today was protected through various clearances and security special access programs for many years, especially in the seventies through the nineties, and into the early 2000s. Nonetheless, one cleared with sensitive information must always proceed with caution. In that regard, I use generalities as much as possible.

Satellite imagery and its analysis have many applications that enable users in numerous government and commercial organizations to understand better the significance of the data it provides, the timeliness of the data, the utility, and especially the resultant product when it is complemented with other data.

Satellites are used for many applications in military operations: essential secure and unsecured communications; weather and navigational data for ground, air, and fleet operations; and threat warnings. Both ground-based and space-based systems monitor ballistic missile launches around the globe to guard against a surprise missile attack on North America. It is no surprise that the United States, and other nations, have satellites that watch each other.

Remote sensors operated by governments and businesses worldwide collect satellite images of the earth. Satellite-imaging companies sell photos by licensing them to governments and businesses such as Apple Maps and Google Maps.

I'll stick to satellite imagery and its utility to the tactical community since that was the focus of my job at the Pentagon. The satellites that supported the TENCAP program continue to mature in their capabilities and usefulness. It was essential to understand the physical constraints of satellites—their orbit times (and thus revisit time over a specific location), their fields of view (FOV), instantaneous fields of view (IFOV), and many other parameters.

Like digital photographs, satellite images contain tiny dots called pixels. The width of each pixel is the satellite's spatial resolution. Commercial satellites have a spatial resolution of down to fifty centimeters per pixel; the most detailed NASA images show ten meters in each pixel. The interpretation of satellite imagery and aerial photography involves the study of various primary characters of an object with reference to spectral bands, which is helpful in visual analysis. The essential elements of shape, size, pattern, tone, texture, shadows, location, association, and resolution can be determined from the imagery.

Metadata means "data for the data," the data that describes these images: What time were they taken? What was the sensor's geometry at that time—its FOV, sun angle? Where exactly on earth is the image? The metadata answers these kinds of questions.

Many earlier spy satellites are in the public domain. In the 4 June 2012 issue of *Space.com* staff published a list of several satellites. It illustrated some in the National Museum of the US Air Force in Dayton, Ohio, and the National Reconnaissance Office (NRO) release of a graphic depiction of Cold War–era surveillance vehicles in orbit between 1971 and 1986.

The National Reconnaissance Office (NRO), funded through the National Reconnaissance Program (NRP), is a member of the US intelligence community and an agency of the US DoD. It designs, builds, launches, and operates the reconnaissance satellites of the US federal government, and provides satellite intelligence to several government agencies, particularly signals intelligence (SIGINT) to the National Security Agency (NSA), imagery intelligence (IMINT) to the National Geospatial-Intelligence Agency (NGA), and measurement and signature intelligence (MASINT) to the Defense Intelligence Agency (DIA).

In 1961, the CIA and the AF agreed to establish the NRO, which is considered, along with the CIA, NSA, DIA, and NGA, one of the "big five" US intelligence agencies. The NRO has its headquarters in Chantilly, Virginia.

The director of the NRO reports to both the director of national intelligence (DNI) and the secretary of defense. The NRO's federal workforce is a hybrid organization consisting of some three thousand personnel, including NRO cadre and AF, army, CIA, NGA, NSA, navy, and US Space Force personnel. A 1996 bipartisan commission report described the NRO as having by far the largest budget of any intelligence agency, and, "virtually no federal workforce," accomplishing most of its work through "tens of thousands" of defense contractor personnel.

The NRO acquired and operated satellites to collect intelligence from orbits, starting with the Corona program that gathered volumes and precise intelligence about Soviet strategic facilities. Corona satellites launched film canisters from space back to the earth, where skillful crews used specially configured C-130s to retrieve them as the payload parachuted over the ocean. AF imagery analysts in the reconnaissance technical groups and the CIA's NPIC would process the film. The resultant images depicted the status of Soviet facilities a few weeks before. Now the race was to narrow that process from imagery tasking to useable intelligence from weeks to days, and with threat mobility on the rise, to downlinking the data to hours.

The NRO's current director, Dr. Christopher Scolese, was a key speaker at the annual United States Geospatial Intelligence Foundation (USGIF) Geospatial

Intelligence (GEOINT) symposium in October 2021 in St. Louis, Missouri. In keeping with the technological expertise and emerging advancements in space vehicles, Dr. Scolese discussed two areas that would give the NRO an advantage in space: innovation and commercial capabilities. He discussed how the NRO has innovated since it began in 1961 and the steps needed to continue innovating to ensure it stays technologically ahead of adversaries and delivers capabilities faster than its competitors.

My interaction with the NRO, its directors, and its components spanned eleven years. I marveled at its talented staff and capabilities. It was one of the most sophisticated and advanced technological organizations I have had the pleasure to work with, and I appreciate their vital role in maintaining our edge in space surveillance.

■ HELPING THE TACTICAL COMMUNITY

During my four years at the Pentagon, our office accomplished significant achievements in the TENCAP program. Delivering national satellite data to the tactical community is a complex set of tasking, collecting, downloading, processing, analyzing, and data disseminating within a time frame that makes the information actionable.

There are seventeen intelligence organizations, some of which I mentioned previously, that acquire specific data to serve their customers—everyone from the intelligence analysts in various services, up through higher headquarters, intelligence organizations at multiple levels, commanders, national agencies, and further to congressional committees and the president.

There is tremendous competition for national satellite data daily among the IC and the DoD. There is a need for national asset intelligence to assess threats, strategic and tactical targeting, war planning, and political posturing, among others. Further, it aids US focus on technology and advancement required to stay ahead of new, emerging threats and existing ones.

Given the diverse thirst for national intelligence, the TENCAP program had a monumental challenge to ensure that the products from our national resources could be allocated wherever and whenever they were needed for tactical operations. Furthermore, since tactical operations include fighter and support activity at the squadron level right up through complex interservice joint operations in an area of responsibility (AOR) or a specific theater—Pacific, Atlantic, Europe, Middle East—it becomes imperative to tap the national resources properly.

Year 1: August 1983–May 1984

During the first six months, I ramped up my knowledge of current and future national space systems. I had to learn how the Air Staff functioned, how satellites operated, and to correlate weapons' functions and reconnaissance needs. The goal was to become an expert in defining the proper force mix ratio between space and aircraft surveillance systems.

Once I became comfortable with the functions and procedures in Space Operations, I was the official representative to the OJCS to solve problems associated with the policies and frequency of JCS special project exercises. These exercises would demonstrate the strengths and weaknesses of interservice theater operations, where national imagery exploitation and dissemination were used at the tactical level. As my expertise grew, I eventually drafted correspondence for DCS/Plans and Ops, which established the USAF recommendations for improving the utility of JCS special exercises of national space systems.

In one focused effort, I managed contractor efforts for an advanced Air Force Systems Command digital imagery system/reconnaissance study, a CENTAF imagery distribution demo, and a tactical target analysis study. This study led to the development of a sound program for imagery exploitation and dissemination at the tactical level for the air component of USCENTCOM. It effectively relieved the pressures of short suspense and interagency conflicts.

I presented briefings at HQ TAC, Langley AFB in Virginia, and 9th AF at Shaw AFB in South Carolina for imagery demos in upcoming joint service exercises with the primary goal of defining the proper mix ratio between space and aircraft surveillance systems.

Year 2: June 1984–May 1985

Having gained detailed knowledge in all aspects of the complex field of national support to tactical commanders greatly aided me in developing an outstanding rapport with workers and senior management in operations and intelligence. We extended our services to the USAF Special Operations Forces. I was a key planner for a demo that showed the critical satellite data utility at forward deployment bases.

I was the project manager for another effort with CENTCOM. I directed a very successful national imagery demo that coordinated a staff of fifteen at five locations worldwide. It demonstrated responsive national support from the collector to PACAF readout, CENTAF weapon allocation, and TAC fighter-wing bombs. The test plan development, site surveys, live demo, wrap up, and brief out directly impacted a nearly

$200 million in both army and AF budget initiatives, and used the CENTCOM model to direct analysis and demo of national support to deployed area of focus (AOF) forces for the MAC.

From the funding/equipment side, I coordinated resources (money/material) from HQ USAF, HQ MAC, four separate subordinate units/agencies, and contractor support. I presented briefings on the CENTCOM imagery demos to the three-star level at Air Staff and TAC and received praise for the effort and outcomes.

All the exercises and demos provided excellent data for a lengthy USAF input I prepared for the Product Dissemination Alternative Study, which addressed the economic distribution of satellite data across the tactical user community.

During this period, my boss, Col. Brown, applied for approval for me to wear the basic space badge. It was approved in May 1985, and to my surprise, the badge I received had been flown on the space shuttle *Discovery* as part of the official flight kit on mission 51-C (24–27 January 1985), the first DoD-dedicated space shuttle mission. A NASA letter dated 11 February 1985, certified that 367 space badges flew on that mission. They were a combination of master, senior, and basic space badges. I proudly wore one of them. Later, after more years in Space Operations, I became authorized to wear the senior space badge.

My senior space badge.

Year 3: June 1985–May 1986

It was always a privilege and opportunity to brief the most senior generals on the Air Staff. During my time at the Pentagon, the highest officer I briefed was the AF vice chief of staff (the number 2 guy) regarding USAF TENCAP support to CENTCOM. This presentation helped establish a new JCS/AF strategy for remotely sensed data.

I was also responsible as the primary planner and organizer for the 1985 Annual TENCAP Conference—support to USAF warfighting MAJCOMs. The focus was on developing new imagery dissemination networks for MAC, TAC, and USAFE to bring essential battlefield information to the warfighter.

In planning for the comprehensive exercise JCS Special Project Night Surge, we orchestrated the employment of over seventeen imagery terminals from various service and DoD agencies. And, on short notice, provided advice to HQ ESD for a major imagery intelligence program that was in jeopardy.

Our office would occasionally brief specific TENCAP programs to the AF chief scientist. We also wrote sections of CONOPs and detailed test plans for several JCS exercises. I was the AF/XO rep for numerous OSD, service, and DoD documents on national recce systems.

Our assistance in JCS Special Project 86 brought divided command positions of CENTCOM and HQ TAC to a mutually agreeable solution. Mending ways between and among higher headquarters was a significant challenge at times, but we prevailed in bringing them closer together.

Also in this third year, our detailed planning for JCS Project 87 led to building the framework to enable component commands of EUCOM to benefit from national reconnaissance systems directly in support of multiservice tactical operations in their theaters.

On Tuesday, 15 April 1986, I got an opportunity to monitor a live operation that used satellite imagery intelligence. Many of the operations staff in the Pentagon viewed Operation El Dorado Canyon, as F-111 Aardvarks, launched from a base in the United Kingdom, conducted a surprise strike on Muammar Qaddafi's compound near Tripoli, Libya. We had visual confirmation of the bomb damage via an electronic feed through secure communications from the aircraft's advanced Pave Tack electro-optical targeting pod. This operation employed numerous air and sea resources—a real-world excellent example of all the joint service projects TENCAP planned and supported.

Year 4: June 1986–May 1987

In my last year at the Pentagon, I was the AF/XO rep at all important interservice and OSD forums on national imagery. The previous three years of work among the commands and services, mainly through operational exercises, contributed to earning the credentials necessary to perform in that capacity.

To this point, our office focused primarily on the imagery products that were derived from the visible part of the electromagnetic spectrum (EMS), that is, the region with ultraviolet (UV) to the left of the range and infrared (IR) to the right. It is a form of electromagnetic radiation that can be subdivided into seven colors. It is the most familiar because it is the only region on the spectrum visible to most human eyes.

As technology progressed and the AF began to exploit the advantages of newer technology, the TENCAP office extended its expertise into another part of the EMS— multispectral imagery. Multispectral imagery measures and captures information about a world with many more dimensions than just the colors of the rainbow. It "sees" past the limits of what our eyes perceive.

Unlike a continuous hyperspectral image, multispectral sensors measure the electromagnetic spectrum in discrete, discontinuous bands. Multispectral sensors are capable of relative material delineation. The thermal wavelength range of the multispectral survey senses heat energy from the earth's surface and can distinguish among many types of objects. This data is precious information to operations in various theater environments, such as dense jungles, desert conditions, hidden moisture, and rough terrain.

An analysis and precise evaluation of multispectral target nominations for HQ USAFE's participation in JCS Special Project Power Hunter prevented the failure of a critical exercise objective. They contributed to the AF's status as the lead service in assessing the tactical application of multispectral imagery technology.

TENCAP also orchestrated the employment of over thirty imagery terminals in theater-wide organizations during comprehensive exercises in JCS Special Projects Night Surge and Power Hunter, USFK exercise Foal Eagle, including over twenty organizations, national agencies, and Green Flag 87-3. Our TENCAP team gained wide respect from the Air Staff and MAJCOM staff for our support of national intelligence in these exercises.

Another project I thoroughly enjoyed occurred on short notice. I researched several AF TENCAP programs and technical documents outside my area of expertise to brief six US astronauts. They presented me with a signed photo that depicted the first landing of the space shuttle *Challenger* (mission 41-B), landing 11 February 1984 at the Kennedy Space Center. It was the first shuttle to land there.

In this busy last year at the Pentagon, I also completed Air War College, which I started soon after I arrived for this assignment. Once I got comfortable in the TENCAP program, I participated in the seminar program in the Pentagon for this final PME level. Unlike the previous two PME levels I completed by correspondence, the seminar involved interaction among the students. As part of the requirements, I submitted written reports, which are listed in appendix A2. I received my AWC certificate on 10 March 1987.

A gift to me from US astronauts commemorating the first shuttle landing at Kennedy Space Center.

Another exciting project required SAP clearance. There were only three of us in the TENCAP office with access—Col. Al Brown, Maj. Chris Caravello, and me. Chris and I had to present new and challenging ideas regarding the tactical utility of multi-spectral imagery to more than fifty aircrews and intelligence analysts. Among those were aircrews of the then-secret Lockheed F-117 Nighthawk stealth attack aircraft in a remote facility in Nevada.

Chris and I flew to Las Vegas and made our way to Nellis AFB before proceeding to the site of the F-117s. Under the cover of darkness, aircrews escorted us to the hangars where the F-117s were located. They rolled back the colossal hangar doors, and it was like the theme from *2001: A Space Odyssey* (released in April 1968) was playing. The aircraft was so out of the ordinary in its design and surface features that we marveled at the engineering and systems integration that went into its development.

We had a couple of days with the aircrews that proved to be very helpful to their understanding of how national imagery, particularly multispectral imagery, would enhance their mission and effectiveness.

The F-117 Nighthawk.
Photo: Courtesy of DVIDS—Defense Visual Information Distribution
Service, Corporal Danielle Rodrigues, 21 October 2003.

During the program's early years, from 1984 to mid-1992, the F-117A fleet was based at Tonopah Test Range Airport, Nevada, where it served under the 4450th Tactical Group. Because the F-117 was classified during this time, the unit was officially located at Nellis Air Force Base, Nevada, and equipped with A-7 Corsair II aircraft. The F-117 reached initial operating capability status in 1983, and the aircraft was operated in secret from Tonopah for almost a decade.

Its first mission was during the US invasion of Panama in 1989 (Operation Just Cause). In 1991, the F-117 flew approximately 1,300 sorties and scored direct hits on 1,600 high-value targets in Iraq during the Gulf War.

Finally, AF TENCAP's contributions to the HQ MAC TENCAP command unique initiative final report convinced the MAC staff to procure equipment to employ national intelligence products. My time spent at the Space Operations office witnessed a steady increase in AF organizations at every level embracing the utility and value of data from our national space assets.

■ THE PARALLEL ACTIVITY: ESTABLISH A HOME (AGAIN)

During my first year working in Space Operations, we decided to build a new house in Burke, Virginia, located in Fairfax County, about seventeen miles from the Pentagon. It was in a friendly community called Longwood Knolls, close to Cherry Run Elementary, where Joe and Jeannie would attend, and Lake Braddock High School, where Bill would start his junior year. It was a four-bedroom house with a basement and two-car garage. And it fell within our price range.

It would be the home we established and lived in while our children progressed through elementary, high school, and college, and through the marriages of our children: Bill to Rebecca in October 1993, Joe to Angie in April 2003, and Jeannie to Danny in May 2005. Fast-forward a bit. We lived in that house for twenty-two years, before Fran and I moved to the next county, Loudoun, in March 2006. There are many joyful and sad memories from when we lived there—the longest time spent in any of our homes while I was on active duty.

My daily commute to the Pentagon was fun due to carpooling with Boyd Lease (my next-door neighbor), Ken Walsh (around the corner), and occasionally, Rich Cardiel (not far from our house). We took turns driving and avoided the slug lines, where commuters lined up to enter a carpool that would enable them to take the HOV (high-occupancy vehicle) lanes along I-95/I-395 to the Pentagon and return. We left early, around 0630 hours, and the clear advantage was coming home when we would leave the office at 1630 sharp to meet up for the drive home.

We were never at a lack of fun as we told each other stories of the day, antics that went on, or a joke here and there. The challenge was to see who could make others laugh the most. Ken came up with a perfect one as he rode shotgun on the way home one day. He stuck the end of his uniform tie in the top part of his window, rested his head against the window with his tongue hanging out, and eyes crossed. A woman driving parallel to us looked over and did a double-take with horror on her face! Ken then looked at her and smiled. Grown men looking for a release from the daily pressures of the job.

Our neighbors were great. We developed relationships, generally with those who had children near the ages of ours. One couple, however, did not have children. Chip and Barbara lived in the house up the hill behind us. Barbara was a school counselor, and Chip was the Secret Service agent assigned to Barbara Bush when her husband was the VP to President Reagan.

In June 1985, I had a TDY to Hickam AFB in Hawaii. We arranged for Fran's parents to come from New York to stay with our kids, while Fran came with me on the trip. We planned to take a few personal days after my official business was done at the base. We had a whole week there, and it was an excellent opportunity for some downtime. We saw many sites, including the USS *Arizona* Memorial in Pearl Harbor. We took time there to fully appreciate and honor the sacrifices made on 7 December 1941. We kept in touch with the folks back in Virginia, and all was going well there.

When we returned, and as Fran's parents prepared to return to New York, Chip offered to take us all on a personal tour of the White House. Fran's parents delayed their return trip; they did not want to pass on the opportunity for this visit. Chip took us through the historic home, visiting several rooms before we were at the door to the Oval Office. We did not go in but could see the entire room from our vantage point. What an opportunity that was!

Suddenly, Chip and other Secret Service agents received a communication that President and Mrs. Reagan were returning from Camp David and would be landing via helicopter (*Marine One*, of course) on the White House lawn in a few minutes. We scrambled to the outside near the entry door President Reagan and his wife would enter. Only a handful of people were present since this was an exceptional tour arranged by a few Secret Service agents for their families and friends.

President and Nancy Reagan walked toward us, smiling and waving. Eventually, they were right in front of where we stood. Mrs. Reagan stopped briefly and pointed at Jeannie, eight years old at the time, or to be more precise, at the blue-and-white muumuu we bought for Jeannie while in Hawaii. She remarked on how nice it looked! All smiles! They then proceeded into their home.

While we were elated and talked about the encounter at the White House, it was Fran's father, J. Vincent Micucci, who had come to America from Italy when he was only eighteen, and was overwhelmed with excitement—to have been at the White House and see a president he thought very highly of, to be in the same space with him, even if so briefly. This visit was a story he would tell many others with pride.

▪ TDY GALORE

During my four years at the Pentagon, TDY travel was extensive, with seventy-five trips to military organizations worldwide at all levels—AF MAJCOM HQ to numbered AFs, wings, squadrons, intelligence centers, army facilities, R&D centers, and contractor facilities.

After only two months in the Pentagon—during the beginning of my education in the world of space, satellites, multiorganization interfaces, budgets, and security measures—I went on several TDYs between October and December 1983 to begin the planning for some upcoming joint exercises between the army and the AF. The planning required my visits to 9th AF at Shaw AFB, South Carolina; Fort Bragg in North Carolina; MacDill AFB in Florida; HQ TAC at Langley AFB, Virginia; and a contractor facility in Palo Alto, California.

In 1984, I traveled every month except May and June on nineteen trips across twelve states, including Hawaii, and one trip to Ramstein AB in Germany. Most of these were 2–5 days long, with a slightly more extended stay in Hawaii and Germany.

In 1985, I visited many of the same sites over twenty-two trips, adding visits to contractor facilities in Palo Alto, Valley Forge, Pennsylvania, and Sunnyvale, California. The stop in Sunnyvale was with Lockheed Martin, the largest defense contractor in the world, which I would get to know in much greater depth during my assignment after the Pentagon.

In 1986, I made eighteen trips and was TDY every month as I completed many revisits, including Hawaii and Germany. Only that year, I also went to Korea: Seoul, Osan AB, and Taegu AB to coordinate the USKF exercise Foal Eagle.

In my last year at the Pentagon, between January and May 1987, I completed eleven trips. I went to Ramstein three times; Los Angeles; Ann Arbor, Michigan; and St. Louis, Missouri. Many of these were to contractor sites to coordinate contractor support for comprehensive joint exercises using TENCAP-provided services.

The interactions among the services, higher management staff, contractors with their leading-edge technology and capabilities, and responsibilities within a higher level of security and national trust were an enriching part of my career. It would open the door to my next assignment.

The experience I gained was the perfect foundation to work in a program that would be revolutionary for multiple DoD service operations, intelligence organizations within the services, intelligence agencies, and the overall national capability to provide real-time (RT) and near real-time (NRT) remote sensor (satellite) intelligence.

The Boat Show Trip

This was my personal TDY trip, and one of my most cherished since it was with my brother, Rob, to go to a boat show in Newport, Rhode Island. We both loved boats and owned them from time to time. I had never been to Rhode Island, and making this trip would earn me the "all fifty states" badge as I had visited or passed through all the others during my AF career.

I called my brother, "Hey Rob, want to go to the boat show in Newport with me?"

Without any hesitation, he replied, "Yeah, when?" I told him that I would take a couple of days off, fly to New York, and pick him up. We decided on a day for the four-day show.

I said, "OK, here's the plan. I'll fly into JFK, rent a car, and pick you up in Hicksville. Then, we'll drive out to get the ferry at Orient Point [Long Island] to New London, Connecticut. From there, we'll drive to the Newport Marriott. Then, it's just a short walk to the boat show. We'll grab dinner and spend the next day at the show!" He was all in and as excited as I was. We don't see each other often, so this was an excellent opportunity to get together and enjoy something we both loved.

The day of departure was stormy, and the weather conditions delayed my flight out of Washington Reagan Airport. I notified Rob and said we would have to hightail it to Orient Point before the last scheduled ferry departed. I arrived at JFK airport too late, so we went to plan B, which was to drive west after I picked him up at his home, and make our way to the Throgs Neck Bridge to cross from Queens into the Bronx, and then through New Rochelle, New York. Then we'd go to Connecticut and finally enter Rhode Island—a long several hours. It was our only option.

Along the way, Rob would drift off into sleep. I snapped, "Hey, stay awake, would ya? Don't go to sleep on me!"

He popped his eyes open and said, "I am awake," as he propped himself up in his seat.

"No, you were sleeping. You were snoring!"

My brother is always quick on his feet (and in this case, as he sat). "Sometimes I snore when I'm awake!" I just gave him a look.

"Stay with me. We have a long way to go!" Rob tried his best, but it took only a few seconds before I heard the familiar sound again … Zzzz.

We arrived at the Newport Marriott around 11 p.m. I had a ton of Marriott points, so I used them for the reservations there. We were tired and needed to get to sleep. We had a room with two twin beds. We briefly discussed that we would rise at about 8 a.m. and have a nice breakfast before we walked to the boat show. "Sounds good," I said. "See you in the morning."

A few seconds after the lights went out, I heard this very low, childish voice say, "Billy?"

I snapped back, "What is it?"

He said even more softly, "Billy, can you read me a story?"

Amid the darkness, we both laughed pretty hard for a while before I replied, "Please go to sleep. And try not to snore!"

These shenanigans always happened when we got together, and they did not stop there. We had our breakfast, checked out of the Marriott, but left our car there while we had a great day at the boat show, climbing all over the boats that had all the latest gear and technology. At the end of the day, we drove to the New London ferry that would take us to Orient Point on Long Island.

We boarded the ferry, which surprisingly had only a small number of passengers and vehicles. Once our car was secured, we went to the upper deck and sat awhile. Now underway, as dusk took over, a full moon began to brighten the night sky, which was crystal clear. The ferry trip would take well over an hour, and as it proceeded, we went to the bow and hung over the rail, looking toward Long Island. But we could not see any indication of land yet.

Ten or fifteen more minutes passed by. The moon was now very bright; many more stars were visible, and some Long Island lights began to appear. It was magical—quiet, as only the water against the bow could be heard. I felt an eerie feeling that I was being watched. I turned to my brother, standing next to me. He was looking at me. A few seconds later he said, "This is very romantic. You are looking very attractive right now!"

"Stop that," I said loudly. We both cracked up! My brother would always come up with something hilarious, which would lead to more teasing and challenges to see who could make the other laugh the most. He was the king of that department! And it was times like these that made me appreciate my brother very much.

SELECTED FOR RESTON AFB BY A ROLE MODEL

During part of my time at the Pentagon, Col. Kenneth Israel was also located there. He was the special assistant to the director, and division chief of Plans, Programs, and Policy for Electronic Combat. I didn't know much about him at first but later learned about his distinguished career.

Ken was a navigator, and through the years of his assignments after UNT graduation in April 1968, he went directly to SEA to fly as an EB-66 electronic warfare officer. His follow-on assignment in the same aircraft was at Spangdahlem AB, Germany, for three and one-half years before he transferred to the B-52 at Anderson AFB, Guam.

Ken became more experienced in Strategic Air Command, with a B-52 assignment to Barksdale AFB, Louisiana, and senior executive staff positions at numbered AFs and HQ SAC. During this time, he was promoted to the rank of lieutenant colonel. He held positions such as aide-de-camp to the commander of the 8th AF and commander of the 2nd Avionics Maintenance Squadron. He went to the National War College at Fort McNair in Washington, DC before taking on the role I described earlier, when we were both at the Pentagon.

Ken was very familiar with the TENCAP program and our team's work in Space Operations. In May 1985, he transferred to become the deputy commander for Intelligence and C3CM Systems and Tactical Exploitation of National Capabilities Officer, Electronic Systems Division, Hanscom AFB, Massachusetts. With this role, he had control over military positions with IDEX—Image Data Exploitation—a national imagery-related program.

Toward the end of my assignment at the Pentagon, Ken selected me for the role of DoD director for the IDEX II program, managed from the DC metro area. I would become the deputy director to Program Director Mike Dillard, who worked for another agency. The overall organization that managed IDEX was called Softcopy Exploitation Systems/Joint Program Office (SES/JPO)—a mouthful of complexity in the terminology and the diverse interaction of management that the term implied.

Ken Israel referred to my location for this new job as "Reston AFB, Virginia." No such base existed, which only emphasized the secrecy and sensitivity of this program and activity. Ken's ability as a supervisor, personality, actions, and example stood out with lasting influence on me. He remains a unique role model and friend!

SES/JPO

◼ MEET THE DIRECTOR

This chapter contains a bombardment of acronyms, more so than previously, so while I apologize for that, I will add that this is the nature of lingo in the military and the intelligence community (IC). Just try to adapt!

It was July 1987. I wore my civilian attire: a suit, a neatly pressed shirt with a tie that Fran picked out, and polished dress shoes. This would be my predominant "uniform of the day," as I gave my AF uniforms a break during this new assignment. My interaction with other agencies and contractors would require a bit of stealth now and then, and civilian clothing allowed me to blend in well with the masses.

I drove north on US Route 123 through Vienna, Virginia, before taking a right turn onto Follin Lane SE to proceed a few blocks to a building with a guarded gate. The Navy Federal Credit Union was nearby, so I suspected they were serving government customers in the vicinity. Once I mentioned my appointment and identified myself, I gained access and met someone in the lobby to take me to meet the director of SES/JPO, my new boss, Michael Louis Dillard—Mike.

Mike Dillard, Director SES/JPO.
Photo: Courtesy of Mike Dillard.

Mike was a seasoned manager, a senior intelligence service (SIS) level 1, equivalent to a brigadier general in the AF. The CIA selected Mike to lead the joint office due to his broad experience in satellite imagery and the many organizations necessary for tasking, collecting, processing, analyzing, disseminating, and everything in between.

Mike started his career at the National Photographic Interpretation Center (NPIC) in Washington DC, where he was a scientist in the photogrammetry/image science area. He led the design and technology development for satellite ground systems, including image data processing, storage, communications, compression, and other imagery-related disciplines. I would quickly learn how well he was respected in the IC, having earned the trusted reputation he built over his years in the agency.

My first and perpetual impression of him made me feel like an immediate member of his team and that I would be working with an expert, a professional. His smile, personality, and interaction all contributed to a welcome first day in the new job. He informed me at a very top level what SES/JPO's task was, and that the office would move to Reston, Virginia, along with other organizations in the CIA. So while I met Mike in Vienna, I never set foot in that building again.

The office in Reston is what Col. Israel referred to as "Reston AFB." *Pretty cool*, I thought.

People would ask, "Where do you work, Bill?"

"At Reston AFB," I would reply.

"Where is Reston AFB? Never heard of it."

"Can't tell you. It's classified. If I tell you, I will have to kill you." This phrase about disclosing classified information with the need to kill someone immediately afterward would be repeated many times during this assignment when similar questions popped up from those with no need to know. People usually get the message loud and clear. If not, I would repeat the words of the initial defense counsel in the movie *My Cousin Vinny* while I waved my index finger: "No more questions!"

Mike was a dedicated family man, married to Wanda. They had three children—two boys and a girl, like Fran and me. He lived in Burke, Virginia, near us. Mike and I had the same master's degree in systems management, mine from USC and his from George Washington University. The similarities continued until you got to our origins: Mike and Wanda were from Georgia—the Peach State; Fran and I, we're New York folks. This difference did not matter a bit. I am happy to report that being NY Yankee fans did not drive a wedge of any kind between us.

Of course, I am biased, but I could not think of a better team to manage this joint national agency program through development, delivery, initial operational capability (IOC), and operations and maintenance (O&M) in the years ahead. Mike's background made him perfect as the director; I was his deputy, with groundwork and experience in the TENCAP program, but also had the title of DoD director.

From my first meeting with Mike, I eagerly anticipated working together. Much confidence had been placed in us both to make Image Data Exploitation (IDEX) II a successful and revolutionary capability in imagery intelligence productivity. And our challenges were ahead of us.

■ AN EXTENDED ORGANIZATION FABRIC

To some degree, all the organizations I worked with during my time in the AF TENCAP program remained vital during the development of the IDEX II. The services now included the navy, AF, and army. The SES/JPO, where Mike and I directly worked, fell within the CIA's Collections Program Group (CPG), an organization of over one hundred personnel. It was nested under the CIA's Office of Development and Engineering, which, in turn, fell under its Science and Technology Directorate.

The Air Force Intelligence Office, AF/INY, was the designated Air Staff intelligence organization that selected an AF colonel to chair the DoD Softcopy Steering Committee (DSSC), which represented the interests of DoD customers for IDEX II. They would rotate this position, usually every year.

The National Reconnaissance Office (NRO) was a vital component of the program since it managed all satellite development and operations. Imagery satellite capabilities and interfaces with IDEX II needed to sync well since our program would exploit the national imagery products from those collectors. A close association was necessary.

The Defense Intelligence Agency (DIA), in Washington DC, was also an essential component as it provided intelligence across a broad scope of customers within the DoD.

HQ, Electronic Systems Division, Air Force Systems Command at Hanscom AFB, right outside Boston, managed my AF position within the program. In effect, I had three "bosses." I use "bosses" only because it became a relative term with respect to the chairman of the Softcopy Steering Committee. Naturally, I intended to make the committee's goals and utility for IDEX a high priority. After all, they are a significant representative of the user community that had documented requirements for advanced capability in imagery exploitation. But they had a minor input on my performance reports, as far as I determined.

Since I worked directly for Mike daily, and my AF boss, Col. Israel, was at Hanscom, I focused on keeping them happy. Col. Israel wrote my officer effectiveness reports (OERs) with input from Mike and CIA managers above him. I knew my priorities. They were clear-cut: Make these two guys happy!

Col. Israel said it best when he wrote in my first OER for this job, "Seems to have more 'bosses' in Washington than Carter has pills. Peaks in pressure cooker environment but never wilts." He always had a unique way with words, and he was spot on because many thought they *were* my boss!

▪ PRE-IDEX II

What led to the development of IDEX II? A brief history of the need for strategic intelligence during the Cold War can provide simple answers.

NPIC was established in January 1961 under the director of Central Intelligence to provide efficient and timely exploitation of photography as a source of foreign intelligence in response to national security needs. Dwight D. Eisenhower, in the final days of his presidency, created the center, which combined the CIA's Photographic Interpretation Center and DoD assets.

Previous obscure divisions were founded on the assumption that competent photo interpreters exploiting high-quality, up-to-date photography of strategic targets, with the aid of all-source collateral information, could produce definitively important information concerning the capability and, to some extent, the immediate intentions of potential enemies of the United States to initiate military action against our country and its allies.

As the Vietnam War drew to a close, Congress looked for ways to consolidate military and intelligence organizations. The Defense Mapping Agency (DMA) emerged in the DoD in mid-1972 to increase efficiencies and economies by bringing into one organization the mapping, charting, and geodesy (MC&G) activities of the services. This new organization absorbed the AF's Aeronautical Chart and Information Center operations, the oceanographic and charting services of the US Naval Hydrographic Office, and the Army Map Service.

The DMA provided MC&G support to the secretary of defense, the joint chiefs of staff, the military departments, and other DoD components. This support included the production and worldwide distribution of maps, charts, precise positioning data, and digital data for strategic and tactical military operations and weapon systems. On 1 October 1996, the DMA was folded into the National Imagery and Mapping Agency (NIMA), which later became the National Geospatial-Intelligence Agency (NGA). At that point, NGA also absorbed the resources from NPIC.

Going back a few years, by 1954, gaps in US intelligence that precluded adequate knowledge of Soviet capabilities and intentions concerning the possible launching of a nuclear attack on us generated strong pressure to find some means to fill the gaps. Though aerial photography ranked high on the list of prospects, enthusiasm for using a promising sensor—a reconnaissance aircraft—was tempered by considering the possible consequences of a shootdown of an American military aircraft deep within Soviet airspace.

At this critical juncture, intensive work on the problem began to point to a possible solution. The first inkling came in a report dated 30 September 1954, issued by the Special Study Group of the Hoover Commission, which was investigating the covert activities of the CIA. Under the chairmanship of General James H. Doolittle, this group urged the use of all possible techniques to increase the capability of gathering intelligence information utilizing high-altitude photoreconnaissance. The report added that no price paid would be too high to emphasize the overriding need for such capability.

Project Aquatone, the code name for the Lockheed-built U-2 Dragon Lady reconnaissance aircraft program, was born. The first U-2 photo reconnaissance mission flew over eastern Europe on 20 June 1956 and the Soviet Union on 4 July that same year. The U-2 system was not conceived on the spur of the moment; several studies of military intelligence problems during the early 1950s set the stage.

U-2 Dragon Lady, strategic reconnaissance.
Photo: Courtesy of DVIDS—Defense Visual Information
Distribution Service, Heide Couch, 14 May 2022.

A task force had the responsibility of exploiting Aquatone imagery, although, at that time, this force was not considered "permanent" or even an organizational entity. Instead, a group of people, initially about 150, assembled to work together under one management to exploit U-2 photography. At the time, no one could say just how long the collective effort would continue or how long it would be needed.

The U-2 was not the only game in town. During this period of the 1950s, Project Jackpot, the name given for the exploitation phase of Genetrix, would take overhead photo intelligence primarily over the Soviet Union and China. Huge plastic balloons were released in Scotland, Norway, Germany, and Turkey, and carried by prevailing westerly air currents in the upper troposphere.

They were instrumented to parachute their loads to earth whenever they dropped below thirty thousand feet, and it was believed that most of them would succeed in reaching the Pacific, where they could be captured in the air using a line and hook, which each payload was equipped with, or by retrieval from the ocean.

The U-2s flew out of a USAF base near Wiesbaden, Germany. The exposed film from the first flights was flown to Rochester, New York, for processing and to Washington for exploitation. Still, the agency deemed it necessary to set up a film-processing and exploitation facility at the base, at least on a standby basis. It was felt that such a facility would be needed to supply current intelligence should an international crisis develop within the flying range of Western Germany.

Through the 1960s and 1970s, analysts used electronic light tables (ELTs) for imagery viewing. Working at an ELT for hours required focus and stamina, but eventually, thousands of imagery analysts would become experts in their craft using these devices. The term *NIIRS* (pronounced "nears") became an important parameter that NPIC analysts would use—National Imagery Interpretability Rating Scale.

The aerial-imaging community utilizes NIIRS to define and measure the quality of images and performance of imaging systems. Through a process referred to as "rating" an image, the NIIRS is used by imagery analysts to assign a number that indicates the interpretability of a given image. The NIIRS concept provides a means to directly relate the quality of an image to the interpretation tasks for which it may be used. Although the NIIRS has been primarily applied in evaluating aerial imagery, it provides a systematic approach to measuring the quality of photographic or digital imagery, the performance of image-capture devices (such as satellites), and the effects of image-processing algorithms.

The ratings range from 0 to 9, where 0 for visible, radar, infrared, and multispectral imagery interpretability is precluded by obscuration, degradation, or very poor resolution. On the other end, with a rating of 9, as it applies to visible, radar, and infrared, the detail of the imagery is significantly enhanced. Everything in between is merely a degradation of refinement as the scale goes up. Images can have ratings between the digits, such as 5.5, 7.2, and so on.

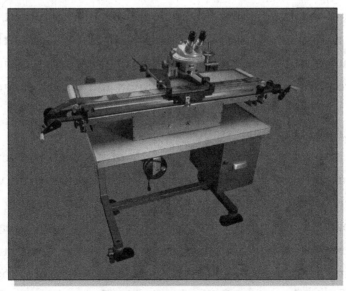

Imagery analyst light table.
Photo: Courtesy of the National Air and Space Museum (NASM).

IDEX II followed the first generation of successful but limited IDEX I, built by E-Systems in Garland, Texas. IDEX I was the first system to display digital data on a cathode ray tube (CRT), a vacuum tube containing one or more electron guns. The beams are manipulated to display images on a phosphorescent screen. They were deployed from 1981 to 1991 and were limited to only two locations—HQ Strategic Air Command at Offutt AFB, Omaha, Nebraska, and the NPIC in Washington DC.

IDEX I was the initial program to explore the ability to transfer the intelligence activity of imagery analysis from old technology of light tables, where analysts painstakingly spent hours staring at and studying imagery through magnifying devices. It would parallel the advancements in computer technology and enable an analysis of satellite imagery through computer processing and monitors to display and manipulate the imagery products.

IDEX II was a national-level intelligence program that addressed the nation's first robust softcopy imagery exploitation system for the DoD and CIA. Following the delivery of IDEX I, the CIA established a team in OD&E to design the next-generation softcopy exploitation system to be called IDEX II. Mike Dillard supported these initial efforts as a representative from NPIC and the NRO ground team.

Before I arrived at the JPO, Mike had inherited the program, which was two years behind schedule and nearly $150 million over budget. He also had a deputy he recognized would not be strong enough for the job. He contacted Col. Ken Israel, whom he had met earlier at HQ ESD, when he was invited to attend a major event there on behalf of the NRO. Mike described the qualifications he needed in a deputy. Ken selected me, and after a discussion with Mike, they agreed to my assignment for the job.

The role as deputy was expansive. I would be responsible for all DoD relationships, informative updates, the satisfaction/incorporation of diverse and unique requirements into the development process, and related budgets.

The program's purpose was to be ubiquitous in its ability to display multiple types of imagery at very high resolutions, with stereo capability and precise measurement. It was a tough competition among contractors for the prime role. Lockheed won by its commitment to build a production line to eventually reduce the cost of workstation production. The concept was to commercialize the IDEX II design to make it available in thousands of units.

To set the stage even further, it is essential to understand the historical technological context that led to a more sophisticated imagery exploitation system. For over 150 years, armies relied on various sources to spy on their enemies—everything from human intelligence (HUMINT), surveillance by balloons, and aerial photos from early reconnaissance aircraft.

When IDEX was conceived and executed, technology in many areas was nonexistent. There were no cell phones, Microsoft was in its infancy, Apple was a tiny company, and digital imagery display was on such a small scale that most people knew nothing about it. Therefore, the move to digital display on a large scale was historical. The concept of thousands of lines of resolution on a display screen was unheard of, not to mention making the display in stereo to ascertain more than just a two-dimensional image.

The internet began to emerge, but no one had desktop computers, and laptops were nonexistent. Computer chip designs were nascent. IDEX represented capabilities that far exceeded the norms of image data storage, quality, and speed at that time. The IDEX program had to invent new methods and capabilities to handle imagery in a digital world, such as image data tagging, icons, measuring tools, viewing techniques, applications, ergonomics, display tools, graphical user interface (GUI) tools, image manipulation, bandwidth systems, multi-bit pixel depth, and the unique ability to navigate the electromagnetic spectrum on a display screen. This had never been done before. The progression to digital displays was historic!

The challenges for IDEX would parallel those of building the satellites that acquired the imagery it would exploit. The technologies that IDEX unfolded are now commonplace—high-resolution digital TV, streaming services, apps, icons, densely packed mobile phones, and high-resolution laptops; the list goes beyond all that.

Get ready. Here's IDEX II, a revolutionary program we developed, went worldwide, and helped set the stage as a rock-solid foundation for even more-sophisticated exploitation of imagery intelligence as our national overhead assets became more advanced and diverse in the new century!

◾ IDEX II: THE PROGRAM

From 1991 to 2003, US intelligence agencies used Lockheed's IDEX II system to analyze digital imagery returned from photoreconnaissance satellites and aircraft. There were 105 IDEX IIs deployed to sites at DoD and intelligence agency locations worldwide. They were used to analyze mostly high-interest targets and images that needed enhancing, such as haze removal and contrast and brightness manipulation to fully exploit the data. A list of IDEX II sites is in appendix H.

When I joined the SES/JPO, the development of IDEX II was in its very early stages based on the consolidated requirements, which would eventually number over two thousand from the diverse intelligence user community. Every organization had its interests as a priority for this revolutionary change in how they would do business for their respective imagery exploitation. Our job in the JPO was to ensure we delivered a system that would meet *all* their requirements. Lockheed Martin, our prime contractor at their Sunnyvale, California facility, was ready with their team to make the program a success.

The user organizations were designated by site numbers 1 through 15, with specifically identified DoD and national sites that stretched from Hawaii east to the intelligence centers in the United Kingdom and Germany. The majority were located in the Washington DC area. Each location would require a facility built to support the IDEX II workstations. The workstation took up a small footprint. Some organizations received a few workstations, while others received more than twenty-five.

An IDEX II workstation.
Photo: Courtesy of the National Air and Space Museum (NASM).

The central processing area (CPA) contained the complex hardware that made up the architecture supporting the workstations. It included a secure workflow management infrastructure with multiple database servers, an imagery archive of optical disk storage, magnetic tape storage, image file servers, HIPPI (very high-speed data transfer protocol) switches, and a connectivity enclave for direct electrical connection for query/order and processor/product services. A display broker would enable the workstation analyst to interface with the architecture component to allow much-advanced imagery analysis and timely dissemination of imagery products.

The CPA required a designated space in the user's organization that would be secure, built to support hardware weight specifications, able to access proper power and cooling, and many other requirements. When someone sees the workstation, it is easy to overlook the tremendous back-office support from the CPA necessary to make the workstation "work." Our program office personnel would conduct site surveys to determine the adequacy to support IDEX II equipment at each location.

Many of the achievements in technology for IDEX II were way ahead of their time. For example, today—and this is an oversimplification—when you order internet service and your provider states you can download data to your computer at 100 megabytes/ second (MB/s), you think, *Wow, that's fast!* Lockheed's IDEX II image data transfer rate in the late 1980s to a large storage disk was 100 MB/s! Yes, we achieved these rates more than thirty years ago!

The IDEX systems permitted imagery enhancement to achieve more complete and precise analyses. They also made the storage, retrieval, and dissemination of imagery much easier and quicker. There will always be a need to strive for real-time/near-real-time (RT/NRT) intelligence. As threats become more mobile with a quicker ability to strike, it becomes increasingly important to collect, retrieve, process, and disseminate actionable intelligence more quickly. It is of no value if the intelligence is too old or too late!

A color monitor was on the left of the workstation, and a high-resolution black-and-white monitor was on the right. Electronic goggles enabled the imagery analyst to view images stereoscopically to determine the height and depths of terrain and numerous other terrain features that were not accessible from a light table. Subcontractors were limited, but we did rely on Watson Labs for the original design of the imagery monitors. Another company produced the goggles.

We had the multilayer processing boards manufactured in Austin, Texas, due to the higher cost of producing them in California. These boards had up to eleven layers of circuitry when the industry standard at that time was only two to three! As an alternative means for storage and distribution of image data, we also assessed the viability of a system called EMASS—an E-Systems robotic data storage system they developed for wide use by defense and intelligence agencies to store massive amounts of data tape cartridges.

Some of the significant achievements of the IDEX II program included the first digital display for high-quality satellite imagery. Jimmie Hill, who served as the NRO deputy director for fourteen years (1982–1996), viewed the first IDEX II images, the first digital display system for electromagnetic spectrum data (visible, radar, infrared, multispectral), the first interactive stereo single-screen display, the first nine-layer processing board for the display monitors (the eleven-layer boards were in other IDEX II CPA components), and the first displays with 1,500 × 1,500 lines of resolution.

PROGRAM MANAGEMENT

Mike had the overall responsibility for the SES/JPO and the IDEX II program. As his deputy, I represented the AF assistant chief of staff for intelligence (ACS/I) at the DoD contingent at SES/JPO to execute the National Foreign Intelligence Program (NFIP) Softcopy Exploitation Systems Program. The NFIP provides integrated intelligence covering broad national policy and national security aspects.

My experience as a Space Operations officer in the Pentagon Air Staff for TENCAP certainly provided broad and in-depth knowledge of DoD and national intelligence communities, their systems, and programs. This foundation was necessary to be effective in the deputy position.

Together, we would lead a team of seventeen program office personnel (military and CIA) and staff of over 350 contractor personnel—which sometimes peaked closer to five hundred—for technical engineering design (hardware and software), development, testing, verification (product assurance), hardware manufacturing, recorder system program management, detailed discrepancy report work off, configuration control, installation readiness, security accreditation, operations demonstrations, and systems acceptance. The military program office (PO) staffing was as low as 60 percent when I joined the office, but we managed the program for the DoD with this reduced support. I acquired 100 percent staffing within a couple of years, when it was especially needed for site deliveries.

I was very fortunate to have a high-caliber talented military team in the PO. Four AF captains came with all the energy and determination needed to support the program in many tasks. They were the hands-on representatives of our office to the DoD sites, intimately involved in the site's requirements. They needed to be thoroughly conversant in the program technology and aware of program status in all areas of development, integration, factory testing, verification, and site readiness via transition readiness reviews (TRRs), site IDEX II concepts of operation (CONOPS), and equipment delivery. They represented a very critical facet of the SES/JPO to the DoD user community. I was honored to have them on my team.

IDEX II military program office staff.
L to R: Captains Jim Watson, Darren Smith, me, Captains Mike Buck, and Suzanne Roseberry.

The majority of the JPO were CIA civilians who comprised our team's remainder—administration support, development engineers, design experts, interface test engineers, configuration control managers, security experts, and O&M personnel. These were complemented by a mature independent systems integrator team of around fifteen personnel from General Electric in Valley Forge, Pennsylvania.

My responsibilities included: management of all DoD administrative functions in the PO, including interviewing and hiring; selected by Mike as the prime PO spokesman to the DoD, other program offices, and selected CIA organizations; briefing the SAC/IN, GDIP manager, ESD commanders, OSD, and at exploitation technology conferences; determine scope and agenda for JPO division meetings; attend CIA OD&E group management meetings, configuration control meetings as a Customer Configuration Control Board (CCCB) voting member, and senior intelligence services conferences. During the first week of November 1987, I completed a week-long OD&E manager's course at the GE Systems Integrator facility in Valley Forge to help me understand the environment and infrastructure of this CIA office.

More of my duties included: establishing a cooperative interface between ESD/IC and OD&E on a broad range of intelligence programs; acting as the contracting officer technical representative (COTR) for a science applications international corporation (SAIC) contract to support Air Staff and the DSSC; setting and implementing contractor policy and management over $25 million in contractor support; act as director of a strategic planning team to update a memorandum of agreement between the DoD and the CIA, for future PO development/acquisition of national softcopy capabilities; assist the DSSC in the validation of softcopy requirements for organizations such as USSPACECOM; and participate in DoD user groups, IDEX II transition/integration working groups, DSSC meetings, and other principal program offices.

Among the many trips our support staff took to administer the IDEX II program, it was vital to meet with the prime contractor frequently to review progress in all development activities I previously described. We held monthly program management reviews (PMRs) in Sunnyvale. We amassed a ton of United Airlines miles during this program! The PMRs usually took a minimum of two days as we needed to cover a contractor-prepared stack of briefing charts in the hundreds. No detail was too small.

Mike and I, and key Lockheed managers, would sit at the head table with an audience of up to 150 personnel behind us who represented others from our PO, military sites, contractor support personnel, and other agencies interested in how IDEX II related to their organizations and programs.

At the end of these more public and classified sessions, a smaller group from our PO met privately with Lockheed managers to cover any issues, problems, or changes in direction that we did not want to advertise too early. It also allowed us to meet with Lockheed executive leadership to discuss the program's status and other related programs Lockheed developed, including satellites.

Dr. Vance Coffman was the CEO of Lockheed at the time. We occasionally met with him and some of his closest senior executives. Recognize that Lockheed is a world leader in global security and aerospace technology and that most of its business is with the US DoD and federal government agencies.

Despite Lockheed's diverse business and complexity, Vance always seemed to have time for us. Our visits with him were always cordial and friendly, and "beyond wild" fascinating as we were escorted through many of their secure facilities wearing white robes, booties on our shoes, and other protective clothing—not for us, but for their hardware. No dust or tiny particles were allowed as we walked across tacky mats to collect any foreign substances off our shoes before we entered the rooms that contained highly technologically advanced systems!

We built a great relationship with Lockheed, and they treated us very well. Of course, we were their customer, and they wanted to meet our demands and goals. They always had a great food spread for us on the first day of the PMR, or the occasional BBQ at a local park after the workday, where they grilled tri-tip steaks, and we challenged them to a volleyball game.

On the off days, when we went locally for lunch, a group of us would head over to

Kal's BBQ, a short distance from the Lockheed facility. Kal was a Korean gentleman who owned the shop and cooked some of the best BBQs I have tasted. He knew us by name and was delighted to see us each month and to serve us our lunch at the picnic tables outside.

I occasionally got a jog in for a few miles before dinner with a small group. I also sometimes played handball with someone so inclined. We would drive over to NAS Moffett Field, slightly over three miles away, to our reserved court to get in a few games—great workouts! As we approached from a distance, we would see the hangars that once housed Goodyear's G-class, L-class, and K-class blimps. The hangars looked big from a few miles away, but as you got close, they were beyond huge. They covered as much as eight acres!

These diversions helped to balance the workload with some fun. Our priority was to make progress each month and ensure that our program funds were applied correctly and efficiently. Program funding came from various sources. The General Defense Intelligence Program (GDIP) provided funding for the DoD portion (AF, navy, army, and DIA) of the IDEX II program.

Funding was already approved through the fiscal year 1989. Each year, I would go to the Pentagon to brief the GDIP manager, Marty Hurwitz, to convince him to continue the funding in the out years, especially since the current budget had some shortfalls for the years ahead. It was my responsibility to procure and manage the funding from DIA and the services.

I always prepared detailed charts to give him a program status and summary of the Softcopy Steering Committee requests as their requirements would sometimes drift. We called this "requirements creep." Marty always had a few questions, which I addressed, and he provided 100 percent support as needed for fiscal years 1990 through 1992. It was great working with him.

Other monetary resources, managed by Mike, came from the CIA, NRO, and the National Reconnaissance Program (NRP).

Mike and I inherited a $150 million overrun for the IDEX II program from the previous director, who did a terrible job. The original program budget was planned at $200 million, with a cost for each IDEX station at one million. Through replanning and additional requirements—add-ons—the total cost for our program was around $500 million.

The overall management of the IDEX II budget that Mike and I controlled always contained the element of defense against program budget reduction recommendations from congressional intelligence committees. We managed to maintain our funding support, even though we experienced two overruns for the program over three years.

I teased Mike with the question, "We had two cost overruns for IDEX II, and you still managed to get two promotions! How is that possible?" When Mike left the IDEX II program, he was an SIS level 3!

HQ, SAC at Offutt AFB in Omaha, Nebraska, was site 1 for IDEX II delivery. It was vital for our first delivery to be a success because we would have many more deliveries to follow and would be judged accordingly.

Before I describe my meeting with Maj. Gen. Clapper, I digress a bit to explain my interactions with the site representatives, which I had in several sessions with different agendas months before I visited him. I have always considered my management style as one of diplomacy, fairness, focus, and genuine concern for every customer. I had great relationships with everyone. But time and again, another "Lt. Quattro" entered the scene—the type of guy I described in chapter 10 when I was at Udorn AB, Thailand. This time it was Capt. J. C.

Capt. J. C. represented the user organization at SAC, Offutt AFB. We were at an IDEX II user meeting at one of SAIC's buildings in Falls Church, Virginia. The group numbered from twenty to thirty, as I recall. It was one of many opportunities for users to hear program updates and ask questions. I was there to chair the meeting with my military team.

Capt. J. C. began a series of questions addressed to me at one point. I did my best to respond but pointed out that some of them would require research, and I would get back to him. This did not satisfy Capt. J. C. He persisted with the same questions and more while implying that our office was not performing well enough. I did my best, again diplomatically, to mitigate the trend that transitioned from, "concern for my site," to, "challenge the colonel" in front of a large group. As it got more disruptive, I calmly stated, "Now would be a good time for a restroom break. Let's take fifteen minutes and regroup."

I left the room, went to the nearest phone (which was in the hall), and called Capt. J. C.'s immediate supervisor at Offutt AFB. As I dialed, J. C. saw me and seemed to know what I was about to do. I told him I was calling his boss and that he was not allowed back in the room. I told him to go home. He apologized and pleaded that I not make the call. I told him I gave him every opportunity to settle down in the room, and it was too late. I explained the situation to his boss, who agreed with my decision.

I hate it when events unfold this way. I have always exhibited a lot of patience and have given others the benefit of the doubt. But when you can't get through with some calm discussion and a sincere obligation to respond to one's concerns, you pick up the two-by-four and smack 'em in the head!

Back to site 1. Maj. Gen. James Clapper was the deputy chief of staff for intelligence for SAC. He had concerns about the IDEX II's capability, primarily due to his experience with intelligence systems from two previous tours. He did not provide details but was clearly apprehensive about IDEX. From June 1985 to June 1987, he was the assistant chief of staff for intelligence, Republic of Korea, and US Combined Forces

Command. From July 1987 to July 1989, he was the director for intelligence, at HQ US Pacific Command at Camp H. M. Smith in Hawaii.

I digress once more. A few months prior to my visit to HQ SAC, I attended a ceremony at Andrews AFB, Prince Georges County, in Maryland. Fran and my family were there, Fran's mother, Col. Israel, and Mike Dillard. General Brandt officiated at the ceremony. It was my promotion to colonel! The pinning ceremony was held at 1400 hours on Friday, 31 March since the effective date would be 1 April 1989, on the weekend.

As in most large organizations, it is wide at the bottom of the pyramid, and it narrows at the top. Each prior promotion, at least to major and lieutenant colonel, involved a bit of competition. The statistics for promotion to colonel become more significant and evermore defining beyond that.

Gen. Brandt (now deceased) and Fran pinning on my eagles at Andrews AFB, Maryland.

On a trip to Hanscom AFB, Massachusetts, in September 1987, Col. Israel announced that I was selected for promotion to colonel. This was eighteen months before I pinned on my eagles. *Air Force Times,* 48 (7), dated 28 September 1987, posted the results: A total of 814 line officers (not special categories such as judge advocate, chaplain, medical service) out of 1,872 were selected by a review board that met on 11 August that year. This represented a promotion rate of 43.5 percent.

I received a personal note of congratulations from Lt. Gen. Melvin Chubb, the commander of the Electronic Systems Division at Hanscom AFB. The statistics at HQ AFSC were 190 eligible, 69 promoted for a 36.3 percent rate; at HQ ESD, fifteen officers were eligible, and three were promoted for a 20 percent rate.

Back to site 1 (again). Maj. Gen. Clapper arrived at HQ SAC in July 1989. I went to HQ SAC for a two-day visit, 16–17 August 1989, to personally brief him and address any issues he had. I expected that he would have a staff of officers with him for my informational briefing on IDEX II. But it was just the two of us in his conference room, a colonel and a general face-to-face.

I assured Gen. Clapper that SAC was getting a very robust team with the delivery of twenty-four workstations and the CPA. I explained the entire process of site surveys and preparation for system delivery. I also told him that we put together a first-class team of hardware and software engineers, configuration control personnel, and other support assets that would be part of our IDEX II delivery to SAC. Additionally, I explained the process we would complete at the Lockheed facility to pretest and certify his system before shipment. His anxiety seemed to fade as I addressed his many questions. He didn't act at all like Capt. J. C.

When Gen. Clapper became the AF assistant chief of staff for intelligence (ACS/I) in the Pentagon, I represented him at the DoD contingent of the SES/JPO. I would meet Gen. Clapper later in his career, after I retired. He earned his third star, promoted to lieutenant general while serving as the director of the DIA and General Defense Intelligence Program. He eventually became the civilian director of NIMA, which he transformed into the present-day NGA.

I had the opportunity to brief him again while he was at NIMA. He remembered me as we briefly discussed IDEX II's success for HQ SAC. After serving in several other key intelligence assignments, he became the civilian DNI for the sixteen intelligence agencies. The DNI oversees the integration of these agencies, spearheads the support the intelligence community provides to the military and senior policymakers across the government, and serves as a principal adviser to the president. Clapper's book, *Facts and Fears; Hard Truths from a Life in Intelligence*, tells a compelling story.

Our delivery to HQ SAC was a complete success. Capt. Suzanne Roseberry was our program representative to HQ SAC, and she deserves significant credit for this critical first delivery. Suzanne had completed many trips to ensure we would meet requirements, perform site surveys, and work with the SAC customer and the Lockheed team to leave no issues unresolved. I could not ask for a better representative from our PO for this first delivery.

We maintained our delivery schedule, but as Operations Desert Shield (2 August 1990–17 January 1991), the operations leading to the buildup of troops and defense of Saudi Arabia, and Desert Storm (17 January–28 February 1991), in response to the Iraqi invasion of Kuwait, provided the focus of military activity, we ramped up and accelerated operational capability at HQ SAC and CIA sites to support these operations.

We also accelerated IDEX II delivery to FICEURLANT to support extended Desert Storm contingencies. This provided rapid and effective intelligence production available for field and national commanders in response to hostile activities in the Middle East. Gen. Norman Schwarzkopf commented that "We had extraordinary data to draw on: ever since the tanker war, the United States had kept the region under stepped-up surveillance, both human and high-tech, so each day brought a huge haul of fresh information." Much of that technical information was provided by intelligence analysts using IDEX II for satellite imagery of the Area of Responsibility (AOR)!

Much has been done to improve the processing, exploitation, and dissemination (PED) efficiency since Desert Storm, but expectations for PED efficiency have also risen. The ability to supply near-real-time intelligence has engendered a greater demand for near-real-time intelligence. Process timelines that would have been considered efficient in 1991 would be considered broken today.

The CIA delivered numerous awards for those who supported the Persian Gulf crisis. Recipients were in various organizations, and our IDEX II office was duly recognized. Here is my certificate signed by the director of Central Intelligence, William H. Webster, sometimes referred to as "Judge Webster."

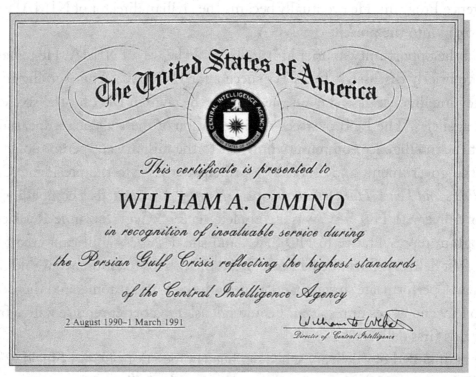

My certificate, recognizing "Invaluable Service during the Persian Gulf Crisis."

By September 1991, we had delivered IDEX II to nine sites among the AF, navy, CIA, DIA, and a highly classified facility. The remaining site deliveries would follow in early 1992. I had always embraced the opportunity to meet with every IDEX II site commander to understand their issues and apply the proper attention for resolution before system delivery.

The intelligence facility consolidating sites in Europe and Hawaii caused us to replan those baseline deliveries as the DSSC issued an RFC—request for change. This, in effect, canceled a delivery to Germany and consolidated sites in Hawaii as our Customer Configuration Control Board reviewed and received approval for the engineering and integration changes.

I briefed the CINCPAC/J2, Brig. Gen. Jackson, twice on the issues of the consolidation decision and directed the engineering of the CPA to accommodate a remote site (548th Reconnaissance Technical Group at Hickam AFB) remoted off the Joint Intelligence Center Pacific (JICPAC) at Makalapa, Pearl Harbor, Hawaii. Operations would begin in mid-June 1992.

As the utility of IDEX II grew and supported operations and intelligence, we initiated several improvements and cost-saving measures from lessons learned. In parallel, we completed a reorganization of SES/JPO and established the Customer Systems Support Center (CSSC) in Newington, Virginia, a transfer from Reston in early June 1991. This move represented a transition of SES/JPO from a development environment and organization to a new facility for long-term customer systems support to operations for all IDEX II and recorder systems customers. It also included a transition of most of the west coast-based factory support personnel to the CSSC to reduce overall operations and maintenance (O&M) costs to the government.

This planning and implementation of organizational changes to combine all PO functional activity and center operations into a consolidated division under a single manager resulted in increased efficiency and management of resources; more responsive customer service, and O&M; and better focus on future system enhancements.

We established a robust O&M program in the field, at the factory in Sunnyvale and at the CSSC for repair, spares, logistical support, testing, trend analysis, training, and engineering of problem analysis. This resulted in the reliable performance of fielded IDEX II systems at all intelligence centers.

Prior to IDEX II, the Computer-Aided Tactical Information System (CATIS) was the primary Host Data Base System (HDBS). Over the years of delivery, our interface testing would allow a connection for IDEX II with newer tactical and national strategic databases. We also endeavored to drive down the costs for IDEX II. Achieved through studies of broader community requirements, we directed the effort to reengineer the workstation and the analysts' interface with it. These changes resulted in the development and delivery of a low-cost workstation (LCWS) and low-cost interface unit (LIU).

These efforts to expand the IDEX II architecture through appropriate interfaces contributed to IDEX II stability and operability and kept with the spirit of coordination with the DSSC for emerging requirements and system configurations to meet operational scenarios of the future.

Throughout the years, as we sought to develop, deliver, and maintain, we were inundated with meetings in many focus areas: the monthly program reviews; budget meetings; staff meetings in the IDEX II PO, and CPG; transition/integration working groups; formal semiannual user-participation reviews; CCCB meetings; weekly action items meetings; DSSC meetings; readiness review meetings; and the list goes on and on.

I am proud to state that Mike and I, with the support of our dedicated PO staff, in-depth and technologically advanced contractor team, funding organizations, and the user community, met the challenge to deliver a revolutionary intelligence capability at a critical time for our DoD and national intelligence agencies.

After four years on the program, with successful IDEX II deliveries and contributions to real-world warfighting, as in Desert Shield/Desert Storm, the CIA held a meeting in August 1991 for CPG and others in their "Bubble" auditorium right outside the main CIA building in Langley, Virginia. This was a month before Mike Dillard would depart the program for a new assignment.

The agency congratulated the composite team of CPG and IDEX II and issued many thanks and awards. I received another framed certificate signed by the CIA director, William H. Webster. Many others received similar recognition.

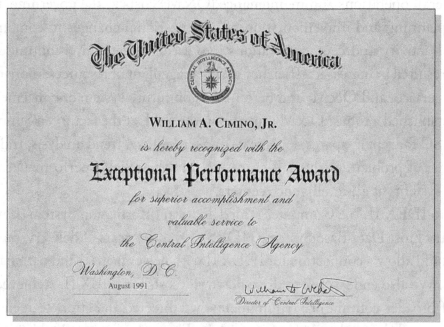

My exceptional performance award for superior accomplishment and valuable service to the Central Intelligence Agency.

In September 1991, Mike left the IDEX II program, having led our team for four years through a remarkable journey of technological change and capabilities for numerous intelligence organizations worldwide. He had met the challenges that looked insurmountable back in 1987, but he was never daunted by the difficulties associated with the effort. He was a great manager, revered by all. I did not want him to leave, but I was happy to have worked with him and gotten to know him well.

Now at the SIS 3 level within the CIA, he was presented with a new and much more challenging role. The agency asked him to join Robert "Rae" Huffstutler, the executive director at CIA headquarters, to create an agency-wide information technology organization. Mike had proved his worth, and this was a perfect follow-on assignment that could leverage all his unique talents, knowledge, and experience.

CIA Director Robert Gates, Mike Dillard, and Robert Huffstutler.
Photo: Courtesy of Mike Dillard.

About a year later, Rae and Mike established the CIA's first CIO office, officially titled, chairman, information policy board. Mike took over that role and reported directly to CIA Director, Robert Gates, who later became the secretary of defense, initially appointed by President George W. Bush, and retained for service by President Barack Obama.

Mike retired from the CIA on 14 August 1995. He went on to work successfully in the defense and intelligence industry for over twenty-five years. Mike and I maintain our friendship to this day, having witnessed our families progress through thirty-six years and our journeys through civilian jobs. We have been in business together since 2005, in the information technology/defense industry after IDEX II. But that is another story.

■ TDY GALORE × GALORE

I thought that the seventy-five TDY trips I took while assigned at the Pentagon were excessive, but it became less impressive compared to the 114 that I completed during my time with the IDEX II program. These visits were all over the map and frequent. A quick summary:

- 1987: Ten trips, including Sunnyvale, California; Offutt AFB, Nebraska; Valley Forge, Pennsylvania; Germany; Hanscom AFB, Massachusetts; and Hawaii.
- 1988: Twenty-two trips, including Sunnyvale; Langley AFB, Virginia; Wright-Patterson AFB, Ohio; Offutt AFB, Nebraska; San Francisco/Denver; Hanscom AFB; Austin, Texas; and Germany.
- 1989: Twenty-five trips, including Dallas, Texas; Sunnyvale; Langley AFB, Virginia; Hawaii; Hanscom AFB; Colorado Springs, Colorado; Wright-Patterson AFB; Offutt AFB; Germany; and Valley Forge.
- 1990: Twenty-four trips, including Hanscom AFB; Sunnyvale; Offutt AFB; Langley AFB; Hawaii; and Valley Forge.
- 1991: Fifteen trips, including Sunnyvale; Hawaii; Hanscom AFB; Langley AFB; Wright-Patterson AFB; Norfolk, Virginia; and Offutt AFB.
- 1992: Eighteen trips, including Sunnyvale; Offutt AFB; Hawaii; Wright-Patterson AFB; Langley AFB; the United Kingdom; Hanscom AFB; San Antonio, Texas; and San Jose, California.

Many of these trips—forty-two to be exact—were to our prime contractor, Lockheed's facility in Sunnyvale, where we maintained continuous oversight and management of the IDEX II program. Overall support there was excellent, with only minor hiccups that did, in fact, include the replacement of the Lockheed program manager and a few other mid-level managers to get some aspects of the program back on track.

One instance when I exhibited a bit of anger was when I did not see the proper application of the one million dollars I allocated to Lockheed to develop specific security measures to be built into the software. I recognized this as a significant mismanagement of funds. Banging my hand on the table was rare, but it got someone's attention.

I simply stated that by the next PMR, which would be in one month, I wanted to see this corrected. And it was.

All these trips were exciting, productive, and contributed to good experiences. However, some created special memories.

September 1987: This was my first trip to SAC at Offutt AFB, Omaha, Nebraska, to participate in a technical exchange meeting (TEM) for IDEX II and brief Maj. Gen. William Doyle Jr., the SAC/IN.

March 1988: I had a busy month. I went to Wright-Patterson AFB, Ohio, from 2–4 March; then to HQ SAC at Offutt AFB from 10–11 March; and on the 14–19 March trip that started at Lockheed in Sunnyvale, I stopped in Denver on my way home to give a talk to the AFROTC cadets of the 105th Cadet Wing at the University of Colorado at Boulder.

Fran's brother, Col. Vince Micucci, was the commander of the ROTC detachment and asked if I could give his cadets a speech during their leadership lab. Of course, I said yes and planned an overnight stop. I received a letter of invitation from his cadet protocol officer, Cadet Capt. Jeffries, expressing interest in my experiences in the navigator, reconnaissance, and intelligence fields. They also invited me to dinner at Banana's restaurant to follow the presentation. Had a great time there!

After about a twenty-minute presentation on 17 March in the university lab, I addressed the numerous questions they had. It was exhilarating to engage with these intelligent college students at the lab and at dinner. They were full of ambition, curiosity, and excitement. I sent a letter of thanks and best wishes and received a letter of thanks from the Cadet Wing commander, Cadet Col. Copello. It is always rewarding to commingle with our future AF leaders. I also thanked Vince for the opportunity.

September 1988: Briefed the AF Systems Command commander, Gen. Randolph during his visit to ESD, Hanscom AFB, Massachusetts.

November 1988: Col. Israel invited me to be one of many speakers at the Air Force Association (AFA)/Intelligence Technology Symposium at Hanscom AFB. He sent me a letter of thanks, stating in part, "Results are pouring in from the 350 participants ... and uniformly the comments are complimentary and soliciting us for another conference next year. One lady sent a picture in, asking for your phone number, but I threw it away. Hope you don't mind. All in all a great effort, lots of fun and couldn't have done it without you. Thanks again for a first class effort, or should I say ... nonpareil." Again, he always had a way with words. I wonder who the lady was.

Shortly afterward, I received a unique gift tied to a bit of history. The Paul Revere Chapter of the AFA gave me a beautifully framed certificate of appreciation that contained a "notable artifact," a bronze nail that was wrought in the foundry of Paul Revere and used to fasten the copper sheathing to the outer hull below the waterline.

It was retrieved from the USS *New Hampshire*—a 2,100-ton, 196-foot ship that was the first training ship of the US Navy and the New York Militia. It sunk on 27 July 1922 and remains in eight fathoms of water off Graves Island, Massachusetts. The nail was brought up in July 1984 by Dennis M. Loger, a marine conservationist, explorer, and divemaster.

A representative of the AFA, Paul Revere Chapter presenting a
Thank-you gift for my support at the AFA/Intelligence Technology Symposium.

May 1989: This was another busy month with three TDYs. I had many months where I would travel multiple times. My first trip this month, from 1–3 May, was to ESD at Hanscom AFB for routine updates and administrative purposes. I went back to Hanscom on 11–12 May to be present for Col. Israel's departure from ESD. He was about to report to the IG's office at AF Systems Command, Andrews AFB, Maryland. His work there would enable him to become a brigadier general (one-star) a year later.

There is no way to overstate the significance of Ken Israel and the impact he made on many people, me included. Lt. Gen. Gordon Fornell, commander of ESC at Hanscom, presided over the ceremony for Col. Israel. Ken's wife, Annetta, was present along with about seventeen other distinguished guests, among many others. Among

those were senior AF officers from the base and senior executives in the defense industry. These included: Vic DeMarines, VP for special programs, MITRE Corporation,
Jeff Hallahan, Hughes Aircraft Company; Tony Durante, assistant program director
to Colonel Israel; and Jack Segal, his chief engineer.

Segal's poem captured everyone's attention and spoke to the character we all recognized as Ken Israel. I am honored to share it here with Jack's permission:

Ode to a Colonel

It was back in the past, four long years ago,
That life changed dramatically, and we became stars in the show.
There came a loud knock on our inner office door.
We sprang from our chairs as the view graphs hit the floor.
And into our vault came Colonel, "You-Know-Who."
His hat in one hand, and his moose in the other,
He smiled when he saw the place all in clutter.
He pulled up a chair and motioned us down,
And then his eyes narrowed with a serious frown.
He said, "I'm Israel, not the land but Ken.
I'm looking damn hard for the IC good men."
I knew then and there that this man would be great
And decided to join him to go to my fate.
. We started out small, with very few in our band,
So we handled the work by touring the land.
The MITRE support was always fearless and ready,
And by juggling the numbers, the program was steady.
From 85-89 the programs covered strategic and tactical,
But Col. Israel always stayed flexible and practical.
He juggled his people with polish and verve,
And watched IC grow as a result of his nerve.
During the past four years he's led a spectacular IC band,
Which he trades in now for a tour in Systems Command.
For us who remember that first day long ago,
And have participated with him in the four-year show,
Have tears in our eyes as we watch the man go.

Jack Segal
12 May 1989

The third trip in May 1989 was to Lockheed in Sunnyvale again, but this time to be part of a group that briefed and provided a tour for Edward "Pete" Aldridge Jr. Pete was a former secretary of the air force (1986–1988) and director of the NRO (1981–1988).

October 1989: There never seemed to be a lack of excitement when we visited our team in California. A few days before our October trip, the entire nation learned of the Loma Prieta earthquake that occurred on 17 October in the Santa Cruz area south of San Francisco. The entire Bay area was affected. The earthquake measured from 6.9 to 7.1 on the Richter scale (depending on different reports) and lasted ten to fifteen seconds. It happened during game 3 of the World Series between the San Francisco Giants and the Oakland Athletics in Candlestick Park (now 3-Com Park). I remember the news and seeing the reactions of the players and spectators at the game!

After our all-day session on Tuesday, 24 October, at Lockheed's facility with a large audience, a smaller management group of us assembled in a conference room with windows for a more private discussion. After a few minutes, we sensed something that quickly developed into an aftershock from the earthquake that rolled through the room like we were surfing a wave. The window frames buckled, going from a rectangular shape to a trapezoidal shape back and forth several times! I wondered why the windows didn't break! It only lasted a second or two, but it definitely got our attention!

The earthquake triggered a sprinkler system in some of the critical IDEX II contractor-designated areas. We heard that some of the senior executives scrambled to lift heavy manhole covers to shut off valves that supplied the system with water. Additionally, some of the Lockheed managers' homes were so badly damaged they had to move out until repairs could be completed—some, many months later.

October 1989: I was again asked to brief at the Exploitation Technology Conference held in Valley Forge, Pennsylvania, hosted by our systems integrator, GE. I gave a status update on the IDEX II program to the attendees.

April 1990: Immediately after Gen. Ronald W. Yates became the commander of AF Systems Command at Andrews AFB, Maryland, I gave him a short IDEX II briefing at ESD, Hanscom AFB during his visit there, one of many he would make in his new role.

August 1992: I made another visit to HQ SAC at Offutt AFB. I arrived a day before my meetings, which included a walking tour of IDEX II for one of the generals and a few others. I was pleased to get a VIP room at the base—a two-room suite with many amenities. SAC had some of the best visiting quarters in the AF. I decided to run a few miles that afternoon; I brought my running gear. After a few miles, my left heel developed a slight ache, so I walked back to my room. After dinner, I prepared a bit for the next day and went to bed early.

In the early hours of the next day, I woke up with severe pain in my foot. I had plantar fasciitis! I could barely walk to the bathroom. *How the hell am I going to go on a walking tour?* I wondered. I soaked my foot, took some mild pain medication, and tried to get some sleep. Eventually, I made it to the meeting but told no one of my ailment. Once the discussion in the meeting room ended, we set out to tour the IDEX II facility. I hobbled along and was behind the group the whole way. I finally had to disclose why it seemed I didn't want to be anywhere near the others as we walked. They were somewhat compassionate but more focused on the general!

■ FAMILY FOCUS

While I was knee-deep in IDEX II management and travel, with a frequency of every other week from 1988 through 1990, plenty was going on at the home front that deserved attention.

When I started my job in the IDEX II program, our kids were spread across the academic community. Our son Bill entered his sophomore year at George Mason University (GMU) in Fairfax, Virginia. Joe started his freshman year at Lake Braddock High School in Burke, and Jeannie began sixth grade at Cherry Run Elementary School in Burke. In the years ahead, Fran and I would face the escalating costs of college tuition and related expenses. Fortunately, part of that was offset by our college savings, which we set up when they were born.

During this assignment, Bill would graduate from GMU in 1990, Joe from high school in 1991, and Jeannie would advance to a junior in high school in the 1992–1993 academic year. In parallel with that, Fran had begun working as a teacher at Burke Presbyterian Pre-School from 1986–1989. In the fall of 1988, she entered a program to attain a graduate degree. Her workload increased considerably with this new commitment.

Fran worked very hard to complete the four-year study program locally to receive her master's degree in social work in May 1992 from Virginia Commonwealth University, based in Richmond. This provided the credentials she needed to be a social worker. Our family celebrated her graduation at the university campus in Richmond.

With this important qualification, she began working in Prince William County public schools as a school social worker for a middle school and two elementary schools. In this new role, Fran was part of the interdisciplinary team that evaluated students for special education services. She also worked closely with the guidance department and school staff to provide the best counseling to students. She interfaced closely with students' parents to hear their concerns.

Fran received her MSW at VCU, Richmond, Virginia.

Fran had some very tough challenges with middle-school students who came from dysfunctional families and tough neighborhoods, and who had poor self-respect and sometimes indicated they might want to hurt themselves. They could not see the light ahead. She did a magnificent job earning their trust, and they benefited from her genuine and personal care. This was exhausting work. Fran would tell me some of what she faced but never revealed names to protect the confidentiality between her and "her" kids.

Fran was also her mother's primary caregiver. She had moved from Rhinebeck, New York, to Virginia. Fran's father passed away right after Christmas 1987. He had been ill, and we were on our way by car to see him. Since we did not have mobile phones at that time, we learned, sadly, when we called from the motel in Rhinebeck that he passed away in the hospital mere hours before we arrived there. He was eighty-five years old. He immigrated to America when he was eighteen.

Fran's mother, Jean, had a stroke in spring 1986. Since that time, Fran and her father talked about moving to Virginia to be near us. That subject became more imminent since her mother had a limited disability that required she walked with a cane and was alone. Jean had many friends in Rhinebeck, New York, but she wanted to be near family. The decision was easy. She would come back to Virginia with us to ascertain options.

Shortly after we brought her back to Rhinebeck, we made plans to move her to Burke, Virginia, in early 1988 to a small condominium she liked. She was very independent, and while she managed with her disability, her mind was as sharp as ever.

She had the equivalent of a PhD with her teaching credentials and had taught for many years.

She did not want to move in with us. Independence, although perhaps not total, was important to her. Her condo was three miles from us, which was convenient for visits, Sunday dinners, or taking her to medical appointments, shopping, or visiting others. It worked out very well.

During this assignment, our family experiences were like those of many other families. There were happy times—celebrations, work satisfaction, learning, and various achievements—and sad and stressful moments. One big celebration deserves a bit of narrative.

In June 1992, Fran and I celebrated our twenty-fifth wedding anniversary, and we wanted it to be special. We arranged a trip to New York City for a few days, and I made reservations to stay in quarters at the Coast Guard facility on Governor's Island, a 172-acre island in the heart of New York Harbor, only eight hundred yards from Lower Manhattan, and even closer to Brooklyn. We could bring our car and leave it there while we visited the city. The ferry often ran between Battery Park and the island, and the subway could take us anywhere we wanted to go.

I also arranged a unique anniversary ring for Fran from a jeweler we had used for a few years. I coordinated it with Fran so as not to screw it up. I'm sure she would have liked anything I brought her (as she did with all the previous jewelry I had purchased, especially the custom-made ones from Thailand). It was a fourteen-carat white gold channel ring with fifteen round diamonds set edge to edge that went halfway around the ring. I had ordered this custom ring many weeks before we left for New York. It was supposed to be ready long before our departure, but it was not. I was not happy and told the jeweler when I was leaving, and asked how he would get it to me. He said it would be done, and he would get it there before our anniversary on 24 June.

We were in the city, and the twenty-fourth was approaching. And no word from the jeweler. I called him from a phone booth while we toured the city. Now he really got me angry because while he assured me before we left that it would be done, he now told me it wasn't ready yet, and he could express mail a temporary ring that I could use on our anniversary. *A TEMPORARY RING!* It's in caps because that's the way my brain immediately started to function, and my words to him were no less emphatic!

"What do you mean, a *temporary ring*?" I asked. Maybe I raised my voice so half of NYC could hear me. I did not give him a moment to explain this away. I went through the entire prior discussion we had going back to when I ordered it and emphasized when I needed it. I told him where we were staying and that I had an anniversary dinner planned at Windows on the World restaurant on the 107th floor of the North Tower of the World Trade Center. I wanted the ring to give to Fran there.

I think ten minutes went by before I came up for air. I told him one more thing before I hung up. I don't remember the exact words, but it was very close to this: "Look, I don't care if you have to fly that ring here yourself, ride a horse all day and night, or hire someone to drive it here. I want it delivered to the Coast Guard accommodations on Governor's Island before I leave for dinner on the twenty-fourth!" *Click!*

On the morning of the twenty-fourth, I received a call from the reception desk. "Mr. Cimino, there is a package for you that came by overnight express mail." I picked it up and vowed if it was anything but the ring I ordered, the first thing I would do when I got home was … well, maybe I shouldn't say! I opened it, and a huge smile squelched any residual anger.

As planned, I presented the ring to Fran as we enjoyed the fine dining and sites from one of the most memorable locations in NYC. She has worn it ever since that day. We were very fortunate to have that experience, and we remain devastated and saddened that others will not get the same opportunity to view NYC as we did that day.

■ ONE FOR THE SMITHSONIAN

A new director came on board as Mike departed for his next challenge. Dennis Adams arrived from another CIA organization to lead the IDEX II PO in the fall of 1991. I accompanied him when he attended an orientation visit in November 1991 at Lockheed's facility in Sunnyvale. I worked as his deputy for the remainder of my time with the program.

After about twelve years of service to the intelligence organizations that used IDEX II, the National Geospatial-Intelligence Agency transferred the IDEX II workstation to the National Air and Space Museum (NASM) of the Smithsonian Institution, located at the Stephen F. Udvar-Hazy Center in Chantilly, Virginia, in April 2005. It is located near the many space systems that tourists marvel at when visiting the museum.

The system had great utility as it adapted to more incredible collected intelligence data evolution. It was eventually replaced by a system that GDE Systems, a Rancho Cordova, California, company won in a wide competition with much larger defense organizations. After my retirement, I worked for that company in Virginia, wrote the O&M portion of our bid, and was on the eight-person oral team to present our solution to the government.

On 5 April 2005, a small management group of us met with Joe Anderson, who retired in January 2001 as a major general in the marines and became associate director at the museum. It was a great day with Joe as we toured the IDEX II area, followed by a meeting in his conference room, where he showed us some of the very private historical videos and artifacts that are not open to the public. Pretty fascinating!

L to R: Randy Blystone, Dennis Adams (now deceased),
Maj. Gen. Joe Anderson, Marine Corps-Retired, Bill Cimino, Mike Dillard, Brian Bartelt.

A few years later, I received a call from the museum to ask if I would address a group of tourists who specifically wanted to learn more about IDEX II. I called on Brian Bartelt to accompany me. A museum representative gave a short briefing on the history of IDEX II to a group of about twenty. They had many questions that the rep, Brian, and I addressed. It was fun and rewarding to engage with the folks at the museum and tell them what a critical role the system played in our nation's intelligence reconnaissance effort. More recently, I would tell people who asked about IDEX II, "Our system is so old it's in a museum!"

More recently, James David, curator at the NASM, responded to my request to visit the museum and take some photos at the IDEX II workstation exhibit located in the Space section. He requested that Dr. Chuck Byvik, a NASM volunteer, accompany me. I met with Chuck for nearly two hours to trade stories of our experiences with programs and technology. Chuck is a physicist and scientist with a fascinating background in laser technology.

NASM volunteer Chuck Byvik and me at the IDEX II workstation display, 1 November 2022.
Photo: Courtesy of Chuck Byvik and the National Air and Space Museum (NASM).

■ IDEX II OPENED DOORS

As my time in the JPO approached four years, I added a desire for a follow-on assignment to my inputs in a job summary my boss requested. I expressed an interest in a tour of duty at HQ Air Force Systems Command in Maryland for two to three years as a division chief or other appropriate position for an O-6 (colonel). These are usually a shot in the dark, but I hoped it would get someone's attention.

In late 1991, I received a call from Ken Israel, who was now a brigadier general assigned as the AF program executive officer for the C-3 PO of the Secretary of the AF at the Pentagon. Ken had completed his nearly two-year assignment in the IG Office at Andrews AFB, Maryland (May 1989–February 1991), and was promoted on 1 July 1990.

His call told me immediately that he was looking out for me and had my best career interest in mind. He always expressed his strong support for me verbally, through letters, and in my performance evaluations. Ken also knew my family well. He stated that Gen. Fornell, who was still the commander of ESD at Hanscom AFB, had a job offer for me and wanted to know if I would accept it. At this point, I had been in the SES/JPO for four and a half years. The IDEX II deliveries were complete, and we were in an O&M phase working out of the CSSC in Newington, Virginia. So it made sense that a new assignment would soon follow.

The position was the chief of staff for the Operations Office of the Atlantic Command in Iceland. This office had operational oversight of all military operations from Newfoundland to Greece. Ken explained that it was a two-year remote tour of duty, and I could not bring my family. He also commented that previous colonels in the position achieved their first stars, meaning promotion to brigadier general. This was a great opportunity!

As his words swirled in my head, in a matter of seconds, part of my brain recalled all the opportunities I had been given throughout my AF career. For the most part, I went where I was told to go. I recalled the day I raised my hand and recited the oath of office and that I was government property and would jump when and where and how high the AF told me to do so. Of course, I took steps to shape that career as much as possible, my application to UNT a prime example.

However, as Ken proposed this opportunity to me, I was given a choice. There are always other colonels who can fill the job, and this was in *my* hands now. As we spoke on the phone, my mind was already made up; I knew in an instant. But I asked Ken if I could have some time to think about it before getting back to him and Gen. Fornell.

He said, "Sure. You have until tomorrow."

Wow! Tomorrow! OK. I thanked Ken and told him I truly appreciated being considered for the job and would certainly call him back the next day. I was not even off the phone before I knew my decision was the right one. Opportunities come and go throughout life. Each one is important and requires careful consideration given the context within the time it happened, the potential outcome, and any consequences.

I knew in a heartbeat that I would not accept the offer. I was delighted to be considered for this enormous opportunity, but my decision was not based on whether the assignment was good for me. I knew it would be. The decision was based on the collective "us"—our family. There was not a shred of doubt in my mind that it was more important to be home with the family at this time. Fran worked in a job and was also working toward her master's degree, she cared for her mother, and we had teenagers at home. The house upkeep was also a responsibility that was no small concern.

There was no way I would put her in jeopardy by leaving for an extended remote tour. I had been on a remote tour, and I determined one was enough. Once home, I explained the call to Fran and immediately told her my decision. No further discussion was necessary. I called Ken the next day, thanked him, and asked him to extend my thanks to Gen. Fornell. I explained my thought process, and he fully understood, which I knew he would.

Do I think of that decision and wonder what might have happened if I accepted the assignment? Of course I do. I would be a fool to admit otherwise. But do I *regret* my decision? That is the better question, and the answer is absolutely not. I have never once regretted my choice because I would always put my family first. I had no manifestation of apprehension about this opportunity. I repeat what I wrote in the "Introduction":

In life, opportunities come and go. It's essential to recognize opportunities and to carefully assess whether to embrace them or not.

I have great admiration for Ken Israel. I consider his example, his career, and his leadership as unique. Ken was promoted to major general on 1 July 1993. In December 1993, he became Assistant Deputy Undersecretary of Defense for Airborne Reconnaissance, and director of the Defense Airborne Reconnaissance Office (DARO) in Washington DC.

He has always had my best interest as a priority, and I will always have immense appreciation and respect for him. He rightfully belongs to a very small, distinguished group of AF navigators who have attained general officer status. He remains a significant role model for me for all he represents and has accomplished.

Maj. Gen. Kenneth R. Israel retired 1 October 1998.
Photo: Courtesy of Maj. Gen. Ken Israel.

The years of experience I had with my assignments in the Pentagon for AF TENCAP and the SES/JPO for IDEX II opened a new world for me, one connected with national reconnaissance assets, emerging technologies, multiple contractors, numerous intelligence organizations, and hundreds of personal contacts in the associated industries. I immediately had a new opportunity from this point forward. I could apply everything I had learned, and had honed into expertise, and use those credentials in the civilian world. It was an opportunity to transition from military life to civilian life. I decided I would consider retiring from the USAF.

TRANSITION

■ TIME TO RETIRE

It was not long after Ken Israel called me that I began to assess the possibilities of spending more time in the AF. What would I do? What job would be meaningful for me? What control would I have going forward? What was the likelihood of another family relocation after living comfortably in Virginia for nearly seven years? The questions kept coming.

As the close of 1991 approached, the subject of a reduction in force (RIF) emerged that might take place in mid-1992. If it included me in that action, I might find myself out of the AF more rapidly than if I had some control over when the RIF might become effective. I would then be subject to a shorter time frame to transition into a civilian job. This scenario contained an element of uncertainty. Although my previous years in the AF had many uncertain circumstances, I ascertained that this time, it would be better to have greater control of my destiny.

When one retires from the AF, you may have up to a year to submit your retirement paperwork. For a while, the AF extended this to thirteen months. It was not much more, but I welcomed every extra month available to plan for retirement. I carefully thought through this circumstance as I weighed every reason in both directions: remain in the AF for a few more years or make a dramatic change and start a new career.

The high priority for me was to adapt best, either way, to maintain the lifestyle we enjoyed and continue my part in supporting my family. How do I do this best? This was not a decision to take lightly. The points important in my rationale for my decision included where I was in life—my age, my potential in future work environments, my type of employment, my control in determining my future, and the time available to plan. I'm big on planning things!

Regarding age, I was now going on forty-seven years old. My thoughts were that I was probably a little more than halfway through my life (at least statistically). If I maintained good health and was very lucky (luck is always a factor), I would have good many years ahead. Why not jump into civilian life sooner than later, when I may be more competitive and have more "running time" in a new career?

Concerning the uncertainty of any AF actions, including RIF, assignments that may send me to undesirable locations, or even just because we did not want to be ripped once again from a lifestyle and location we loved, why not go out on my terms? I could apply for retirement early and have a solid year to look and prepare for a job, interview with many companies, and consider the type of role I wanted to have, whether that would be in a small company, a large company, a private company, and the like.

My terms! I preferred that. By December 1991, I had convinced myself that retirement from the AF was the right choice. Naturally, I had some apprehension. Who wouldn't after years of military life that determined a considerable part of one's very being? But I learned how to manage uncertainty by becoming bigger than the anxiety itself. I maintained more control over it than it did over me. I knew building more permanency in our family's household was paramount, and I could manage my way through civilian life as I did in the military. I submitted my application for retirement on 30 December 1991. It was approved the next day. This would allow me to retire on 1 February 1993.

While many of my OERs stated the endorsements for promotion, assignment to greater challenging jobs, and highlighted my potential for advancement, my last OER in 1992 stated that I planned for retirement in early 1993. There would be no further need to suggest things previously stated. They only described how well I did my current job, and that was more than I could ask for from my superior officers.

During my years with SES/JPO, I traveled every other week for nearly two years straight. And with heavy travel in the remaining years, I had built up a significant amount of leave. As my retirement date was established as 1 February 1993, I could finish my AF career with an extended "terminal leave" of the maximum allowed time of sixty days. This would enable me to complete any work by the end of November and have all of December 1992 and January 1993 on leave with full pay and benefits. Based on this schedule, my retirement ceremony was planned for late November 1992.

■ RETIREMENT CEREMONY

The date, time, and place were set: 1400 hours (2 p.m.), Friday, 20 November 1992, at the Officer's Club, Potomac Room, Bolling AFB, Washington DC. Brig. Gen. Ken Israel, who would preside over the ceremony, had sent out formal invitations to 108 guests. Most were local; others were from out of town. There were seventy-two in attendance. The notice also indicated a reception to follow in the Arnold Suite at the club.

My family, Fran's mother, and Bill's fiancée, Rebecca Hervey, were there. Bill and Rebecca's wedding was planned for 2 October 1993. From New York, my brother, Rob, and his wife attended. Others at the ceremony were friends, personnel from our IDEX II JPO (including our previous director, Mike Dillard), representatives from HQ ESD, Hanscom AFB, members of CIA's CPG, Lockheed Martin, SAIC, and other government agencies. It was a full house!

The AF is big on ceremonies such as these, and protocol defines the procedure. Gen. Israel left no detail undone as he prepared the official proceedings with my replacement, Lt. Col. Kirk Washington, and Suzanne Roseberry and Darren Smith, who were members of my staff. Each had a role in the ceremony that would begin after a brief meeting my family and I had with Gen. Israel in the Old Club Room. In his usual professional and warmhearted manner, Gen. Israel greeted my family and spoke of the ceremony that was about to begin.

Lt. Col. Washington and Capt. Roseberry took their places. Maj. Leon Mable, ceremony coordinator for Gen. Israel, and Capt. Darren Smith escorted my family to their reserved seats on both sides of an aisle in the front rows of the Potomac Room. The ceremony began at 1400 hours sharp with an introduction by Lt. Col. Washington:

> Good afternoon, ladies and gentlemen. Today the men and women of the United States Air Force pay special tribute to Col. William A. Cimino on the occasion of his retirement from active duty with the United States Air Force. The host official for today's ceremony is Brig. Gen. Kenneth R. Israel, Air Force Program Executive Officer for Command, Control, and Communications Programs. Ladies and gentlemen, please rise.

Capt. Smith played the entrance music as I followed Gen. Israel down the center aisle to the flags and turned to face the audience. Darren then played the National Anthem. I scanned the room. My family, friends, the many people I had worked with over the last few years, and those I worked with and knew longer than that all stood there, facing my role model and me. I was proud to stand there with Gen. Ken Israel.

Ken welcomed my family and guests and talked a bit about me before he presented me with the Legion of Merit, my highest medal, handed to him by Suzanne Roseberry, and after Kirk Washington read the award citation that spoke of my performance while assigned on the IDEX II program. After Ken pinned the medal to my uniform, we shook hands and exchanged salutes.

Suzanne handed the retirement certificate to Gen. Israel, who presented it to me. Kirk Washington read the retirement orders and certificate:

> By direction of the Secretary of the Air Force, Col. William A. Cimino is retired from active duty with the United States Air Force, effective 01 February 1993, after more than twenty-five years of faithful and honorable duty.

Following this, Kirk read the Presidential Certificate of Appreciation, a standard document granted to those retiring. My certificate is signed by George H. W. Bush, commander in chief.

Some of my retirement ceremony photos follow. They capture a memorable point in my military career.

Gen. Israel pins the Legion of Merit.

Gen. Israel presents the retirement certificate.

The Legion of Merit certificate.

After everyone took their seats, Gen. Israel invited Fran to join us. He commented on Fran's contributions during my career, highlighting her enduring support. He then directed Kirk to read the certificate he would present to her.

Kirk read, "As a gesture of our sincere gratitude for assisting your husband during his long and impressive career, Mrs. Cimino, the Air Force is pleased to present you with this certificate." I was so proud of all that Fran had contributed and sacrificed over the years and was happy she received recognition in front of all those who were present. Earlier, I had asked Suzanne to hold a bouquet for me. She handed it to me to present to Fran.

Gen. Israel presents a certificate of appreciation to Fran.

Flowers for my sweetheart.

Others came forward to make statements and present gifts. This generated a lot of laughter as one after the other told interesting and comical stories. The formality of the ceremony drifted into a format in which guests could say whatever they wanted. And to sum it up, it was fun!

Bob Dumais, CPG director.

Tony Durante, HQ ESD/IC.

Lt. Col. Kirk Washington.

Marilyn Conrad.

I then took the podium to make some remarks. I had developed a habit of writing key phases or just a few words on an index card I kept in my pocket. When I began my comments, I pulled out the card and placed it on the podium. But I did not look at it until after I made some quick opening remarks, thanking all those who attended the ceremony from far and near, supported me in the last few years, and especially Gen. Israel and my IDEX II team. And naturally, my family.

The card list ensured I did not leave anyone out. You never want to omit someone or a group and regret it later, so I think I had it all covered. I extended thanks to ceremony planners and supporters, military and civilian teams, program directors, contractors, secretaries, and others.

After my presentation, Kirk made closing remarks that expressed appreciation for my service and granted well wishes for the future. We adjourned the ceremony and went to the Arnold Suite for some food and refreshments. As we departed the Potomac Room, Darren played the "Air Force Song" on the boom box! It was a wonderful and memorable ceremony!

I wrote two letters dated that same day: one for Gen. Israel and one for Gen. Fornell, expressing my appreciation. These letters are in appendices I and J, respectively.

My retirement date of 1 February 1993 marked the end of my AF career after twenty-five years, six months, and twenty-six days of service. It held so many memories and experiences for which I am eternally grateful.

■ ENTER THE CIVILIAN WORKFORCE

Early in 1992, I began a series of interviews with several companies. My goal was to find a middle-management job where I could lead a group of employees for a particular effort, a program that would require all the expertise I had developed in the last years of my military career. These included leadership and communication skills, conflict resolution, risk management, interpersonal skills, organization, delegation, scheduling and time management, technical expertise, planning and strategic thinking, problem-solving, decision-making, commercial awareness, and mentoring.

I had months before I would need to begin my new job. I could even start in December while I was on terminal leave since I would no longer be committed to serving in the AF after my retirement ceremony and a few days to do some early out-processing. Any remaining administrative tasks could be completed in late January 1993.

I decided to take all the terminal leave without committing to a new job until February 1993. I attended interviews locally at first, with an easy schedule through 1992. Two companies presented the highest interest to me.

Aerospace Corporation had offices on the West Coast and in Virginia. They are an independent, nonprofit corporation operating the only federally funded research and development center (FFRDC) for the space enterprise, which provided objective technical analysis and assessments on all aspects of space missions to military, civil, and commercial customers.

The other company was GDE Systems, Inc., located in Rancho Cordova, California, near San Diego. They also had an office in Reston, Virginia, called the Northern Virginia Office (NVO). The Carlyle Group, an American multinational, private equity, alternative asset management, and financial services corporation, bought GDE Systems from General Dynamics Corporation in 1992.

Dr. Terry Straeter was a corporate director of technical software at General Dynamics who was promoted to corporate vice-president and general manager of their electronics division, DGE, which became GDE Systems. GDE would eventually drift through acquisitions and mergers with Tracor, Inc., Marconi Integrated Systems, and finally end up in BAE Systems, Inc., the US subsidiary of BAE Systems plc, an international defense, aerospace, and security company. I worked within these companies, all considered one for retirement purposes, for twelve and a half years after retirement from the AF.

Terry Straeter had occasionally visited Mike and me at our IDEX II office and intended to acquire business with us. While we never did engage his company's services, we maintained a good relationship. I leveraged that relationship when I began my search for a civilian job. I notified Terry that I would retire, and he immediately expressed an interest in hiring me.

He notified his HR office in Rancho Cordova to arrange a paid flight and accommodations to visit GDE for a few days to meet and interview with his senior vice presidents. Terry told me that he wanted me in GDE but would go through the normal hiring process. The interviews went well, and shortly after I returned, I received a job offer from them.

Before my trip, I had received a job offer from Aerospace Corporation. It was a good offer with a decent salary and benefits. However, the position was for a project manager. The job offer I received from GDE was at a slightly lower salary and had similar excellent benefits, but the position was a program manager. A big difference! Project management is on a much lower scope in terms of objective comprehensiveness, resources dedicated to the task, and level of responsibility at a minimum.

I evaluated both carefully but knew the GDE position was the one best for me, given my experience. I responded to GDE HR and told them I was very interested but that I also had an offer from Aerospace at a higher salary, which I said I could provide the documentation if they needed it. GDE sent me a new proposal that didn't quite meet the Aerospace offer but was a few thousand dollars more than their original offer. That was good enough for me, and I would have the job I wanted at the NVO. I accepted their offer and would start in February 1993.

Terry Straeter was very happy I joined his team of about 2,200 employees. I must provide some highlights of what that job meant to me even though it occurred after my retirement, which is when this memoir ends. Terry Straeter was a one-of-a-kind civilian manager. He knew all his employees by their first names and had rare charisma in the defense industry. We bonded very well. Anytime he was coming to the East Coast, he would call me and say, "Bill, I'm coming to the East Coast for a few days. Please set up the following meetings for me, and I want you to come to some of them with me." One such meeting was at the old Defense Mapping Agency (DMA) in Bethesda, Maryland. Former US Secretary of Defense Frank Carlucci was in attendance.

I could relate many stories about my interactions with Terry Straeter, who graduated at the top of his high school class, magna cum laude from college with a BA in math, a PhD in applied math, and worked in NASA's Langley Research Center in Hampton, Virginia. There, he contributed to major technological breakthroughs in aviation and avionics, working his way up the corporate ladder. He was exceptionally well recognized at NASA.

He has served as an adviser to the Senate Select Committee on Intelligence; on the board of directors of the Aerostructures Corporation and the United States Marine Repair, Inc.; on the board of governors of the Electronic Industries Alliance; and as chairman of the board of directors of the Government Electronics & Information Technology Association.

Sadly, Terry had a stroke a few years before he passed away on 6 November 2007.

Before his death, a few thousand of his devoted admirers—including Fran and me—attended a celebration of his life at the Smithsonian Institution after he stepped down from work. We all watched as his mother pushed the wheelchair that Terry occupied into the building that displayed "The Bronze Bust."

The bronze bust of Dr. Terry Straeter—sculpted by Ruth Hayward—mathematician and engineer who worked for General Dynamics' Electronic Division.

Photo: Courtesy of Ruth Hayward.   *Photo Courtesy of Ritenour High School Hall of Fame, St. Louis, Missouri.*

After my retirement ceremony, I enjoyed the Thanksgiving, Christmas, and New Year holidays with my family as I have never done for so many years—without reporting to work! However, I could not merely be without something to do since I had adapted to a mode of always being busy. In the past, I had finished part of the basement to include a bedroom with a closet for our oldest son, Bill, and a family room with partially paneled walls, carpeting, and electrical connections throughout. I studied how to do the wiring and obtained a permit from the county to install it.

We wanted to add a bathroom with a shower, but that was a little beyond my expertise. So I called on the only one I could absolutely trust in this regard—my brother, Rob. Rob lived in Hicksville, New York, on Long Island, in the home our parents purchased in 1959 after we moved from Brooklyn. He had done several different jobs in his earlier years but developed his skills as a master craftsman in repairing and building everything related to a home or commercial building. His ability to size up a project and initiate a plan toward completion was nothing less than amazing!

He was delighted to come down from New York to help me with the project. He drove his work van down with what I often described as containing "every tool known to mankind." He spent about a week and a half with us. He didn't want to be paid, but we insisted, "This is a job. It's your time, and you need to be paid." That was one of the most enjoyable times I had with my brother. We only saw each other briefly during the occasional visits while I was on active duty with the AF over the years.

Rob stood there and looked at the space where we wanted the bathroom—one side facing a finished basement area, the other facing a storage area. Overhead were air vents and pipes and a mess of other things that needed to be enclosed and finished. He studied it for about five minutes, after which he said, "OK, I know what to do." *You do? That fast?* Of course he did. He was a master craftsman.

I ordered major components before his arrival, like the toilet, sink with cabinet, shower stall, and other fixtures. I would run out to get other items if we needed anything while he worked away. I had never spent so much time laughing as I did with Rob the whole time he visited. He was younger than me by ten years but was six feet four inches tall and weighed over 250 pounds. He was strong as you can imagine. So regarding his size and age, I called him my "Big Little Bro."

As we grew up, we would play this game of one-on-one. We would each, in turn, punch each other in the upper arm to determine who was the strongest. As he outgrew me and became much stronger, I knew he was gaining the upper edge.

The inevitable day came when he said, "Let's play one-on-one!" The little brother in him never dwindled.

"No, you will hurt me! You're an animal," I said. One-on-one became a thing of the past. He converted this lovable show of affection for his brother into bear hugs instead. Those hurt me too. I couldn't breathe!

One day as we worked and it approached lunchtime, I asked, "Rob, you hungry? I can go to Bozzelli Brothers. They have great subs—Italian, chicken Parmesan, meatball. Which do you want?" This is what Italians do; they opt for the good stuff!

He responded with a smile and raised eyebrows, indicating he was getting famished, and said, "Yes!"

I asked, "Yes, what? Which one do you want?"

With a serious stare at me, he replied, "All of them!" I would have gladly brought him all three, but he picked one, and we broke out into laughter once again.

That's how our time would go as we worked to build the bathroom—one joke after another. He loved Fran, and if I ever even hinted that I might be angry with her for some reason, he would protect her and threaten me. He liked to "threaten" me. He was this lovable big teddy bear.

The teddy bear did a magnificent job completing the bathroom while he was in Burke with us. He completed all the structural work, installation, plumbing, wood trim, doors, and connections. He didn't care much for finishing details, like painting. He left that for me. We spent the latter part of the day having dinner and just relaxing before another all-day-at-work. He was proud of his work, and so were we. We were sorry to see him return to New York.

I never thought this would happen, ever, my brother predeceasing me. Rob passed away suddenly on 4 September 2020 due to a heart attack. He was sixty-four years old. We miss him and mention his name every evening during a brief prayer before dinner. I especially miss the texts we sent each other now and then. He would always end his texts with an icon of red lips indicating a kiss for his brother. I would jokingly text back, "I don't mind the kisses; just don't make them too wet!"

Rob would quickly text back, "Oh, I will send you many kisses, and they will be very wet!" He always wanted to one-up me! I continue to save on my mobile phone some of the last texts we exchanged just days before he passed. It keeps me linked in with him, as does the photo array of him that Fran and I cherish in our home. He was the sweetest man I have ever known!

Robert Cimino (Rob, "Big Little Bro")
1956–2020

◼ TIME FOR REFLECTION: EVERYONE IS A NAVIGATOR

As I have done in the past, at each turn in my career, at the end of each assignment, at the beginning of a new role and place for me in the AF, I find it very natural to determine what those twenty-five years plus meant. What did my career do for the AF, my country, my family, and me? I can be realistic, or I can be grandiose about it. Grandiose is not my style, so I will attempt to be honest and realistic as much as possible. And the only way to do that is to reflect on what it *meant* to me rather than what I did.

Having a career in the AF was an honor. It was a privilege for me to serve my country. I believe it is one of the most incredible opportunities a citizen can have, and I am proud to stand with the many who have done so in whatever capacity that was.

Achieving any level of success requires the help and support of others; no one does it entirely on his or her own. We need family and professionals in our work environments, those who can lead the way, provide support and encouragement, and demonstrate through their actions, not entirely by words. We need role models.

The phrase, "Cooperate and Graduate" not only applies to formal training, as I have mentioned while in OTS, UPT, UNT, and other training programs. It is relevant in everyday activities when you are on a quest to achieve a goal or reach an objective. We all are trying to go somewhere or reach something. I gave thought to titling this memoir *Cooperate and Graduate* or *Everyone Is a Navigator.* I stuck with *Manifestations of Apprehension* because it was central to the drive I developed to go forward, to rise above the failure from my earlier, darker days when I was filling barf bags in the skies over southwestern Texas.

MOA is a scar. It's like a branding from a hot iron. It is still there and will never completely disappear, but years of cosmetics from support, encouragement, steadfastness, and achievements, have rendered it barely visible.

Everyone *is* a navigator. They don't all have USAF-rated officer certifications or wear navigator wings. Still, they work their way through life at their own speed, progressing from A to B and beyond, trying to reach each initial point to the target of each quest, and then make any necessary course changes to reach their goals. Like professional navigators, sometimes they get off course and need to adjust and make corrections. But they are always mindful of their goals.

Another appreciation I have is that my career was at a time when the AF needed navigators for its diverse aircraft and associated missions. Tactical reconnaissance is a dying breed due to sophisticated technological advancements, such as GPS, drones, and unmanned and persistent overhead reconnaissance. The days of the RF-4C and similar aircraft are virtually over. I was fortunate to go through UNT and follow-on training that taught me a profession I loved and admired.

My career in the AF exposed me to so many values, and I do value each one. It's challenging to capture them all. It presented challenges at all levels and barriers to success, but it also presented resources to meet each challenge and be successful. Sometimes it worked. Sometimes it did not.

The AF is a lot of things: equipment and aircraft, armament—missiles, rockets, bombs, and so on—strategic and tactical war plans, intelligence systems, multilevel organizations worldwide; the lists go on and on. But most important, it's people, dedicated people, a diverse force.

Diversity is one of the most essential components of our AF, or any branch of the military for that matter. People with different backgrounds, different beliefs, different faiths (or no faith at all), different ethnicities, differently colored skin, different accents, all shapes and sizes and textures. I didn't matter. We were all in it together for the mission entrusted to us. Tremendous collective talent comes from a diverse force.

Education never ends. You can always learn more; you can never know enough. And more important, never think you have learned enough and are above it all. The AF has given me many opportunities to learn through training and experience.

Respect for authority is paramount if we want to function effectively in the military *and* society. While many recognize that sometimes those in power should not be there, we still should adhere to authority to the best of our ability and judgment. The chain of command is sacred in the military. It allows us to know our places in the fabric of the mission. Organization, structure, and discipline usually fall into place when we understand where we are in the chain of command.

When one understands and accepts a role in the military for a given assignment, dedication and loyalty to the mission, teamwork, and perseverance contribute to the success of the branch one serves. These components developed quickly when I transitioned from civilian to military life back in 1967. But their value grew in family life during my military career and was reinforced when I transitioned back to civilian status in 1993. So I live by much of what I learned in the AF and applied those lessons, I believe, to the best of my ability. I adapted what my career taught me into a loose set of rules—Bill's eleven rules.

▪ BILL'S ELEVEN RULES

Why eleven? Why not ten? We often hear of ten rules: the ten rules of etiquette, the ten rules of good financial investing, the Ten Commandments. Those are good practices, too, ten good rules, no doubt. So why eleven? Because that's what I have—eleven!

These are in no particular order only because I didn't want to take the time to try and prioritize them. They are all important, at least to me.

Discipline: Everyone needs some level of discipline, some code of behavior, and punishment to correct bad behavior. I have witnessed bad behavior many times, and I admit, I'm not exempt. And it needs to be addressed. Rule: *Get some discipline in your life.*

Learning: We are indeed fortunate that we can turn to an infinite number of things about which we can learn. Rule: *Don't be brain dead: Learn something* (especially from mistakes or failure).

I digress a bit here to emphasize a little more how I view failure since it was a key motivation to write this book. Since I don't have any great quotes about failure that I can call my own, I give credit to those who have made meaningful statements. There are hundreds of individuals from all walks of life—world leaders, politicians, scientists, authors, entrepreneurs, physicians, and on and on. They remind us that failure is an outcome, and it may occur many times in one's life. More important, it's part of a process that may lead to success. The one common thread—the message I observe in all the quotes about failure—is that to get beyond it, one must try again. Don't give up. Learn from it, and keep going.

Back to the rules.

Be a role model: We all could use them. Someone needs you to be the person he or she wants to become, to live the way you live by your good example. Rule: *Be a role model, a good example. Give others something for which they can be proud to follow.*

Diversity: How boring would it be if we were all clones of one another? Embrace the diversity in our humankind. Rule: *Accept diversity: Give the world a hug.* It may just hug you back.

Opportunities: Assess every opportunity that comes your way. Or better yet, create them. The opportunities you meet that you mature into achievements help to define you. Rule: *Don't turn your back on opportunities.*

Optimism: I've always found optimism to have a greater advantage over pessimism. An attitude of hopefulness and confidence feeds the mind in a favorable way. Rule: *Make optimism your default attitude.*

Problem Perception: We all have problems to some degree. Don't make your problems bigger than they really are, and stop whining about them. A leak from your water heater is nothing compared to the loss of an entire neighborhood due to a fire, as in the terrible fires in communities near Boulder, Colorado, in 2022. Also, don't make your minor physical maladies compare in any way to someone who lost a limb, is confined to a wheelchair for life, or lost their sight. Rule: *Put your problems in proper perspective, and stop your habit of whining.*

Appreciation: Show those who support you some appreciation. Sometimes that's all they want in return—some recognition that you truly benefited from their help. Don't take anyone for granted. A simple, "Thank you," goes a long way. Rule: *Be generous with showing appreciation.*

Values: This is one that sort of overlaps with others, but I think of them more abstractly. As an aside, when our kids were young, they teased Fran and me about our occasional talks with them about the need to have values. They occasionally still bring it up, even as adults, when we reminisce. But those lessons took root! It is very rewarding to see them teaching *their* children, our grandchildren, those same values today. Loyalty, humility, compassion, respect, honesty, kindness, integrity, selflessness. More? Determination, generosity, courage, tolerance, trustworthiness, equanimity, altruism, spirituality, empathy, and self-reliance. They are all important values and contribute to defining you as an individual. Rule: *Seek as many values as possible.*

Perspective: There is always another point of view, a different perspective, another side of the story that deserves to be heard. We are not experts in everything. In fact, we are probably experts in nothing by our need to keep learning. Perspective is a close relative to learning. Rule: *Develop some perspective.*

Improvise: "Bumps in the road": They happen. Find solutions—a path forward, around, under, whichever way works best. If you can't proceed, perhaps you need to find another road. Rule: *Don't give up. Go back to the rule on learning (and failure).*

There you have it, my eleven rules. If I ponder this some more, I'm sure I could add a few more. But why bother? These will do just fine, at least for me. You should decide what rules work best for you. (I suggest all eleven!)

I am happy to state that Fran and I have worked together to instill these core rules in our three children. They are married with two children each, so we also enjoy witnessing how they have transferred the rules to our six grandchildren, aged thirteen to twenty-seven. They all make us enormously proud.

I revert to my AF career. What a valuable experience of learning, appreciation, respect, order, structure, problem-solving, teamwork, value-building, and all the elements that I believe have made me, *me*. I owe an immense debt of gratitude to all those who have made my career enjoyable, successful, meaningful, and a very significant and memorable part of my life.

My sincere hope is that readers of this memoir will come to learn of the immense appreciation I have for those who were part of my career in the AF and dwell less on anything I may have accomplished. My AF career is over. It's behind me. But my friends and family—those I admired, trusted, relied on, respected, and much more—remain.

■ CONTROL OVER APPREHENSION

I would never be so bold as to claim that I defeated apprehension anytime in my life. Defeat is too decisive of a word and implies that I no longer have anxiety. I *will* assert, however, that I have developed a means to control this foreboding feeling. Learning to overcome apprehension often depended on the severity and time I had to tackle each issue.

In UPT, there was no way to recover, and I had to accept that. The program had its own speed, and I could not keep pace by successfully completing the flying phase. Plain and simple, I failed! The training report contained a simple statement: "Manifestations of Apprehension (not due to factors over which he had control)." While that was a devastating blow, I had no choice but to look forward, not backward. I faced new assignments and accepted that each had some level of apprehension. And although I may not have admitted that from time to time, they all contained some level of uncertainty. That alone can cause anxiety.

However, as each new challenge came, I managed to gain traction, enlisting the support I needed along the way and building the confidence I required to continue through my years in the AF. I learned how to gain control, and I dove into every assignment with determination and excitement to succeed and do the best job possible.

My assignments after UPT, at Lowry AFB and Kadena AB, were confidence builders as I learned a new skill and applied it operationally. Working my way through UNT at Mather AFB was a tremendous challenge of studying and testing, as well as a great opportunity in a leadership role as class commander.

The advanced aircrew training I received at Shaw AFB in the RF-4C was the first in a series of steps toward becoming combat-ready as I would become certified at Bergstrom AFB. The operational training there prepared me for my tour in SEA at Udorn RTAFB, where I contributed to our efforts at the end of the war in Vietnam.

As a navigator instructor at Mather AFB, my self-confidence and skills increased as I tackled many tasks—flying, teaching, leading, and seeking advanced education. My selection for the AF-CF Exchange Program added diversity to my assignments, including a role as ambassador before I returned to Shaw AFB to fly once again in the RF-4C. Only this time, I managed and had key operational tasks as chief, wing Stan/Eval, and chief of wing training, filling positions typically held by pilots.

My last two assignments—in the AF TENCAP Office for Space Operations at the Pentagon and the IDEX II program via the Softcopy Exploitation System/Joint Program Office (SES/JPO), opened a vastly greater complex world of DoD, the intelligence community, and contractor interaction. These afforded me the ability to hone my skills as a senior manager and leader, which prepared me well as I shifted into civilian life.

In every one of these assignments, the most important takeaway for me was that whatever I did was as part of a team. It was me giving my best for the team, and in the end, to the organization that had its specific mission. Contributing to the team was a great feeling, and while earning the occasional award or medal here and there, it was most rewarding when the unit I served was awarded recognition. That was primary; individual recognition was secondary. I can never overstate how highly I value my AF career and what it means to my life.

So here I am. Approaching seventy-eight years of age in October 2023, I fully realize how fortunate I am to have reached this point. I also know with almost complete certainty that I have more years behind me than ahead of me. (I would never claim 100 percent certainty about anything other than death, taxes, software upgrades, and changes in PCS assignments.) Of course, add to this my love for my family. That's in a category by itself, an absolute certainty.

There are two things that I contemplate almost daily: death and my next adventure in life, two things so opposed to one another. As one gets older, it's only natural to wonder, *How much more time do I have?* We know what our bodies "tell" us, and we realize the physical limits we once had may no longer be achievable. At least this cognition indicates my mind is still functioning well enough. I am so fortunate and grateful for that!

What lies ahead? Apprehension? Of course, there is some level of apprehension. Does it manifest itself in me in a detrimental manner? No! I would be a fool not to admit that I worry about death. Most people do, I suppose; it's part of life. But I am confident that my experience with apprehension better enables me to apply perspective and create positive diversions from such thoughts. I focus on remaining positive.

I am always thinking of what I will do next, what *we,* Fran and I, will do next. What project will I start? The possibilities energize me! You only get one shot at this thing called life. I read for pleasure. I have some favorite authors whose writing amazes me. Maybe I'll write something else—maybe fiction. I have one idea for a story that is beginning to interest me. I'll see if it gels. There is no question my writing style and storytelling can improve. I need to read more. Fran reads so much more than I do, so I have a long way to go to catch up to her. I will probably never get there, but I can try.

I must remain busy with something. I like to fix things. If something breaks, I'll do my best to fix it before I call on the so-called experts, who often do not turn out to be experts or much help. So I'll keep trying—until I'm desperate.

I love to fly fish for trout! I enjoy this pastime several times a year in all weather conditions, sometimes alone, other times with my sons, grandson, son-in-law, or friends. And every time I catch one, I silently say, "Thanks Dad," as a reverent gesture for all he taught me about the sport. I could always try to break my one-day record of twenty-nine trout! No worries. I gently put them all back in the river. It was catch and release only on that cool day, 22 February 2021, at the Rose River Farm in Madison County, Virginia, in view of the beautiful Shenandoah Mountains.

I know one thing for sure: I am anxious to get started on the next adventure. While a little apprehensive about it, I'm confident that my zeal for something new will dominate my mindset and steer my actions forward.

SPECIAL TRIBUTES

Photo: Courtesy of Atul Kumar Pandey, AtulHost American Flag Images and Wallpapers.

In Memoriam: Gone, But Not Forgotten

Since I retired from the AF, I have learned of the passing of several individuals. Each relationship was special to me in its distinct way. These men were taken from their families far too soon, and they all deserve to be honored for their commitment and service to our country. I have great admiration and respect for their friendship, support, and devotion to duty.

ANTHONY (TONY) CAMERON SHINE

20 May 1939
Pleasantville, Westchester County, New York

MIA: 2 December 1972
Promoted posthumously to lieutenant colonel.

Tony, a young man full of zeal and determination.

Captain Tony Shine, one hundred missions in SEA in the F-105.

In chapter 9, I wrote that "A Friend is Missing," when communications with Tony failed after he descended in his A-7D aircraft through the clouds in North Vietnam near the Laotian border on 2 December 1972. He was declared MIA on that day, which launched a long and painful search for many years by his family for answers.

The Shine family never gave up in their pursuit to explain why Tony and his plane disappeared. There had to be an answer. Planes just don't disappear. Tony's wife, Bomette, known to all as Bonnie, persistently pressed the AF and our government to provide information. Tony's daughter, Colleen, was only eight years old when her dad went missing. As years passed with no relevant information, Colleen took on the primary role of investigation that would eventually lead to a memorial service for Tony at Fort Myer and burial at Arlington National Cemetery, in Arlington County, Virginia on 11 October 1996, twenty-four years later!

The story of Colleen's determination and courage cannot be overstated. Over the years, the military repeatedly told her that any further searching was useless.

Undaunted, Colleen continued to press for information despite what she and her family had heard. She said:

"Finally in 1995, they told me they found his crash site. They believed there was nothing more we can learn...he was killed in action. Any parts of the aircraft would have been scavenged by villagers for scrap metal and any remains would have been washed away in floods and erosion. And so, I went to Vietnam...to have peace with knowing, in war, there will be casualties where you never have an answer, and I thought that would be the case." But instead, she found answers and proof of where her father perished.

"I found parts of my father's plane, serial numbers. I found my dad's helmet that had his name in it. ... It was held by a Vietnamese villager in his 60s who kept it as his memento of the war, and when I turned it over and saw my father's handwritten name inside, I asked if I could take it home, that it would be helpful for me in the search in knowing if my father was alive or dead, and he gave it to me."

That led to recovering his remains, verified through DNA testing, and in 1996, Lt. Col. Anthony Shine came home to his country and his family. Colleen was the family member who accepted the findings of the DNA testing. When asked what it's like to see her father's name on the Vietnam Veterans Memorial Wall, Colleen said, "I think one of the most amazing qualities of the wall is you see yourself in it. I see my father's name here, and he's no longer living, and his legacy is living. That reflection is me, and that's how I honor his service, and his sacrifice is how I live my life."

Vietnam Veterans Memorial
Washington DC
panel 1W, row 93

Pencil rubbing of Tony's name on the Memorial Wall.

Fran and I attended Tony's memorial service in October 1996 with his friends and family. Among those were Sheila Rockholt and her husband, Bob. Tony is buried in Arlington National Cemetery, section 60, site 7772.

In 1980, Bonnie established an award in honor of her husband and those missing in Vietnam. Tony's dedication, service, and sacrifice as an AF fighter pilot are commemorated annually in this special award, the Lt. Col. Anthony C. Shine Award, which is given to fighter pilots and presented by his daughter, Colleen. Tony was a fighter pilot's fighter pilot!

Bonnie passed away on 7 January 2018, after a long battle with cancer. Along with Tony's father and later her daughter, Colleen, she contributed directly and powerfully to the National League of POW/MIA Families' efforts to achieve the fullest possible accounting for those Americans listed as POWs or MIA.

Tony's parents, Helen and George Shine, were proud parents who taught their children to love their country. All four of their children served in the military: Tony in the AF and Al, Sarah, and Jonathan in the army. Tony was the oldest. His younger brother, Al, was wounded in Vietnam. Tony's sister, Sarah, served as a nurse and has passed away. The youngest sibling, Jonathan, USMA Class of 1969, was killed in action in South Vietnam on 15 October 1970; he was twenty-three years old. Tony took on the important responsibility of escorting his brother's body home for burial at West Point, where Jonathan was an army cadet.

Jonathan's story is also remarkable as he instilled lifelong influence and inspiration in many others. The book *Out of the Valley*, by Jonathan's close friend Barry Willey, describes Jonathan's interactions with others through his faith. The testimonials of Jonathan's faith, courage, and honor in the book express the extraordinary effect Jonathan had on others.

On 29 August 2021, Fran and I had the pleasure to meet Colleen for lunch. We shared many personal stories from the years since we last saw her at her father's memorial service, and even before that, in July 1972, in Myrtle Beach, South Carolina, a few months before Tony went missing. We recalled when she was almost eight years old, had blonde hair, a big warm smile, and so graciously offered us some cookies. The Shine family is an inspiration.

Colleen Shine, eight years old.
Photo: Courtesy of Colleen Shine..

Our lunch meeting with Colleen.

■ DAVID LEE NICHOLS

18 January 1934–5 April 1997
Iola, Allen County, Kansas
USAF Lieutenant General

When I first met Dave, he had arrived at the 18th TFW at Kadena AB in Okinawa. He was an AF major who had flown the F-105 for one hundred missions in Vietnam and was assigned as the chief of safety for the wing. Even though I served under Dave for slightly less than a year, in that time, I understood his ability to combine his work ethic, style of leadership, and personal friendship that enabled him to advance in his AF career quickly. Before I departed Okinawa

T-33 pilot instructor, Vance
AFB, Enid, Oklahoma

in March 1971, Dave had been promoted to lieutenant colonel. After I departed, he became the F-105 squadron commander at Kadena AB.

Along with other senior officers, he encouraged me and gave me the confidence and ability to seek higher goals. Dave rewarded me for my performance in wing safety, but his recognition of Fran in her supportive role meant something extra special. His actions and personal touch characterized his inner substance, which engendered greater admiration.

On a visit in November 1970 that Dave and his wife, Jan, made to our off-base house in Awase, he was incredibly warmhearted in his interaction with our son, little Bill, twenty-nine months old at the time. As he handed Bill a toy in his room, Bill showed a little leadership of his own as he pointed and "demanded" that Dave, "Put it down here!"

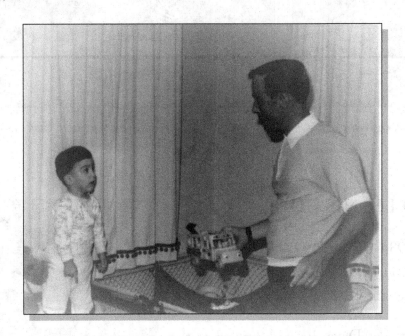

The next occasion I met Dave was during my USAF exchange officer assignment with the Canadian Forces. One of the many tours we took to military facilities and the defense industry was to Eglin AFB, Florida. We arrived there on Friday evening, 30 March 1979. On Saturday, I stopped by Dave's on-base house for a quick visit to catch up on the last six years. Dave was cutting his lawn when I drove up. It was great to see him again and reminisce.

I was truly fortunate to connect via email and phone with Dave's gracious daughter, Pam Nichols Jenison, in November 2021. This was made possible through Sheila Rockholt who, as I said before, stayed connected with all the old crew from Kadena, and their children in many cases. Former President Ronald Reagan was known as "The Great Communicator." I consider Sheila "The Great Connector."

Pam and I shared some stories about our time in Okinawa. We discussed her father's career and learned a little about each other's families. She was fourteen years old when I worked with her father, and she had a perfect recollection of their time on that assignment. I felt a welcomed connection to her father during my conversation with her after so many years.

Photos: Courtesy of Pam Nichols Jenson, daughter of Lieutenant General Dave Nichols.

Dave graduated from Iola High School in 1952. He earned a bachelor of science degree from Oklahoma State University in 1964 and a master of science degree in systems management from the University of Southern California in 1973. He completed Air Command and Staff College in 1966 and Air War College in 1973, both as a distinguished graduate.

After completing F-105D training at McConnell Air Force Base, Wichita, Kansas, in January 1967, he was assigned to the 357th Tactical Fighter Squadron, 355th Tactical Fighter Wing, Takhli Royal Thai AFB, Thailand, where he completed one hundred combat missions over North Vietnam in an F-105D Thunderchief, aka the "Thud."

From 29 April 1977 to 19 July 1979, he was assigned to Eglin AFB, Florida, as commander of the 33rd Tactical Fighter Wing, equipped with F-4Es and F-15s.

Returning from overseas to the United States in August 1983, General Nichols was named assistant deputy chief of staff for plans and operations at Air Force Headquarters (the Pentagon). In June 1984, he became deputy chief of staff for plans and operations. He also served as the air force operations deputy to the Joint Chiefs of Staff.

On 27 September 1985, Dave became the commander of Alaskan Air Command, and of Alaskan American Aerospace Defense Command Region at Elmendorf AFB, Alaska. He was also responsible for the overall defense of mainland Alaska.

He was promoted to lieutenant general on 28 June 1984. He retired on 1 July 1988 as a command pilot with over 8,800 flying hours.

Dave Nichols passed away at the young age of sixty-three due to a second heart attack. His wife, Jan, contracted ALS and lived with Pam and her family in Charlotte, North Carolina, until she passed away at age sixty-seven. Dave and Jan are buried in Arlington National Cemetery, section 6, site 9125-EH.

DOUGLAS M. ALEXANDER

19 March 1936–8 January 2015
USAF Lieutenant Colonel

Doug was an AF major when I first met him in the 18th TFW Safety Office at Kadena AB, Okinawa. He flew the EB-66 electronic warfare aircraft with duty as acting chief of safety before Dave Nichols came to the office. He remained my immediate supervisor for over two years and was a mild-mannered officer who gave me tremendous support.

Doug always encouraged me to seek a career as a rated officer in a fighter aircraft. He supported me in my application for UNT and in that respect, shared mutual endorsements from Dave Nichols, Tony Shine, Denny Jarvi, and Colonel Monroe Sams.

I regret that I lost touch with Doug after Okinawa. Sheila Rockholt sent a note to Fran and me in early 2015 after not receiving her usual Christmas card from him. He had congestive heart failure and passed away just before his seventy-ninth birthday. It was an honor to work with him. As a young officer, I had the opportunity to work and socialize with those who have had lasting influences on me. Doug and his family were among the small group that meant so much to me.

■ THOMAS EUGENE CROOK

29 September 1947–13 November 2021
Rossland, British Columbia, Canada
USAF Lieutenant Colonel

Fran and I always communicated with Tom and his wife, Pat, through Christmas cards and occasional holiday letters. I sent a letter to Tom in early July 2021, when I was writing this book, and asked him for some help in locating other RF-4C aircrews. Tom responded immediately, excited to help, and provided valuable information that led me to others.

We maintained routine communications through early November. We had a tremendous eighty-minute phone call on 24 August. After several email exchanges, I learned he was having health issues. We last spoke for a short time on 2 November, when Tom had difficulty with coughing. He had been in the hospital suffering from cancer, Parkinson's disease, and heart failure. I sent an email on 12 November to ask how he was doing but did not receive a reply.

I sensed that something wasn't right since Tom always responded very quickly. We had sent a Christmas card to the Crooks a few days before receiving a card and notice from Pat. Tom passed away on 13 November. Sadness filled our house in Chantilly, Virginia, that day, and I think of Tom often.

Tom atop the RF-4C.

*Receiving a retirement certificate
from Lieutenant General James Clapper.*
Photos: Courtesy of Pat Crook, wife of Tom Crook.

In the memorial note for Tom, his family wrote that he, "was respected and liked by everyone who knew him," and that he was, "intelligent, capable, hardworking, honest, intrepid, inventive, skilled, woodworker, worldly, family man, fighter, no-nonsense, humorous, lover of life, loud, a born leader." Absolutely accurate in all respects. And concerning "loud," I would emphasize it was a welcomed and enjoyable "loud," not an annoying one!

Tom received his commission in January 1971 as a second lieutenant through OTS. After UNT, he trained in the RF-4C at Shaw AFB, South Carolina, and went to his first operational assignment in the 91st TRS at Bergstrom AFB, Texas, where we met.

Tom was one of the fellow officers who made our jobs fun every day, was always loyal and supportive, and developed expertise in his role as an RF-4C WSO and navigator instructor when we were stationed again at Mather AFB. While at Mather, Tom completed his master's degree in educational systems management.

He went to Zweibrucken AB, Germany, where he served as a flight commander and leader of other aircrews. He moved up to the wing executive officer at Zweibrucken, and in 1981, worked with NATO evaluations teams while assigned to HQ USAFE. He followed this assignment at Alconbury AB, in the United Kingdom, as the 10th TRW chief of inspection and later, the deputy base commander.

Tom moved to AF/INXYT, Air Force Intelligence Collection Division, at the Pentagon and was the only rated aircrew officer in that office. After five years, he retired in February 1992. Tom told me he always got the assignment he wanted. After his service in the AF, Tom began his second career as a high school teacher, where he taught engineering design, woodworking, applied math, and applied physics. I could easily see Tom in this teacher role; he was a natural. I'm certain his students loved him as they had at UNT. He deserves admiration for his service. He remains in my mind and now in my heart.

■ JOHN WILLIAM HEIDE

14 November 1940–2 June 2020
Austin, Minnesota
USAF Lieutenant Colonel

Photo: Courtesy of Betts Heide, wife of John Heide.

While I was there, John Heide was also stationed at Bergstrom AFB, Texas. However, we were in different operational TAC recce squadrons. I knew of John but got to know him better when he arrived at the 14th TRS at Udorn AB, Thailand. He was my senior by a few years and became the 14th TRS commander shortly before we deployed all the RF-4Cs back to the States in July 1975.

We jokingly referred to him as "Chief Turkey in Charge," which he received comically because he knew we respected him in his leadership role. We gave him a plaque with that title. I am sure it brought back many memories of his aircrews in Thailand.

When I tried to contact John through an email on 27 September 2021, I received a reply from his wife, Betts, the next day. I was sorry to learn that John passed away on 2 June 2020. He suffered from Parkinson's disease for fifteen years and is buried in the National Cemetery at Fort Bliss in El Paso, Texas, where he retired. Betts and Fran were in the same bridge club in Austin when John and I were on the remote tour of duty in Thailand.

After returning from Thailand, John then went to "career-broadening" at McConnell AFB in Wichita, Kansas, for a year before he was tasked with an assignment to La

Paz, Bolivia, as one of the C-12 pilots for the military group there. John told them he would take the assignment, but they needed to send him to language school because he hadn't used his Spanish in twelve years.

John went to language school for nine months at the Defense Language Institute to hone his communications skills before working in La Paz for two years. He then returned to an assignment at the 9th Air Force at Shaw, where he was attached to an RF-4C squadron for flying duty. He ultimately became the squadron commander of the RF-4C academic squadron and transitioned the squadron to Bergstrom AFB, Texas.

Advancing in his career, John became the wing chief of safety at Bergstrom AFB after giving up the academic squadron. His next assignment was at a NATO facility in Germany, where he was community commander for the Americans and Canadians in a bunker. His last assignment before retirement was with the III Corps at Fort Hood, Texas, during Desert Storm, teaching the army how to use airpower.

He retired in 1991 to El Paso, Texas, where he returned to school and earned his credentials to teach fifth-graders for eleven years. Betts remarked that John always said teaching fifth grade was much harder than flying jets! I was honored to serve with John in a job we both held in the highest regard.

John Heide was greeted by his fellow squadron aircrew members after his last flight at Bergstrom before going to Udorn AB, Thailand.
Photo: Courtesy of Betts Heide, wife of John Heide.

■ MICHAEL S. JOYAL

25 September 1965– 22 April 2012
Oroville, California
USAF Lieutenant Colonel

Michael S. Joyal, a highly decorated USAF officer with command pilot wings.
Photo: Courtesy of Suzanne Roseberry, wife of Mike Joyal.

Mike was born in Oroville, California. After graduating from Placer High School, he attended the Air Force Academy and was commissioned in 1987. He opted for service in intelligence rather than pilot training due to complications with an allergy diagnosis at that time.

Suzanne Roseberry was my IDEX II representative to the first site that would receive our advanced imagery exploitation system. She made trips to HQ SAC at Offutt AFB, Nebraska, often in support of this delivery. However, another, and perhaps higher priority was Mike Joyal, who she met while doing IDEX II testing, and who was the OIC of the intelligence section of the 544th Strategic Intelligence Wing that would receive the first IDEX II system.

Suzanne and Mike dated after the delivery of IDEX II to the wing at Offutt. Shortly after that, in mid-1991, Mike entered pilot training at Columbus AFB in Mississippi, having been inspired by U-2 pilots he briefed while in Korea before his assignment in Nebraska.

Fran and I, with other AF members of the IDEX II PO staff, attended the beautiful wedding of Suzanne Roseberry and Mike Joyal in July 1992, in Altoona, Pennsylvania. Mike served for twenty-three years in the AF. His last assignment was flying the Twin Otter, a plane used for parachuting at the Air Force Academy. Mike had over 5,200 hours of flight time, including ninety-eight sorties as an Air Force Two pilot for the vice president of the United States. He retired on 1 January 2011.

After his retirement, Mike sought a job as a civilian pilot during a rough time in that industry. Undaunted, Mike found a part-time aviation consulting position with Convergent Performance in Colorado Springs, Colorado. He also focused on training for triathlons and being home more for his and Suzanne's two daughters. He enrolled for the Boise Half Ironman scheduled for June 2012.

Mike trained exceptionally hard for this, and after he and his family visited friends in Denver on 22 April 2012, Mike decided he would ride his bike from there to their home in the northern section of Colorado Springs. Suzanne and her daughters stopped to see him and check on him on their way home. Shortly after they arrived home, Mike called Suzanne to pick him up. Suzanne and their oldest daughter, Jackie, left their home to give Mike a ride the rest of the way home.

On the way, and at a location where Suzanne would pick Mike up, she found several cars pulled off the road. She approached and found someone performing CPR on Mike! A driver had struck Mike and was later charged with vehicular homicide and multiple DWI charges. Mike was pronounced deceased after about thirty minutes, a time Suzanne described as the most horrible period in her life.

Suzanne related a long-written narrative to me regarding the many months of her interactions with county courts, hearings on the case, attempts by the defense to lower the charges based on circumstances that certainly did not lessen the gravity to Suzanne and her family, and her final statement in the sentencing of the driver on 19 December 2012.

Suzanne's statement was compelling and communicated her desire for justice for Mike, but also her wish for fairness to the defendant. She stressed that the tragedy did not occur due to "maliciousness or ill will." Suzanne stressed it was from a complete lack of judgment. This statement and balance of fairness took incredible courage from Suzanne.

Suzanne's statement said in part:

> So what do I want? I want Michael's death to not be an end but a beginning. If he died for nothing and we can't rise out of this better for having known him, it would be the worst of all tragedies. So how do

you balance punishment for wrongdoing and reform? I am sure every judge in this building struggles with the hope that their decisions will correct the behaviors that led to the wrongs committed. I have no idea what sentence would ensure that, and I completely defer to you to make that determination.

Mike would be proud of Suzanne's perspective. The driver began her sentence at 0830 hours on 21 December 2012.

I only met Mike briefly and primarily knew him through Suzanne. But his exemplary character and integrity were loud and clear to me. I am honored to mention him in this special section and thankful for his distinguished service.

Mike at the controls, with Mount Fuji in the distance.
Photo: Courtesy of Suzanne Roseberry, wife of Mike Joyal.

■ A PENSIVE VISIT

On 2 December 2021, I completed a long-overdue visit to the Arlington National Cemetery to pay my respects to Tony Shine and Dave Nichols. I chose this date due to its special meaning: It was the forty-ninth anniversary of Tony's status as MIA. I spoke to both men through my heart and mind as I visited each grave.

To Tony, I expressed my sorrow for what happened to him and for the years of anguish his family endured. I told him how proud he would have been of his daughter, Colleen, for her untiring efforts. But, in my heart, I am confident he knows that. If I ever visit Myrtle Beach, South Carolina, again, I'll be sure to stop to see Shine Avenue and the Lieutenant Colonel Tony Shine Marker, both established in his honor.

I expressed similar feelings of sadness to Dave but also communicated my deep appreciation for his leadership and guidance. I was fortunate in my early career to work for Dave and later at the Pentagon, where he was in Headquarters Air Force Plans and Operations, first as a major general, followed by receiving his third star and promotion to lieutenant general. He had oversight of the Space Operations Division and the TENCAP program, where I worked.

I stood there, in turn, at the final resting places for these men. It was quiet as the sun gained dominance over a cloudy morning, and the fallen leaves were scattered over the acres of headstones as far as the eye could see. I am not ashamed to admit I shed a few tears as the reality of their passings took over my thoughts. I delivered a final respectful salute to them both before I leisurely walked back to the main building that contained beautiful exhibits of the cemetery's history.

As I made my way home, my thoughts were focused on our nation's most hallowed ground, where more than 400,000 people are laid to rest. I turned my attention to all those friends who have served with me, supported me, made me laugh, may still be alive, or may no longer be with us. There are some friends I was not able to find in my search. I regret that but must emphasize that they are in my thoughts and prayers, and I am grateful for having them in my life. They may be gone but never forgotten.

In Memoriam:
Military Service in My Family

In 2019, as I produced the family video tribute to my parents, I learned more about the military service of my paternal grandfather and uncles on my father's and mother's side. My father wanted to serve in WWII. However, rheumatic fever in his younger years affected his heart, and he could not qualify to serve due to that physical condition. I have great admiration and respect for my family's service to our country.

▪ GRANDPA CIMINO

My grandfather, William Vito Cimino, served in WWI. He entered the US Army on 27 March 1917, at the age of eighteen, and fought in Europe. He was wounded slightly in his upper arm from gunfire while fighting the Germans in France. I remember seeing his wound as a young kid but never thought much about it. He never made it a topic of conversation. He received the Purple Heart medal.

Grandpa Cimino, US Army, WWI

1898–1969

A side note: George Washington created the badge for military merit in 1782. Only three soldiers received the award in the Revolutionary War, and they were personally presented by General Washington, commander in chief of the Continental Army, in 1783.

The Purple Heart was officially established in 1932. However, approximately 320,000 military personnel who served in WWI, which ended in 1918, received the award. How was this possible? General Douglas MacArthur signed General Order No. 3, which awarded the medal *retroactively* to US Army personnel wounded in combat in WWI or who were presented with a Meritorious Service Citation certificate.

During my search for data on my family to create the latest video, I found a document on Ancestry.com that verified Grandpa Cimino's service and injury while fighting in WWI.

Source: Ancestry.com–NY Abstracts of WWI Military Service: 1917–1919.

■ MY FATHER'S BROTHERS—MY UNCLES

Carmine (Tommy) Cimino
1925–2013
US Navy, WWII

Angelo Cimino
1926–2005
US Marines, WWII

Vincent Cimino
1933–1990
US Marines, Korean War

■ MY MOTHER'S BROTHERS—MY UNCLES

Three of my mother's four brothers served.

Andrew Costa
1923–2008
US Army, WWII

Freddie Costa
1926–1972
US Army, WWII

Rudy Costa
1932–2013
US Army, Korean War

▪ STAMINA AND LONGEVITY: MY FATHER'S BROTHER

I had held on to the hope that my father's surviving brother and my only remaining uncle, Uncle Dom, would be able to read this memoir. He served after WWII, and he would occasionally talk with me about some of his fascinating experiences. Unfortunately, he passed away before this book was published, but he was blessed with a long life. I think he would have liked my book; he always showed a genuine interest, no matter what the subject. He would tell me stories about my father, things I had never heard before that were interesting, sometimes comical, and always told with the love and admiration he had for Dad, his oldest brother. Uncle Dom, like all my uncles, was terrific and always had a warm smile. I looked forward to talking with him whenever I could. May he be at peace.

Dominick Cimino
1929–2022
US Marines, post-WWII

To this "Special Tributes" collective group,
you have my most profound admiration and respect.

I salute you one and all.
Thank you for your service!

ACKNOWLEDGMENTS

Fran

To simply state that my wife of fifty-six years has supported me throughout my career and that I am eternally grateful would be a monumental understatement. Her contribution of love, caring, dedication, and sacrifice over these many years has had no bounds and has been the source of my inspiration to do the best I could for her, our family, and in my career in the USAF and beyond.

From the very beginning, while we were at St. John's University, she had a unique influence on me, like no other, and it created the foundation that we share today in our mutual love that continues to grow upon it.

Fran worked extremely hard to achieve a position in the New York City Public School system. She loves children, and she loves teaching. All her work at SJU was focused on that end. Instead, she always stood by my side, beginning even before the early years of my air force career. She gave up her dream of teaching to become a wife and mother but would regain her yearning for helping students with their learning, solving difficult personal problems, and working in libraries.

She simultaneously earned an advanced degree, worked at teaching jobs, and cared for her mother, our children, and me. She does not have a selfish bone in her body. She always thinks of others first and makes their interests her top priority.

Through the years.

While I fully appreciate all those in my career who have been supportive and encouraging, Fran is my most important source of strength, not only when I fail at something, but anytime I have needed it. So how do I show Fran proper acknowledgment? I simply continue to take care of her in every possible way. She deserves much more.

My Family's Service in the Military Makes Me Proud

Grandpa Cimino (in memoriam), thank you for your service and sacrifice in WWI.

Uncles Andy, Freddie, Rudy, Tommy, Angelo, Dom, and Vincent (all in memoriam), thank you for your service.

Vince Micucci, (Colonel, USAF-Ret), my brother-in-law, thank you for lighting the spark of my interest to join the air force, for all the handball games (I lost), and for sharing in our service.

Officer Training School

My fellow officer trainees and instructors, thank you for your contribution to Cooperate and Graduate. Together we achieved our student goals of commissioning in the AF.

Undergraduate Pilot Training

My instructor pilots, thank you for your patience and for providing me with enough barf bags.

Lowry AFB, Denver, Colorado

My son, Bill, you were the highlight of my assignment at Lowry. The way you live your life makes me immensely proud.

Okinawa

Tony Shine (in memoriam), you and your family are enduring memories. Thank you for all your support and friendship, your service and sacrifice. I will always appreciate your influence on me early in my career.

Denny Jarvi, thank you for your support, your service, friendship, and the T-33 rides that got my aviation blood flowing again. And thank you and Becky for caring for our son Bill when Fran and I went to Hong Kong, and for contributing to this memoir.

Doug Alexander (in memoriam), you and your family are enduring memories. Thank you for your supervision, your service, friendship, and support. I will always appreciate your endorsement of my potential for flying.

Dave Nichols (in memoriam), you and your family are enduring memories. Thank you for your leadership, your service, friendship, and support. Your AF career has been an inspiration.

Colonel Monroe "Sabre" Sams (in memoriam), thanks for being a great wing commander, your support, service, endorsements, and the handball games. You are a legend I will never forget.

Sheila Rockholt, I cannot thank you enough for your support during the writing of this book. Your lifelong friendship (and Bob's), and your ability to remain connected with so many have contributed in a special way to this memoir.

Dave Drewry, thank you for your friendship and support when I arrived in Okinawa, for your service, for contributing to this memoir, and for the great memories we shared recently and hope to continue.

Undergraduate Navigator Training

UNT Class 72-13, I was proud to be your class commander. Thank you all for your Cooperate and Graduate contribution as we all drove forward to earn our navigator wings.

Shaw AFB, Sumter, South Carolina

Bob Morris, thank you for your service and for demonstrating the power of focus, passion, and skill in RF-4C training, and how you have honed these traits throughout your remarkable professional life. My short time sharing the same aircraft with you will always be a unique and favored memory.

Dickie Bauer, thank you for your service and for all the laughter you provided. It was a much-needed diversion from all the RF-4C training, testing, and check rides. I cannot tell an air force story without including you and Andrea, our White Lake visit, and especially all the crazy things we did together.

Bergstrom AFB, Austin, Texas

My son, Joe, you were the highlight of my assignment at Bergstrom. The way you live your life makes me immensely proud.

Tom Crook (in memoriam), you are an enduring memory, and your family—Pat and children—will always be special to Fran and me. Thank you for all the fun you created, your fellowship as an RF-4C WSO, your lifetime friendship, your contribution to this memoir, and your service.

Jim Mills, thank you for your friendship, all the crazy fun we had (especially on the TDYs), your keen piloting skills, for contributing to this memoir, and your service. I will never forget you and Sheila, especially each time I try to eat chocolate mints.

The men and women of the 91st TRS, thank you for being a team in our tactical reconnaissance operations and mission. Your contributions made me proud to be part of our squadron.

Udorn RTAFB, Udon Thani, Thailand

Guy Munder, when I think of Udorn, I immediately think of you and your friendship, piloting skills, level-mindedness, trust, and all the fun we shared. Finding you after many years has been a highlight amid all the worry and sadness brought on by the pandemic. Thank you for contributing to this memoir, for your service, and for staying connected.

Russ Metzler, it was good to have a familiar friend at Udorn at the outset, especially someone with the RF-4C WSO experience you brought. Thanks for your friendship and service, and for contributing to this memoir. I am glad we connected again after many years.

Bill Bowman, somehow, we never flew together at Udorn. But I appreciate our friendship there, your contribution to our mission, this memoir, and your service, and I am thankful that we were able to connect again recently after many years.

John Heide (in memoriam), thank you for your service. I am thankful that we were able to connect again later in our careers. Your spirit of fun at the job will always remain an enduring memory of you.

The 14th TRS, thank you for being a team in our tactical reconnaissance operations and mission in SEA (Cambodia and South Vietnam), especially during the tense moments of Operations Eagle Pull and Frequent Wind, and the *Mayaguez* incident.

Mather AFB, Sacramento, California

My daughter, Jeannie, you were the highlight of my second assignment at Mather. The way you live your life makes me immensely proud.

Tom Crook (in memoriam), being stationed with you again and going through navigator instructor training together could not have been more enjoyable. I will cherish our time together always. Thank you for your service and for being part of my life.

Gregg Hughes, thank you and Janet for your enduring friendship, your service, and working together as we made our way toward, and achieving our USC master's degrees. Thank you for contributing to this memoir, and thank you and Janet for attending my air force retirement ceremony.

CFB Winnipeg, Manitoba, Canada

Canadian couples, thank you to the many Canadian men and women who embraced Fran and me and our children as friends. We will always have pleasant thoughts of our three years with you, eh!

CFANS officers, instructors, and students, thank you for the experiences we had in Canada, the camaraderie, and for sharing common goals of achieving the best joint military strength of our nations.

Shaw AFB, Sumter, South Carolina

John Heide (in memoriam), thank you for your service. I am grateful that we flew together, especially on my practice check ride. Your spirit of fun on the job will always remain an enduring memory of you.

Russ Metzler, thank you for all the great work you did in life support, your service, and for contributing to this memoir. I always knew I could rely on you.

Father Tony, you are an enduring memory of our time in Sumter. Thank you for your devotion, for contributing to this memoir, and for being a lifelong friend and inspiration to many.

To the many families and friends at Sumter who enriched our lives there, especially the Cardiels, and the Doyles.

The Pentagon

Colonels Ron Knecht and Al Brown, thank you for your leadership in the AF TENCAP office, the opportunities you provided, and your trust in me.

To the members of AF TENCAP, especially Chris Caravello and Denny Haynes, Thank you for your service and your contributions to our team. We accomplished a lot.

To my Burke, Virginia, neighbors Boyd Lease and Ken Walsh, I will never forget our commutes to and from the Pentagon. And thank you for your friendship and service.

SES/JPO

Maj. Gen. Kenneth R. Israel, thank you for your support, trust, and inspirational service. Working for and with you was a privilege. You have been a leader and role model from day 1, and the one who carved new capabilities into the history of surveillance and reconnaissance for the air force. Having you officiate at my retirement was an honor.

Lt. Gen. Gordon E. Fornell, thank you for your support, the opportunities you provided to me, and your service.

Lt. Gen. James R. Clapper, thank you for your support for IDEX II at HQ SAC and your extraordinary career in intelligence.

Mike Dillard, thank you for your leadership and teaming in an exciting program for the DoD and the Intelligence Community, for providing specific IDEX II information, for attending my retirement ceremony, for your service, and for thirty-six years of friendship. Working with you has always been a privilege.

Suzanne Roseberry, thank you for your contributions to the IDEX II program, your service, and your participation in my retirement ceremony.

Jim Cromer, thank you for your contributions to the IDEX II program and your service.

Mike Buck, thank you for your contributions to the IDEX II program and your service.

Darren Smith, thank you for your contributions to the IDEX II program, your service, and your participation in my retirement ceremony.

Jim Watson, thank you for your contributions to the IDEX II program and your service.

IDEX II civilians, thank you for your support in the IDEX II program, your service, and your attendance at my retirement ceremony.

Bob Dumais, thank you for your leadership in CPG, your support, your service, and your participation in my retirement ceremony.

Jeff Harris, thank you for your leadership in CPG, your support, your service, and your attendance at my retirement ceremony. (Later, after US Senate confirmation, Jeff became the Honorable Jeffrey K. Harris, the Director for the National Reconnaissance Office and Assistant Secretary of Air Force for Space.)

Nick Aleyanis, thank you for your support of the IDEX II program at the 480th at Langley AFB, Virginia, your service, and your friendship all these years.

Steve LaFata, thank you for your support of the IDEX II program at the 480th at Langley AFB, Virginia, your service, and your friendship all these years.

Lockheed Martin managers, thank you all for your contribution to the IDEX II program that provided a new intelligence exploitation capability for the DoD and IC.

Dr. Vance Coffman, thank you for your attention to the IDEX II program, the support of your excellent team, and the great tours of Lockheed capabilities I will never forget.

Jim David, thank you for responding to my request for photo access of exhibits at the Smithsonian, National Air & Space Museum (NASM) annex at the Steven F. Udvar-Hazy Center, Chantilly, Virginia.

Dr. Chuck Byvik, thank you for a great meeting and personal tour at the NASM, and for sharing stories of your career.

My sweet granddaughter, Allison Cimino (employee at the NASM), thank you for your assistance in connecting me with the staff that led to coordinating with Jim David for my photo access to museum exhibits.

Transition

To the participants and attendees at my AF retirement—my family, Major General Ken Israel, Mike Dillard, Dennis Adams, Lt. Col. Kirk Washington, Suzanne Roseberry, Darren Smith, Marilyn Conrad, Bob Dumais, Jeff Harris, Tony Durante, members from Lockheed Martin, SAIC, CPG, other AF and civilian friends—my sincere thank you.

Special Tributes

Colleen Shine, thank you for sharing an important part of your life, your courageous journey for answers about your father, for providing a huge contribution to this memoir, and for your unwavering service to the memory and families of POW/MIA service members. It was an honor to work with your father.

Al Shine, thank you for providing an inspiring book, *Out of the Valley*, which related another dimension of the Shine family that I will always admire. And thank you for your service. It was an honor to work with your brother, Tony.

Sheila Rockholt, thank you for your consistent willingness to help with this memoir, especially for this section, the information you provided, and your and Bob's life-long friendship.

Ann-Mills Griffiths, thank you for connecting me with Colleen Shine and your work for the POW/MIA families.

Pam Nichols Jenison, thank you for sharing information about your parents and our memorable phone call. It was an honor to work with your father.

Pat Crook, thank you for providing information about Tom for this section and your friendship over the years. It was an honor to work with Tom. I miss him and will always cherish my phone calls with him.

Betts Heide, thank you for providing information about John for this section and your friendship. It was an honor to work with John.

Suzanne Roseberry, thank you for providing information about Mike for this section. I will always admire Mike's service.

Support from Others

T.Sgt. Ashley Nicole Taylor, media specialist at AFPAA/SAF/PAON, the Air Force National Media Engagement Office in New York City, thank you for your help in numerous areas of permission requests.

Lisa M. Riley, public affairs specialist at the National Museum of the US Air Force, Wright Patterson AFB, Ohio, thank you for your help in gaining access to many air force images.

Amanda Saunders, Director of Media Relations, Encompass Digital Media, Inc., thank you for your assistance in aiding me in obtaining membership in the Defense Visual Information Distribution System (DVIDS), which provided me with many images.

Gloria Kelly, 17 Wing Public Affairs, Department of National Defence/Government of Canada at CFB Winnipeg, Manitoba, Canada, thank you for your help with the Canadian elements of this memoir.

The Canadian Embassy, thank you for your assistance in connecting me with the Canadian Armed Forces Transition Group (CAFTG) of the Military Personnel Command Canadian Armed Forces.

Robert Nolan, master warrant officer (Retired) at CAFTG, thank you for your assistance in attempts to locate Canadian personnel.

Central Intelligence Agency Prepublication Classification Review Board (PCRB), thank you for your review, assessment, and clearance to publish this memoir.

Defense Office of Prepublication and Security Review (DOPSR), thank you for your review, assessment, and clearance to publish this memoir.

To the Men and Women of the US Armed Forces,
thank you for your dedication, loyalty, and service to our country.

APPENDICES

APPENDIX A1
EDUCATION: COLLEGES

Education Institution	Degree or Certificate	Graduated - Period Taken
St. John's University (SJU), Jamaica, NY (1963-1967)	B.S. Mathematics (major) Physics (minor)	11 June 1967
University of Texas (UT), Austin, TX	MBA	Incomplete due to remote tour assignment
UT Graduate Courses		
Fundamentals of Financial Accounting		Summer 1973
Introduction to Economics I		Fall 1973
Business Course, First Course		Spring 1974
Business Course, Second Course		Summer 1974
University of Southern California (USC), Los Angeles, CA (Mather AFB location)	M.S. Systems Management	2 September 1978
USC Courses		
Psychological Factors in Systems Management		Summer 1976
Man-Machine Factors in Systems Management		Fall 1976
Deterministic Models in Decision Making		Fall/Winter 1976/77
Probalistic Models in Decision Making		Winter/Spring 1977
Problems in Systems Technology		Spring 1977
Man-Environment Factors in Systems Management		Summer 1977
Planning Technical Systems		Summer/Fall 1977
Systems Analysis		Fall/Winter 1977/78
Systems Integration		Winter/Spring 1978
Fiscal Aspects of Systems Management (elective)		Spring 1978
Systems Management and Organization Theory		Summer 1978
Organizational Behavior and Administration (accepted elective from UT, Austin, TX)		Summer 1978

APPENDIX A2
EDUCATION: PROFESSIONAL
MILITARY EDUCATION (PME)

Professional Military Education (PME)	Method - Certificate	Completion Date
Squadron Officer School (SOS)	Correspondence (at Bergstrom AFB, Udorn AB)	March 1975
Air Command and Staff College (ACSC)	Correspondence (at Mather AFB, CFB Winnipeg, Shaw AFB)	14 September 1981
Air War College (AWC)	Seminar (at the Pentagon)	10 March 1987
AWC Papers Submitted		
A Critical International Issue and its Effect on U.S. National Security		September 1986
NATO Strategy and Forces		February 1987
Other Education	Method - Certificate	Completion Date
Aerospace Systems Course (ASC) 31	AF Exchange Program with Canada: Canadian Forces Air Navigation School, CFB, Winnipeg, Manitoba, Canada	4 July 1979
ASC 31 Course Content - See Appendix 2a-2d		
ASC 31 Course - Papers/Reports Submitted		
A Study of Canadian Forces Requirements for VTOL Aircraft - 1980 to 2000. (An extensive analysis and assessment of state-of-the-art VTOL technology and its application to forecast Canadian VTOL requirements - classified SECRET (Co-authored with other students)		June 1979
Canadian Forces Air Navigation School Conference Report 2nd Annual Conference on Electro-Optical Systems & Technology, Boston MA		24 November 1980
Canadian Forces Air Navigation School Individual Report 9102, Sensors for Tactical VTOL Aircraft		22 March 1979
Visit to Hughes Aircraft Company, CA (Technical Report)		February 1979
Visit to Smith Industries in the UK (Technical Report)		May 1979
Air Command (Canadian) Electronic Warfare Course Institute	CFB, Winnipeg, Manitoba, Canada	8-19 September 1980

APPENDIX A2A
EDUCATION: MILITARY EDUCATION, CANADA

(Course Material)

Aerospace Systems Course 31	
MATH & APPLIED SCIENCE	
Mathematics	*Statistics*
Algebra	Organization of Data
Trigonometry	Probability
Calculus	Distributions
Matrices and Vectors	Hypothesis Testing
Differential Equations	Regression and Correlation
Fourier Transforms	Error Theory
Control Theory	Reliability and Redundancy
Physics	*Communications Theory*
Mechanics	Principles of Communication
Wave Theory	Modulation Techniques
Properties of Materials	Information theory
Thermodynamics	Communications Security
Aerodynamics	*Electronics*
Fluid Dynamics	Basic Electrical Concepts
Subsonic Aerodynamics	Magnetism and AC Circuits
Supersonic Aerodynamics	Electromagnetic Radiation
Propulsion Plants	Electrical Machinery
Stability and Control	Vacuum Tubes
Aircraft Performance	Solid-State Devices
Vertical/Short TO & Landing	Electronic Circuits
Automatic Flight Control	Electromagnetic Compatibility
Human Factors	*Computer Programming*
Human Body	Computer Fundamentals
Degradation of Human Performance	Computer Language
Human Factors Engineering	

APPENDIX A2B
EDUCATION: MILITARY EDUCATION, CANADA

(Course Material)

Aerospace Systems Course 31		
SYSTEMS STUDIES		
Radar Systems		*Computer Systems*
Radar System Fundamentals		Electronic Computer Applications
Specialized Radar Techniques		Systems Integration
Airborne Radar Systems		
Ground Environment Radar Systems		
Electro-Optical Systems		*Weapon Systems*
Infrared Radiation		Weapon Components
Camera Systems		Weapon Aerodynamics
Television Systems		Weapon Effects
Infrared Systems		
Laser Systems		
Electro-Optical Contermeasures		*Communications Systems*
Navigation and Guidance Systems		
Air Data Devices		
Gyroscopic and Magnetic Compass Devices		*Electronic Warfare Systems*
Stable Platforms		
Inertial Navigation		
Radio Aids to Navigation		*Display Systems*
Landing Guidance Systems		Display Devices
Inertial Navigation and Weapons Release Systems		Man-Machine Interface

APPENDIX A2C
EDUCATION: MILITARY EDUCATION, CANADA

(Course Material)

Aerospace Systems Course 31
OPERATIONS AND STAFF DUTIES
Research, Development, Test & Evaluation
Operations Research
Performance Specifications
Testing and Evaluation Programs
Testing and Evaluation Techniques
Operational factors
Fundamentals of Aeronautics
Fundamentals of Astronautics
Weapons Planning and Delivery
Logistic Support
Staff Duties
Report Writing
Audio-Visual Presentations
Military Organization
Capital Equipment Acquisition
Network Analysis

APPENDIX A2D
EDUCATION: MILITARY EDUCATION, CANADA

(Course Travel)

Aerospace Systems Course 31	
Aerospace Industry	*Military Units/Other Agencies*
Canadian Avionics Electronics	CF Maritime Warfare School
General Electric (Aircraft Engine Group)	CF Maritime Proving and Evaluation Unit
General Electric (Aircraft Equipment Division)	Various CF Operational Units and Headquarters
Sanders Associates (Electronic Warfare Division)	NORAD Headquarters
Sikorsky Aircraft	Strategic Air Command Headquarters
Boeing-Vertol	Armament Development & Test Center, Eglin AFB, FL
Litton Systems (Canada)	US Army Aviation Center, Fort Rucker, AL
Bell Helicopter	Naval Air Development Center, Westminster, PA
Texas Instruments	Defence-Civil Institute of Environmental Medicine (CF), Toronto
E-Systems	AF Systems Command Space Division, Los Angeles, CA
Motorola	NASA Ames Research Center
Sperry Flight Systems	Armament Experimental Establishment (RAF)
Hughes Aircraft Co.	RAF College Cranwell
Hughes Helicopter	RAF Wittering
Rockwell International	CF Europe
British Aerospace (UK)	Air Force Systems Command Electronic Systems Division, Hanscom AFB, MA
Westland Helicopter (UK)	US Readiness Command, MacDill AFB, FL
Rolls-Royce (UK)	Nellis AFB, NV
Smith Industries, Ltd (UK)	
Grumman Aerospace Corp.	
Westinghouse (Defense and Electronic Systems Center)	
Sperry (Electronics Division)	
Raytheon (Electromagnetic Systems Division)	

APPENDIX B
PROMOTIONS

Air Force Officer Rank	Effective Date	Location
2nd Lieutenant	29 September 1967	OTS, Lackland AFB, TX
1st Lieutenant	29 March 1969	18th TFW, Kadena AB, Okinawa
Captain	29 September 1970	18th TFW, Kadena AB, Okinawa
Major	31 July 1979	CFANS, CFB Winnipeg, Manitoba, Canada
Lieutenant Colonel	1 December 1983	HQ USAF, Pentagon, Washington, DC
Colonel	1 April 1989	SES/JPO, Washington, DC area

Appointed to the Regular Air Force: 29 September 1975

APPENDIX C
PCS ASSIGNMENTS

PCS Location	From	To	Assignment
Lackland AFB, San Antonio, TX	Jul-67	Sep-67	Officer Training School (OTS)
Laughlin AFB, Del Rio, TX	Oct-67	Jan-68	Pilot Training
Lowry AFB, Denver, CO	Feb-68	Aug-68	Aerospace Munitions Officer Course
Kadena AB, Okinawa	Oct-68	Mar-71	Wing Weapons Safety Officer (Nuclear and Conventional Weapons)
Mather AFB, Sacramento, CA	Mar-71	Jan-72	Undergraduate Navigator Training
Shaw AFB, Sumter, SC	Mar-72	Aug-72	RF-4C Tactical Reconnaissance Course
Bergstrom AFB, Austin, TX	Sep-72	Aug-74	91st Tactical Recce Squadron
Udorn RTAFB, Thailand	Aug-74	Jul-75	14th Tactical Recce Squadron
Mather AFB, Sacramento, CA	Jul-75	Jul-78	323rd Flying Training Wing
USAF Exchange Program with Canadian Forces in Winnipeg, Manitoba	Jul-78	Jul-81	AF Exchange Program with Canadian Forces Winnipeg
Shaw AFB, Sumter, SC	Aug-81	Sep-83	363rd Tactical Fighter Wing
Air Staff, Pentagon, Washington, DC	Sep-83	Jul-87	Air Force TENCAP Program
Softcopy Exploitation Systems Joint Program Office (SES/JPO), Washington DC area location	Jul-87	Feb-93	DOD Director, SES/JPO for IDEX-II Program

APPENDIX D
RF-4C WSO'S OFFICE ILLUSTRATIONS

Much of the WSO's preparation for a mission included intelligence briefings of known or suspected threats along the target route; assembling maps that cover the route; drawing and marking the detailed route with checkpoints, headings, turn points, groundspeed, initial points inbound to the target and target points; and folding it for easy access in a tight cockpit.

The WSO and pilot would review the route and actions required of each in detail; no detail is too small to omit. Then and only then would the crew proceed to their respective "offices" to conduct the mission.

The RF-4C WSO's office was in the rear cockpit directly behind the pilot by a few feet. Many of the instruments in the front cockpit were repeated in the rear cockpit, and the WSO could fly the aircraft if needed. The major differences are that the sensor controls for cameras, side-looking radar, infrared, and most of the aircraft circuit breakers were in the rear cockpit.

The WSO's environment in the cockpit was like the pilot's, with an abundance of controls and indications crammed into a tiny bit of acreage. This was the nature of a fighter-type aircraft aircrew's office. The office chair was the ejection seat, which was another complex component. It did not matter if you were at the office sitting upright, flying straight and level, in a tight high-G turn, or upside down. You performed your duties, nonetheless.

Illustrations of the WSO's office space follow.

The RF-4C WSO's office (1).

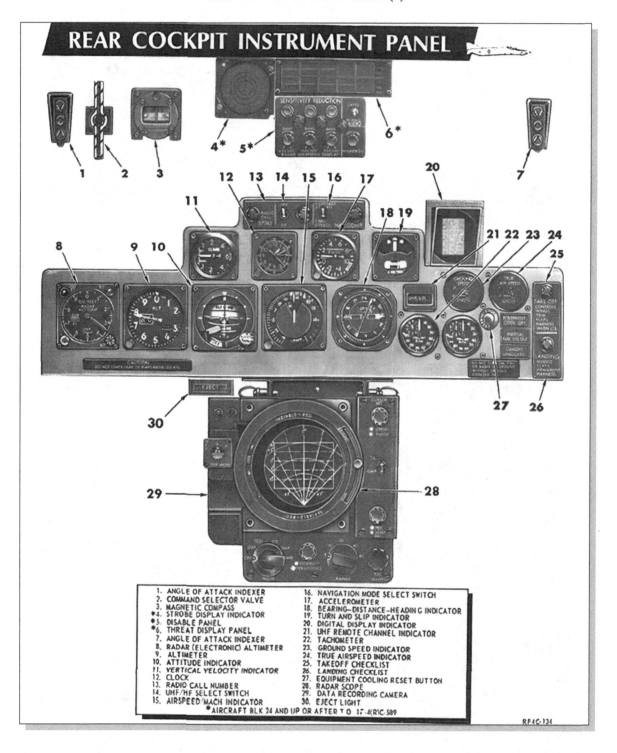

REAR COCKPIT INSTRUMENT PANEL

1. ANGLE OF ATTACK INDEXER
2. COMMAND SELECTOR VALVE
3. MAGNETIC COMPASS
*4. STROBE DISPLAY INDICATOR
*5. DISABLE PANEL
*6. THREAT DISPLAY PANEL
7. ANGLE OF ATTACK INDEXER
8. RADAR (ELECTRONIC) ALTIMETER
9. ALTIMETER
10. ATTITUDE INDICATOR
11. VERTICAL VELOCITY INDICATOR
12. CLOCK
13. RADIO CALL NUMBER
14. UHF/HF SELECT SWITCH
15. AIRSPEED/MACH INDICATOR

16. NAVIGATION MODE SELECT SWITCH
17. ACCELEROMETER
18. BEARING–DISTANCE–HEADING INDICATOR
19. TURN AND SLIP INDICATOR
20. DIGITAL DISPLAY INDICATOR
21. UHF REMOTE CHANNEL INDICATOR
22. TACHOMETER
23. GROUND SPEED INDICATOR
24. TRUE AIRSPEED INDICATOR
25. TAKEOFF CHECKLIST
26. LANDING CHECKLIST
27. EQUIPMENT COOLING RESET BUTTON
28. RADAR SCOPE
29. DATA RECORDING CAMERA
30. EJECT LIGHT
*AIRCRAFT BLK 24 AND UP OR AFTER T O 1F-4(R)C-589

RF4C-134

369

The RF-4C WSO's office (2).

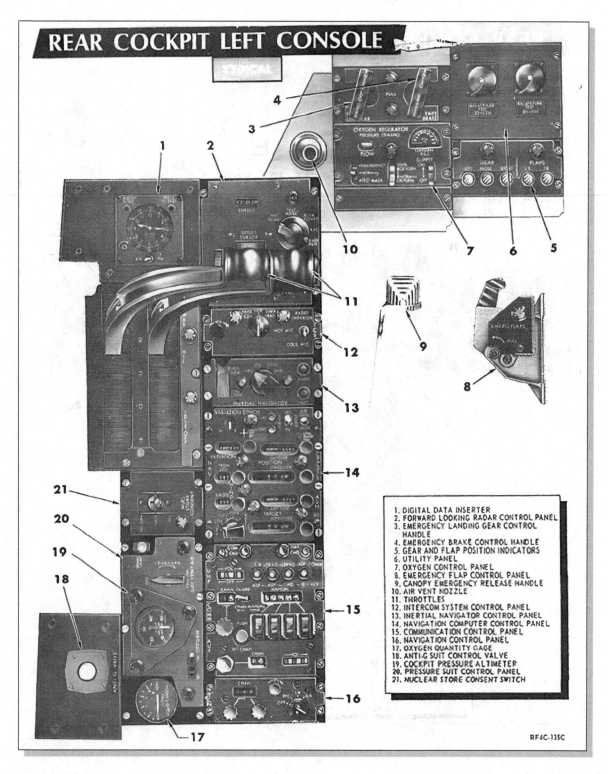

REAR COCKPIT LEFT CONSOLE

1. DIGITAL DATA INSERTER
2. FORWARD LOOKING RADAR CONTROL PANEL
3. EMERGENCY LANDING GEAR CONTROL HANDLE
4. EMERGENCY BRAKE CONTROL HANDLE
5. GEAR AND FLAP POSITION INDICATORS
6. UTILITY PANEL
7. OXYGEN CONTROL PANEL
8. EMERGENCY FLAP CONTROL PANEL
9. CANOPY EMERGENCY RELEASE HANDLE
10. AIR VENT NOZZLE
11. THROTTLES
12. INTERCOM SYSTEM CONTROL PANEL
13. INERTIAL NAVIGATOR CONTROL PANEL
14. NAVIGATION COMPUTER CONTROL PANEL
15. COMMUNICATION CONTROL PANEL
16. NAVIGATION CONTROL PANEL
17. OXYGEN QUANTITY GAGE
18. ANTI-G SUIT CONTROL VALVE
19. COCKPIT PRESSURE ALTIMETER
20. PRESSURE SUIT CONTROL PANEL
21. NUCLEAR STORE CONSENT SWITCH

RF4C-135C

The RF-4C WSO's office (3).

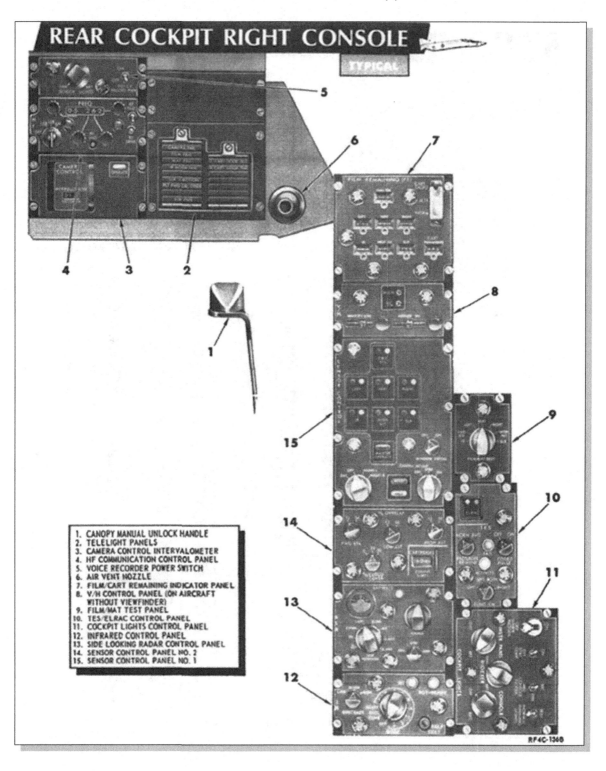

REAR COCKPIT RIGHT CONSOLE

TYPICAL

1. CANOPY MANUAL UNLOCK HANDLE
2. TELELIGHT PANELS
3. CAMERA CONTROL INTERVALOMETER
4. HF COMMUNICATION CONTROL PANEL
5. VOICE RECORDER POWER SWITCH
6. AIR VENT NOZZLE
7. FILM/CART REMAINING INDICATOR PANEL
8. V/H CONTROL PANEL (ON AIRCRAFT WITHOUT VIEWFINDER)
9. FILM/MAT TEST PANEL
10. TES/ELRAC CONTROL PANEL
11. COCKPIT LIGHTS CONTROL PANEL
12. INFRARED CONTROL PANEL
13. SIDE LOOKING RADAR CONTROL PANEL
14. SENSOR CONTROL PANEL NO. 2
15. SENSOR CONTROL PANEL NO. 1

RF4C-1340

The RF-4C WSO's office (4). Bottom section is CB panel 2.

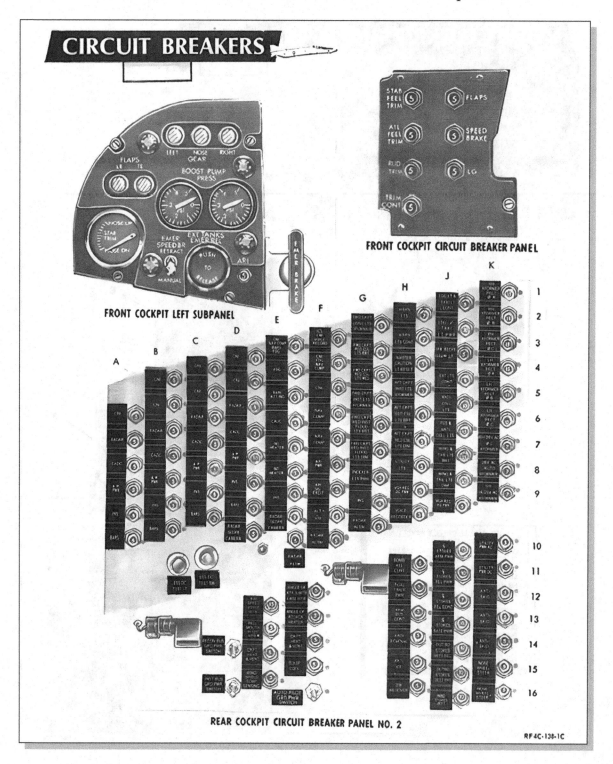

The RF-4C WSO's office (5).

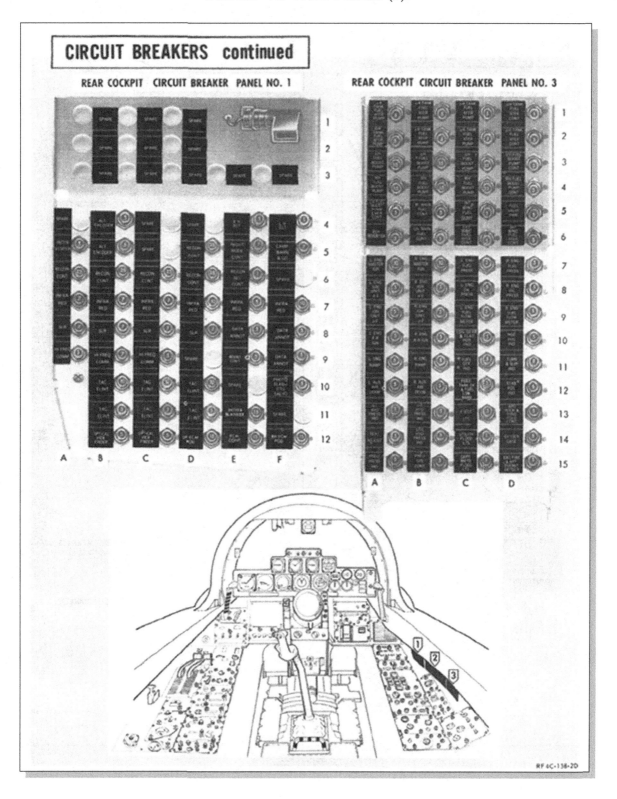

The RF-4C WSO's office (6).

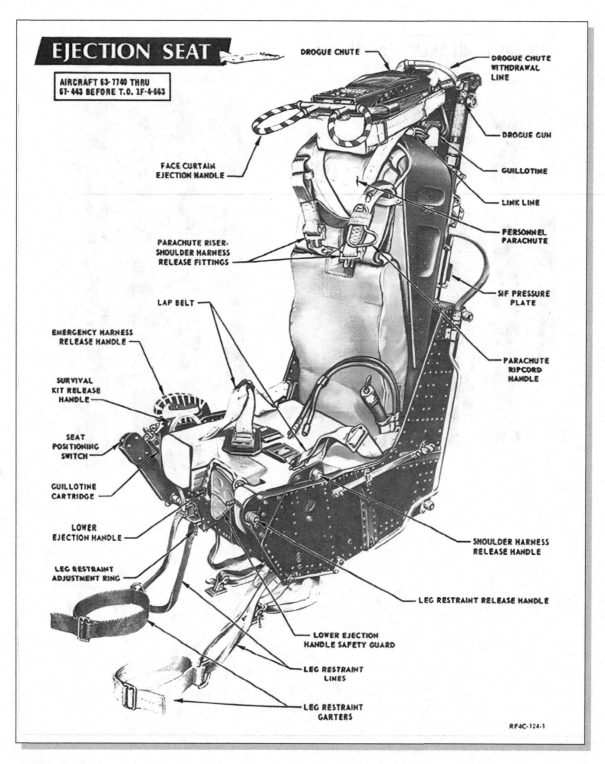

EJECTION SEAT

AIRCRAFT 63-7740 THRU
67-443 BEFORE T.O. 1F-4-663

DROGUE CHUTE

DROGUE CHUTE
WITHDRAWAL
LINE

DROGUE GUN

GUILLOTINE

LINK LINE

PERSONNEL
PARACHUTE

SIF PRESSURE
PLATE

PARACHUTE
RIPCORD
HANDLE

FACE CURTAIN
EJECTION HANDLE

PARACHUTE RISER-
SHOULDER HARNESS
RELEASE FITTINGS

LAP BELT

EMERGENCY HARNESS
RELEASE HANDLE

SURVIVAL
KIT RELEASE
HANDLE

SEAT
POSITIONING
SWITCH

GUILLOTINE
CARTRIDGE

LOWER
EJECTION HANDLE

LEG RESTRAINT
ADJUSTMENT RING

SHOULDER HARNESS
RELEASE HANDLE

LEG RESTRAINT RELEASE HANDLE

LOWER EJECTION
HANDLE SAFETY GUARD

LEG RESTRAINT
LINES

LEG RESTRAINT
GARTERS

RF4C-124-1

APPENDIX E
14TH TRS HISTORY: NARRATIVE, JUNE 1942–JULY 1975

(As written, author unknown)

Tonight, our last sawadee, we pay honor to the 14TRS bunnies. Bunnies of the past, bunnies of the present and possibly in another place and at another time bunnies of the future. In the next few weeks, the fighting 14th will finish yet another chapter of its big book. As we leave SEA, it can be said, "the squadron has done well and we have accomplished our mission." The phrase is not only known to ourselves but also to past bunnies for more than 33 years.

Thirty-three years ago (PAUSE) WWII and the Air War over the skies of Europe; a different place, different war, different time than today but those early bunnies were a close kin to us as displayed symbolically through our squadron emblem. Our patch shows an aircraft composed of lightening bolts representing speed, stratospheric flight, and the striking power of the 14TRS. Cinc Bunny, obviously drawn by a pilot as a very aggressive and elusive creature capable of scampering over any target and then out maneuvering his foe for an always successful RTB.

Our missions in 33 years hasn't really changed. The men have changed, but not the attitude. The theater, tactics, and aircraft have changed, but the mission is still "get the pictures"; and "Get the Pictures" is exactly what the 14TRS has done since its origin.

Constituted in June 1942, the 14th Photographic Squadron began its colorful career at Colorado Springs Army Air Field, Colorado. By mid-October the pilots' training flights consisted of mapping the south Texas area to perfect navigation techniques. In March 1943 the Colorado Springs Field was renamed Peterson Field in honor of Lt Edward J. Peterson, a pilot of the 14th Squadron who was killed when his F-4 Mustang crashed during takeoff.

Following its parent group—the 3rd Photographic Group—the squadron departed Peterson Field in April 1943 for Mount Farm, a former Royal Air Force Reconnaissance Base near Oxford, England. Pilots were trained in local operational conditions, radio procedures, escape and evasion techniques, safety and related subjects. Crew flew training missions over British coastlines in borrowed Spitfire aircraft until the squadron's F-4's Mustangs and F-5's Lightnings arrived in late July.

Reassigned from the 3rd to the 7th Photo Group, the squadron flew its first combat mission in August 1943. Using Spitfire XI and F-5 aircraft, the squadron pilots flew numerous long-range photo missions over Germany. By January 1944 all F-5 aircraft were transformed and the 14th became the single Spitfire Squadron of the 7th Group.

A 14th pilot was credited as the first American to obtain bomb damage assessment aerial phots of Berlin in early March 1944. During the same period, several members of the squadron were detached for service with a photo unit operating in Russia.

A Distinguished Unit Citation marked the squadron's activities for pre and post D day operations. German V-weapon sites were uncovered by the squadron's reconnaissance flights in July. August 1944, was the squadron's busiest month with a total of 528 missions. During the remaining months of 1944, numerous missions were flown over Holland, recording the Battle of the Bulge.

P-51 aircraft were added to the squadron's inventory in January 1945. Long range missions, several into Czechoslovakia, were flown in March. In early April all Spitfires were reassigned and the 14th returned to the F-5 as its primary aircraft. By late April 1945 reconnaissance missions dwindled. The last combat mission was flown on 23 July 1945. Villacoublay, France became the 14th in October 1945 and by year's end, the unit returned to the United States and deactivated.

For its accomplishments the squadron was awarded seven Campaign Streamers: Air Defensive, Europe; Normandy; Northern France; Ardennes-Alsace; Central Europe; Air Combat; and a foreign decoration, the French Croix de Guerre with Palm.

General Hap Arnold stated, "Fighter Planes Win Battles But recce Teams Win Wars."

The Squadron's precent form took shape on 3 April 1967 when the unit was reactivated and assigned to the 75th TRW at Bergstrom AFB, Texas. The unit's new aircraft, the RF-4C Phantom II, began arriving in late April and the crews followed a highly intensified upgrading and training program. Six months later the squadron had passed its first ORI and was ready for its new assignment in Southeast Asia. The deployment began on 25 October and by 28 October all (16) sixteen assigned aircraft had arrived at Udorn and joined the 432TRW. The day prior to our arrival the 20TRS with RF101s had departed Udorn and we swapped facilities, parking spaces and even hooch areas.

The war at this time was extremely active and would remain so until the end of Phase I, on 31 March 1968. The bombing of North Viet Nam was partially stopped during this period and was totally halted in November of 1968. This period, referred to as Rolling Thunder Operation, is the first of four (4) distinct periods for the 14TRS Bunnies operations, purpose, and mission employment. It is difficult to describe the Bunnies total operation except to state that the mission was mainly North Viet Nam pre-strike, post-strike, target development, night radar and IR operations. The average daily frag was nineteen (19) lines with a surge capability of twenty-three (23). Crew strength was thirty (30) and, needless to say everyone was damn busy. Tactics were generally present day European; low level, terrain masking with target pop. Aircrew losses were fairly high during this period; six (6) bunnies never came home.

Phase II began 1 November 1968. This phase was named "Tester Phase" and it was an accurate description; RF-4C's were teamed with Spectre gunships, infrared photography was thoroughly tested in the SEA environment, Loran stations were established and used on an everyday basis, Laser guidance was also introduced during this phase with Recces carrying out BDA immediately after strikes. While these new systems were being introduced and evaluated, the Recces still had to perform their normal jobs, though somewhat lessened with the coming of the bombing halt of North Viet Nam in November 1968. During 1969 the 14TRS was commanded by three squadron commanders. Before the SEA tour would end the a4th would be commanded by 15 dedicated leaders. There were no combat losses during this time frame but battle damage to aircraft was extremely high. The RF-4C definitely proved its ruggedness and dependability during this time while flying in Route Pack I SVN, and Laos, performing considerable visual reconnaissance, BDA, and quick strike concept.

The first half of 1970 was continuation of Phase II. The US was drawing down in SEA and aircraft were making daily runs into Cambodia. During this period the Recces passed 20,000 hours of accident-free flying. There were no combat losses during this period either. But by July of 1970 there was beginning to be a feeling of increased activity though not statistically apparent. Sortie numbers decreased somewhat but the targets were more difficult. The 14th during this time also incurred an increased responsibility with the rotating of her sister squadrons back to the United States. The 14th accepted her responsibility with pride and ran 18 lines per day anywhere and everywhere to meet her mission requirements for all of Southeast Asia.

These last six months of 1970 took their toll on the 14th. Four bunnies were missing in action and two more were confirmed killed in action.

The year of 1971 was one in which the Bunnies fulfilled their responsibility almost perfection. Flying 18 sorties per day under the command of Lt Col Reeves they entered into full scale Cambodian operation. By mid-71 the Bunnies had surpassed 50,000 hours of combat flying in some 22,500 sorties since arriving in SEA. The bunnies continued their task and by the end of 1971 only one Bunnie did not return from action, but still one too many had been lost.

The year of 1972 was not as gracious to the Bunnies as 1971. In May, the Recces made their first run to Hanoi in five years. And on 11 May the high-risk Linebacker I was initiated. The Cambodian operation was terminated and Phase II ended. With the initiation Linebacker into NVN and the Barrel (Hanoi), Phase III was almost instantaneously in high gear. Within the first four months of the new campaign four bunnies were lost and one more was a known POW. By the end of 1972 there would be two more bunnies missing in action. But the 14th never stopped supplying the important information necessary to sustain a strong effort against its foe. The PPIF reflects the success of the Bunnies in its statistics for the year of 1972. Over 10,000,000 feet of film had been processed and published. This doesn't even include the time and effort interpreting each frame and producing IPIR's and prints.

On 23 October, Linebacker one ceased and conferences were held to release American POWS. Somehow this message didn't get across to our opponent and on 19 Dec Linebacker II went into action for 10 days and Recces reported everything first hand. On 30 Dec, the POW release talks resumed with good results, and early in 1973 a total of four bunnies had been reunited with their families after spending time at Hanoi Hilton. During this same period the RF-4 had passed 50,000 hours of major accident-free flying.

1973 was moving towards a Phase IV. 15 January marked the termination of flying over North Viet Nam and Recce again in "First In–Last Out." The bunnies assumed the task of flying into Cambodia and Laos on a daily basis. But political activity in February resulted in a decreased tasking for the Bunnies with the bombing halt of Laos and by mid 1973 the Phase III shifted to Phase IV, one of surveillance and draw down.

The fourth (4th) and final phase began after Linebacker II and continues through the collapse of Cambodia, South Viet Nam and finally ends with the S.S. *Mayaguez* incident. This period, which lasted two and one half (2 1/2) years is termed Final Draw Down and Surveillance Phase. It is distinctly different from the historic TAC Recce mission of target development, pre and post strike BDA. Surveillance activity, long familiar to SAC's high flying Black Birds, is new to the Bunnies but our high resolution photo equipment plus new IR sensors were key to systems for detect[ing] truck parks and insurgent activity. The question of North Viet Nam intent was well understood but the where, when\, how, and to what degree were the big questions that remained to be answered. It became quite obvious after September 1973, the final Southeast Asian bombing halt, that new aggressive moves were in the making. The trail was closely monitored and revealed a four-lane major highway completely constructed with even a Howard Johnson! On 30 November 1973, just one month after the completion of the highway, massive truck convoys were moving. Day after day the convoys were counted and each one had over one thousand trucks in each string. The implications were now apparent, and the enemy's timing was perfect.

Cambodian surveillance activities can best be described with just one word— FRUSTRATING. Trying to save an impossible situation while drawing down and flying under extreme fuel shortage left their mark on a strong and very proud unit. The bunnies took it in stride and accepted the term "Combat Support" while flying daily missions over a territory that was completely controlled by an extremely savage and near fearless aggressor.

The PPIF also did their thing during this time by introducing Hunt's Extended Range Chemistry. This revolutionary processing chemistry was an important element in allowing the aerial film to practically see into the many shadows of the Southeast Asia tree and jungle infested topography. Without a doubt, their work generally goes unappreciated but only by those that are not familiar with what it takes to make the Recce team.

The war in Southeast Asia is now a closed book. The Bunnies' effort and "can do" attitude is recorded in detailed form that would take hours, if not days to relate. Combat hours flown were *75,777*, combat sorties *41,456* and award and decorations just another large number. Aircrew lost is *20*, POWs returned ___ and MIA's stand presently at ___.

In summary, you can see the story of the 14TRS is an involved set of complex events linked over 33 years and two wars. Our mark on history is not written in words alone or merely tallied in combat statistics but is simply the achievement of a very important and unique type mission. A mission that took the work, dedication and skill of many people. People from the PPIF, the PIs and processors, the maintenance, administrative, and supply personnel. The crew chiefs, camera personnel, life support and whole host of others. Soon the book will close on another chapter of the 14th Tactical Reconnaissance Squadron Bunnies and all that will remain in a few pages of words and the knowledge of having done our mission well. This finally is what counts and what has been important to ourselves; bunnies of the past and bunnies never to return again. Tonight I propose a Toast. "To the proud bunnies of the 14th, Bunnies of the past, Bunnies of the present and Bunnies of the future."

14th Tactical Reconnaissance Squadron Commanders (SEA)

1.	Lt. Col. Dale L. Flowers	3 April 1967
2.	Lt. Col. Aloysius P. McHugh	20 April 1968
3.	Lt. Col. Robert R. Heaton	2 December 1968
4.	Lt. Col. Laverne H. Griffin	6 June 1969
5.	Lt. Col. James C. Rankin	1 October 1969
6.	Lt. Col. Robert H. Williams	20 May 1970
7.	Lt. Col. Charles W. Bryan	6 October 1970

8.	Lt. Col. Robert W. Reeves	7 June 1971
9.	Lt. Col. Harry L. Brown	29 October 1971
10.	Lt. Col. Howell E. Jones	9 April 1972
11.	Maj. Sidney D. Rogers	20 July 1972
12.	Maj. Rian H. Currie	1 December 1972
13.	Lt. Col. Giles D. Harlow	26 November 1973
14.	Lt. Col. Thomas N. Gibson III	21 November 1974
15.	Maj. John W. Heide	10 June 1975

APPENDIX F
MY AF PATCHES

A representative sample of the many patches I've worn during my AF career.

APPENDIX G
MY NAVIGATOR WINGS, SPACE
BADGE, RIBBONS, MEDALS

Narrative states:
In Honor of
William A. Cimino
Colonel, USAF

This flag proudly flew over the customer systems support center in November 1992 to mark the occasion of his retirement from the United States Air Force.

The men and women of the CSSC offer this small, but deeply sincere, token of gratitude and appreciation for his many years of uniformed service. His last five years at the Softcopy Exploitation Systems/Joint Program Office culminate a long and distinguished career in the service of his country.

APPENDIX H
IDEX II SITES

SITE NUMBER	ORGANIZATION	LOCATION	NOTATION
1	544th Strategic Intelligence Wing, HQ Strategic Air Command	Offutt AFB, Omaha, NE	
2	Classified	Classified	
3	Atlantic Intelligence Command (Navy)	CINCLANTFLT, Norfolk, VA	
4	National Photographic Interpretation Center (NPIC)	Bldg 213, Washington, DC	
5	Office of Imagery Analysis (OIA)	CIA HQ, Langley, VA	
6	480th Reconnaissance Technical Group	Langley AFB, Hampton, VA	
7	USEUCOM Joint Analysis Center (JAC)	Stuttgart, Germany	Eliminated due to consolidation of intelligence organizations in Europe
8	Army Intelligence Tactical Analysis Center (ITAC)	Bldg 213, Washington, DC	
9	Defense Intelligence Agency (DIA)	Bldg 213, Washington, DC	
10	Defense Intelligence Analysis Center (DIAC)	Bolling AFB, Washington, DC	Remoted off Site 4
11	DIA	Pentagon, Washington, DC location	Remoted off Site 2
12	496th Reconnaissance Technical Squadron	RAF Molesworth, UK	Became the Joint Analysis Center for EUCOM in October 1991
13	548th Reconnaissance Technical Group	Hickam AFB, Hawaii	Remoted off Site 14
14	Joint Intelligence Center Pacific (JICPAC)	CINCPACFLT compound, Makalapa, Pearl Harbor, HI	
15	Foreign Technology Division (FTD)	Wright-Patterson AFB, Dayton, OH	FTD was the predecessor organization to the National Air and Space Intelligence Center (NASIC)

APPENDIX I
THANK-YOU LETTER

To Brig. Gen. Kenneth R. Israel

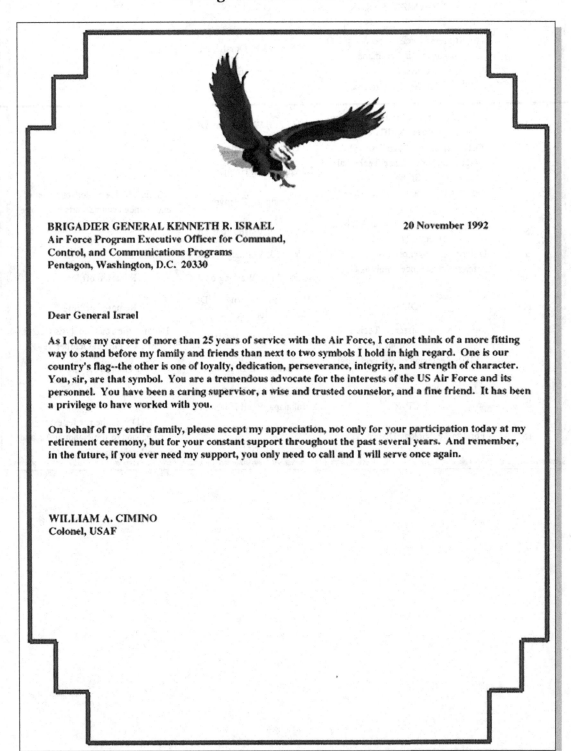

BRIGADIER GENERAL KENNETH R. ISRAEL   20 November 1992
Air Force Program Executive Officer for Command,
Control, and Communications Programs
Pentagon, Washington, D.C. 20330

Dear General Israel

As I close my career of more than 25 years of service with the Air Force, I cannot think of a more fitting way to stand before my family and friends than next to two symbols I hold in high regard. One is our country's flag--the other is one of loyalty, dedication, perseverance, integrity, and strength of character. You, sir, are that symbol. You are a tremendous advocate for the interests of the US Air Force and its personnel. You have been a caring supervisor, a wise and trusted counselor, and a fine friend. It has been a privilege to have worked with you.

On behalf of my entire family, please accept my appreciation, not only for your participation today at my retirement ceremony, but for your constant support throughout the past several years. And remember, in the future, if you ever need my support, you only need to call and I will serve once again.

WILLIAM A. CIMINO
Colonel, USAF

APPENDIX J
THANK-YOU LETTER

To Lt. Gen. Gordon E. Fornell

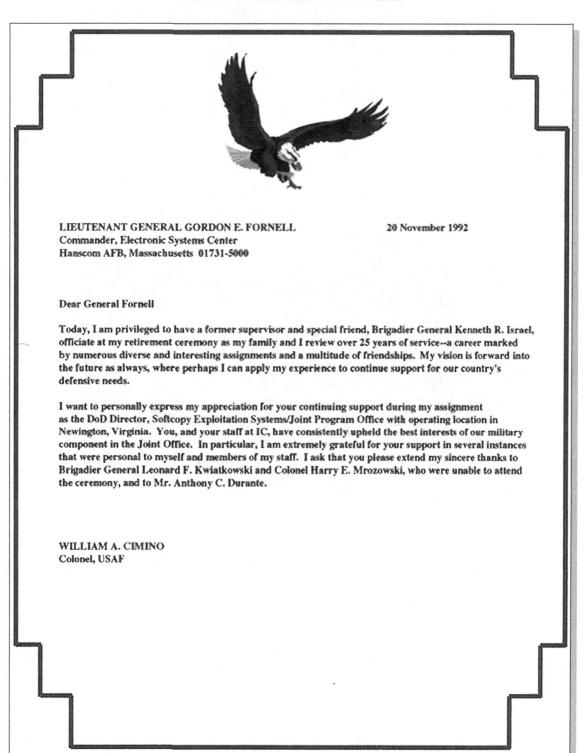

LIEUTENANT GENERAL GORDON E. FORNELL   20 November 1992
Commander, Electronic Systems Center
Hanscom AFB, Massachusetts 01731-5000

Dear General Fornell

Today, I am privileged to have a former supervisor and special friend, Brigadier General Kenneth R. Israel, officiate at my retirement ceremony as my family and I review over 25 years of service--a career marked by numerous diverse and interesting assignments and a multitude of friendships. My vision is forward into the future as always, where perhaps I can apply my experience to continue support for our country's defensive needs.

I want to personally express my appreciation for your continuing support during my assignment as the DoD Director, Softcopy Exploitation Systems/Joint Program Office with operating location in Newington, Virginia. You, and your staff at IC, have consistently upheld the best interests of our military component in the Joint Office. In particular, I am extremely grateful for your support in several instances that were personal to myself and members of my staff. I ask that you please extend my sincere thanks to Brigadier General Leonard F. Kwiatkowski and Colonel Harry E. Mrozowski, who were unable to attend the ceremony, and to Mr. Anthony C. Durante.

WILLIAM A. CIMINO
Colonel, USAF

APPENDIX K
OFFICIAL USAF PHOTO

Colonel William A. Cimino
18 December 1991

ABBREVIATIONS

AAA—Anti-Aircraft Artillery

AAM—Air-to-Air Missiles

AAR—Air-to-Air Refueling

AB—Air Base

AC—Alternating Current

ACS/I—Assistant Chief of Staff for Intelligence

ACSC—Air Command and Staff College

ACT—Air Combat Training

ADCAP—Additional Duty Career Advancement Program

AETC—Air Education and Training Command

AF—Air Force

AFA—Air Force Academy

AFA—Air Force Association

AFB—Air Force Base

AFCM—Air Force Commendation Medal

AFHRA—Air Force Historical Research Agency

AFIT—Air Force Institute of Technology

AFMPC—Air Force Military Personnel Center

AFOQT—Air Force Officer Qualifying Test

AFOTEC—Air Force Operational Test and Evaluation Center

AFROTC—Air Force Reserve Officers' Training Corps

AFSC—Air Force Specialty Code

AFSC—Air Force Systems Command

AGL—Above Ground Level

AHC—Aircraft Handling Characteristics

AIRC—Annual Instrument Refresher Course

ALS—Amyotrophic Lateral Sclerosis (Lou Gehrig's Disease)

ANG—Air National Guard

AO—Aeronautical Order

AOF—Area of Focus

AOR—Area of Responsibility

APO—Army Post Office (used with army and AF installations overseas)

ARTCC—Air Route Traffic Control Center

AS—Air Station

ASC—Aerospace Systems Course

ASL—Above Sea Level

ATAF—Allied Tactical Air Force

ATC – Air Traffic Control

ATC—Air Training Command

AU—Air University

AWACS—Airborne Early Warning and Control System

AWC—Air War College

BCE – Before Common Era

BDA—Bomb Damage Assessment

BFM—Basic Flight Maneuvers

Bldg.—Building

BMT—Basic Military Training

BOQ—Bachelor Officer Quarters

BRAC—Base Realignment and Closure Commission

C3CM—Command, Control, and Communications Countermeasures

CAT—Civil Air Patrol

CATIS—Computer-Aided Tactical Information System

CBPO—Consolidated Base Personnel Office

CCCB—Customer Configuration Control Board

CENTAF—US Air Forces, US Central Command

CENTCOM—US Central Command

CF—Canadian Forces

CFANS—Canadian Forces Air Navigation School

CIA—Central Intelligence Agency

CINCLANTFLT—Commander in Chief, US Atlantic Fleet

CINCPACFLT—Commander in Chief, US Pacific Fleet

COTR—Contracting Officer Technical Representative

CPA—Central Processing Area (for IDEX II)

CPG—Collections Program Group

CRT—Cathode Ray Tube

CSO—Combat Systems Officer

CTO—Compensatory Time Off

CTP—Course Training Plan

CTS—Course Training Standard

DARO—Defense Airborne Reconnaissance Office

DCM—Defensive Combat Maneuvers

DCO—Deputy Commander for Operations

DCS—Deputy Chief of Staff

DEROS—Date Estimated Return from Overseas

DIA—Defense Intelligence Agency

DIAC—Defense Intelligence Analysis Center

DMA—Defense Mapping Agency

DNI—Director of National Intelligence

DoD—Department of Defense

DOPSR—Defense Office of Prepublication and Security Review

DR—Dead Reckoning

DSSC—DoD Softcopy Steering Committee

DVIDS—Defense Visual Information Distribution System

ECM—Electronic Countermeasure

ELT—Electronic Light Table

EMS—Electromagnetic Spectrum

EO—Electro-Optical

EOD—Explosive Ordnance Disposal

EOT—End of Tour

ESC—Electronic Systems Command

ETC—Emergency Terrain Clearance

EUCOM—United States European Command

EWO—Electronic Warfare Officer

EWOC—Electronic Warfare Operations Course (Canadian)

FAA—Federal Aviation Administration

FFRDC—Federally Funded Research and Development Center

FICEURLANT—Fleet Intelligence Center, Europe and Atlantic

FLIR—Forward-Looking Infrared

FOD—Foreign Object Debris

FOL—Field of View

FOL—Forward-Operating Location

FTD—Foreign Technology Division

G—Gravity

GDIP—General Defense Intelligence Program

GEOINT—Geospatial Intelligence

GMU—George Mason University

GPA—Grade Point Average

GPS—Global Positioning System

GS—Ground Speed

GUI—Graphical User Interface

HAF—Headquarters Air Force

HF—High Frequency

HIPPI—High-Performance Parallel Interface

HOV—High Occupancy Vehicle

HQ—Headquarters

HR—Human Resources

HUMINT—Human Intelligence

IAS—Indicated Airspeed

IAW—In Accordance With

IC—Intelligence Community

ICBM—Intercontinental Ballistic Missile

IDEX—Image Data Exploitation

IFOV—Instantaneous Field of View

IFR—Instrument Flight Rules

IG—Inspector General

IHPS—Infantile Hypertrophic Pyloric Stenosis

IP – Initial Point

IP—Instructor Pilot

IPIR—Immediate Photo Interpretation Report

IR—Infrared

ITAC—Intelligence Tactical Analysis Center (Army)

IUNT—Interservice Undergraduate Navigator Training

IWSO—Instructor Weapon Systems Officer

JAC—Joint Analysis Center

JCS—Joint Chiefs of Staff

JICPAC—Joint Intelligence Center, Pacific

JUSMAG—Joint US Military Advisory Group

LCWS—Low-Cost Workstation

LIRR—Long Island Railroad

LIU—Low-Cost Interface Unit

LLLTV—Low-Level Light Television

LOP—Line of Position

LORAN—Long-Range Navigation

MAC—Military Air Command

MAJCOM—Major Command

MARS—Military Auxiliary Radio Station

MASINT—Measurement and Signature Intelligence

MB/s—Megabytes per Second

MC&G—Mapping, Charting, and Geodesy

MEI—Management Effectiveness Inspection

MIA—Missing in Action

MMS—Munitions Maintenance Squadron

MOA—Manifestations of Apprehension

MPC—Military Personnel Center

MSL—Mean Sea Level

NAC—National Agency Check

NAS—Naval Air Station

NASA—National Aeronautics and Space Administration

NASIC—National Air and Space Intelligence Center

NASM—National Air and Space Museum

NATO—North Atlantic Treaty Organization

NBT—Navigator Bombardier Training

NFIP—National Foreign Intelligence Program

NIIRS—National Imagery Interpretability Rating Scale

NIMA—National Imagery and Mapping Agency

NLT—Not Later Than

NOE—Nap of the Earth

NORAD—North American Aerospace Defense Command

NOTAM—Notice to Airmen

NPIC—National Photographic Interpretation Center

NRO—National Reconnaissance Office

NRP—National Reconnaissance Program

NRT—Near-Real Time

NSA—National Security Agency

NYC—New York City

O&M—Operations and Maintenance

OLC—Oak Leaf Cluster

OT—Officer Trainee

OD&E—Office of Development and Engineering

OER—Officer Effectiveness Report

OIA—Office of Imagery Analysis (CIA)

OIC—Officer in Charge

OJCS—Office of the Joint Chiefs of Staff

OODA—Observe, Orient, Decide, Act

ORI—Operational Readiness Inspection

OSD—Office of the Secretary of Defense

OTER—Officer Trainee Effectiveness Report

OTS—Officer Training School

PACAF—Pacific Air Forces

PACAFR—Pacific Air Forces Regulation

PCRB—Prepublication Classification Review Board (CIA)

PCS—Permanent Change of Station

PED—Processing, Exploitation, Dissemination

PFP—Partnership for Peace

PGM—Precision-Guided Munitions

PI—Photo Interpreter

PLF—Parachute Landing Fall

PM—Program Manager; Project Manager

PME—Professional Military Education

PMR—Program Management Review

PO—Program Office

POW—Prisoner of War

PPIF—Photo Processing and Interpretation Facility

PRF—Pulse Repetition Frequency

PT—Physical Training

R&D—Research and Development

RAF—Royal Air Force

RCAF—Royal Canadian Air Force

RFC—Request for Change

RHAW—Radar Homing and Warning

RHCA—Reciprocal Health-Care Agreement

RIF—Reduction in Force

ROI—Return on Investment

ROK—Republic of Korea

ROTC—Reserve Officers' Training Corps

RSO—Runway Supervisory Officer

RT—Real-Time

RTAFB—Royal Thai Air Force Base

RTB—Return to Base

SAC—Strategic Air Command

SAFE—Selected Areas for Escape (or Evasion)

SAM—Surface-to-Air Missile

SANC—Senior Air Navigation Course (Canadian)

SAP—Special Access Program

SCI—Sub-Compartmented Information

SCIF—Sub-Compartmented Information Facility

SEA—Southeast Asia

SEFE—Standardization Evaluation Flight Examiner

SERE—Survival, Evasion, Resistance, and Escape

SES/JPO—Softcopy Exploitation System/Joint Program Office

SIGINT—Signals Intelligence

SIOP—Single Integrated Operational Plan

SJU—Saint John's University

SOF—Supervisor of Flying

SOFA—Status of Forces Agreement

SOS—Squadron Officers School

SS—Schutzstaffel (German "Protection Echelon")

STAN/EVAL—Standardization/Evaluation

SUNT—Specialized Undergraduate Navigator Training

TO—Technical Order

TAC—Tactical Air Command

TACAN—Tactical Air Navigation

TAWC—Tactical Air Warfare Center

TDY—Temporary Duty

TEM—Technical Exchange Meeting

TENCAP—Tactical Exploitation of National Space Program Capabilities

TENCAP—Tactical Exploitation of National Capabilities (more recent)

TFS—Tactical Fighter Squadron

TFW—Tactical Fighter Wing

TGIF—Thank God It's Friday

TI—Theater Indoctrination

TRR—Transition Readiness Review

TRS—Tactical Reconnaissance Squadron

TRTS—Tactical Reconnaissance Training Squadron

TRW—Tactical Reconnaissance Wing

UHF—Ultra High Frequency

UNT—Undergraduate Navigator Training

UPT—Undergraduate Pilot Training

USAF—United States Air Force

USAFE—United States Air Forces in Europe

USAFMPC—United States Air Force Military Personnel Center

USC—University of Southern California

USCINCEUR—United States Commander in Chief, Europe

USFK—US Forces Korea

USGIF—United States Geospatial Intelligence Foundation

USMA—United States Military Academy (West Point)

USS—United States Ship

USSPACOM—United States Space Command

UV—Ultraviolet

VFR—Visual Flight Rules

VHF—Very High Frequency

VIP—Very Important Person

VIRIN—Visual Information Record Identification Number

VOR—Very High-Frequency Omni-Directional Range

VTOL—Vertical Takeoff and Landing

WMD—Weapons of Mass Destruction

WSO—Weapon Systems Officer

BIBLIOGRAPHY

The primary sources of material for this memoir are my military records, recollections, and personal letters between my wife, Fran, and me. I have complemented that material with references that I listed for each chapter, many of which led to permissions to include information (text, stories, images, and so on) that I did not create. All the information is factual to the best of my knowledge.

Chapter 1: A Memorable Decade

Courses.lumenlearning.com. "Conclusion: Change in the 1960s."

History.com, editors. "The 1960s History." History.com, June 26, 2020.

History.com, editors. "Vietnam War Timeline," 26 February 2020; original 13 September 2017.

Nalty, Bernard C., *Air War Over South Vietnam, 1968–1975*. AF History and Museums Program, US Air Force, Washington DC, 2000.

The PeopleHistory.com. "What Happened in the 1960s." Additional flavor to the 1960s.

SongFacts.com. "The Twist by Chubby Checker." Statement by Chubby Checker.

StJohns.edu. "History and Facts: Saint John's University."

Wikipedia.org. "The 1960s." A description of the 1960s—trends, political and cultural changes.

Wikipedia.org. "Swinging Sixties." Further description of the 1960s.

Chapter 2: No Wedding in October

Dept. of the Air Force, Headquarters Lackland Military Training Center (ATC), Lackland Air Force Base, Texas, 20 March 1967. Officer Training School selection letter.

Wikipedia.org. "Eisenhower Park." Formerly Salisbury Park, it was the location of the Salisbury Country Club, where our wedding reception was held.

Chapter 3: USAF OTS

AF.mil. "Officer Training School, US Air Force, Fact Sheet Display," 11 February 2015.

AirForce.com. "US Air Force—Officer."

Cimino, William A. AF personal records, July to September 1967.

Fran's letters to me dated from 6 July to 19 September 1967.

Letters from me to Fran, dated from 6 July to 17 September 1967.

Wikipedia.org. "Air Force Officer Training School. Description of AF OTS."

Wikipedia.org. "Fort Hamilton." Site of my enlistment into the AF.

Chapter 4: UPT Assignment

AF Aeronautical Order 181, 24 October 1967 (authorization to fly between 24 October 1967 to 15 November 1968).

AF Aeronautical Order 198, 21 November 1967 (suspension from flying training).

AF Form 475, 14 December 1967. Training Report.

ATC Form 240, 30 November 1967. Summary Record of Training (flying).

ATC Message, 16 January 1968. Assignment to navigator training (UNT denied).

ATC Message, USAFMPC, Randolph AFB, Texas, 23 January 1968. Assignment to Lowry AFB, Colorado (to attend Aerospace Munitions Officer Course).

Baseops.net/military pilot/upt. "Air Force Pilot Training Topics."

BogiDope.com. "UPT Phases." Description of pilot training phases.

Cimino, William A., AF personal records, October 1967 to January 1968.

FAS.org., Military Analysis Network. "T-41 A/C Mescalero." Description of the T-41, the first trainer in AF pilot training.

Special Order A-1205, 27 November 1967. Appointment of Wing Faculty Board to review my pilot training.

Technical Order 1T-41C-1. *Flight Manual, USAF Series T-41C/D Aircraft*.

Wikipedia.org. "Cessna T-41 Mescalero." More description of the T-41.

Wikipedia.org. "Cessna T-37 Tweet." Description of the first jet used in modern pilot training.

Wikipedia.org. "Northrup T-38 Talon." Description of the advanced jet aircraft used in AF pilot training.

Chapter 5: A New Career Path

AF.mil. "B-52H Stratofortress." Description of the B-52 aircraft bomber.

Boeing.com. "B-52." Description of the B-52.

Cimino, William A. AF personal records, February to September 1968.

Nationwidechildrens.org. "Pyloric Stenosis: Causes, Signs and Symptoms, Diagnosis."

Quora.com, 25 April 2018. "Why is the B-52 Bomber referred to as the BUFF?"

Special Order AA-1184, 2 July 1968. Assignment to 18th TFW, Kadena AB, Okinawa.

USAF Training Certificate, 17 August 1968, Aerospace Munitions Officer Course, Lowry AFB, Colorado.

USAF Training Certificate, 24 September 1968, Nuclear Safety Officer Course, Lowry AFB, Colorado.

Wikipedia.org. "Fitzsimons Army Medical Center." Hospital where our first son, Bill, was born.

Wikipedia.org. "Boeing B-52 Stratofortress." Description of the B-52.

Chapter 6: Okinawa

AF.mil/About Us/Biographies. "Lieutenant General David L. Nichols, US Air Force."

Award of the AF Commendation Medal, 16 October 1968–15 March 1971. (Awarded at UNT, Mather AFB).

Cimino, William A. AF personal records, October 1968 to March 1971.

Dept. of the Air Force, USAFMPC Letter, 25 May 1970, Application for Undergraduate Flying Training, 1st Lt. William A. Cimino, SSN.

Drewry, Dave. Phone calls, email exchanges, 29 July to 6 August 2021; lunch meeting 30 July 2021; biography received 5 August 2021.

Everything.explained.today.com. "1968 Kadena Air Base B-52 Crash." More news coverage and analysis.

Fran's letters to me dated from 12 October 1968 to 15 January 1969.

Graham, Gordon M., Lt. Gen. Fifth Air Force commander, letter, 2 February 1971, Commander's Individual Weapons Safety Award for Captain William A. Cimino.

Gwulo.com. "Old Hong Kong: Juno Revolving Restaurant 1980." Description of Juno's restaurant, one of our visits while in Hong Kong.

History.com, editors. "*Pueblo* Incident."

Howell, Philip V., Jr., Col. Eighteenth TFW commander, letter, 28 December 1970, nomination for Fifth Air Force Commander's Individual Weapons Safety Award for Captain William A. Cimino.

Jamison, Pam Nichols (daughter of Jan and Dave Nichols). Email/text exchange 6 to 27 November 2021; phone call 28 November 2021.

Jarvi, Dennis W. *MS-513, Dennis W. Jarvi Aviation Collection, Special Collections and Archives, University Libraries, Wright State University, Dayton, Ohio,1942–1997*. The collection was donated by Dennis W. Jarvi on 18 February 2016. Additions were received 1 July and 8 September 2016.

Jarvi, Denny. Email exchanges, 3 August 2021 to 28 June 2022, and 3 and 4 June 2023; phone call 6 August 2021.

Kadena.af.mil. "Kadena Air Base, Typhoon Alley." Description of the vulnerable position of Okinawa with respect to typhoons in the Pacific.

Letters from me to Fran dated from 15 October 1968 to 12 January 1969.

Newspapers.com. "B-52 Crash, 19 November 1968, Kadena AB, Arc Light Mission." News coverage of a B-52 crash at Kadena AB.

Nichols, David L., Lt. Col., chief of 18th TFW Safety, letters of recognition for William A Cimino and Fran Cimino, 16 and 17 February 1971, respectively.

Officer effectiveness reports for William A. Cimino, USAF 2nd Lt. to Captain, 14 August 1968 (overlaps with Lowry AFB training period) to 26 February 1971.

Ove, Stephen, 18th Wing Historian. "The Battle of Okinawa: 70 Years Later," 1 April 2015.

Pioneersofstealth.org. *Pioneers of Stealth*. An organization to which Denny Jarvi contributes a significant amount of his time and effort.

Project CHECO (Contemporary Historical Evolution of Combat Operations) Report, "The Pueblo Incident, 15 April 1968" (approved for public release).

Rockholt, Sheila. Email exchanges, 17 July 2021 to 26 May 2022, updates on 18th TFW personnel since 1971.

"Service in the USAF: DATAW Historic Foundation, Colonel Monroe Seabrook Sams." Authorization from Bill Riski, Dataw Historic Foundation, and his coordination with Tom Sams (son of Colonel Sams), email, 20 May 2022.

Shine, Anthony, Colleen, Shannon, and Bomette "Bonnie." "Overcoming Incredible Odds" (a reference to Tony Shine).

Shine, Colleen (daughter of Bonnie and Tony Shine). Email exchanges, 27 July 2021 to 24 May 2022; lunch meeting, 29 September 2021.

TDY log for William A. Cimino, USAF, 2nd Lt. to Captain, November 1968 to December 1970.

USAF Training Certificate, 4 August 1969, Annual Aircrew Survival Training IAW PACAFR 50-22, Kadena AB, Okinawa.

USAF Training Certificate, 27 January 1970, Air-Launched Tactical Missiles Safety Officer Course, Lowry AFB, Colorado.

Wikipedia.org. "Hong Kong." General information about Hong Kong.

Wikipedia.org. "Kadena Air Base." Description of Kadena AB, Okinawa.

Wikipedia.org. "1968 Kadena Air Base B-52 Crash."

Wikipedia.org. "Kwang-Ju Air Base, South Korea." Description of Kwang-Ju AB, South Korea.

Wikipedia.org. "Lockheed T-33 Shooting Star." Description of the T-33 aircraft.

Wikipedia.org. "Okinawa." Description of the island of Okinawa.

Wikipedia.org. "Typhoon Alley." More coverage of typhoon activity in the vicinity of Okinawa.

Wikipedia.org. "Typhoon Cora." A description of Typhoon Cora.

Chapter 7: Recovery, Phase 1

AF Form 702, Individual physiological training record. Initiated during UNT, Mather AFB, California. (Included wet-ditching drills, parasailing, ejection seat training, and altitude chamber sessions).

AF Manual 50-5, July 1970. Course N-V6A. A description for UNT.

AFCEC.af.mil. "Mather History—Air Force Civil Engineer Center." A history of Mather AFB.

AOPA.org. "Technique—Pilotage and Dead Reckoning." More on simple determination of position.

ATC Form 240-5, Summary Record of Training (UNT), 28 January 1972, for Captain William A. Cimino, Mather AFB, California.

Awards: ATC Commander's Trophy (highest overall UNT grade); Husik Memorial Trophy (highest-flying average); Outstanding Graduate Letter.

Brighthubengineering.com. "Chip Log Explained—An Ancient Navigation System." Description of how sailors accounted for positioning on the seas.

Callander, Bruce D. "Navigators with a Difference." *Air Force Magazine*, 1 December 1987.

Certificate of Aeronautical Rating, 28 January 1972, for Captain William A. Cimino.

Cimino, William A., AF personal records, March 1971 to January 1972.

Curiousself.com. "The Natural Navigator: How to Navigate using the Stars." The importance and utility of stars in navigation.

Graduate Program, USAF UNT, Air Training Command. Graduation program for UNT Class 72-13.

History.com. "Why Is a Ship's Speed Measured in Knots?" The origins of the word *knot* and its relevance to speed.

Localwiki.org, *Mather Air Force Base*. General information about Mather AFB.

MG.CO.UK. "Longitude Found—the Story of Harrison's Clocks." Information regarding the accomplishments of John Harrison regarding longitude and navigation.

Nationalgeographic.org. "Coriolis Effect." What Coriolis does to navigation.

NY.Vanderbilt.edu. "Plotting a Line of Position." The importance of lines of position and how they intersect to provide a more accurate position during navigation.

Reconnaissancemusings.wordpress.com. "The T-29 'Flying Classroom.'" The aircraft trainer for UNT, 8 March 2016.

SACmuseum.org, Strategic Air Command & Aerospace Museum: "T-29A 'Flying Classroom.'"

SGP.FAS.org. "Base Closure and Realignment (BRAC): Background and Issues for Congress." *Congressional Research Service Report*, 25 April 2019, p. CRS-22.

Simler, G. B., Lt. Gen., Commander, Air Training Command, Randolph AFB, Texas. Letter, 28 January 1972, commendation for William Cimino's selection as outstanding UNT graduate.

Timeandnavigation.si.edu. "The Untold Story of Getting from Here to There; Dead Reckoning." A simple account of determining position.

UNT Class 72-13. Assignments List.

UNT Class 72-13. Computer Printouts—Class Standing. Several class status reports.

Weems-path.com. "History of Navigation." General information about navigation.

Weiss, Jay A., Captain. "Celestial Techniques," *The Navigator Magazine*, AFRP 50-3, 25(1), 1978, pp. 20–21.

Wikipedia.org. "Mather AFB." Description of Mather AFB.

Chapter 8: Recovery, Phase 2

AF Flight Records. Flight records while assigned to RF-4C training at Shaw AFB, South Carolina.

AF.mil. "USAFSAM Aerospace Physiology Training Optimizes Airman's Performance." A description of the training that helps aircrews recognize the effects of hypoxia (oxygen deprivation) in a loss of cabin pressure, or loss of oxygen supply from an aircraft while wearing an oxygen mask.

AFHRA.af.mil. "Shaw Air Force Base." Facts about Shaw AFB.

Aircrew Familiarization (RF-4C) Course 40FF1325F-1, 24 March 1972, Shaw AFB, South Carolina.

Airplane-Pictures.com. "Simulator McDonnell Douglas RF-4C Phantom II." Photo of an RF-4C simulator.

Brandt, C. R., Captain. "RF-4C Inertial Navigation." *The Navigator Magazine,* 18(3): 20, 1971.

Cimino, William A. AF personal records, January to August 1972.

Flight Manual, USAF Series, RF-4C Aircraft, T.O. 1F-4(R)C. A complete technical document that covers everything an RF-4C aircrew (pilot and WSO) must know. It is the primary AF publication for RF-4C training.

Intelligence Resource Program. "RF-4," Irp.fas.org. Additional information on the RF-4C aircraft.

Jedik, Rocky "Apollo." Goflightmedicine.com, "Pulling Gs—The Effects of G-Forces on the Human Body." Goflightmedicine.com, 5 April 2013.

Joe.Baugher.com. "McDonnell RF-4C Phantom II." More description of the RF-4C aircraft with an explanation of sensors.

Masse, Richard F., Major. "RF-4C Radar Predictions." *The Navigator Magazine,* AFRP 50-3, 27(3): 12–14, 1980.

Michini, Albert. *Water Survival on Biscayne Bay.* USAF Art Collection. Picryl.com. Depicts pulling an aircrewman over the Bay where he will be released to parachute to the water.

Murphy, Terrence M., Major, and Bridges, James T., Captain. "Training for the Future, the TAC WSO." *The Navigator Magazine,* AFRP 50-3, 25(3): 13, 14, 1978.

Nationamuseum.af.mil. "McDonnell Douglas RF-4C Phantom II." Description of the RF-4C aircraft.

Norvell, John E. (F-4 WSO). "At Fairchild 1972). Jenorv66.wordpress.com, 2 August 2020. A vivid description of an aircrew member who went through winter survival and POW camp when I did in January 1972.

OIresource.com. "G-suit Basics and Complete Guide at OI Resource." A good summary of G-suits used in high-performance aircraft.

RF-4C Summary of Training, Captain William A. Cimino, 21 August 1972.

SACmuseum.org. "RF-4C 'Phantom II'." More information on the RF-4C aircraft.

Schultz, Michael J., Captain. "Where Will We Be without TACAN." *The Navigator Magazine*, AFRP 50-3, 25(3): 11, 12, 1978.

Survival Training Course, S-V80-A (Winter Survival). 14 February 1972, Fairchild AFB, Washington.

Training Report: Tac Form 89, Student Flying Training Record.

USAF Tactical Reconnaissance Training Course, 132105F/N, RF-4C, 8–21 March 1972.

Water Survival Training Course, S-V-86-A, 5 March 1972, Homestead AFB, Florida.

Wikipedia.org. "Area Control Center." A description of Air Route Traffic Control Centers (ARTCCs).

Wikipedia.org. "Air Traffic Control." A description of the service provided for aircraft on the ground and through controlled airspace.

Wikipedia.org. "Airspace." A description of airspace classes for flying.

Wikipedia.org. "RF-4C." More RF-4C information.

Wikipedia.org. "Shaw Air Force Base." Coverage of Shaw AFB in Sumter, South Carolina.

Wikipedia.org. "Survival, Evasion, Resistance, and Escape (SERE).: A description of the techniques necessary for aircrews who may have ejected into enemy territory.

Chapter 9: Tactical Operations

AFHRA.af.mil. "Bergstrom Air Force Base." Facts about Bergstrom AFB.

Boyne, Walter J. "Red Flag." *Air Force Magazine* 1 November 2000. Describes why Red Flag was developed.

Cimino, William A. AF personal records, September 1972 to August 1974.

Colvin, Rod. *First Heroes: The POWs Left Behind in Vietnam*, 2013. Chapter 17 is written by USAFR Lt. Col. George Shine, the father of Tony Shine, who was listed as MIA on 2 December 1972. He describes the service of his and his wife, Helen's, children—three sons and a daughter—in the military, the loss of two sons, their journey to get answers about Tony, and their family's dedication to military service.

Crook, Tom, First Lieutenant, artist. "First in Tac Recce, 91st Tac Recon Sq: The Professionals." Christmas card depiction.

Flight logbook for William A. Cimino, USAF Captain, while assigned to 91st TRS, Bergstrom AFB, Texas.

Luft, Alastair. "The OODA Loop and the Half-Beat." Thestrategybridge.org, 17 March 2020.

Laslie, Brian Daniel. "Red Flag: How the Rise of 'Realistic Training after Vietnam Changed the Air Force's Way of War, 1975–1999'." Kansas State University, 2013. Krex.k-state.edu.

Letter/email exchanges with Tom Crook from 5 July to 12 November 2021; and phone calls on 24 August and 2 November 2021. Sadly, Tom passed away on 13 November 2021. I honor him in the "Special Tributes" section.

Militarybases.com. "Aviano Air Force Base in Aviano, Italy." History of the Allied base.

Officer Effectiveness Reports for William A. Cimino, USAF Captain, 22 August 1972 to 25 July 1974.

Phone call with Jim Mills on 26 August 2021, and some emails in August and September 2021.

Quora.com. "What Is Terrain Masking? How Is It Achieved, and What Are Its Advantages and Disadvantages?"

Saceneedle.com. "Space Needle." Information on the Seattle Space Needle.

Techtarget.com. "What Is OODA Loop?" A description of the OODA Loop process.

TDY Log for William A. Cimino, USAF Captain, November 1972 to June 1974.

The University of Texas, Division of Extension, Student Grades slips, William A. Cimino.

Wikipedia.org. "Bergstrom Air Force Base." A brief history of Bergstrom AFB.

Wikipedia.org. "Death Valley National Park." Description including the lowest point at 282 feet MSL.

Wikipedia.org. "Exercise Red Flag." Describes advanced aerial combat-training exercises between Blue (friendly) and Red (enemy) forces.

Wikipedia.org. "Nap-of-the-Earth.: Describes this as a very low-altitude flight course to avoid enemy detection in a high-threat environment.

Wikipedia.org. "Olympia Brewery." Describes the Old Olympia Brewery in Tumwater, Washington.

Wikipedia.org. "Space Needle." More Space Needle information.

Wikipedia.org. "Terrain-Following Radar." Description of radar navigation at a low level in hilly terrain and using terrain masking as a means to avoid detection.

Xbradtc2.com. "Smokey SAM—Bring the Heat." 18 September 2014. Describes the GTR-18 (Smokey SAM) as a solid rocket that simulates the visual signature of an enemy SAM.

Chapter 10: Southeast Asia

AF Form 702, Individual Physiological Training Record. Updated at Udorn RTAFB, Thailand. (Included wet-ditching drills.)

AFHRA.af.mil. "Udorn Royal Thai Air Force Base." Facts about Udorn RTAFB.

AFHRA.af.mil, "432 Wing (ACC)," Air Force Historical Research Agency, 19 June 2017. The lineage of the 432 Wing since the mid-1940s.

Author Unknown. "14TRS History, Narrative Form (June 1942 to July 1975)."

Award of the AF Commendation Medal, 1st OLC, 31 August 1974–6 July 1975. (Awarded at Mather AFB).

Award of the Air Medal, 6 November 1974–5 May 1975. (Awarded at Mather AFB).

Berry, F. Clifton, Jr. "Tactical Reconnaissance at a Turning Point." *Armed Forces Journal International.* July 1979.

Cimino, William A. AF personal records, August 1974 to July 1975.

Dunham, George R., Major, and Quinlan, David A., Colonel. *US Marines in Vietnam— The Bitter End—1973–1975.* History and Museums Division, HQs US Marine Corps, Washington DC, 1990. Marines.mil. Description of Operations Eagle Pull, Frequent Wind, and the *Mayaguez* incident.

Flight Logbook. Flight log entries while assigned to the 14th TRS, Udorn AB, Thailand.

Frisbee, John L., "Valor: The Mayaguez Incident." *Air Force Magazine*, AirForcemag. com, 1 September 1991.

History.net. "These Phantoms Flew 'Unarmed and Unafraid' Over Vietnam."

HistoryByDay.com, *The Unknown Story of the King of Cool; Steve McQueen;* sub-story, *A Feud with his Next Door Neighbor* (Keith Moon of *The Who*), Alva Yaffe, date unknown.

Hushkit.net. "The RF-4C: Last manned USAF Tactical Reconnaissance Aircraft, Col Eileen Bjorkman, 25 May 2020."

Jenorv66.wordpress.com. "An American Family." Party suits, patches, and jewelry— the well-dressed fighter jock. The business managed by "the Maharajah," Amarjit Singh Vasir, better known as "The Thief."

Jungle Survival School Course S-V 88-A, 11 September 1974, Clark Air Base, Philippines.

Letters from Fran to me, dated from 9 September 1974 to 24 June 1975.

Letters from me to Fran, dated from 3 September 1974 to 4 July 1975.

Madera Tribune. "Pygmies Teach Jungle Survival to Fliers," 75(112), 21 October 1966. An article about some of the world's greatest game stalkers. Cdnc.ucr.edu.

Nalty, Bernard C. "Air War Over South Vietnam, 1968–1975," AF History and Museums Program, US Air Force, Washington DC 2000.

Officer Effectiveness Reports for William A. Cimino, USAF Captain, 26 July 1974 to 10 June 1975.

Operation Eagle Pull call sign "Spear Lead" to "Cricket." Tape recording.

Pacific Stars and Stripes newspapers, various articles from 1974 to 75.

Phone call with Bill Bowman, 3 February 2022. Contact with Bill after nearly forty-seven years. Emails/text exchanges 27 January to 3 February 2022.

Phone call with Guy Munder, 27 October 2021. Contact with Guy after nearly forty-seven years. Emails/texts exchanges 27 October 2021 to 15 April 2022.

Phone call with Russ Metzler, 23 October 2021. Contact with Russ after nearly thirty-nine years. Emails/texts exchanges 23 October 2021 to 14 April 2022.

Project CHECO (Contemporary Historical Evolution of Combat Operations), Southeast Asia Report, "USAF Tactical Reconnaissance in Southeast Asia," reclassified from secret to confidential 15 June 1989 by—the authority of HQ USAF, CHOR Letter, 22 July 1986; declassified IAW E.O. 12958, AF Declassification Office and Approval for Public Release, 15 August 2006.

Reddit.com. "Steve McQueen and Keith Moon Story. McQueen fires a shotgun to settle a problem with his neighbor, Keith Moon of The Who.

Special Survival Training Course S-V83-B-O, 29 March 1975, Udorn RTAFB, Thailand.

Squadron Officer's School (SOS) certificate, 15 March 1975, completed by correspondence.

Stvmcqueen.tripod.com. "McQueen." McQueen clashed with Moon. Another article regarding McQueen's solution to the Keith Moon light bulb problem.

Wikipedia.org. "Operation Frequent Wind." Covers evacuation of American civilians and at-risk Vietnamese from Saigon.

Wikipedia.org. "Pattaya." Resort city in Thailand, where Guy Munder and I took a few days off.

Wikipedia.org. "S-75 Dvina" (SA-2 Guideline SAM). Describes one of the major surface-to-air missiles used against US air forces in Vietnam. S-75 Dvina photo licensed via Creative Commons Attribution-Share Alike 4.0 International: https://commons.wikipedia.org/wiki/File:S-75_Dvina.jpg.

Wikipedia.org. "United States Air Force in Thailand." Some history of bases in Thailand, Lao Civil War, and USAF withdrawal from Thailand.

Wikipedia.org. "*Mayaguez* Incident." An account of the Khmer Rouge (Cambodia) seizure of the US container ship SS *Mayaguez*, President Ford's reaction, and joint military rescue efforts.

Youtube.com, *Alone, Unarmed, and Unafraid*. A 39-minute video narrated by actor Robert Stack describing the RF-4C's tactical reconnaissance mission in SEA.

Chapter 11: Multichallenges

AF Form 702, Individual Physiological Training Record. Updated at Mather AFB, California. (Included refresher training.)

ATC Form 240-5, Summary record of training for Captain William A. Cimino, Mather AFB, California, 4 December 1975.

ATC Instructor Training (Navigator) Course B-V7D-A, 2 September to 4 December 1975, Mather AFB, California.

Bulletin of the University of Southern California, Institute of Safety and Systems Management, 1975–1976.

Buzanowski, J. G., Senior Airman. "Air Force Eliminates Commissioned Officer Distinctions," *Air Force Print News*, 31 January 2006, AF.mil.

Certificate of Master Instructor in Flying Training for completion of 900 hours of navigator instructor training to UNT students, 25 April 1978, Mather AFB, California.

Cimino, William A., AF personal records, July 1975 to July 1978.

DVIDShub.net. My registered account for defense-related video, photos, and text information pertaining to the first six women in Undergraduate Navigator Training, Mather AFB, California, 1977.

Email exchanges and phone call with Gregg Hughes 4 November 2021. We shared family updates, and Gregg also provided some notes on the USC master's program in systems management, which we took together. He and Janet would later attend my retirement from the AF.

Flight Logbook. Flight log entries while assigned to the 452nd Flying Training Squadron, Mather AFB, California.

Kester, Marissa N., Captain, USAFR. *There from the Beginning: Women in the Air Force.* Maxwell AFB, Alabama: Air University Press. Airuniversity.af.edu.

Letter/email exchanges with Tom Crook from 5 July to 12 November 2021; and phone calls on 24 August and 2 November 2021. Sadly, he passed away on 13 November 2021. I honor him in the "Special Tributes" section.

Officer Effectiveness Reports for William A. Cimino, USAF Captain, 11 June 1975 to 21 July 1978.

Regular Air Force Appointment certificate, 29 September 1975.

NYtimes.com. "Air Force to Train Six as Women Navigators." *New York Times* Archives, 13 June 1976.

Travis.af.mil. "Women in the Air Force: March Celebrates Women's Contributions to Military Then and Now," 17 February 2006. A list of first accomplishments for women in the military.

USC Master of Science in Systems Management (Systems Technology). Description of program, courses, admissions, study centers (Mather AFB, one of eighteen military locations). See appendix A1.

USC master's degree in systems management completed at Mather AFB, California; awarded on 2 September 1978, while stationed at CFB, Winnipeg, Manitoba, Canada.

Wikipedia.org. "Boeing T-43." Navigator trainer referred to as the "Gator" and "Flying Classroom," as its predecessor, the T-29.

Chapter 12: Canadian Forces, A Different Military

AF Form 1887, Award of Senior Navigator Wings, effective on 28 January 1979.

Air Command (Canadian) Electronic Warfare Course Institute, CFB Winnipeg, Manitoba, Canada, 8–19 September 1980. Referenced in appendix A2.

Air Command (Canada) EWOC Certificate of Completion, 8–19 September 1980.

Air Force Special Order AS-2287, 1 July 1979, promotion to major effective 31 July 1979.

Air Force Special Order T-33, 1 June 1981, for Permissive TDY to Shaw AFB, South Carolina to search for housing between 8 and 14 June 1981.

AEWA.org. "The Wonderful Game of Crud." A complete description of the game of crud.

"ASC Course Mutterings." Silly sayings during ASC 31 by officer classmates and instructors.

ASC 31 Certificate of Completion, 4 July 1979.

Award of AF Commendation Medal, 2nd OLC, 23 August 1975–20 July 1978. (Awarded at CFB Winnipeg).

CA.USEmbassy.gov. "US Consulate Winnipeg." Interface with US Consul General assigned in Winnipeg, Manitoba, Canada.

Canada.ca. "Canadian Armed Forces." Information about the Canadian Armed Forces.

Canadian Forces Air Navigation School, Aerospace Systems Course 31, Course Content, appendices A2, A2A through A2C.

Canadian Forces Air Navigation School Conference Report, 2nd Annual Conference on Electro-Optical Systems and Technology, Boston, Massachusetts, 24 November 1980. Referenced in appendix A2.

Certificate of Merit, Manitoba Marathon, June 1980.

Certificate of Recognition, 323rd Flying Training Wing Flight Safety Award, 6 September 1978. (Awarded at CFB Winnipeg).

Cimino, William A., AF personal records, July 1978 to July 1981.

Cimino, William A., Captain. "Technical Report, Visit—Hughes Aircraft Company, California," February 1979. Referenced in appendix A2.

Cimino, William A., Captain. "Canadian Forces Air Navigation School Individual Report 9102, Sensors for Tactical VTOL Aircraft, Confidential," 22 March 1979. Submitted as part of ASC 31 written requirements for a coauthored analysis and assessment of state-of-the-art VTOL technology and its application to forecast Canadian VTOL requirements. Submitted in whole as a secret document, "A Study of Canadian Forces Requirements for VTOL Aircraft—1980 to 2000," June 1979. Referenced in appendix A2.

Cimino, William A., Captain. "Technical Report, Visit—Smith Industries, London, UK), May 1979. Referenced in appendix A2.

Cimino, William A., Major. CF Aerospace Squadron Course Development Officer Memorandum 4660-1, 19 January 1981. Validation of: Canadian Forces Aerospace Systems Course (ASC), Senior Air Navigation Course (SANC), Electronic Warfare Operations Course (EWOC), and all course training plans.

Cimino, William A., Major. CFANS, CFB Winnipeg, Final Report, USAF-CF Exchange Officer, 12 May 1981. Copies to Commandant (CFANS), CFB Winnipeg, Manitoba; AIRCOM HQ/SSO PERS, CFB Winnipeg, Manitoba R2R0T0; NDHQ/DMMD-6, Ottawa, Ontario K2P0E8; Chief, USAF-CF Officer Exchange Program, 141 Cooper Street, Mezzanine Floor, Ottawa, Ontario, Canada K2P0E8.

Cimino, William A., Major. AF Form 90, Officer Career Objective Statement, 4 August 1981. A summary of preferred follow-on assignments submitted to AF Military Personnel.

Email exchanges with Canadian Master Warrant Officer (Ret'd.) Robert Nolan, Canadian Armed Forces Transition Group, November 2022.

Email exchanges with Gloria Kelly, Canadian Forces 17 Wing Public Affairs, CFB Winnipeg, October–November 2022.

Hirsch, Steve. *Sergei Sikorsky: Born to Aviation*. Rotomedia.com, 21 January 2019. Describes the life of Sergei Sikorsky, son of the aviation pioneer Igor Sikorsky of Sikorsky helicopters.

NPS.edu. "DoD and Civilian Health Care under International Agreements." Includes health-care benefits for those military and their families who fall under the following categories: NATO—North Atlantic Treaty Organization, SOFA—Status of Forces Agreement, PFP—Partnership for Peace, RHCA—Reciprocal Health Care Agreement, and some non-NATO countries.

Officer Effectiveness Reports for William A. Cimino, USAF Captain to Major, 22 July 1978 to 4 July 1981.

Phone call with Canadian Embassy on 9 November 2022, which led to connection with the Canadian Armed Forces Transition Group in Ottawa, Ontario, Canada.

State.gov. "US Department of State: US Relations with Canada. Bilateral Relations Fact Sheet," 7 July 2021.

TDY travel trips as a student during Canadian Forces Air Navigation School, Aerospace Systems Course 31, 30 October 1978 to 18 May 1979. See appendix A2D.

TDY travel trips as an instructor during Canadian Forces Air Navigation School, Aerospace Systems Course 32, 8–28 February 1980. See appendix A2D.

TDY to Ottawa, Ontario, Canada, to attend the AF Exchange Officers Conference in May 1981.

TheCanadaGuide.com, March 2020. "Canadian Armed Forces 101." A brief summary of the structure of the Canadian Armed Forces.

USAF-CF Officer Exchange Program Incoming Briefing, Ottawa, Ontario, Canada, 21–23 August 1978. A comprehensive information briefing on serving as an AF Exchange Officer in Canada, protocols, expectations, and challenges.

Wikipedia.org. "Canada." General information about Canada, its ten provinces, three territories, population, and more.

Wikipedia.org. "Crud." Description of the popular game loosely based on billiards (or pool) originated in the Royal Canadian Air Force.

Wikipedia.org. "Manitoba." General information about this province of Canada.

Wikipedia.org. "Winnipeg." General information about the capital of Manitoba.

Wikipedia.gov. "Curling." A description of the sport of curling, popular in Canada.

Winnipeg Free Press. "Complete Marathon Results Listed," 16 June 1980.

Chapter 13: Return to Operations

AF Form 369, Aircrew/Mission Flight Data Document. The record of my last RF-4C flight at Shaw AFB, South Carolina, and for my flying career.

AF Form 475, Education/Training Report, 5 July to 21 December 1981. (The training report start date picks up from the day after my last OER at CFB Winnipeg).

Air Command and Staff College Certificate, 14 September 1981, completed by correspondence.

Award of the AF Meritorious Service Medal, 8 August 1978–31 July 1981. (Awarded at Shaw AFB).

Boeing.com. "Aero 13—Runway Arresting Systems." Description of several types of aircraft arresting systems used in emergencies.

Boyne, Walter J. "Red Flag," *Air Force Magazine,* 1 November 2000. Describes why Red Flag was developed.

Cimino, William A., AF personal records, August 1981 to September 1983.

Flight Logbook. Flight log entries while assigned to the 363rd Tactical Fighter Wing, Shaw AFB, South Carolina.

Key.aero.com. "Dissimilar Air Combat Training (DACT)." Explanation of both DACT and ACT air combat training.

Letter/texts/emails between me and Russ Metzler, 17 October 2021 to 24 January 2022.

Metzler, Russ. "Detail of Wing Life Support Duties and Accomplishments."

Officer Effectiveness Reports for William A. Cimino, USAF Major, 22 December 1981 to 31 July 1983.

Tactical Reconnaissance Aircrew Training Course, RF400XOOAS, 15 September to 12 November 1981, Shaw AFB, South Carolina.

Tactical Reconnaissance Course, RF4OOIOOWS, 5 January to 2 March 1982, Shaw AFB, South Carolina.

TDY Log for William A. Cimino, USAF Major, October 1981 to September 1982.

Wikipedia.com. *Dissimilar Air Combat Training*. Explanation of introduction of DACT as a formal part of US air combat training.

Xbradtc2.com. "Smokey SAM—Bring the Heat," 18 September 2014. Describes the GTR-18 (Smokey SAM) as a solid rocket that simulates the visual signature of an enemy SAM.

Letter of congratulations for promotion to lieutenant Colonel from the 363rd Tactical Fighter Wing Commander, Colonel Richard E. Carr, 23 September 1982.

Letter to me and others in appreciation for hosting Air Force Academy Cadets from Brig. Gen. Anthony J. Burshnick, Commandant of Cadets, AF Cadet Wing, USAF Academy, Colorado Springs, Colorado, 17 September 1982.

Letter to me in appreciation for hosting Air Force Academy Cadets from the 363rd Tactical Fighter Wing Commander and Deputy Commander for Operations, Colonels Richard E. Carr and Gerald A. Daniel, respectively, 4 and 5 October 1982.

Chapter 14: AF TENCAP—Space Operations

"14 Fascinating Facts You Never Knew About the Pentagon" by Joe McKinley originally published on RD.com. Copyright © 2018 by Trusted Media Brands, Inc. Used by permission. All rights reserved.

Advanced Imagery Interpretation Orientation Course, G30RP8016, Offutt AFB, Nebraska.

Air War College, 10 March 1987, completed by the Air War College Seminar Program at the Pentagon.

Award of the AF Meritorious Service Medal, 1st OLC, 2 August 1981–19 September 1983. (Awarded at the Pentagon).

Beitler, Stu. "Air Force Investigates Jet Crash; Two Likely Killed," Gatlinburg, TN Air Force Crash, Jan 1984, Copyrighted 2002. Associated Press, 4 January 1984.

Boyce, Walter J. "El Dorado Canyon, *Air Force Magazine,* 1 March 1999.

Cimino, William A. AF personal records, September 1983 to July 1987.

Clapper, James R. (2018). *Facts and Fears, Hard Truths from a Life in Intelligence,* New York: Viking, Penguin Random House, LLC.

Crockett, Christopher. "What is the Electromagnetic Spectrum," 7 September 2019. EarthSky.org.

DCMilitary.com. "The Pentagon," 19 February 2016. Some elements of Pentagon information.

Department of the Air Force, Washington, Special Order, AB-3046, 1 December 1983, promotion to Lt. Col.

ESRI.com. Chapter 3, "Imagery Fundamentals."

GEOINT Symposium, 7 October 2021, keynote speaker, Dr. Chris Scolese.

Historic Archaeology. "Fighter Jet Crash in the Great Smokies," 11 March 2018.

HQ Air Force letter, Shuttle Mission 51-C Space Badge Recipients, 12 February 1985. Award of Space Badge.

Hunter, Jamie. "40 Years of the Nighthawk," 15 June 2021, Skiesmag.com.

Israel, Kenneth R., USAF Maj. Gen. "US Air Force Biography." Retired, 1 October 1998.

Kitfield, James A. "The Secret Doings at Tonopah." *Air Force Magazine,* 1 January 1993 (reference for F-117 Nighthawks).

NASA Mission 41-B Photo: First Landing at KSC. Presented to me for briefing several astronauts.

NASA letter, 11 February 1985, certification of Space Badge aboard Mission 51-C, 24-27 January 1985, the first DoD-dedicated Space Shuttle mission.

National Reconnaissance Office. "Above and Beyond, Dr. Christopher Scolese, Director of the NRO."

Obituary for David F. Greggs, aged twenty-eight, Newspapers.com

Officer Effectiveness Reports for William A. Cimino, USAF Lt. Col., 1 August 1983 to 31 May 1987.

Phone call with Maj. Gen. John Storrie and Mary Ann, 9 December 2022. Contact with General Storrie after thirty-nine years. Emails/texts exchanges followed.

Pwalyk, Oriana. "The Myth vs. Legend of the Air Force's Purple Water Fountain," 17 January 2016 (Early Bird Brief editor, 2015, for *AF Times*).

Pentagontours.osd.mil. General Pentagon information.

Schriever.Spaceforce.mil. "Air Force Tactical Exploitation of National Capabilities."

Space.com Staff. "Gallery: Declassified US Spy Satellite Photos & Designs," 4 June 2021.

Swedberg, Edwin C., USAF Maj. US Army Command and General Staff College thesis, *The Effect on Operational and Tactical Surprise by US Military Forces Due to the Proliferation of Unclassified Satellite Imaging Systems* (data for Operation El Dorado Canyon), 1995.

TDY log for William A. Cimino, USAF Lt. Col., October 1983 to May 1987.

White, Ed, Air Force Space Command Affairs, "Air Force TENCAP Celebrates Three Decades of Impressive Warfighter Support Programs," 26 August 2008.

Wikipedia.org. "Lockheed F-117 Nighthawk." Discussion of this twin-engine stealth attack aircraft.

Chapter 15: SES/JPO

"1,099 Selected for Promotion to Colonel." *Air Force Times*, 48(7), 28 September 1987.

AF Association, Paul Revere Chapter president Lyle T. Niswander's appreciation gift to me for speaking at the AFA/Intelligence Symposium at Hanscom AFB, Massachusetts, in November 1988.

Air Force Association, Paul Revere Chapter. USS *New Hampshire*. The artifact from this ship was a part of a gift of appreciation to me from the Air Force Association, Paul Revere Chapter, Mass.gov.

AF.mil. "Edward C. Aldridge Jr." The sixteenth secretary of the air force.

AFROTC, 105th Cadet Wing Letter, 8 February 1988, Cadet Captain Rhett W. Jeffries, Protocol Officer, request for speaker services at Cadet Leadership Lab, University of Colorado, Boulder, Colorado.

AFROTC, 105th Cadet Wing Letter, 8 April 1988, Cadet Wing Commander, Brian C. Copello, thanks for speaker services at Cadet Leadership Lab, University of Colorado, Boulder, Colorado.

Airandspace.si.edu. "IDEX II Workstation." Located at the Udvar-Hazy Center, Smithsonian National Air and Space Museum, Chantilly, Virginia.

Airandspace.si.edu. "Udvar-Hazy Center." The Smithsonian National Air and Space Museum.

Artnalls.com. Maj. Gen. Joe Anderson (USMC, Retired), associate director of Udvar-Hazy Center.

Award of the AF Meritorious Service Medal, 2nd OLC, 27 September 1983–15 July 1987. (Awarded in the Washington, DC area).

CIA Certificate to William A Cimino for services supporting the Persian Gulf Crisis, 2 August 1990 to 1 March 1991.

CIA Certificate to William A. Cimino for accomplishments and service to the CIA, August 1991.

Cimino, William A. AF personal records, July 1987 to January 1993.

Clapper, James R. *Facts and Fears, Hard Truths from a Life in Intelligence.* Viking, Penguin Random House, LLC, 2018.

Colonel Pinning Ceremony Memorandum, 20 March 1989, Major Jene E. Curell, Deputy Chief of Protocol, HQ AFSC, Andrews AFB, Maryland.

Dillard, Michael L., former director SES/JPO (1987–1991) and former CIA, chairman, Information Policy Board (1991–1995). IDEX II supplemental information and notes.

Dillard, Michael L. IDEX II program information provided by Mike in response to comprehensive questions.

ESPN.com. "MLB—A Look Back at the 1989 World Series."

Faga, Martin C. "Military-History." Fandom.com. Declassification of the existence of the NRO.

Flickr.com. "Lockheed's Image Data Exploitation (IDEX II) System." Digital imagery analysis system.

Fran Cimino's MSW from Virginia Commonwealth University, Richmond, Virginia, May 1992.

GlobalSecurity.org. Image Data Exploitation System (IDEX).

GlobalSecurity.org. Electronic light tables.

Governmentattic.org. The Directorate of Intelligence Historical Series, *National Photographic Interpretation Center, volume 1: Antecedents and Early Years, 1952–56, Secret, NPIC-2, December 1972,* Declassified in part. Sanitized copy approved for release, 9 July 2012.

"History of E-Systems, Inc.," EMASS.

History.army.mil. "Operation Desert Shield—US Army Center of Military History." Overview of military response to the Iraqi invasion of Kuwait.

IDEX II sites. See appendix H.

Invitee list for departure of Colonel Israel to HQ AFSC, Andrews AFB, Maryland, May 1989.

IRP.FAS.org. "IMINT—NIIRS National Image Interpretability Rating Scale." Reason for NIIRS and an explanation of rating scales.

Israel, Kenneth R., USAF Maj. Gen. "US Air Force Biography, Retired 1 October 1998."

Laurie, Clayton, and Suk, Michael. NRO.gov, *Leaders of the NRO, vol. II, 1993–2001.* Second revised edition, NRO.gov.

Letter of Congratulations, 17 September 1987, from Lt. Gen. Melvin Chubb, Jr., Commander, Electronic Systems Division, Hanscom AFB, Massachusetts, for my promotion to colonel.

Letter of Endorsement to Colonel Kenneth R. Israel, ESD, Hanscom AFB, Massachusetts, 26 April 1988, Michael L. Dillard, Director, SES/JPO.

Letter from Col. Kenneth R. Israel, 6 June 1989, thanks for attending his departure ceremony at Hanscom AFB, Massachusetts. and for the gifts as he prepared to go to Andrews AFB, Maryland, for his new assignment in AFSC/IG.

Letter of Endorsement to Lt. Gen. Gordon E. Fornell, commander, Electronic Systems Division, Hanscom AFB, Massachusetts, 6 June 1990, Julian Caballero, Jr., Director, OD&E.

Letter from Col. Kenneth R. Israel, 1 December 1988, thanks for support and participation in Air Force Association/ESD Intelligence Technology Symposium, HQ ESD, Hanscom AFB, Massachusetts.

L3HarrisGeospatial.com. "What Makes a PED, a PED?" A description of a PED cell and its goals, 5 June 2012.

Lockheedmartin.com. "The U-2 Dragon Lady."

Lyonairmuseum.org. "A Brief History of the U-2 Spy Plane Program."

Medical Records for William A. Cimino, August 1992, re: left heel injury while TDY to HQ SAC, Offutt AFB, Omaha, Nebraska.

Memorandum for Correspondence, 18 September 1992, re: declassification of the existence of the NRO and its funding by the NRP. DoD No. 264-M.

National Geospatial-Intelligence Agency. "NGA in History—Defining Moments, Defense Mapping Agency," NGA.mil.

National Security Archive. "Out of the Black: The Declassification of the NRO," 18 September 2008.

National System for Geospatial-Intelligence. *Geospatial Intelligence (GEOINT) Basic Doctrine,* publication 1.0, Springfield, Virginia, April 2018.

NGA.mil. "National Photographic Interpretation Center." Establishment of the NPIC.

OD&E's Manager's Course Certificate of Completion, 9 November 1987.

Officer Effectiveness Reports for William A. Cimino, USAF Lt. Col. to Col., 1 June 1987 to 31 May 1992.

Powell, Colin. *My American Journey.* Random House, 1995.

Rand.org. "Special Operations Forces and Elusive Ground Targets."

RAND.org/t/RRA341-2. *Technology Innovation and the Future of Air Force Intelligence Analysis, vol. 2, Technical Analysis and Supporting Material.*

Request for speaker by Col. Vince Micucci, commander of AFROTC cadets of the 105th Cadet Wing, University of Colorado at Boulder.

Schwarzkopf, Norman H. *General H. Norman Schwarzkopf, The Autobiography, It Doesn't Take a Hero.* Bantam, p. 293.

Segal, Jack, HQ ESD, Chief Engineer. "Ode to a Colonel," 12 May 1989.

TDY log for William A. Cimino, USAF Col., July 1987 to October 1992.

Thompson, Loren. "Air Force's Secret 'Gorgon's Stare' Program Leaves Terrorists Nowhere to Hide. " Forbes.com, 10 April 2015.

Trajectory Magazine, 2016, the official magazine of the United States Geospatial Intelligence Foundation.

Wikipedia.org. "1989 Loma Prieta Earthquake."

Wikipedia.org. "Governor's Island." Description of 172-acre island off southern NYC in New York Harbor.

Wikipedia.org. "Gulf War." War waged by coalition forces from thirty-five nations, led by the United States.

Wikipedia.org. "Moffett Field Airship Hangars."

Wikipedia.org. "Windows on the World." The restaurant that existed on the 107th floor of the North Tower (Building One).

Chapter 16: Transition

AF Special Order AL-000334, Notice of Relief from Active Duty, effective 31 January 1993, and retirement effective 1 February 1993.

Air Force retirement certificate. Awarded to me by Brig. Gen. Israel at my retirement ceremony.

Appreciation certificate for Fran. Awarded to her by Brig. Gen. Israel at my retirement ceremony.

Award of the Legion of Merit Medal, 16 July 1987–31 January 1993. (Awarded at my retirement ceremony, Bolling AFB).

Bill's Eleven Rules, derived from decades of learning from others—individuals and organizations—which are made up of individuals.

Blog.Hubspot.com. "55 Inspirational Quotes about Learning from Failure," 14 December 2021.

Certificate of Appreciation for Services in the Armed Forces of the United States, with imprint signature from the commander in chief, George Bush.

Gregory, Debbie. "65 Famous Quotes from Famous People on Failure," Vamboa.org.

Legacy.com. "Terry Straeter Obituary," 2007. A summary of accomplishments and notice of death for Dr. Terry Straeter.

Lifehack.org. "30 Powerful Success and Failure Quotes That Will Lead You to Success."

List of invitees to my Air Force retirement ceremony.

List of attendees at my retirement ceremony.

Mintz, John. "Tracor Buying GDE Systems from Carlyle." WashingtonPost.com, 14 October 1994.

My letter of appreciation to Brig. Gen. Kenneth R. Israel, 20 November 1992. See appendix I.

My letter of appreciation to Lt. Gen. Gordon E. Fornell, 20 November 1992. See appendix J.

Official Air Force Officer Record Brief, William A. Cimino, 10 January 1992.

Official invitation from Brig. Gen. Kenneth R. Israel for the retirement ceremony of Colonel William A. Cimino, 20 November 1992.

Photo array in our home of my brother, Rob.

Photo of Dr. Terry Straeter, courtesy of Ritenour High School Hall of Fame, St. Louis, Missouri.

Retirement ceremony protocol. A detailed list of steps through the retirement ceremony.

San Diego Union-Tribune, 14 November 2007, "Straeter, Terry Anthony."

Wikipedia.org. "Tracor." The acquirer of GDE Systems.

Wikipedia.org. "Ruth Howard." An engineer, sculptor, and philanthropist known for her work, especially in the San Diego area, and for the bronze bust of Dr. Terry Straeter.

Special Tributes

Anthony (Tony) Cameron Shine

Colvin, Rod. *First Heroes: The POWs Left Behind in Vietnam*, 2013. Chapter 17 is by George Shine, USAFR lieutenant colonel and father of Tony Shine, who lost two sons, their journey to get answers about Tony, and their family's dedication to military service.

DPAA.mil. "DPAA Family/VSO Quarterly Call and Update Notes, 29 July 2021, "Fulfilling Our Nation's Promise." Agenda Item: POW/MIA chair of honor. Key speaker, Colleen Shine, daughter of Lt. Col. Anthony Shine.

Email exchange with Ann Mills-Griffiths, chairperson for National League of POW/MIA Families, Falls Church, Virginia. Ann provided contact information for me to connect with Colleen Shine.

Lunch meeting that Fran and I had with Colleen Shine on 29 September 2021.

McFarland Flint, Jennifer. "What Remains: A Vietnam Pilot's Daughter and Her Fight for Answers," Repository.Wellesley.edu.

MilitaryHallofHonor.com. "Lt. Col. Anthony Cameron Shine—Military Hall of Honor." A short description of Tony's MIA status on 2 December 1972, twenty-four years later, and the Shine family.

The National League of POW/MIA Families: www.pow-miafamilies.org. The League's sole mission is to obtain the release of all prisoners, the fullest possible accounting for the missing, and repatriation of all recoverable remains of those who died serving our nation during the Vietnam War.

Other emails/websites/articles/phone calls: Colleen Shine, between 27 July 2021 and 24 May 2022.

Phone call with Al Shine, Tony's younger brother, on 16 October 2021.

POW-MIAFamilies.org. "National League of POW/MIA Families: Langley Hosts Shine Fighter Pilot Award Ceremony," 15 June 2018. Award established by Bonnie Shine and the USAF.

POWMIAMemorial.org. "Colleen Shine." Ms. Shine is a spokesperson for the POW/MIA issue, responding to national and international media interest in the POW/MIA issue.

Shine, Colleen. "Accounting for US POW/MIAs in Southeast Asia: Hearing before the Military Personnel Subcommittee of the Committee on National Security House of Representatives, 104th Congress, First Session, 28 June 1995. Statement by Colleen Shine regarding her father's status as MIA and efforts to seek answers for him and all Vietnam War missing.

The Vietnam Veterans Memorial Fund, www.vvmf.org. A nonprofit organization established on 27 April 1979 by Jan Scruggs, a Vietnam army veteran.

The Vietnam Veterans Memorial wall rubbing of Tony Shine's name, located on Panel1W, Row 93.

Wiley, Barry E., Colonel, USA-Ret. (2007), *Out of the Valley*. Officers' Christian Fellowship of the USA, 2007. The book was provided by Tony's brother, Al Shine. An inspiring story of Tony and Al's younger brother, Jonathan, who was killed in Vietnam, and who had a tremendous influence on the lives and Christian faith of many others.

Youtube.com, VVMF Colleen Shine, *At the Wall*. The Education Center. A powerful five-minute video where Colleen Shine describes what the wall (which contains the names of her father and uncle) represents to her, her family, and the country.

David Lee Nichols

AF.mil. "Biographies, Lieutenant General David L. Nichols."

Email/text exchange with Pam Nichols Jenison, daughter of Dave and Jan Nichols, between 6 and 27 November 2021.

Phone call with Pam Nichols Jenison on 28 November 2021.

Photos of Lt. Gen. David Nichols, courtesy of his daughter, Pam Nichols Jenison.

Wikipedia.org. "Lieutenant General David L. Nichols, photo."

Douglas M. Alexander

Handwritten note from Sheila and Bob Rockholt, 19 March 2015, contained the notice of death of Lt. Col. Douglas Alexander, 8 January 2015, from his children, Jim Alexander and Vicki Alexander Hensley.

My photo of Doug Alexander from a party in Okinawa.

Thomas Eugene Crook

Email exchange with Tom from 11 July to 2 November 2021.

"In Loving Memory" memorial program for Thomas Eugene Crook, "Aim High," provided by Pat Crook.

Joint assignments with Tom at Bergstrom AFB, Texas, and Mather AFB, California.

Narrative: "Tom's Life, September 29, 1947–November 13, 2021," from Pat Crook.

Phone calls with Tom on 24 August and 2 November 2021.

Photos and TAC Recce Roster from Tom Crook.

Photos of Tom courtesy of his wife, Pat Crook.

John William Heide

Details of John's assignments in the Air Force and his career after his military retirement.

Email exchanges with Betts Heide, John's wife, from 27 September to 10 December 2021.

Joint assignments with John at Udorn AB, Thailand and Shaw AFB, South Carolina.

Photos of John courtesy of his wife, Betts Heide.

Michael S. Joyal

Email exchange with Suzanne Roseberry from 17 to 30 January 2022.

Letter from Suzanne Roseberry, 27 January 2013. Her reply to my correspondence with details of the accident that took Mike's life.

Memorial and short biography of Michael S. Joyal from Suzanne Roseberry.

My letter to Suzanne Roseberry, Mike's wife, on 1 December 2021.

Photos of Mike courtesy of his wife, Suzanne Roseberry.

A Pensive Visit

ArlingtonCemetery.mil. "Find a Grave—Arlington National Cemetery." Grave locations by section and plot, map of the cemetery, and visit instructions.

Collectively, inputs/bios/emails/photos/and so on from Colleen Shine, Sheila Rockholt, Pam Nichols Jenison, Suzanne Roseberry, Pat Crook, and Betts Heide.

Information provided by Sheila Rockholt for Tony Shine's memorials in Myrtle Beach, South Carolina: Shine Ave, and Lt. Col. Tony Shine marker.

Washington.org. "Guide to Visiting Arlington National Cemetery." Specific information about the cemetery.

Wikipedia.org. "Arlington National Cemetery." General information.

The Cimino and Costa Families

My family records and my ancestry research: Ancestry.com, BeenVerified.com, personal family photos, data collected for my 2019 video, *Costa—Cimino, Our Family Story, A Son's Perspective.*

APPENDICES

A1: Education—Colleges

College transcripts and documentation: Saint John's University, the University of Texas at Austin, the University of Southern California.

A2: Education—PME

Certificates from AF formal education: Squadron Officers School, Air Command and Staff College, Air War College, Canadian Forces Aerospace Systems Course, Air Command (Canadian) Electronic Warfare Course Institute.

A2A–A2D: Education—ASC Detail (courses and travel)

Canadian Aerospace Systems Course 31 detailed subject matter for Math and Applied Sciences, Systems Studies, Operations and Staff Duties; ASC 31 Travel to Aerospace Industry, Military Units and Other Agencies.

B: Promotions

Promotion records, special orders, letters of congratulations, specific rank pinning ceremonies: 2nd lieutenant through colonel.

C: PCS Assignments

Personal records, PCS orders, training assignments, from 5 July 1967 to 31 January 1993 (retired on 1 February 1993).

D: RF-4C WSO's Office Illustrations

Flight Manual, USAF Series, RF-4C Aircraft, T.O. 1F-4(R)C—1. A complete technical document that covers everything an RF-4C aircrew (pilot and WSO) must know. It is the primary AF publication for RF-4C training.

E: 14th TRS History: Narrative, June 1942–July 1975

14th TRS history by an unknown author.

F: AF Patches
My AF personal patch sample collection.

G: Navigator Wings, Space Wings, Ribbons, Medals
My shadow box depicting navigator wings, space wings, ribbons, medals, and the US flag that flew at the IDEX II Customer Systems Support Center, Newington, Virginia, in November 1992.

H: IDEX II Sites
List of IDEX II sites where SES/JPO delivered the IDEX II system.

I and J: Thank-You Letters
My thank-you letters to Brig. Gen. Kenneth R. Israel and Lt. Gen. Gordon E. Fornell, respectively.

K. Official USAF Photo
My official photo as Colonel.